# Elvis For Dummies

## Elvis's Number-One Singles

In Elvis's lifetime, 18 singles reached the top of the *Billboard* Hot 100 chart. These ranking airplay and sales. Such statistics are a measure of a singer's success, albeit an imperfect one. Comparing Elvis's accomplishment to that of other singers is tricky, because both the industry and the criteria for reaching number one have changed. Also, some sources only count American charts, while others count both U.K. and U.S. charts. And, a list of number-one hits isn't the same as number-one singles. Here are Elvis's singles in chronological order:

- "Heartbreak Hotel" (1956)
- "Don't Be Cruel" (1956)
- "Hound Dog" (1956)
- "Love Me Tender" (1956)
- "Too Much" (1957)
- "All Shook Up" (1957)
- "Teddy Bear" (1957)
- "Jailhouse Rock" (1957)
- "Don't" (1958)
- "Hard-Headed Woman" (1958)
- "A Big Hunk O' Love" (1958)
- "Stuck on You" (1960)
- "It's Now or Never" (1960)
- "Are You Lonesome Tonight" (1960)
- "Surrender" (1961)
- "Good Luck Charm" (1962)
- "Suspicious Minds" (1969)
- "Burning Love" (1972)

As a point of comparison, the Beatles are the only musical act to surpass Elvis with 20 number-one hits, though the songs weren't all single releases. Frank Sinatra had less than five number-one singles, and Elvis's contemporary Jerry Lee Lewis never had a number-one pop single.

## The Grammy Awards Elvis Won

Nominated 14 times, Elvis won three Grammy Awards during his lifetime. Given his nickname "King of Rock 'n' Roll," it's ironic that the awards he won were all for gospel recordings. Here are the three recordings he received Grammys for:

- *How Great Thou Art* (1967)
- *He Touched Me* (1972)
- *How Great Thou Art* (live recording, 1974)

In 1971, Elvis also was recognized with the Bing Crosby Award, which was a lifetime achievement award from the Grammy association (National Academy of Recording Arts and Sciences, or NARAS). Six of Elvis's recordings have been inducted into the NARAS Grammy Hall of Fame, which "honors recordings of lasting qualitative or historical significance." The following recordings were inducted:

- "That's All Right" (1955)
- "Heartbreak Hotel" (1956)
- "Don't Be Cruel" (1956)
- "Hound Dog" (1956)
- "Are You Lonesome Tonight" (1960)
- "Suspicious Minds" (1969)

**For Dummies: Bestselling Book Series for Beginners**

# Elvis For Dummies®

*Cheat Sheet*

## Reviewing Elvis's Unique Accomplishments

- **Setting a charitable example:** In 1961, Elvis gave a benefit performance at Hawaii's Bloch Arena, which raised $65,000 toward the U.S.S. *Arizona* memorial. Fundraising efforts for the memorial had crawled to a standstill, but Elvis's concert raised awareness as well as money, and the memorial was built within a year.

- **Getting the star treatment:** Elvis starred in 31 feature films in 13 years, averaging three per year, which was an amazing output. Also, during his lifetime, he was the subject of two feature documentaries.

- **Reigning as the King of Vegas:** Elvis's return to the concert stage at the International Hotel in July/August 1969 — a four-week, 57-show engagement — broke all existing attendance records in Las Vegas.

- **Being named an Outstanding Young Man:** On January 16, 1971, Elvis was named one of the "Ten Outstanding Young Men of the Nation" by the Junior Chamber of Congress (Jaycees) for outstanding personal achievement in his arena of endeavor, patriotism, humanitarianism, and community service.

- **Selling out the Garden:** In June 1972, Elvis became the first performer to sell out four consecutive shows at Madison Square Garden.

- **Setting a TV record:** In January 1973, Elvis's television special *Elvis: Aloha from Hawaii* was broadcast live by Globecam satellite to several countries in the Far East. It was then shown by broadcast delay to 30 other countries. A taping of the special aired in the U.S. in April of the same year. In all, the special was seen by between 1 and 1.5 billion people in about 40 countries, a record that hasn't been surpassed by any television special.

- **Becoming a triple hall-of-famer:** Posthumously, Elvis was elected into the Rock 'n' Roll Hall of Fame, the Country Music Hall of Fame, and the Gospel Hall of Fame. He's the only performer to date to become a member of all three.

- **Outselling everyone else:** Estimations purport that Elvis Presley has sold more than one billion records worldwide without touring outside of the U.S. and Canada, which is more than anyone in record-industry history.

- **Going gold, platinum, and multi-platinum:** Including his albums (LPs), singles, and extended play albums (EPs), Elvis Presley has more Recording Industry Association of America (RIAA) certifications than any other group or artist. As of 2005, 81 of Elvis's albums have been ranked as gold, platinum, or multi-platinum by the RIAA. Sales requirements for gold and platinum status have changed over the years; otherwise Elvis's record sales would be even higher.

Wiley, the Wiley Publishing logo, For Dummies, the Dummies Man logo, the For Dummies Bestselling Book Series logo and all related trade dress are trademarks or registered trademarks of John Wiley & Sons, Inc. and/or its affiliates. All other trademarks are property of their respective owners.

Copyright © 2009 Wiley Publishing, Inc. All rights reserved. Item 7202-6.

For more information about Wiley Publishing, call 1-877-762-2974.

## *For Dummies: Bestselling Book Series for Beginners*

PATIENT'S LIBRARY
ST ANDREW'S HOSPITAL

12 APR 2010

0 1 AUG 2011

83\10

WWH 4\11

DISCARDED
Northamptonshire Libraries

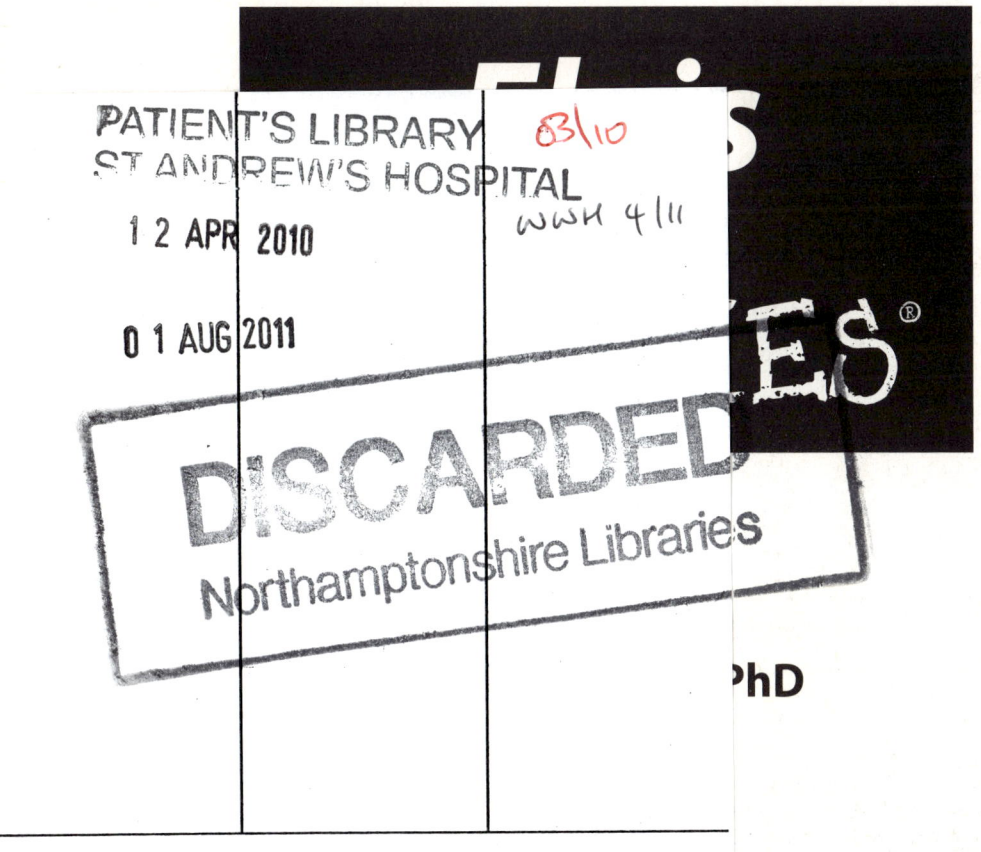

PhD

Please return/renew this item by the last date shown. Books may also be renewed by telephoning, writing to or calling in at any of our libraries or on the internet.

Northamptonshire Libraries and Information Service

**Northamptonshire**
County Council

www.library.northamptonshire.gov.uk/catalogue

**WILEY**

Wiley Publishing, Inc.

80003139735

**Elvis For Dummies®**

Published by
**Wiley Publishing, Inc.**
111 River St.
Hoboken, NJ 07030-5774
www.wiley.com

Copyright © 2009 by Wiley Publishing, Inc., Indianapolis, Indiana

Published simultaneously in Canada

No part of this publication may be reproduced, stored in a retrieval system or transmitted in any form or by any means, electronic, mechanical, photocopying, recording, scanning or otherwise, except as permitted under Sections 107 or 108 of the 1976 United States Copyright Act, without either the prior written permission of the Publisher, or authorization through payment of the appropriate per-copy fee to the Copyright Clearance Center, 222 Rosewood Drive, Danvers, MA 01923, (978) 750-8400, fax (978) 646-8600. Requests to the Publisher for permission should be addressed to the Permissions Department, John Wiley & Sons, Inc., 111 River Street, Hoboken, NJ 07030, (201) 748-6011, fax (201) 748-6008, or online at http://www.wiley.com/go/permissions.

**Trademarks:** Wiley, the Wiley Publishing logo, For Dummies, the Dummies Man logo, A Reference for the Rest of Us!, The Dummies Way, Dummies Daily, The Fun and Easy Way, Dummies.com, Making Everything Easier, and related trade dress are trademarks or registered trademarks of John Wiley & Sons, Inc. and/or its affiliates in the United States and other countries, and may not be used without written permission. All other trademarks are the property of their respective owners. Wiley Publishing, Inc., is not associated with any product or vendor mentioned in this book.

| Northamptonshire Libraries & Information Services SA | |
|---|---|
| Askews | |

**LIMIT OF LIABILITY/DISCLAIMER OF WARRANTY: THE PUBLISHER AND THE AUTHOR MAKE NO REPRESENTATIONS OR WARRANTIES WITH RESPECT TO THE ACCURACY OR COMPLETENESS OF THE CONTENTS OF THIS WORK AND SPECIFICALLY DISCLAIM ALL WARRANTIES, INCLUDING WITHOUT LIMITATION WARRANTIES OF FITNESS FOR A PARTICULAR PURPOSE. NO WARRANTY MAY BE CREATED OR EXTENDED BY SALES OR PROMOTIONAL MATERIALS. THE ADVICE AND STRATEGIES CONTAINED HEREIN MAY NOT BE SUITABLE FOR EVERY SITUATION. THIS WORK IS SOLD WITH THE UNDERSTANDING THAT THE PUBLISHER IS NOT ENGAGED IN RENDERING LEGAL, ACCOUNTING, OR OTHER PROFESSIONAL SERVICES. IF PROFESSIONAL ASSISTANCE IS REQUIRED, THE SERVICES OF A COMPETENT PROFESSIONAL PERSON SHOULD BE SOUGHT. NEITHER THE PUBLISHER NOR THE AUTHOR SHALL BE LIABLE FOR DAMAGES ARISING HEREFROM. THE FACT THAT AN ORGANIZATION OR WEBSITE IS REFERRED TO IN THIS WORK AS A CITATION AND/OR A POTENTIAL SOURCE OF FURTHER INFORMATION DOES NOT MEAN THAT THE AUTHOR OR THE PUBLISHER ENDORSES THE INFORMATION THE ORGANIZATION OR WEBSITE MAY PROVIDE OR RECOMMENDATIONS IT MAY MAKE. FURTHER, READERS SHOULD BE AWARE THAT INTERNET WEBSITES LISTED IN THIS WORK MAY HAVE CHANGED OR DISAPPEARED BETWEEN WHEN THIS WORK WAS WRITTEN AND WHEN IT IS READ.**

For general information on our other products and services, please contact our Customer Care Department within the U.S. at 877-762-2974, outside the U.S. at 317-572-3993, or fax 317-572-4002.

For technical support, please visit www.wiley.com/techsupport.

Wiley also publishes its books in a variety of electronic formats. Some content that appears in print may not be available in electronic books.

Library of Congress Control Number: 2009928715

ISBN: 978-0-470-47202-6

Manufactured in the United States of America

10 9 8 7 6 5 4 3 2 1

WILEY

# About the Author

**Susan Doll, PhD,** is a film and popular culture historian who has written several books on Elvis Presley. Born in Ohio, she received a B.A. in Art History from Kent State University and an MA in Art History from Ohio State University before seeing the light and changing her career path to focus on art forms from the 20th century. She then received an MA and PhD in Radio, Television, & Film Studies from Northwestern University.

Currently Susan works as a researcher and writer for Facets Multi-Media in Chicago, an organization devoted to showcasing foreign, independent, and documentary films. She also teaches film studies at Oakton Community College and writes extensively on film and pop culture. She writes regularly for the Turner Classic Movies Web site and has authored many books, including *Elvis: A Tribute to His Life; Best of Elvis; Elvis Album; The Films of Elvis Presley; Understanding Elvis; Marilyn: Her Life and Legend; Florida on Film;* and *I Love Lucy.*

# Dedication

This book is dedicated to Bill Burk (1933–2008), a Memphis newspaper reporter who covered Elvis for over 20 years before founding *Elvis World* magazine. In 13 books on Elvis, Bill specialized in uncovering information no one else could get or in finding the truth behind the myth. A mentor, supporter, and friend to me, Bill Burk is missed in the world of Elvis's fans, writers, and colleagues.

# Author's Acknowledgments

I'd like to thank my literary agent, Julie Hill of Julie A. Hill and Assoc. LLC, for helping me find this great project. I would also like to acknowledge all of the people at Wiley Publishing who helped bring out the best in me, including acquisitions editor Stacy Kennedy, my patient and encouraging project editor Sarah Faulkner, my efficient copy editor Jessica Smith, and the technical editor Peter Nazareth. Finally, a special thanks to Rockin' Robin Rosaaen who was always there with a quick answer when I needed clarification on the finer points of Elvis lore and literature.

**Publisher's Acknowledgments**

We're proud of this book; please send us your comments through our Dummies online registration form located at http://dummies.custhelp.com. For other comments, please contact our Customer Care Department within the U.S. at 877-762-2974, outside the U.S. at 317-572-3993, or fax 317-572-4002.

Some of the people who helped bring this book to market include the following:

*Acquisitions, Editorial, and Media Development*

**Project Editor:** Sarah Faulkner

**Acquisitions Editor:** Stacy Kennedy

**Copy Editor:** Jessica Smith

**Assistant Editor:** Erin Calligan Mooney

**Editorial Program Coordinator:** Joe Niesen

**Technical Editor:** Peter Nazareth

**Editorial Manager:** Christine Meloy Beck

**Editorial Assistants:** Jennette ElNaggar, David Lutton

**Art Coordinator:** Alicia B. South

**Cover Photo:** Elvis images used by permission, Elvis Presley Enterprises, Inc.

**Cartoons:** Rich Tennant (www.the5thwave.com)

*Composition Services*

**Project Coordinator:** Patrick Redmond

**Layout and Graphics:** Reuben W. Davis, Joyce Haughey, Christine Williams

**Photographs:** Elvis images used by permission, Elvis Presley Enterprises, Inc.

**Proofreaders:** John Greenough, Bonnie Mikkelson

**Indexer:** Glassman Indexing Services

---

**Publishing and Editorial for Consumer Dummies**

    **Diane Graves Steele,** Vice President and Publisher, Consumer Dummies

    **Kristin Ferguson-Wagstaffe,** Product Development Director, Consumer Dummies

    **Ensley Eikenburg,** Associate Publisher, Travel

    **Kelly Regan,** Editorial Director, Travel

**Publishing for Technology Dummies**

    **Andy Cummings,** Vice President and Publisher, Dummies Technology/General User

**Composition Services**

    **Debbie Stailey,** Director of Composition Services

# Contents at a Glance

Introduction .................................................................... 1

## Part 1: From Rockabilly to Rock 'n' Roll ........................ 7
Chapter 1: Introducing Elvis Presley ........................................... 9
Chapter 2: Walking a Mile in His Shoes: Examining Elvis's Early Years ...... 27
Chapter 3: Touring As the Hillbilly Cat and the Blue Moon Boys ............. 49
Chapter 4: Shocking America: Elvis Becomes a National Sensation ............ 63
Chapter 5: What's the Ruckus About: The Impact of Elvis the Pelvis ......... 83

## Part II: From Hot-Headed Rebel to Hollywood Leading Man .................................................. 99
Chapter 6: Taming the Rebel: Elvis Goes to Hollywood ...................... 101
Chapter 7: Reinventing His Image: Elvis Becomes the Leading Man .......... 115
Chapter 8: Sinking to a Low Point in Hollywood ............................ 137
Chapter 9: Looking Beyond the Presley Travelogue .......................... 147
Chapter 10: Defending Elvis's Movies: They're Not That Bad ................ 159

## Part III: From the Las Vegas Stage to the End of the Road ................................................... 173
Chapter 11: Making the Comeback of a Lifetime ............................. 175
Chapter 12: Viva Las Vegas: Returning to Live Performances ................ 189
Chapter 13: Savoring Elvis in Concert ..................................... 197
Chapter 14: Enjoying a Professional Peak .................................. 219
Chapter 15: Fading Away ................................................... 231

## Part IV: From the King of Rock 'n' Roll to American Cultural Icon .......................................... 247
Chapter 16: In the Aftermath of Death ..................................... 249
Chapter 17: Examining the Jokes, Stereotypes, and Negative Influences ..... 259
Chapter 18: Appreciating Elvis as a Cultural and Historical Figure ........ 275
Chapter 19: Visiting the Sites: The Elvis Tourist ......................... 291
Chapter 20: Understanding Elvis Today ..................................... 303

## Part V: The Part of Tens ................................................................. 313
Chapter 21: Ten Best Elvis Songs ........................................................... 315
Chapter 22: Ten Best Elvis Albums .......................................................... 321
Chapter 23: Ten Best Elvis Moments ......................................................... 327
Chapter 24: Ten Best Elvis-Related Movies .................................................. 333

## Appendix: Cast of Characters ........................................... 339

## Index ........................................................................... 347

# Table of Contents

## *Introduction* ........................................................................ 1

About This Book ..................................................................... 2
Conventions Used in This Book ............................................. 2
What You're Not to Read ........................................................ 3
Foolish Assumptions .............................................................. 4
How This Book Is Organized ................................................. 4
    Part I: From Rockabilly to Rock 'n' Roll ........................ 4
    Part II: From Hot-Headed Rebel to Hollywood
       Leading Man ................................................................ 5
    Part III: From the Las Vegas Stage to the
       End of the Road ........................................................... 5
    Part IV: From the King of Rock 'n' Roll to American
       Cultural Icon ................................................................ 5
    Part V: The Part of Tens ................................................. 6
Icons Used in This Book ........................................................ 6
Where to Go from Here .......................................................... 6

## *Part 1: From Rockabilly to Rock 'n' Roll* ......................... 7

### **Chapter 1: Introducing Elvis Presley............................. 9**

Identifying a Cultural Icon ..................................................... 9
Uncovering the Roots of Elvis's Music ............................... 10
    Recording for Sun Studio ............................................ 11
    Gaining a fan base ........................................................ 12
Gyrating Across America ..................................................... 13
Changing Elvis's Notorious Image ...................................... 14
    Shooting his first films ................................................. 15
    Serving in the army ...................................................... 15
Becoming a Leading Man in Hollywood ............................. 16
    Starting out as an actor ............................................... 17
    Finishing as a movie star ............................................. 18
    Evaluating a Hollywood career ................................... 19
Capitalizing on a Turning Point ........................................... 19
    Making a comeback with the '68 Comeback Special ..... 20
    Reinventing the music ................................................. 20
    Taking time for a personal life .................................... 21

Returning to Live Performances ..................................................21
    Attending an Elvis concert: Teddy bears and underwear ..............22
    Dressing a star: The jumpsuits............................................22
    Appreciating the World's Greatest Entertainer: "Vegas Elvis" ......23
    Taking a toll: A personal and professional decline ........................24
The End of the Road for the King ................................................25
Tracing Elvis Presley's Continued Popularity ............................................25

## Chapter 2: Walking a Mile in His Shoes: Examining Elvis's Early Years ............27

Growing Up in Tupelo ....................................................28
    Introducing Elvis's parents....................................28
    Examining the family's greatest misfortune ............................30
    Considering Elvis's earliest musical influences and experiences....31
Walking in Memphis: Elvis the Teenager.........................................32
    Making the move...........................................................32
    Getting through high school................................................33
    Absorbing a medley of musical influences .....................34
    Understanding Southern musical genres............................36
Making Music and History at Sun Studio............................................37
    Taking that first step: Elvis, Marion, and the Memphis Recording Service ..................................................................37
    Meeting Sam Phillips ........................................................39
    Cutting "That's All Right"............................................40
    Releasing additional Sun Studio recordings............................42
Making His Radio Debut with Deejay Dewey Phillips ....................45
Performing in Public for the First Time ............................................46

## Chapter 3: Touring As the Hillbilly Cat and the Blue Moon Boys ....49

Introducing the Blue Moon Boys ..................................................50
Dressing As the Hillbilly Cat.........................................................51
Hitting the Road on the Country-Western Circuit .....................53
    Failing at the Opry ............................................................53
    Hopping aboard the Louisiana Hayride ............................54
    Adding a drummer: D.J. Fontana...........................................55
    Acquiring a manager: Bob Neal................................................55
    Becoming a hard act to follow ..........................................56
Recognizing the Importance of Touring ........................................56
    One in a million: Standing out from the crowd .....................57
    Establishing a diverse following ...........................................58
    Shakin' and gyratin': Honing a performing style............................60

## Chapter 4: Shocking America: Elvis Becomes a National Sensation ............63

Meeting Colonel Tom Parker..............................................64
    Uncovering the Colonel's true background..............................64
    Waiting in the wings to sign Elvis ..............................................65
    Making Elvis his sole client.....................................................66

## Table of Contents

Finding a Home at RCA ..................................................................... 68
    Working with Steve Sholes ........................................................ 68
    Recording for RCA for the first time......................................... 69
    Releasing an album: Elvis Presley.............................................. 72
    Tweaking Elvis's sound .............................................................. 72
    Considering the role of Hill and Range ..................................... 74
Taking Television by Storm............................................................... 75
    Appearing on *Stage Show*......................................................... 76
    Tearing up *The Milton Berle Show* ........................................... 77
    Clowning around on *The Steve Allen Show*............................. 78
    From the waist up: Tackling *The Ed Sullivan Show* ................ 79

### Chapter 5: What's the Ruckus About: The Impact of Elvis the Pelvis . . . . . . . . . . . . . . . . . . . . . . . . . . . . . . .83

Anatomy of a Controversy ............................................................... 83
    Weighing the backlash: Generational conflict and sex ........... 85
    Weighing the criticism: Rock 'n' Roll versus Tin Pan Alley........... 87
    Weighing the subtext: It's the Civil War all over again .............. 90
Cooling the Controversy.................................................................. 92
    Countering the bad publicity .................................................... 92
    Merchandizing Elvis like other pop culture figures ..................... 93
    Going Hollywood........................................................................ 94
    Buying Graceland....................................................................... 94
    Serving in the army now ........................................................... 95
    Controlling the media's access to Elvis ..................................... 96
Noting Two Touchstones in Elvis's Personal Life ............................. 96
    Suffering a terrible loss: The death of Gladys Presley .............. 97
    Meeting Priscilla......................................................................... 97

## Part II: From Hot-Headed Rebel to Hollywood Leading Man...................................................... 99

### Chapter 6: Taming the Rebel: Elvis Goes to Hollywood . . . . . . . . . .101

Embarking upon a Movie Career ................................................... 102
    Signing with Hal Wallis ............................................................. 102
    Following in the footsteps of Sinatra....................................... 103
    Evaluating *Love Me Tender* .................................................... 103
Telling Elvis's Life Story: How His Movies Act As Autobiography ........ 105
    Looking at *Loving You* ............................................................ 106
    Exploring *Jailhouse Rock* ....................................................... 108
    Turning *King Creole* into an Elvis vehicle .............................. 110
Using Elvis's Movies to Spin His Image.......................................... 111
    Explaining the success myth.................................................... 111
    Seeing the characters of Deke, Vince, and Danny
        as Elvis and vice versa........................................................ 112

Shaping Elvis's music and performing style
into Hollywood production numbers ........................... 113
Co-starring with some well-known actors ......................................... 114

## Chapter 7: Reinventing His Image: Elvis Becomes the Leading Man ....115

Returning to Hollywood to Rebuild a Career ............................................ 116
Using the army as a turning point ...................................... 116
The King meets the Voice .................................................. 118
Singing the *G.I. Blues* .......................................................... 119
Calculating a Successful Movie Formula ........................................... 121
Establishing the Presley formula ......................................... 121
Crediting Hal Wallis as the father of the Elvis musical ................ 123
Making an Elvis film: Add these ingredients and stir .................... 124
Listing the best of the Travelogues .................................... 125
Playing a Leading Man Off-Screen ................................................. 127
Handling the press .................................................................. 127
Dressing like a movie star ....................................................... 128
Taking the South out of the boy .............................................. 129
Hanging with the Memphis Mafia ............................................. 129
Dating his leading ladies ........................................................ 130
Trading Rock 'n' Roll for Pop .......................................................... 131
Living in a pop-music world ..................................................... 131
Recording in the studio again ................................................. 132
Savoring the soundtrack tunes ............................................... 133
Saying goodbye to live performances ..................................... 134
Marrying Priscilla and Settling Down . . . At Least for a While ............. 134

## Chapter 8: Sinking to a Low Point in Hollywood ....137

Examining the Change in Approach to Making an Elvis Movie ............. 138
Dealing with the Devil: Considering the Colonel's New Movie Deals ... 139
Let's make a deal ................................................................... 139
Let's make a movie — fast and cheap .................................... 140
Introducing Sam Katzman: King of the Quickies ............................... 142
*Kissin' Cousins* ....................................................................... 142
*Harum Scarum* ...................................................................... 143
Considering the Movie Music ........................................................... 144
Considering the role of the songwriters ................................. 145
Factoring in poor marketing practices .................................... 145
Focusing on the Fans ......................................................................... 146
Reflecting on Elvis's Movie Career .................................................... 146

## Chapter 9: Looking Beyond the Presley Travelogue ....147

Breaking the Travelogue Mold .......................................................... 147
Delving into the genres and story lines ................................. 148
Exploring Elvis's roles ............................................................. 148
Clashing over the music .......................................................... 148

Considering Four Films from the Early '60s ........................................... 149
    Shooting a western: *Flaming Star* ........................................... 150
    Milking the melodrama: *Wild in the Country* ...................... 151
    Tackling satire: *Follow That Dream* ...................................... 152
    Making a musical drama: *Kid Galahad* ................................. 153
Factoring in the Final Films ......................................................... 153
    Sleeping with the girl (finally): *Live a Little, Love a Little* ........ 155
    Reminiscing with a period piece: *The Trouble with Girls* ......... 155
    Breaking into the Italian western genre: *Charro!* ................... 156
    Getting dramatic: *Change of Habit* ...................................... 157

## Chapter 10: Defending Elvis's Movies: They're Not That Bad ...... 159

Understanding Why the Movies Need to Be Defended ............................ 160
    Factoring in Elvis's dissatisfaction ......................................... 160
    Examining the standard view of Elvis's movies ...................... 162
Appreciating Elvis's Movies As Part of the Teen Musical Subgenre ..... 165
    The typical teen musical ........................................................ 166
    The Presley Travelogues ........................................................ 167
    Revealing how the movie music works .................................. 170
Following in Elvis's Footsteps ..................................................... 171

# Part III: From the Las Vegas Stage to the End of the Road ........ 173

## Chapter 11: Making the Comeback of a Lifetime ................... 175

Getting Back on Track with a New Producer ............................ 176
    Working with producer Felton Jarvis ..................................... 176
    Perfecting Elvis's songs and their sound ................................. 177
    Spreading the Gospel ............................................................. 178
    Savoring the success of *How Great Thou Art* ........................ 179
Creating a Hit: *The '68 Comeback Special* ................................ 179
    Shaping the special ................................................................ 180
    Looking closely at the completed special .............................. 182
    Understanding how the special redefined Elvis Presley ......... 184
Recording *From Elvis in Memphis* .............................................. 184
    Rediscovering Memphis as a recording center ...................... 185
    Establishing a musical direction with his latest album .......... 185
    Selecting the songs for the American
        Sound recording sessions ................................................. 187

## Chapter 12: Viva Las Vegas: Returning to Live Performances ...... 189

Conquering Las Vegas ................................................................ 190
    Preparing for the first concert performance in eight years ..... 191
    Opening night: July 31, 1969 ................................................. 191
    Congratulating Elvis after the show ....................................... 192

Signing the tablecloth deal ............................................................... 193
Breaking records ................................................................................ 194
Returning to Las Vegas ..................................................................... 194
Taking His Show on the Road .................................................................. 195
Playing the Astrodome ...................................................................... 195
Going through a divorce ................................................................... 196

## Chapter 13: Savoring Elvis in Concert .......................... 197

Introducing the Musicians Who Joined Elvis in Concert ...................... 198
Rock 'n' rollers: The TCB Band ........................................................ 198
Gospel singers J.D. Sumner and the Stamps Quartet ................... 201
Female vocal group, the Sweet Inspirations .................................. 202
Soprano Kathy Westmoreland .......................................................... 203
Orchestra director Joe Guercio ...................................................... 203
Examining the Music: Uniquely Elvis ...................................................... 204
Revamping old favorites .................................................................. 204
Performing the new singles ............................................................. 205
Move over Paul Simon: "Bridge Over Troubled Water" ................ 206
Remembering swamp rock: "Polk Salad Annie" ............................ 206
Singin' a song about the Southland: "An American Trilogy" ........ 207
Pondering the Priscilla Songs .......................................................... 208
Singing it his way ............................................................................. 208
Appreciating the Significance of All the King's Jumpsuits ................... 209
Designing the first jumpsuit ............................................................ 210
Considering the jumpsuits as autobiography ............................... 210
Ritualizing the Experience ...................................................................... 213
Making an entrance ......................................................................... 214
Exchanging gifts and tossing underwear ....................................... 214
Romancing his audience ................................................................. 215
Dramatizing his act ......................................................................... 216
Leaving the building ........................................................................ 216

## Chapter 14: Enjoying a Professional Peak ...................... 219

Becoming an Outstanding Young Man .................................................. 220
Went to a Garden Party: Elvis Performs in New York City .................... 221
Performing for the World: Aloha from Hawaii ....................................... 223
Achieving a career pinnacle ............................................................ 224
Broadcasting to the world ............................................................... 225
Tossing the cape .............................................................................. 225
Reliving the concert over and over with the Aloha albums .......... 226
Capturing the Concert Years on Film ..................................................... 226
*Elvis: That's the Way It Is* .............................................................. 226
*Elvis on Tour* ................................................................................... 228
Influencing Las Vegas Entertainment ..................................................... 228
A therapeutic shot in the arm for Las Vegas .................................. 229
Establishing the Vegas-style performance template ..................... 229

## Chapter 15: Fading Away .................................................. 231
Caught in a Trap: Discovering the Downside of Fame ........................ 232
Traveling the Road of Excess .............................................. 232
    Living in a state of arrested development ............................ 233
    Struggling with a drug problem ....................................... 235
    Wrestling with a weight problem ...................................... 237
    Collecting extravagances ............................................. 238
Lost and Weary: Watching the King's Career Decline ........................ 240
    Paying the piper: The high price of the road ......................... 241
    Singing them moody and blue: Elvis records his last albums ........... 241
August 16, 1977: Last Stop on the Mystery Train ........................... 243
    Shocking the world with the news ..................................... 244
    Preparing a Southern-style funeral ................................... 245
    The King is dead, long live the King ................................. 246

# Part IV: From the King of Rock 'n' Roll to American Cultural Icon ............................... 247

## Chapter 16: In the Aftermath of Death ................................... 249
Moving Elvis to Meditation Garden ......................................... 250
    Thieves in the night ................................................. 250
    Coming home to Graceland one last time ............................... 251
Establishing New Rituals .................................................. 251
    Gathering at the gates ............................................... 252
    Returning to Memphis ................................................. 252
    Establishing Elvis Week .............................................. 254
    The evolution of Elvis Week .......................................... 257

## Chapter 17: Examining the Jokes, Stereotypes, and Negative Influences .................................................. 259
Bashing Elvis: The Press versus Presley ................................... 260
    Shaping early opinions: The bodyguard book ........................... 261
    Revealing the ugly truth: Elvis's drug abuse ......................... 262
    Weighing in on weight ................................................ 264
    Spreading rumors: Elvis is alive ..................................... 265
    Treating Elvis with respect: It's about time ......................... 267
Marketing Elvis Presley: Would You Like to Buy Some Elvis Sweat? .......... 267
    Recognizing the Colonel's hand ....................................... 268
    Valuing the Elvis merchandise: From trash to treasure ................ 269
Reading the Memoirs: Elvis, We Hardly Knew Ya ............................. 270
    The Memphis Mafia cash in ............................................ 271
    The cook, the stepfamily, the wife, and her lover .................... 272
Imitating the King: From Impersonators to Tribute Artists ................. 273

## Chapter 18: Appreciating Elvis as a Cultural and Historical Figure .......275

Taking Care of Elvis's Music: BMG-RCA ................................................275
    Cranking out the discs: RCA puts the pressing plants to work ..........276
    Developing new strategies to release Elvis's music .......................277
    Introducing the Masters Series to casual listeners and die-hard fans alike ..........278
    Digging for gold ...................................................................279
    Marketing *ELVIS: 30 #1 Hits* .................................................280
Mythologizing Elvis Onscreen ..................................................281
    Busting the biopics ..........................................................282
    Discovering the documentary: This Is Elvis ..........................284
    Turning Elvis into a symbol in fictional films ........................284
    Showing up in biopics of other celebrities ............................287
Reading Some Worthy Elvis Biographies ....................................289

## Chapter 19: Visiting the Sites: The Elvis Tourist .......291

Graceland: Visiting the King's Palace ........................................291
    Still devoted: Looking at Priscilla's role in managing Graceland ..........292
    Walking through the house ................................................293
    Strolling the grounds ......................................................296
Where Legends Were Born: Stopping by Sun Studio .....................297
    Sun before Elvis .............................................................298
    Sun after Elvis ...............................................................298
Touring Other Elvis Sites in Memphis .....................................300
Making a Pilgrimage to Tupelo ................................................301
Exploring the California Hideaways ........................................301

## Chapter 20: Understanding Elvis Today .......303

Innovator and History Maker: Elvis Changes the Music of the 1950s ..........304
    Integrating regional styles of music ...................................304
    Defying pop music standards ............................................305
    Influencing an important generation ..................................306
Shaping Youth Culture in the 1950s ........................................306
    Forging an identity .........................................................307
    Smells like teen spirit ......................................................307
Offering Something to Everyone .............................................308
    Comparing Rebel Elvis with Vegas Elvis ............................308
    Acknowledging his Southern roots ....................................310
    A taste of forbidden fruit: Examining Elvis's effect on his young female fans ..........310
    Considering other meanings of Elvis's image ......................312

## Part V: The Part of Tens .................................................. 313

### Chapter 21: Ten Best Elvis Songs ................................. 315
"That's All Right" ........................................................................ 315
"Heartbreak Hotel" ..................................................................... 316
"Don't Be Cruel" ......................................................................... 316
"All Shook Up" ............................................................................ 317
"Jailhouse Rock" ......................................................................... 317
"It's Now or Never" .................................................................... 318
"Return to Sender" ..................................................................... 318
"How Great Thou Art" ............................................................... 319
"If I Can Dream" ......................................................................... 319
"Suspicious Minds" .................................................................... 320

### Chapter 22: Ten Best Elvis Albums ............................... 321
*Elvis Presley*: The First Album ................................................. 321
Elvis's Christmas Album: Rock 'n' Roll Controversy ............. 322
*Elvis Is Back!* Home from the Army ......................................... 322
*Blue Hawaii*: The Movie Music ................................................. 323
*How Great Thou Art*: Gospel Roots ......................................... 323
*From Elvis in Memphis*: Back in the Groove ........................... 324
*That's the Way It Is*: Elvis's Heartsongs ................................... 324
*Reconsider Baby*: Ain't Nothin' But the Blues ........................ 325
The Masters Series ..................................................................... 325
*ELVIS: 30 #1 Hits* ....................................................................... 326

### Chapter 23: Ten Best Elvis Moments .............................. 327
Performing "That's All Right" at the Overton Park Shell,
   July 30, 1954 ............................................................................ 327
Performing "Hound Dog" on *The Milton Berle Show,* June 5, 1956 ........ 328
Defying Authority Onstage in Jacksonville, August 11, 1956 ............. 328
Getting Censored on *The Ed Sullivan Show,* January 6, 1957 ............. 329
Performing the Title Song in *Jailhouse Rock,* 1957 ........................... 329
Swinging with Ann-Margret in *Viva Las Vegas,* 1964 ...................... 330
Mesmerizing a Live Audience on *The '68 Comeback
   Special,* December 3, 1968 ..................................................... 330
Opening with "Blue Suede Shoes" at the
   International Hotel, July 31, 1969 ........................................ 331
Shaking Hands with Richard Nixon, December 21, 1970 ....... 331
Performing for the World: *Aloha from Hawaii,* January 14, 1973 ....... 332

### Chapter 24: Ten Best Elvis-Related Movies .................... 333
*Bye Bye Birdie* ............................................................................. 333
*Mystery Train* .............................................................................. 334
*Leningrad Cowboys Go America* .............................................. 335

Wild at Heart ..................................................................................... 335
Honeymoon in Vegas ...................................................................... 335
True Romance .................................................................................. 336
Picasso at the Lapin Agile ............................................................... 336
3000 Miles to Graceland .................................................................. 337
Walk the Line ................................................................................... 337
Hounddog .......................................................................................... 338

# Appendix: Cast of Characters ......................... 339

# Index ....................................................................... 347

# Introduction

*E*lvis Presley needs no introduction, but he does need an updated evaluation of his life and career and a sincere appreciation of his contributions to popular American music. After years of fan hyperbole, accusations and rumors by former friends and associates, and bad jokes about fried banana sandwiches, it's time to give Elvis his due — and that's just what this book does.

Even though Elvis died at age 42, he managed to accomplish more than several entertainers combined. Elvis integrated different styles of music to create the sound called "rockabilly," a musical thread that made up the fabric of a then-new genre referred to as "rock 'n' roll." Openly singing the songs of African Americans (and properly acknowledging their influence on his sound), Elvis helped focus industry and audience attention on blues and R&B. He achieved integration musically, but the country struggled with the concept socially.

Drop-dead handsome and charismatic, Elvis parlayed his rock 'n' roll notoriety into movie stardom. A decade later, after a new generation of rock 'n' rollers had forgotten him, and the mainstream press had written him off as obsolete, Elvis reinvented himself to take the stage once more to become a 1970s superstar. Gaudy, glamorous, and glorious, Elvis filled Vegas hotel showrooms and huge concert venues with old and new fans who wanted to see a legend.

Elvis's career evolved through many phases, absorbed a variety of musical styles, and involved all arenas of entertainment. Some people are fans of his early rock 'n' roll music; others are fans of his movies; still others prefer the gaudy splendor of the Vegas concert performer. Elvis's widespread appeal developed from a diverse career that as the title of one of his albums suggests truly held something for everybody. Likewise, this book about Elvis contains something of interest for everyone, whether you're an Elvis fan, a pop culture enthusiast, a lover of indigenous American music, or someone looking for a fascinating story about fame and fortune.

Elvis left behind no autobiography, memoirs, or even a definitive interview. Throughout much of his career, any interaction with the media was through press conferences, which aren't conducive to revealing personal information. As a matter of fact, you could say that Elvis's approach to the press was to conceal information more than to reveal it. Consequently, direct access to Elvis's personal feelings, beliefs, and opinions on any given topic is rare. Most of the time, information on his feelings and opinions has come to us secondhand through memoirs by former associates and family members, many of whom have agendas or, at the very least, fuzzy memories. I have made every effort to include Elvis's perspective on important aspects of his life and career, but in many cases, it just isn't possible. Ironically, for one of the most written-about entertainers of the 20th century, Elvis lacks a direct voice in his own story.

## About This Book

*Elvis For Dummies* covers all phases of Elvis's career, from his musical influences as a teenager in Memphis and his first recordings for Sun Studio to his final concert and continued popularity even in death. All the celebrated events that everyone knows about are featured as well — his controversial hip-swiveling performing style, the famous *Ed Sullivan Show* appearance, his much-maligned movie career, his marriage to Priscilla Beaulieu, and his fascination with jumpsuits. In addition, I shine a spotlight on little-known details about his life to provide you with a well-rounded portrait of the 20th century's most famous personality.

Also covered are the anniversary celebrations, memorial events, important posthumous record releases, and other post-death phenomena that keep his memory alive and introduce his music to new generations. Most importantly, I explain the significance of the events of his career, analyze the meaning of the music, and put Elvis into a cultural perspective. The question most often asked about Elvis is "why." Why is he still so famous; why does he still sell records; why does he continue to draw new fans; and why does he continue to be the number-one moneymaking celebrity. By the end of this book, you'll understand why Elvis remains such a presence in our culture.

You don't need to read this book in chronological order to discover Elvis. Though the structure follows the chronology of Elvis's life, each chapter is written to stand on its own. Feel free to select any chapter in any part and start reading without worrying about becoming confused. You can move around the book as you like, picking your favorite Elvis topics to read first.

## Conventions Used in This Book

I use several conventions consistently throughout this book, including the following:

- Most of the time, I refer to Elvis by his first name because the entertainment industry, fans, the media, and average Americans tend to recognize him by his first name. Partly because of his level of fame and partly because of the uniqueness of his first name, Elvis usually is the only name needed. However, when making formal declarations (or just for the sake of variety), I sometimes use the full name Elvis Presley and, occasionally, Presley.

## Introduction

- Elvis's longtime manager, Colonel Tom Parker, goes by many names, befitting an old-school carnival manager who was always working an angle. Like those who knew him, I refer to him as the Colonel, Colonel Parker, or simply Parker.

- When chronicling the success of Elvis's records, I refer to their chart status, which refers to *Billboard* magazine's music charts. *Billboard* has been devoted to the music industry since the 1930s, and its charts track the popularity of recordings. The methods of calculation have evolved with the ever-changing music industry, but the *Billboard* charts remain the standard measure for rating songs in the U.S. The two most important charts are the Hot 100, or Top 100, which ranks the top 100 songs, and the *Billboard* 200, formerly called the Top LPs or Top Albums chart, which tracks album sales. When I mention that an Elvis song became number one, or that he enjoyed many number-one records, I'm referring to the first position on the Hot 100.

- Another measure of success for a recording artist is the number of gold, platinum, and multi-platinum records accumulated during a career. The Recording Industry Association of America (RIAA) awards (or certifies) gold, platinum, or multi-platinum status based on the number of records sold through retail and other ancillary markets. Certification isn't automatic, however. The record company must request it and pay to have sales of a given album or single audited. To receive gold status, a single or album must sell 500,000 units. In 1976, platinum status was instituted by the RIAA for albums selling one million units. In 1984, multi-platinum status was announced for records that doubled, tripled, or quadrupled their platinum amounts. Even though Elvis died in 1977, the Elvis Presley Estate and RCA (his record label) asked the RIAA to audit sales of his records to keep his statistics up-to-date.

- I use **bold** text to highlight key words in bulleted lists.

- When I introduce a new term that you may not be familiar with, I use *italics* and define the term within the text.

## What You're Not to Read

My fondest hope is that you pore over every word in this book, but if you're short on time (perhaps because you're busy listening to Elvis's albums and planning your next trip to Graceland), feel free to skip the following:

- **Sidebars:** If you're reading in a hurry or skimming for essential information, you can skip over the sidebars, which appear in gray boxes throughout the book. Although the information I include in the sidebars is fun and interesting, it isn't essential to the main points.

✔ **Any text accompanied by the Trivia icon:** You can amaze your friends and family with the details of Elvis's life and career if you read the text next to the Trivia icons (see the icon pictures at the end of this introduction), but these tidbits aren't essential to understanding Elvis's importance.

## Foolish Assumptions

As I started writing *Elvis For Dummies,* I made some assumptions about the folks who would be interested in this book. First and foremost, I assume the obvious — that you're interested in discovering something about Elvis. I also made some other assumptions. Perhaps one of the following applies to you:

✔ You recognize Elvis Presley and can sing along to "Jailhouse Rock" or another famous tune, but you want to know why he warrants such fame.

✔ You have seen dozens of books on Elvis Presley and were looking for the one that really explains the meaning of Elvis.

✔ You have always wanted to go to Graceland but don't know what to expect.

## How This Book Is Organized

*Elvis For Dummies* is divided into five parts. Four sections relate to the phases of Elvis's career, and one consists of useful reference lists.

### Part 1: From Rockabilly to Rock 'n' Roll

Starting at the beginning with Elvis's childhood in Tupelo, Mississippi, this part discusses the importance of his Southern background in the development of his sound. That sound was evident from his very first recordings in 1954 for tiny Sun Records, a regionally based company owned and operated by Sam Phillips. Phillips helped develop Elvis's musical style, eventually dubbed "rockabilly," which represents the start of Presley's career. Elvis's regional success led to a nationally based record contract in 1956 with RCA, which tweaked his style and called it rock 'n' roll. Elvis's association with rock 'n' roll, combined with his unique performing style, created a furor in the mainstream press and inflamed the public.

## Part II: From Hot-Headed Rebel to Hollywood Leading Man

As soon as producer Hal Wallis signed Elvis to a movie contract in 1956, the young singer talked about nothing but being a serious actor. His 13-year Hollywood career didn't work out quite the way that he wanted it to, but it did help cool the controversy over his musical performing style and change his image from notorious rock 'n' roller to handsome leading man. This part chronicles his entire movie career, from the excitement of *King Creole* to the nonsense of *Kissin' Cousins.* Typically, Elvis's film career is criticized because much of it consisted of formulaic musical comedies, but I offer a different perspective. I acknowledge the good films, dispel misconceptions, and offer a context with which to appreciate them.

## Part III: From the Las Vegas Stage to the End of the Road

In 1968, with the help of a well-received television special on NBC, which was later referred to as *The '68 Comeback Special,* Elvis reinvented himself. No longer challenged by the musical comedies he had been pushed into, he recorded a critically acclaimed album and then returned to live performances in 1969. Eventually, however, the rigors of the road led to a decline in his career and his health. This part covers this last phase of his career, from a career high point when he premiered his live act at the International Hotel in Las Vegas in 1969 to his death in 1977.

## Part IV: From the King of Rock 'n' Roll to American Cultural Icon

Death did nothing to change the popularity of Elvis, and this part proves it by detailing the many ways (positive and negative) that his memory has been kept alive. Each year in Memphis, fans celebrate his life and music on the anniversary of his death by visiting important Elvis-related sites such as his home, Graceland. Over the years, RCA has constructed Elvis's legacy based on key releases of his historically important music. In addition, more notorious events in his life came to light and focused attention on his personality, career, and death. All of this, and more, has combined to keep Elvis in the public eye.

## Part V: The Part of Tens

A trademark feature of the *For Dummies* series, the Part of Tens contains fun and interesting lists of reference-style information. My lists include the obvious, such as the ten best Elvis songs and the ten best Elvis albums. I also include a list of the ten best Elvis moments, which features the high points of his life and career that meant the most to Elvis. I round out this part with a chapter on ten Elvis-related movies, which are fictional films featuring Elvis as a character. Also, don't forget to check out the appendix, which is a cast of characters listing some important people in Elvis's life.

## Icons Used in This Book

In traditional *For Dummies* style, I have chosen some icons to make accessing information even easier. The icons in this book include the following:

This icon signals a fascinating fact or an interesting detail that adds dimension to the main ideas discussed in a given chapter.

This icon highlights an important point that you should remember for the future.

Like adjectives in a sentence, quotes from Elvis or from people who knew him or worked with him add color and an expressive personal perspective.

## Where to Go from Here

I organized this book so you can quickly and easily find the information you're looking for. For main topics and key events in Elvis's life, check out the table of contents or index. Because *Elvis For Dummies* isn't linear, feel free to start anywhere. If you love the Vegas Elvis, start with Chapter 12, which describes his triumphant return to the stage; if you're a rock 'n' roll rebel, flip to Chapter 4 to read about Elvis in 1956 when he tore across the country like a hurricane, redefining musical tastes and upsetting the status quo. It doesn't matter where you start; it's just important that you do.

# Part I
# From Rockabilly to Rock 'n' Roll

## The 5th Wave        By Rich Tennant

1954 - ELVIS PRESLEY INVENTS HIS SWIVEL HIP DANCING STYLE AS A DIRECT RESULT OF HIS WARDROBE PERSON LEAVING THE IRON ON HIS PANTS ZIPPER TOO LONG

*Ho mama...*

## In this part . . .

To explore the beginning of Elvis Presley's musical career is to explore the development of rock 'n' roll and its impact on our culture.

With Sam Phillips, the owner-operator of Sun Records, Elvis developed rockabilly, a cornerstone of rock 'n' roll. And then he introduced it to a nationally based audience that didn't know what to make of the singer, his music, or his performing style. This part goes back to Elvis's youth to reveal his inspirations and then follows his path from Sun Studio, where he cut his first record in 1954, through his controversial performances on national television to his stint in the army in 1958.

# Chapter 1

# Introducing Elvis Presley

*In This Chapter*
▶ Outlining Elvis's place in American history
▶ Summarizing Elvis's life
▶ Tracking Elvis's popularity from beginning to end

On the one hand, Elvis Presley needs no introduction, because his name and face are recognized around the world as the ultimate celebrity. Imitators re-create his act; late-night comedians joke about him; cable channels rerun his movies; and merchandisers exploit his image on everything from T-shirts to lamps. On the other hand, the reasons for his fame have become lost in the trappings of celebrity, especially for younger generations born after his death on August 16, 1977.

For the original fans, who have remained loyal for over 50 years, Elvis earned his reputation as the King of Rock 'n' Roll; for others, discovering why he deserved his fame and a place in American cultural history may be a revelation.

In this chapter, I introduce you to Elvis Presley through the high points of his life and career, including his post-death popularity. This chapter sets up an extensive exploration of Elvis Presley — the cultural icon — that details the events of his life, explains the significance of his music, and contemplates his meaning to American pop culture.

## Identifying a Cultural Icon

Almost everyone knows that Elvis Presley was a famous singer, but many people don't fully understand what he contributed to popular music to earn his widespread fame. Elvis combined different types of music to form a style called *rockabilly,* which became one of the key sounds in rock 'n' roll. To form this musical style, he fused the country-western music of the South with the rhythm and blues of African Americans and the pop music that dominated the radio and recording industries.

**REMEMBER:** The combination of musical genres and sounds into a new style of music was Elvis's true gift and his contribution to popular culture. That this integration of musical styles took place just prior to the civil rights movement, prefiguring social integration, makes this moment in pop culture history seem momentous.

Elvis wasn't the first to sing in a rock 'n' roll style, so he can't be credited with inventing it. But, his version of this new music became widely popular during the mid-1950s. He spread rock 'n' roll music across the country, making it popular to a wide audience, especially teenagers. In that regard, he was a true innovator. (For more information on Elvis's start in music, see Chapter 2).

Elvis also yielded a strong influence on youth culture. During the 1950s, teenagers had begun to think of themselves as being different from their parents' generation. Because of the economic prosperity of the period, teens enjoyed a disposable income that they could spend on themselves instead of contributing toward family survival. With that money they dressed themselves in fashions marketed to their age group, went to movies that featured stars of their generation, and listened to music that appealed to them. So it wasn't a surprise when Presley's rock 'n' roll music, his hairstyle, and his fashion sense became a part of this new culture for teenagers. (For more information on the burgeoning youth culture, see Chapter 5.)

Later in his career, Presley changed his musical style and his personal look to keep up with the times and gain popularity among older audiences. He became a movie star during the 1960s and then returned to live musical performances during the 1970s. Because his career went through so many changes, he was popular with different types of people for different reasons. Even after his death, his popularity remains strong among a wide variety of people. This wide popularity, as well as his important role in American musical history, makes him a cultural icon.

## *Uncovering the Roots of Elvis's Music*

On January 8, 1935, in Tupelo, Mississippi, Elvis Aron Presley was born a half hour after his stillborn twin brother, Jesse Garon. Thus, the occasion was a mixed blessing to parents Vernon and Gladys Presley, who lived in a two-room shotgun shack on the wrong side of the tracks in Tupelo. A true son of the South, Elvis never ventured far from his roots, physically or musically. While a young boy in Tupelo, Elvis learned to play the guitar from relatives, and then he fell under the influence of country-western singer Mississippi Slim.

## Chapter 1: Introducing Elvis Presley

It wasn't until his family moved to Memphis that Elvis's real musical education began. The diversity of music on Memphis's radio stations exposed Elvis to a variety of genres, which eventually influenced his music. Several radio stations played country music, and big band music was broadcast from the famed Peabody Hotel. Rhythm-and-blues artists could be heard on two different radio stations: WDIA and WHBQ. WDIA was owned by two white men, but it was mostly staffed by black disc jockeys who played the locally produced records of hometown bluesmen. WHBQ played a variety of music, but it's best remembered for disc jockey Dewey Phillips's *Red Hot and Blue* program that showcased the recordings of black artists.

Memphis also developed into the center for white gospel music during the 1950s, so the four-part harmonies of the gospel quartets who regularly visited the city became another influence on the teenage Elvis. He and his parents, and later he and his girlfriend, regularly attended the all-night gospel sings at Ellis Auditorium. In addition, the city's Beale Street district was home to the clubs and joints where African American musicians played blues and rhythm and blues. Elvis became familiar with the music of the well-known local R&B artists, including B.B. King, Rufus Thomas, and Big Memphis Ma Rainey. All these Southern-based musical genres inspired Elvis's early singing style, which turned out to be a true fusion of sounds. (For more information on Elvis's early years, see Chapter 2.)

## Recording for Sun Studio

Sam Phillips, owner of Sun Studio and a small Memphis-based record company also called Sun, recorded the music of blues and R&B musicians. He was quoted in local papers as saying, "If I could find a white man who could sing with the sound and feel of a black man, I could make a billion dollars." Little did he know that Elvis would soon walk right through his doorway.

Elvis's ability to integrate Southern musical genres into a blend of beat and rhythm was exactly what Phillips was looking for. However, it took some time before the two walked into the studio together and made history with Elvis's first recording, "That's All Right," which was an old blues tune originally written and recorded by Arthur "Big Boy" Crudup. Elvis's interpretation of the song featured a relaxed vocal style, upbeat tempo, and a driving rhythm as well as these two elements that would make his sound famous:

- Syncopated lyrics using a hiccupping sound
- Reverberation for an echo effect

Elvis's sound became the essence of rockabilly, though no one called it by that name at the time. A few days after his first recording, Elvis and the two musicians who backed him up — guitarist Scotty Moore and bass player Bill Black — recorded the bluegrass classic "Blue Moon of Kentucky" as the flip side to "That's All Right," giving Elvis his first single. (To read more about this single, check out Chapter 2.)

Sam Phillips took this first record to disc jockey Dewey Phillips (no relation to Sam) to play on his *Red Hot and Blue* radio program as well as to other deejays at other stations. By the end of the month, "That's All Right" was shooting up the local charts, and Elvis made his first major public appearance at the Overton Park Shell.

## Gaining a fan base

From the summer of 1954 to the end of 1955, Elvis and his band, who called themselves the Hillbilly Cat and the Blue Moon Boys, enjoyed success as a Southern-based country-western act. Even though their music sounded decidedly different from typical country music, their status as white Southern singers classified them and their music as "country." They cut four more singles for Sun Studio and toured across the South on the same bill as such well-known country acts as Mother Maybelle and the Carter Sisters, Hank Snow, Faron Young, and Ferlin Husky.

Elvis's singing style wasn't the only unique feature of his high-powered act. As he crisscrossed the South, his performing style evolved to become a unique, highly energetic part of an Elvis Presley performance. Dressed in outrageously colorful clothes — such as those worn by R&B artists down on Beale Street — Elvis moved throughout his entire act, bouncing on the balls of his feet, shaking his legs, and swiveling his hips. In addition, bass player Bill Black, something of a comedian, danced and rolled around on the floor with his huge bass fiddle. The trio's frenzied performances were considered by some venues to be too wild, and other country performers hated to follow their act, but their weekly appearances on the *Louisiana Hayride* radio program brought them wide exposure across the South and a loud, raucous, and youthful fan base.

In *The Nashville Sound: Bright Lights and Country Music* by Paul Hemphill, country singer Bob Luman recalls seeing Elvis when Luman was still a teenager in Kilgore, Texas: "This cat came out in red pants and a green coat and a pink shirt and socks, and he had this sneer on his face and he stood behind the mike for five minutes, I'll bet, before he made a move. Then he hit his guitar a lick, and he broke two strings. Hell, I'd been playing for ten years, and I hadn't broken a total of two strings. So there he was, these two strings dangling, and he hadn't done anything except break guitar strings yet, and these high school girls were screaming and fainting and running up to the stage, and then he started to move his hips real slow like he had a thing for his guitar . . . ."

Chapter 1: Introducing Elvis Presley

The antics of the fans, especially the girls, drew the attention of country promoter Colonel Tom Parker (also known as simply "the Colonel"), who believed the strange-looking kid with the big moves could be a national success. By the end of 1955, Parker had succeeded in becoming Elvis's manager, and with that the stage was set for Presley's introduction to Middle America. (For more information on this era of Elvis's career, see Chapter 3.)

## Gyrating Across America

Colonel Parker negotiated a deal with the nationally based company RCA Victor to sign Elvis to a contract. The strategy at RCA involved exposing Elvis to mainstream audiences by promoting him in the nationally based pop market as well as the regionally based country and R&B markets. On January 8, 1956, Elvis recorded his first songs for RCA, including "Heartbreak Hotel." An instant success, the song climbed to number one on the pop and country charts and number three on the R&B chart. (For more information on Elvis's contract with RCA and his first recordings for the company, see Chapter 4.)

Parker's goal from the beginning was to gain the broadest audience possible for his one and only client. In addition to promoting Elvis's records in the pop market to court the teen audience nationwide, he wanted to use television to broaden his "boy's" appeal. Little did he realize that he was about to set off one of pop culture's most famous controversies.

Two weeks after Elvis's first RCA recording session, he appeared for the first time on television as a guest on Tommy and Jimmy Dorsey's weekly variety series *Stage Show*. Compared to the more conventional acts on the show — such as pop singers, dancers, and comedians who dressed, performed, and acted like the singers, dancers, and comedians on other variety shows — Elvis looked strange, alien, even dangerous. If you tuned in to *Stage Show* and saw Elvis performing, the following might have shocked you as it did many in the television audience:

- His ducktail haircut, which was long and slicked back
- His shiny Beale Street suit, which featured wide-legged trousers that shook when he moved
- Eye makeup on his eyelids and under his lashes that must have startled even show business veterans who had seen it all
- His high-energy performance in which he shook, shimmied, and swiveled, causing screams and squeals from the studio audience

During the next eight weeks, he appeared five more times on the program with ever-increasing ratings (though *Stage Show* never beat its competition on NBC, *The Perry Como Show*).

The Colonel continued to book Elvis on the most popular variety shows, including the much-beloved *Milton Berle Show.* Elvis and his band first appeared on the *Milton Berle Show* in April. When he returned for a second appearance in June, he performed "Hound Dog" for the first time on television — and in a particularly provocative manner, sensually thrust his hips toward the microphone. This single appearance ignited a nationwide backlash concerning his performing style. In fact, the performance prompted parents, religious groups, TV reviewers and columnists, and even the PTA (Parent Teacher Association) to condemn Elvis by declaring him indecent and associating his music with juvenile delinquency. The criticism against Elvis became part of the overall condemnation of the new youth-oriented music known as rock 'n' roll.

After the *Milton Berle Show,* Colonel Parker booked Elvis on *The Steve Allen Show.* The high ratings from Allen's program prompted Ed Sullivan to offer the unprecedented fee of $50,000 for Elvis to make three appearances on *The Ed Sullivan Show.* Elvis's final appearance on Sullivan's show in January 1957 features the now legendary moments when the CBS censors demanded that "Elvis the Pelvis," the singer's new nickname in the press, be filmed only from the waist up while singing. More than live concerts or recordings, Elvis's TV appearances fueled the controversy surrounding his hip-swiveling performing style.

The controversy surrounding Elvis's performing style became symbolic of generational conflict, reflecting the rise of the new youth culture (see the earlier section "Identifying a Cultural Icon" for more details on this new culture). However, other social circumstances also added to the conflict over Elvis and his music, including a prejudice against Southern culture and tastes and a racist attitude toward the music of African Americans. (For more information on the controversy generated by Elvis, see Chapter 5.)

# Changing Elvis's Notorious Image

Colonel Parker didn't realize that courting teenage audiences around the country could generate so much controversy and bad publicity (see the preceding section for more on the uproar over Elvis the Pelvis). The notoriety certainly garnered television ratings, but it did little to broaden Elvis's appeal to a mainstream audience. So throughout the rest of the 1950s, Parker and others worked to cool the controversy and broaden Elvis's appeal.

Ever mindful of the value of old-fashioned promotion, which the Colonel called "exploitation," the wily ex-carny generated a lot of publicity designed to counter Elvis's image as a notorious rock 'n' roller. Specifically, he

- Released photos of Elvis participating in charities
- Encouraged interviews in which Elvis talked about his love for his parents
- Negotiated a movie contract with producer Hal Wallis

However, nothing generated acceptance by the mainstream audience like Elvis's service in the army. In the following sections, I look more closely at Elvis's first Hollywood movies and his service in the army, which did more than anything else to change his image.

## Shooting his first films

Negotiating a movie contract for Elvis served Parker's long-term goal of reaching as broad an audience as possible. As a movie star, Elvis could attract regular moviegoers, including those outside the teen demographic, in addition to popular music fans. Producer Hal Wallis was an expert at recognizing star power and constructing screen images for his actors. His handling of Elvis's film career, including developing his film projects and fine-tuning his characters, led to a softening of Elvis's controversial image.

Wallis placed Elvis under personal contract, but the Colonel negotiated for a nonexclusive contract, so Presley was free to make films for other producers and studios.

Elvis made four movies between 1956 and 1958: *Love Me Tender, Loving You, Jailhouse Rock,* and *King Creole.* The first, a Civil War–era western, featured Elvis as the youngest son of a family of homesteaders. The other three films starred Elvis in dramatic stories about young singers with new sounds who are misunderstood by the press and public.

Clearly echoing Elvis's own career and life story, these films helped reshape the singer's image in the eyes of the public, softening the criticism aimed against him and presenting him as just another show business success story. Wallis produced *Loving You* and *King Creole,* while Pandro S. Berman produced *Jailhouse Rock.* (For a detailed account of Elvis's pre-army movies, flip to Chapter 6.)

## Serving in the army

Elvis was drafted in late 1957 at the age of 22, but he managed to postpone his service in the army until March 1958 because of his contractual obligations to finish *King Creole.* When Elvis finally reported to his draft board, Colonel Parker made sure the press was on hand to document every step.

Parker repeated to the press time and again how Elvis could have joined special services in the army or the navy so he could serve his time by performing on bases around the world. However, Parker made it quite clear that Elvis opted to join the regular army and do his duty to serve his country — just like every other young man his age. Elvis spent the bulk of his two years serving in a tank division in Germany.

Instead of killing his career, serving in the army expanded it by attracting the attention of the mainstream audience, which is important to remaining at the forefront of show business. When Elvis was mustered out of the army in March 1960, the Colonel and others who helped manage Presley's career took advantage of his time away from the public eye to recast his image, maturing it to appeal to older audiences while retaining his original fan base. (For more information on the impact of Elvis's army service, see Chapter 5.)

While Elvis was in the army, two events in his personal life occurred that made a permanent impact on his life. In August 1958, near the beginning of his tour of duty, Elvis's mother, Gladys, died unexpectedly. With her death, he lost his biggest supporter. Then in early 1960, near the end of his tour of duty, Elvis met 14-year-old Priscilla Beaulieu, whose stepfather was also a soldier in the service. The two began a relationship that would continue in the 1960s when Priscilla moved to Memphis at Elvis's suggestion, eventually leading to marriage in 1967.

## Becoming a Leading Man in Hollywood

While Elvis was in the service, critics speculated that the two years away from the public eye would seriously damage his career. They proclaimed that his position at the forefront of rock 'n' roll would likely be lost. To some extent, they were right. Elvis didn't return to the forefront of rock music when he was discharged from the army in 1960. However, that absence was deliberate. The Colonel wanted to shift Elvis away from rock 'n' roll, which had endured more notoriety between 1958 and 1960.

Instead, when Elvis returned home, he gradually pursued a more mellow pop-influenced style of music and adopted a more conventional look. The Colonel took advantage of the good publicity over Elvis's tour of duty to promote a new, more mature Elvis Presley. And, he and Elvis turned their attention almost exclusively to the movies as the medium to showcase this new Presley to a mainstream audience. In focusing on movie stardom, Elvis no longer needed high-profile backup musicians, so the Blue Moon Boys as a group were out of the picture. The group actually had stopped being called the Blue Moon Boys after Elvis signed with RCA in order to keep the focus on Elvis, though the trio continued to tour. During the 1960s, Scotty Moore and D.J. Fontana occasionally worked in the studio with Elvis as sessions musicians.

## The movies Elvis didn't make

During the years Elvis was in Hollywood, he was offered opportunities to star in films that were not in the Presley formula — at least according to Colonel Parker. Stories about these opportunities have been exaggerated over the years by highly critical writers and biographers in order discredit the films that he did make. But, there's no doubt that the Colonel turned down some interesting proposals.

For example, in 1956, Parker turned down an offer for Elvis to appear as one of the rock 'n' roll acts in director Frank Tashlin's spoof of 1950s musical crazes, *The Girl Can't Help It,* starring Jayne Mansfield. Apparently, the Colonel didn't want Elvis to share the screen with other notable rock 'n' roll acts, such as Gene Vincent. In the 1970s, Barbra Streisand wanted Elvis to appear in her remake of *A Star Is Born,* but the Colonel refused for reasons unknown.

The Colonel's goal was for Elvis to achieve widespread popularity as a movie star and therefore greater financial success. Elvis, on the other hand, yearned for a career as a serious actor. The Colonel attained his goal, but Elvis didn't.

## *Starting out as an actor*

A few weeks after his discharge from the army, an eager Elvis returned to Hollywood to begin shooting *G.I. Blues,* a story about a singer who's serving in the army in Germany. Producer Hal Wallis borrowed details from Presley's life to flesh out the script just as he had done in the pre-army movies (see the earlier section "Shooting his first films" for details). However, unlike Elvis's earlier movies, *G.I. Blues* is a musical comedy, not a musical drama. Aimed at a family audience, the film presents the new, more mature Elvis Presley.

*G.I. Blues* was enormously successful; it ranked 14th in box office sales for 1960. The soundtrack album reached number one, remaining on the charts longer than any other Presley album. Sadly, Elvis didn't share the fans' enthusiasm for *G.I. Blues*. He felt the movie had too many musical numbers, and he believed that some of them made little sense in context of the plot. He also was concerned that the quality of many of the songs fell short of the music from his earlier films.

The western *Flaming Star,* released in December 1960, gave Elvis the chance to prove himself as a serious actor. In this tense western drama, Elvis held his own with veteran actors John McIntire and Dolores Del Rio. Unfortunately, the film wasn't the box office success it was expected to be.

*Wild in the Country,* a contemporary drama, followed *Flaming Star.* No songs were included in the original script for *Wild in the Country,* but after the disappointing showing of *Flaming Star,* Colonel Parker and some studio executives asked that several musical numbers be shot for the film. Six were shot, but only four made the final cut. *Wild in the Country* didn't lose money at the box office, but it didn't make much either. Both Elvis and costar Tuesday Weld were voted the Damp Raincoat Award for Most Disappointing Performers of 1961 by *Teen* magazine. While this award would hardly ruin anyone's career, it showed the Colonel exactly what kind of movie Elvis's fans didn't want to see. (See Part II for more information on Elvis's movies.)

## Finishing as a movie star

After the disappointing dramas, Elvis returned to musical comedies with *Blue Hawaii,* which was his second most financially successful movie. The movie, directed by Norman Taurog, featured a huge cast of colorful characters who could handle comedy. In response to his fans' cries for more songs, *Blue Hawaii* also contains 14 musical numbers, including the title song and one of Elvis's biggest hits "Can't Help Falling in Love." The songs represent a range of types and styles, from pop-rock ("Rock-a-Hula Baby") to novelty tunes ("Ito Eats") to ballads ("Can't Help Falling in Love").

Released during the Thanksgiving and Christmas holidays in 1961, the film quickly became a box-office hit. The soundtrack album was the fastest-selling album that year. Unfortunately, the success of *Blue Hawaii* restricted Elvis to acting in musical comedy vehicles, because the Colonel, Hal Wallis, and other members of his management team used the box-office figures to convince him that this was the only kind of movie his fans wanted to see him in. This dashed Elvis's dreams of becoming a serious actor.

After *Blue Hawaii,* Presley made 23 more movies, most following the pattern established in this breezy musical comedy. Later, Elvis would bitterly refer to these formulaic films as the Presley Travelogues. Despite his distaste for them, most of Elvis's films were popular successes and highly profitable. At one point in the mid-1960s, Elvis became the highest-paid actor in Hollywood. Even though he failed to become a serious actor, Elvis Presley was an extremely successful movie star.

By 1964, Colonel Parker had persuaded Elvis to focus almost entirely on the movie soundtracks. Many of the songs written for these musical comedies were as formulaic as the films themselves, but some solid pop tunes also were included. However, because the songs on the soundtrack albums weren't well organized and because the albums weren't always marketed wisely, many of the good tunes were lost among the mediocre ones. (See Chapter 7 for more information on the movie music Elvis produced.)

## Evaluating a Hollywood career

Many biographies, rock music histories, and other accounts of Elvis's career analyze his movie years with the benefit of hindsight. The standard interpretation of this period is that Elvis's musical comedy vehicles were disappointments in comparison to his earlier film work and that both his acting and singing talents were squandered by greedy agents and managers, particularly Colonel Parker. Considering the profundity and influence of Elvis's music from the 1950s, this negative opinion of his 1960s pop-oriented sound and movie-star persona almost makes sense. Yet other factors need to be considered.

For example, most of Elvis's movies and albums from the 1960s were financially successful no matter how hastily they were produced. Financial profit is a measure of success in pop culture, particularly in Hollywood, so Elvis and the Colonel had no reason to question — let alone alter — their game plan for Elvis's career. Also, if Elvis had continued singing rock 'n' roll, he may not have survived the changes to the music scene in the 1960s. After all, many pioneering rock 'n' rollers didn't. Finally, if Elvis had continued to make more serious films such as *Flaming Star* and *Wild in the Country,* he wouldn't have been guaranteed success with those either.

Despite the financial success of his films, Elvis became increasingly disappointed and depressed about his Hollywood career. And, there's no escaping the fact that both his movies and the accompanying soundtracks declined sharply during the mid- to late-1960s. (See Chapter 8 for more on the decline of Elvis's film career.)

Personally, Elvis lived an isolated, distorted existence far removed from the real world. The Colonel protected Elvis from the press and public throughout the 1960s, so interviews and articles about his life as a movie star were limited to those orchestrated or controlled by the Colonel himself.

# Capitalizing on a Turning Point

The year 1968 marked a turning point for Elvis professionally and personally. The change began in January when RCA released the single of "Guitar Man." The song didn't chart very high, but it was a non-soundtrack recording that signaled Elvis's willingness and perhaps eagerness to cut material that wasn't related to the movies he was still contractually bound to make.

Colonel Parker then negotiated a deal with NBC for a television Christmas special. The special turned out to be the spark that reignited Elvis's talent and creativity. A combination of his old music and new material, the special reminded Elvis that he had a musical gift and challenged him to use it to regain his stature in the music industry. Proud of the results, Elvis knew he wanted to change the direction of his career. Riding the momentum of the special, Elvis recorded the acclaimed album *From Elvis in Memphis,* which pointed him in a new direction musically.

Elvis's personal life also hit a high point in 1968. Married in the spring of 1967, Elvis and Priscilla became the proud parents of a baby girl, Lisa Marie, in February 1968. In this section, I talk about the important events that turned Elvis's career around, which serendipitously occurred during the happiest time of his personal life.

## Making a comeback with the '68 Comeback Special

In early 1968, the Colonel announced plans for an Elvis Presley television special that would air on NBC in December. It was Elvis's first TV appearance in eight years. Parker planned for his boy to sing several Christmas carols in front of a Yuletide setting, but producer Steve Binder encouraged Elvis to participate in a daring variety program instead.

The special, originally titled *Elvis* but later referred to as *Elvis — the '68 Comeback Special* or simply the *'68 Comeback Special,* consisted of a series of polished production numbers designed to illustrate the roots of Elvis's music. These production numbers alternated with segments featuring Elvis singing live before a studio audience with two of his original backup musicians, Scotty Moore and D.J. Fontana. For the live segments, Elvis appeared in a black leather jacket and pants — a costume that recalled an earlier era without resorting to nostalgia.

The special revealed a side to Elvis that hadn't been seen since 1961 — the part of him that was the rock 'n' roll innovator. It reminded audiences of his music and its importance to the development of popular American music. And, the live segments showcased one of his true talents, which was his ability to excite an audience as a dynamic live performer. (For a detailed account of the *'68 Comeback Special,* see Chapter 11.)

## Reinventing the music

The *'68 Comeback Special* aired on December 3, 1968, earning excellent ratings and favorable reviews. Invigorated by the challenge of doing something different from the movie musicals, he decided to cut a new album that was in no way related to a movie soundtrack. Elvis opted to record in Memphis for the first time since he had left Sun Records.

In January and February 1969, he spent several days recording with producer Chips Moman at the American Sound Studio, resulting in several chart-topping singles and one of his most critically acclaimed albums, *From Elvis in Memphis*. One of the songs from the American Sound Studio sessions was "Suspicious Minds," his first number-one single in seven years and the last one of his career.

The material recorded at the American Sound Studio prefigured his musical style of the 1970s, which was a large-scale sound that revealed the influences of modern country, pop music, and contemporary rock. (See Chapter 11 for more information on Elvis's sessions at American Sound Studio.)

## Taking time for a personal life

Around the time that Elvis was reinventing himself, he married Priscilla Beaulieu, who had been more or less living at the Presley home in Memphis since the early 1960s. A wizard at manipulating the media, the Colonel kept her presence hidden from the press. Elvis and Priscilla married on May 1, 1967, and nine months later to the day, their only child, Lisa Marie, was born. (See Chapter 7 for more information on Priscilla Beaulieu Presley.)

To get the best account of Elvis's marriage and family life, read Priscilla Presley's autobiography *Elvis and Me*. Autobiographies by former members of the Memphis Mafia also offer opinions of Elvis's personal life, but their views of the woman who was competition for their time with Elvis are often jaundiced or self-serving.

# Returning to Live Performances

In the summer of 1969, the opportunity arose for Elvis to play at the newly opened International Hotel in Las Vegas. Elvis's appearance at the infamous hotel marked a new phase of his career that had begun with the *'68 Comeback Special* and the album *From Elvis in Memphis*. At this point, he was still in the process of reinventing himself, and so he decided to return to concert performances with new material and a new image.

Just as he had deliberately changed his image in 1960 to expand his career and launch it in a new direction, he again stood ready in 1969 to reevaluate his goals and alter his musical style to return to live performances. Part of Elvis's long-term success stemmed from his ability to reinvent himself by moving his career in new directions.

## Attending an Elvis concert: Teddy bears and underwear

Elvis opened at the International Hotel on July 31, 1969, and the engagement was so successful that the Colonel inked a deal for Elvis to perform there twice a year for a month each time. The following year, Elvis began to tour when he wasn't playing Vegas. During this time, Elvis established a pattern that he followed for the rest of life: He hit the road two to three times a year but played Vegas for a month in winter and a month in summer. (For more information on Elvis's International Hotel engagement, see Chapter 12.)

As Elvis fine-tuned his act on the road, patterns and rituals were established that defined what a Presley concert was like. In the 1970s, beginning with the show at the International Hotel, Elvis sometimes mocked his sexually provocative 1950s image by comically imitating the pelvic thrusts, the snarling lip, and the other moves associated with Elvis the Pelvis (see Chapter 5). He also established new interactions with his fans; rather than egging them on with sexually provocative gyrations, he began "romancing" them with ballads such as "Love Me Tender." During this song, fans came down to the front of the stage, and Elvis kissed them, touched their hands, or accepted flowers, teddy bears, and other trinkets. Sometimes, he threw them back.

Throwing objects back and forth between the stage and the audience became a common practice with Elvis and his fans. After wiping his brow with a towel or scarf, he would throw it into the audience. This exchange became such a standard part of the show that band member Charlie Hodge would continuously drape towels around Elvis's neck so he could toss them to the audience.

Another interesting ritual between Elvis and his fans in the audience involved throwing underwear onstage, especially in Las Vegas. Women would throw their panties onstage, which Elvis sometimes picked up and made jokes about. (For more information on Elvis's 1970s concerts, see Chapter 13.)

## Dressing a star: The jumpsuits

During the International Hotel engagement, Elvis wore an open-necked black mohair ensemble with a red scarf. Bill Belew, who had designed Elvis's black leather outfit for the *'68 Comeback Special,* put together the mohair suit. After that Elvis always asked Belew to design costumes for his live performances. In fact, it was Belew who fabricated the white bejeweled jumpsuit, supposedly based on a suggestion by Priscilla Presley.

As the years passed, the jumpsuit costume grew more and more elaborate and was often accompanied by waist-length and even knee-length capes. Because Elvis had new jumpsuits designed for each tour, fans can date photos or footage of Elvis performing onstage in the 1970s based on the jumpsuit he's wearing. The jumpsuits are identified by their colorful names, such as the American Eagle, the Black Conquistador, the Peacock, and the Tiffany. You can see Elvis performing in one of his signature jumpsuits in Figure 1-1.

More than anything, the jumpsuit has become associated with Elvis during this phase of his career. Many who know little about Elvis's career and music can recognize him from this iconic outfit of his Vegas years. (For more information on Elvis's jumpsuits, check out Chapter 13.)

Figure 1-1: Elvis donned his White Matador jumpsuit for this 1971 concert performance.

## Appreciating the World's Greatest Entertainer: "Vegas Elvis"

The extravagant costumes and complex rituals of Elvis's period in Vegas fit the scale of the 1970s Presley concert. In Vegas and on the road, Elvis was joined onstage by a gospel quartet, a female backup trio called the Sweet Inspirations, a rock band, and a 35-piece orchestra.

Elvis's repertoire of songs varied throughout the 1970s, but his style of music didn't change. The style wasn't exactly rock 'n' roll, but it wasn't country music or rhythm and blues either. Elvis's style took something from all these genres, and yet it still transcended musical categories to form a sound unique to the singer. Dramatic, potent, and emotional, Elvis's sound — embodied in such songs as "Suspicious Minds" and "Burning Love" — seemed aurally symbolic of Colonel Parker's favorite billing for Elvis, "the World's Greatest Entertainer."

**Part I: From Rockabilly to Rock 'n' Roll**

*REMEMBER*

Elvis enjoyed a number of career highlights during the 1970s, including some record-making accomplishments. (For more information on the high points of the 1970s, see Chapter 14.) Among the most memorable are:

- In June 1972, a handsome, fit Elvis Presley played four sold-out shows at Madison Square Garden. He became the first performer to sell out all of his shows in that venue in advance. Among the attendees were John Lennon, David Bowie, Bob Dylan, and George Harrison.

- MGM produced and released two financially successful documentaries that captured Elvis's live performances, *Elvis — That's the Way It Is* (1970) and *Elvis on Tour* (1972). The latter won a Golden Globe for the Best Documentary of 1972.

- In January 1973, Elvis starred in the television special *Elvis: Aloha from Hawaii,* which was broadcast live via the Intelsat IV telecommunications satellite to countries in the Far East. Two days later, a taped replay was broadcast in Europe, and in April, the special was aired in America. Some estimates claim that 1.5 billion people eventually watched this performance.

## Taking a toll: A personal and professional decline

After his burst of creativity in the early 1970s, a demanding schedule and an unhealthy lifestyle took its toll on Elvis. Endless touring and the exhaustion that accompanied it eventually wore away the enthusiasm and inspiration he had felt after the *'68 Comeback Special.* Repetition and routine began to define his act as Elvis lost his desire to update or change material. Eventually, the concerts became standardized.

Elvis's albums also began to decline in quality as he grew restless with recording. He cut fewer new songs every year; in fact, some years he recorded no new material at all. Yet RCA still managed about three releases per year by relying on live albums of various concerts and by repackaging songs from previously issued albums with what little new material there was. Some of these albums and singles charted well, especially on the country charts, but Elvis lost interest in making music and lacked focus and enthusiasm when the Colonel or producer Felton Jarvis managed to get him to record.

Isolated from the real world and secluded at Graceland when not on tour, Elvis lived a strange life — sleeping all day and staying up all night. Inclined toward excess, including overeating, overspending, and prescription drug abuse, Elvis became increasingly out of shape, unhealthy, and erratic.

Elvis and Priscilla divorced in 1973, which friends and associates claim accelerated the star's drug use, health problems, and bizarre behavior. After 1973, frequent hospitalizations occurred as his health declined. (To read more on Elvis's personal and professional decline, refer to Chapter 15.)

## The End of the Road for the King

On June 26, 1977, Elvis Presley gave his final performance at Market Square Arena in Indianapolis, Indiana. Less than two months later, he was dead at age 42. His girlfriend, Ginger Alden, found his body slumped over in the bathroom at Graceland on August 16, 1977. After paramedics failed to revive him, he was taken to Baptist Memorial Hospital where further attempts to revive him failed. He was pronounced dead by his physician, Dr. George Nichopoulos, who listed the official cause of death as cardiac arrhythmia.

Within an hour of Elvis's death, fans began to gather in front of Graceland. Mourners arrived in Memphis from all the over the world to pay their respects and be with other fans. At the funeral, the speakers included televangelist Rex Humbard, comedian Jackie Kahane, who had often opened for Elvis, and a local Memphis minister. Several prominent gospel performers, including Jake Hess, sang some of Elvis's favorite gospel hymns. After the service, a motorcade of all-white automobiles carried the body to Forest Hill Cemetery. A short time later, a threat to steal Elvis's remains was intercepted, prompting his father to have the body moved to Meditation Garden behind Graceland. His mother's remains were moved there as well. (For more information on Elvis's death, see Chapter 16.)

Elvis Presley's death generated much media attention, some of it positive and much of it negative; it also resulted in extended air play of his records on the radio and prompted rampant sales of his records. And, that was just the beginning.

## Tracing Elvis Presley's Continued Popularity

Elvis's 23 years in show business constituted an extraordinary career. He pursued and conquered different avenues; his achievements were financially lucrative, which is always a barometer of success in the entertainment industry; and he made a major impact on the direction of popular music during the 1950s.

After his death, Elvis's "career" continued to be extraordinary. (See Part IV for a thorough account of the events, celebrations, accomplishments, and rumors surrounding the popularity of Elvis since his death.) His fan base has remained loyal to this day, which isn't surprising, but Elvis's enormous popularity and recognition go well beyond his original fan base. He also has:

- Generated new fans
- Become the focus of a multimillion-dollar business headed by Elvis Presley Enterprises
- Continued to be referenced often in the media, whether in news stories, in jokes, or in a measure of the magnitude of his celebrity
- Often been named the top-earning celebrity of the year — despite being dead for more than 30 years

Simply stated, the reason that Elvis retains such an enormous level of popularity is that he appeals to different groups of people for different reasons. His career was so diverse, his music so innovative, and the post-death phenomenon so strange that everyone finds something interesting or entertaining about the different phases of his life or career. Consider the following groups of Elvis fans:

- **Rock 'n' roll enthusiasts** prefer Elvis the Pelvis, who brought rock 'n' roll to the masses and represented rebellion against mainstream values and tastes.
- **Music historians and scholars** appreciate the cultural significance of his integration of regional influences to achieve a wholly new sound.
- **Country-western fans** embrace his music as an important influence on contemporary country styles.
- **Original fans** remember Vegas Elvis because of his charisma in concert.
- **Family audiences** like the lighthearted wholesomeness of his movies, which they can watch with their children on DVD.
- **Pop culture lovers** find fun in the way Elvis has become an icon of kitsch.

With Elvis Presley, there truly is something for everyone. Behind this simple statement lies a complex set of circumstances accounting for the phenomenon, however. Part sociohistorical context, part fan devotion, part merchandising, and part cultural influence, these circumstances combine to make Elvis Presley *the* American idol. Continue reading this book for a look at the unabridged story, a complete portrait of the man who remains The King of Rock 'n' Roll, and a credible interpretation for the reasons why.

# Chapter 2

# Walking a Mile in His Shoes: Examining Elvis's Early Years

## In This Chapter

- Looking at Elvis's birthplace and its influence
- Taking in the influencing sounds of Memphis
- Investigating Elvis's first recording at Sun Studio
- Reviewing Elvis's radio debut on *Red Hot and Blue*
- Making his first onstage appearance

Considering his first public performance at the Overton Park Shell, much of Elvis Presley's youth and adolescence have been honed into a tidy version of the American Dream through the frequent retelling of his life story in biographies, coffee-table books, music histories, and other writings. The events of his early life are artfully wedged into a mythic narrative about a poor boy with talent who eventually grows up to become the most famous singer in America.

I cast that cliché aside to show that Elvis's early life contains important threads that offer insight into his music, his career path, and his personal choices. His love of family, his Southern identity, and his poverty-stricken childhood, along with the influence of Memphis as a musical center, are all keys to understanding who Elvis Presley was, how his sound developed, and why his career took the path that it did.

In this chapter, I examine Elvis's early life, with a special emphasis on those key threads. I also detail the making of Elvis's first record at Sun Studio, which featured the songs "That's All Right" and "Blue Moon of Kentucky." As I detail the story of Elvis's first record, I analyze the cultural significance of the fusion of musical influences in his revolutionary sound.

## Growing Up in Tupelo

In the early morning hours of January 8, 1935, Elvis Aron Presley was born in rural Tupelo, Mississippi, a small town nestled among the corn and cotton fields in the northern part of the state.

The birth of Elvis was both a happy and sad moment for his parents, Vernon and Gladys Presley. Roughly a half hour before he was born, his twin brother, Jessie Garon, had arrived into the world. However, Jessie was stillborn and that cast a pall over the occasion. Jessie's death had a lasting impact on the Presley family. Elvis was at times haunted by the loss of his twin, who was his only sibling, and Gladys kept her remaining son close to her. Elvis and his mother would maintain an unusually tight bond throughout her short life.

Other tragedies and hardships would befall the close-knit Presleys over the years, keeping the trio in poverty and at times dependent on their extended family. Eventually, the Presleys moved to Memphis, looking for a chance at a better life. (See the upcoming section "Walking in Memphis: Elvis the Teenager" for details about the move and their life in the big city.)

Despite the poverty and hardships, Elvis spoke fondly of life in Tupelo. After all, his interest in music had been sparked in the small town when he was a little boy singing gospel music in church and listening to his first musical influence, Mississippi Slim, on his hometown radio station.

The following sections take a close look at Elvis's parents, his life in Tupelo, and the reasons behind the family's relocation to Memphis. My snapshot of Elvis's childhood reveals some of the reasons Tupelo held good memories for him.

## Introducing Elvis's parents

The daughter of a sharecropper, Gladys Love Smith was born in the farmland of Pontotoc County near Tupelo in 1912. Gladys shared what little the family had with seven siblings and was forced to go to work at a young age because her father had died and her mother was sick with tuberculosis.

Born in Fulton, Mississippi, in 1916, Vernon Elvis Presley grew up in the poorest part of Tupelo. Vernon didn't get along with his father, J.D. Presley, who kicked him out of the house to go work when he was 15. Vernon and J.D. tolerated each other, but J.D. was a hard-drinking hothead who wasn't cut out to be a husband and father. Eventually, he left his wife and children and moved north.

## Chapter 2: Walking a Mile in His Shoes: Examining Elvis's Early Years

> ### Aron versus Aaron
>
> Elvis Presley's middle name causes an undue amount of confusion for fans and historians alike. The traditional spelling of the name is "Aaron," but Dr. William Hunt, the old country doctor who attended the Presley births wrote "Aron" on the birth certificate. No one can say for sure whether Dr. Hunt accidentally misspelled Elvis's middle name, or whether Mrs. Presley had chosen "Aron" to match the middle name of twin Jessie Garon. Elvis was named after a family friend, Aaron Kennedy, but that doesn't mean that Gladys couldn't take creative license with the name. When Presley was an adult, he thought seriously about legally changing the spelling to Aaron, partly because that's the biblical spelling of the name. In the process, however, he learned that state records already listed it as Aaron. When Elvis died, his father chose "Aaron" for the tombstone, because he knew his son would want it that way.

Gladys, a tall, dark-haired beauty, met handsome Vernon Presley in 1933 when she moved to East Tupelo to work at the local garment factory. He was 17, and she was 21; the smitten couple married two months after they met and brought Elvis into the world two years later. (Figure 2-1 shows the Presley family during the Tupelo years.) In those early days, Gladys was an outgoing woman who loved to socialize, and the pair regularly attended the East Tupelo Assembly of God Church. With family and friends from the church, they sang gospel music, often harmonizing together on one of their favorites "The Old Rugged Cross." Gladys and Vernon were part of the church choir, and Elvis followed in their footsteps when he was old enough.

The Presleys lived in a two-room house on Old Saltillo Road, which was in the poorest section of this small, rural town. The tiny home was a type of dwelling known as a "shotgun shack," because it was so small and simply designed that someone could fire a shotgun into the front door and the bullet would fly out the back without hitting anything. Vernon Presley worked as a laborer in Tupelo, which meant he did anything from driving delivery trucks to sharecropping. Gladys worked at the garment factory until about the time that Elvis was born. After he was born, she picked cotton with her son perched on top of her cotton sack.

Like most rural Southerners during the Depression, Vernon and Gladys had quit school as soon as they were old enough to work or help with their families. They took whatever jobs they could find, which wasn't unusual for residents of poor rural communities at that time. In some biographies of Elvis, Vernon is painted as something of a n'er-do-well, because he didn't hold down one job, and he moved his family around a lot. But, these biographers lack a full understanding of what it was like to be poor in the South, and their depictions of Vernon seem more judgmental than accurate.

Elvis and his family may have been poor, but he had a secure childhood in terms of love and support. He was close not only to his mother and father but also to his large extended family of aunts and uncles who helped each other in troubled times. His mother was devoted to his care and safety, watching him carefully to keep him out of trouble and harm's way. Stories abound about how she walked him to school every day and wasn't comfortable allowing him out of her sight. These tales were exaggerated after Elvis's death, but family members and friends have since come forward to offer more accurate portraits of her as a devoted mother, not an obsessive one. As a child, Elvis told his mother that he would always take care of her and his father. True to his word, Elvis took care of his parents financially as soon as he became successful. He also gave money to extended family members or hired them to work for him after he became famous.

**Figure 2-1:** Two-year-old Elvis poses with his mother and father, Gladys and Vernon, not too long before Vernon was sent to Parchman Prison.

## Examining the family's greatest misfortune

Times were difficult for the small family early on, but they became worse in November 1937, when Vernon and two other men were arrested and charged with check forgery. The trio had forged a check to Vernon's landlord, Orville Bean. The forged amount wasn't very much, but the three men were given a harsh three-year sentence at Parchman Prison, a prison farm where the inmates worked the land in chain gangs while serving out their time.

Vernon's prison sentence proved extremely difficult on his tiny family. Gladys was unable to keep up the payments on their house by herself, and so she lost possession of it. She and her son stayed with various relatives until Vernon was released from prison early in February 1939.

After his release, Vernon returned to working odd jobs. Sometimes he landed jobs in other parts of the state, but the family always had a difficult time making enough money. As he moved from one job to another, Vernon moved his family around Tupelo from one rented home to another. The Presleys spoke of these hard times only in very general terms, but Vernon once recalled that after he came home from prison, Elvis didn't want to let him out of his sight.

## Considering Elvis's earliest musical influences and experiences

Elvis expressed an interest in music before he was old enough to go to school, belting out gospel tunes at church. Later, when he was in grade school, he learned to play the guitar from his uncles and neighbors, particularly his Uncle Vester Presley. Vester knew how to play more than just gospel music, because he occasionally sang in Tupelo's honky-tonks, which were small, rough-and-tumble bars that hired local talent to attract customers.

Elvis also showed his talent at the local fair. Each year on Children's Day, the Mississippi-Alabama Fair and Dairy Show sponsored an amateur talent contest, which was broadcast over Tupelo radio station WELO. When Elvis was around 10 years old, the boy entered the talent contest at the county fair at the insistence of a teacher who had heard him sing in class. Elvis's experience in this talent show has been exaggerated over the years. Some insist that he won second place, but various Tupelo residents have come forward to dispute this claim. Whatever the case, the boy was quite young when he sang — with no musical accompaniment — the ballad "Old Shep" for the talent show. In fact, he was so small that he had to stand on a chair to reach the microphone.

Not long after his fair experience, Elvis became a fan of local country-western singer Mississippi Slim, who hosted a couple of radio programs on WELO. Slim's real name was Carvel Lee Ausborn, and he was the brother of one of Elvis's friends, James Ausborn. Through James, Elvis had easy access to the entertainer, and he soaked up Slim's tales of being on the road and singing professionally.

Slim taught the eager Elvis more chords on the guitar and may have provided him with an opportunity to play before an audience on the *WELO Jamboree*, which was an amateur hour hosted by Slim every Saturday afternoon. Like the fair story, however, accounts of Elvis's participation on the *Jamboree* are contradictory and can't be trusted. Historians are sure that he visited the radio station regularly, however.

Mississippi Slim sang pure country music, complete with the twanging guitar and the catch in his voice. So the first major influence on Elvis Presley wasn't the rhythm-and-blues artists of Memphis. Instead, his first influence was from a bona fide "hillbilly singer."

# Walking in Memphis: Elvis the Teenager

During Elvis's day, Memphis, which is nicknamed the River City, was a crossroads of influences from up and down the Mississippi River as well as from the mountains in the eastern part of the state. Blacks, whites, rural folk, city residents, and even Yankees mingled in Memphis. The city's teeming population of different people and cultures was reflected in the diversity of music that thrived there. For more than a century, the city was a virtual breeding ground for new musical trends and sounds.

From the moment the Presleys set foot in the city, Elvis was exposed to the many sounds and styles that later served as influences on his own music. In a way, he received a "musical education" by embracing the sounds of the city while growing up in Memphis. This informal education proved to be more helpful and influential than his official, sanctioned education at L.C. Humes High School.

In this section, I discuss the family's move to the big city, provide an overview of the types of music that inspired the teenage Elvis, and offer a snapshot of his high-school years.

Roughly one of every four inductees into the Rock 'n' Roll Hall of Fame hails from Memphis or its surrounding areas.

## Making the move

By the fall of 1948, Tupelo had become a dead end for the Presleys. Work for Vernon was scarce, so the family decided to move to the city — to Memphis — for better job opportunities. Their move was much like those of rural families who left their farms and small towns for the big cities after World War II.

In a rare candid moment during an interview, Elvis recalled about the family's move to Memphis, "We were broke, man, broke. Dad packed all our belongings in boxes and put them in the trunk and on top of a 1939 Plymouth [actually a 1937 Plymouth]. We just headed for Memphis. Things had to be better."

The family's situation did improve in Memphis, especially after Vernon landed a job at a paint factory. In the fall of 1950, the Presleys moved into a housing project called the Lauderdale Courts, and Elvis attended L.C. Humes High School. While the Courts were designed for families living at the poverty level, they weren't slums. A thriving, bustling atmosphere defined the Courts, and most of the residents worked hard to improve their lives. At one point, when Vernon and Gladys were both working, the family's income exceeded the amount allowed by the Memphis Housing Authority for public housing

## Chapter 2: Walking a Mile in His Shoes: Examining Elvis's Early Years

recipients. The family had to move, but they chose to remain in the same neighborhood as the Lauderdale Courts.

After a time, Elvis's grandmother, Minnie Mae Presley, came from Tupelo to live with her son Vernon, and she remained a fixture in the Presley household for the rest of Elvis's life. She cooked for the family when Gladys was lucky enough to find work, she stepped in to take care of Vernon and Elvis when Gladys died in 1958, and she provided a link to extended family members. Sadly, Minnie Mae, whom Elvis affectionately called Dodger, outlived both her son and grandson.

## Getting through high school

Elvis attended high school and endured adolescence like any other working-class teenager. Though he occasionally got good grades in some subjects, Elvis was largely a "C" student at L.C. Humes High School, also called Humes High. Elvis graduated on June 3, 1953, which was an accomplishment that many in his extended family hadn't achieved. In this section, I offer a brief look at these tender years.

### Hanging with his buddies from the Courts

Elvis hung out with several boys who also lived in Lauderdale Courts and attended Humes High, including Buzzy Forbess, Farley Guy, and Paul Dougher. The group liked to go to the movies together at the Suzore #2 and Rialto Theatres, which were close to the Courts. Sometimes they also rode bikes, played sports, or walked around Memphis. To earn money, the four mowed lawns around the neighborhood with old push mowers. When the boys became old enough, they got part-time jobs. Elvis worked as an usher at the Loew's State Theater for a while.

Sometimes the teens from the Courts held record parties, and witnesses from the era recall Elvis bringing his guitar to these informal get-togethers. He would generally sing one or two songs, so the people in the neighborhood were aware that he could sing.

Some of Elvis's later friends and bodyguards, including George Klein and Red West, attended Humes at the same time, but they didn't know each other very well during high school.

### Adopting a style

In high school, Elvis didn't really stand out and wasn't part of the popular crowd. He tried out for the football team, but he didn't last much past a few weeks of practice. However, by his junior year, he had begun to grow his hair long and dress like the R&B musicians from Beale Street. Elvis never had much to say about high school, but students who remember him recall that he dressed flamboyantly and wore his hair long. Despite being shy, he entered the Minstrel Show (the Humes High talent show) and sang one song, accompanying himself on the guitar.

## Absorbing a medley of musical influences

As he made his way through high school in Memphis, Elvis discovered the different genres of music that were part of the city's music scene. He collected records of diverse artists, listened to a variety of radio stations, and attended live performances to soak up the different performing styles and sounds. Though Elvis may have had the most eclectic interests of any teenager in Memphis, the indigenous sounds and styles of the South — gospel, R&B, and country — made the deepest impression. In this section, I explain the types of music Elvis was exposed to in Memphis and the different outlets that provided it.

### Collecting records

While he was soaking up the musical styles of his adopted hometown, Elvis began collecting records. His tastes were eclectic, revealing a curiosity and passion for all types of music. This curiosity was impressive for someone so young. Like the diversity of music that surrounded him in Memphis, his eclectic record collection could be considered an influence on the way he combined styles and genres in his own sound. Most of Elvis's record collection is still housed at Graceland.

Looking through Elvis's record collection offers an understanding of how music offered him an outlet to express his personal tastes, which were different from teens his age or from other members of his family. How many teenagers of the time would have owned a copy of "Malaguena," which was flamenco dance music arranged by Russian musician Andre Kostelanetz, famous as the "father" of easy-listening music. Most of Elvis's family lacked his interest in pop music, as found in his single of "Witchcraft" by the Spiders, or in blues records such as "Shake a Hand" by Faye Adams. Elvis's copy of the Prisonaires' "Just Walking in the Rain," which was produced by Sam Phillips, suggests that he knew of Phillips's reputation for recording local talent.

### Listening to the radio in Memphis

The River City boasted a multitude of innovative radio stations whose disc jockeys were not only great judges of local talent but also daring in their playlists. Unlike radio today, stations during the 1950s reflected and influenced the tastes and popular culture of the regions they serviced. In a city like Memphis, which was rich with the musical sounds of many groups and cultures, the radio stations disseminated different types of music to all peoples. Disc jockeys, who were experts on the latest music, were free to "spin the platters" of artists they believed in. Thus, some radio deejays yielded a lot of influence on public tastes. The Memphis radio stations made up one of the key outlets for Elvis to experience and learn to appreciate different genres of music.

### Country western

At home, the Presleys listened to country western, and Elvis was known to occasionally attend broadcasts of live entertainment at country-western station WMPS. Country music underwent many changes during the 1940s, and those changes had permanently altered its sound and styles. For example, Ernest Tubb had introduced the electric guitar to the *Grand Ole Opry,* country music's most famous radio program and a favorite in the Presley household. Also, western swing music had combined boogie-woogie with country to form a contemporary sound that appealed to young listeners like Elvis.

Elvis enjoyed country music his entire life, and it played a major role in the development of his music not only in the 1950s but also in the 1970s. (See the later section "Cutting 'That's All Right'" and Chapter 11 for specific information on the influence of country on his music.)

### Gospel

In the 1950s, Memphis became the headquarters of harmony-style gospel music. The top white gospel groups of the era performed at the "All-Night Gospel Singings" at Ellis Auditorium. These sings, which were held about once a month, featured one gospel group after another and lasted into the wee hours of the morning.

Elvis attended these sings whenever possible. The shows featured a variety of gospel styles, but it was the tight harmonies of the gospel quartets that attracted Elvis the most. He was personally acquainted with the Blackwood Brothers, a gospel quartet consisting of four brothers who attended the same Assembly of God church as the Presleys. His favorite group was the Statesmen, whose lead singer, Jake Hess, combined aspects of black gospel music with the harmony style that Elvis grew up with. The Statesmen, headed by the colorful Hovie Lister, dressed flamboyantly for a gospel quartet, their singing style was highly emotional, and their performing style was exciting and energetic. They weren't afraid to move with the music. All these stylistic trademarks proved influential on Elvis.

Elvis performed gospel music for the rest of his life. He enjoyed singing it with family and friends to relax and pass the time. He also recorded several award-winning gospel albums. After he signed with RCA in 1956, he insisted that a gospel group sing backup for him on stage and on recordings. Gospel kept him connected to his Southern roots, which in turn provided him with comfort in times of tension and strife.

### Blues and R&B

Besides "River City," Memphis's other nickname was "Home of the Blues." And Beale Street was indeed home to the seedy clubs and rough joints where African American blues musicians ruled the roost. The joints on Beale Street also gave birth to *rhythm and blues,* or R&B, which combined the heavy beat of blues with a faster rhythm and more sophisticated melodies.

Given Elvis's young age, it's unlikely that he spent a lot of time in the clubs on Beale Street — partly because his church-going mother wouldn't have allowed it and also because Memphis was part of the South, which was still socially segregated. But, he listened to blues and R&B at record shops, such as Poplar Tunes and Charlie's, and he added many R&B singles to his record collection. When Elvis began recording, R&B proved to be a prominent influence on his rockabilly sound. (See "Cutting 'That's All Right'" later in this chapter for more information.) Also, like many R&B musicians of the times, Elvis bought his flashy shirts and slacks at Lansky Brothers clothing store on Beale Street. (Chapter 3 provides more information on Elvis's clothing preferences.)

Poplar Tunes, founded by Joe Cuoghi, epitomized the 1950s record shop. Located near Lauderdale Courts, the shop served as a hangout for teenagers, who could try out new records in the store before buying them. Poplar Tunes sold the records of local artists, including Elvis when he began recording. The shop, which looks much the same as it did in the early 1950s, is still open and still sells Elvis's records.

### Understanding Southern musical genres

Even though Elvis became a fan of singers as varied as pop crooner Dean Martin and operatic singer Mario Lanza, the indigenous musical genres of the South had the strongest influence on his early sound. The South wasn't merely Elvis's geographical birthplace. Elvis's Southern heritage defined him personally and musically. The types of music that inspired him — rhythm and blues, country western, blues, and gospel — are steeped in the unique history and cultures specific to the South.

For example, African Americans and rural white Southerners coexisted in a racially segregated world with a tense atmosphere, but their cultures shared common key values and beliefs, such as strong family ties, religions that focused on earthly suffering and heavenly rewards, and the fervent belief in sin and redemption. These themes, images, and values were naturally reflected in the music and arts of both African Americans and rural white Southerners. Given this common thematic ground, it isn't surprising that the various musical styles and genres were influenced by each other. Elvis's combination of Southern genres and styles in his music extended the influence into integration.

The regionally based musical styles and genres spoke to the peoples of the South in a personal way not characteristic of mainstream audiences and pop music. In other words, a blues lament about working the fields all day at

Parchman Prison farm ("Parchman Farm Blues" by Bukka White) reflects the beaten-down spirit of the victims of the South's harsh penal system. Often, inmates worked from sunup till sundown no matter the weather conditions, and African Americans were subject to the most brutal treatment. African American listeners had firsthand knowledge and experience of their brutal treatment at the hands of the Southern "justice" system and could relate to the song.

Similarly, a country song glorifying trains ("Train Whistle Blues" by Jimmie Rodgers) reveals a reverence for a mode of transportation that provided escape from the poverty, the backbreaking work, and the limited opportunities for poor Southerners. Those rural white Southerners who had escaped the country for the city knew the necessity of leaving such an environment (like the Presleys did), but they still ached for the comfort of "back home."

Elvis strongly identified with the themes, styles, and lyrics of Southern-based music, which had meaning to him that few outside the South ever understood.

## Making Music and History at Sun Studio

If Elvis had plans for a singing career when he graduated, he didn't confide in anyone at that time. But, a few months after graduation, he cut an acetate disc at the Memphis Recording Service, where he was noticed by Marion Keisker, assistant to local record producer and owner of Sun Records and Studio Sam Phillips. A few months later, Elvis returned to cut another disc and caught the attention of Phillips himself, who jotted down his name and information. A few months later, in July 1954, Phillips called him to come to Sun Studio and record a song. And, thus began the most groundbreaking singing career of the 20th century.

In this section, I chronicle the steps leading up to Elvis's first recording at Sun Studio and the pioneering nature of that first single. I also list the other singles Elvis recorded for Sun and detail the start of his career.

### Taking that first step: Elvis, Marion, and the Memphis Recording Service

Shortly after he graduated from L.C. Humes High School in 1953, Elvis, who was working in the small-engine repair department at M.B. Parker Co., walked into the Memphis Recording Service and told the woman behind the desk, Marion Keisker, that he wanted to cut an acetate disc.

**TRIVIA**

In the days before tape recorders were readily available to the mainstream public, recording services existed so the general public could record anything on an acetate disc for a small fee. As a matter of fact, the motto of the Memphis Recording Service was "We record anything, anywhere, anytime," and owner Sam Phillips meant it. Anyone could cut an acetate disc — people who wanted to record greetings for loved ones in the service, those who wanted to get down their personal histories for posterity, or folks who wanted to hear what their singing voices sounded like.

The day that Elvis dropped by, he cut the song "My Happiness," a 1948 ballad that had been made famous by the Ink Spots, on a disc for a fee of $4. Elvis recorded another Ink Spots song, "That's When Your Heartaches Begin," for the other side of the disc. Elvis accompanied himself on his childhood guitar.

**REMEMBER**

The decision to record his voice at the Memphis Recording Service that hot summer day represented Elvis's first step toward a career, though he didn't realize it himself at the time, and it's unlikely that he was following any kind of master plan.

Sam Phillips, the owner of both the Memphis Recording Service and Sun Records (see the upcoming section for details on Phillips), was always looking for new talent. The Memphis newspapers had written about Phillips and the local artists he had recorded several times. More than likely, Elvis was hoping to catch Sam's attention when he walked into the building to record his disc. The Memphis Recording Service, which was open to anyone, and Sun Records, which was for professional musicians, shared the same studio and office space.

Unfortunately, Phillips wasn't there at the time — Ms. Keisker was running the service alone. She noticed Elvis's long, slicked-back hair and sideburns and asked him what kind of music he sang and whom he sounded like. He answered, "I don't sound like nobody," which made her curious. So she taped the young singer on the studio's new master tape recorder while he made his disc.

Phillips had once told Keisker that R&B could become popular with the general public if he could find a white performer who could sing with the sound and feel of a black man. Sam made the same statement to several parties around town. Because Elvis chose two songs made famous by the Ink Spots (a popular African American vocal group), Keisker thought that Phillips might be interested in the polite young man. But, when the producer finally listened to the two recordings, he wasn't impressed.

Presley returned to the Memphis Recording Service in January 1954 to record two more songs: the ballad "Casual Love Affair" and the country-western song "I'll Never Stand in Your Way." This time Phillips worked the controls. The producer took down the young singer's name and address, but he didn't offer Elvis much encouragement.

## Chapter 2: Walking a Mile in His Shoes: Examining Elvis's Early Years

After Elvis became famous, his first encounters with the Memphis Recording Service were molded into a story that was told and retold until it became a legend that simply isn't accurate. When Elvis showed up at the Memphis Recording Service for the second time, he was working for Crown Electric delivering supplies. In the legend, however, Elvis was a truck driver when he happened to stroll into the recording service for the first time to cut a record as a gift for his mother's birthday. But, Elvis was working for a machinist when he made his first disc in the summer of 1953. And, even though he was delivering supplies with a truck when he cut the second disc, he wasn't driving an 18-wheel tractor-trailer, which is what most people think of when they hear the term "truck driver." His mother's birthday was in April, so that part of legend is also untrue.

## *Meeting Sam Phillips*

Sam Phillips owned and operated both the Memphis Recording Service and Sun Studio. He also owned Sun Records, an independent record label that had been recording R&B artists for a couple of years. Phillips enjoyed a national reputation for discovering talented R&B singers. He paid the musicians, financed the sessions, and recorded the artists himself in his little studio on Union Avenue. He generally leased the master recordings to various small record companies across the country, who then released the songs on their own labels.

Phillips had been exposed to gospel and blues music growing up in Alabama, and he, like Elvis, experienced the hard life and poverty common to rural Southerners. When he began Sun Records in 1952, he recorded the blues music of African American artists who wanted to cut singles but couldn't find studios willing to record them. He also recorded country groups, including the Starlite Wranglers. As a record producer, he drew on his life experiences to shape a purely Southern sound that combined R&B, blues, and country-western music with a hardscrabble philosophy born of bad times. The music that he cultivated — that Dixie-fried sound called rockabilly — emanated from Sun Studio throughout the 1950s and became a core sound of rock 'n' roll.

Sam Phillips said this of his desire to record the music of poor Southerners: "I just knew this [music] was culture, and it was so embedded in these people because of hardship . . . Generation after generation, these people have been overlooked — black and white!"

Finally, in June 1954, Phillips called Elvis. The producer thought the kid might be the singer to handle a ballad titled "Without You" that had the potential to be a good record.

Presley rushed down to Sun Studio and gave the song his best effort. However, Elvis couldn't seem to capture whatever it was that Phillips wanted for the ballad, so the producer had him run through every tune that he knew. When nothing panned out, Phillips figured that Elvis needed practice and seasoning. Sam knew everyone in the music business in Memphis, so he contacted Scotty Moore, a guitar player with the Starlite Wranglers, and suggested that he meet with Presley and a local bass player named Bill Black for some practice.

## Cutting "That's All Right"

In early July 1954, the unlikely trio of Elvis, Scotty Moore, and Bill Black decided they were ready to begin work in Sun's tiny recording studio. One evening, after trying a few ballads unsuccessfully, the group finally hit on something while fooling around during a break. Presley started singing Arthur "Big Boy" Crudup's old blues song "That's All Right" with a fast rhythm and a casual style. Moore and Black quickly picked up their instruments and jumped in. Phillips, who was excited by the trio's fresh sound, asked them to start over and refine their playing a bit. Then he eagerly recorded what he thought was surely lightning in a bottle. A few nights later, they recorded their version of Bill Monroe's country bluegrass hit "Blue Moon of Kentucky." Refer to Figure 2-2 to see Phillips and the trio in the studio.

These two songs became the group's first single release. That first record — with a blues tune on one side and a country classic on the other — clearly shows where Elvis's music was coming from. In the following sections, I describe in detail the musical sound of Elvis's first single and then explain its cultural significance.

The label on the single listed "Elvis Presley" beneath the song title and below that in smaller letters the names "Scotty and Bill." From the billing, it was clear that Elvis was the star attraction, but the contributions of the other two musicians were noted.

### Rocking the rhythm

Elvis's versions of "That's All Right" and "Blue Moon of Kentucky" sounded nothing like the originals. His approach was more easygoing, giving his interpretations an air of spontaneity. He replaced the hard vocal delivery and slow rhythm of Crudup's version of "That's All Right" with a relaxed vocal style and fast pace. Likewise for "Blue Moon of Kentucky," the tempo was sped up, and two elements were added that would make Presley famous: syncopation and reverberation. Elvis's syncopation of certain lyrics gave them a hiccuplike effect as he sang, and the reverberation engineered by Phillips during recording created a slight echo.

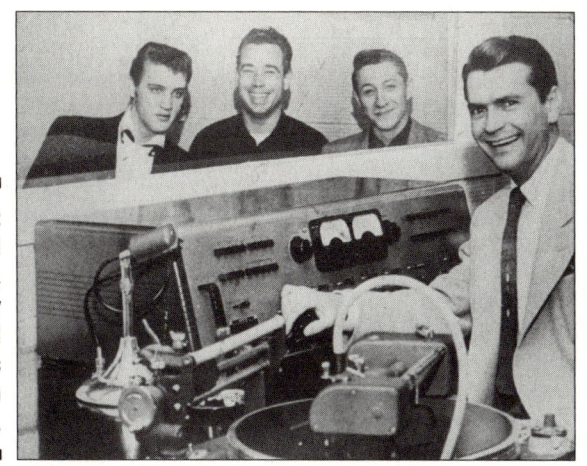

# Chapter 2: Walking a Mile in His Shoes: Examining Elvis's Early Years

**Figure 2-2:** Elvis, Bill Black, Scotty Moore, and Sam Phillips pose in Sun Studio.

Presley's style became known as *rockabilly,* which referred to the mix of country music, commonly called "hillbilly," with R&B that has been relaxed and sped up, or "rocked."

### Achieving musical integration

Elvis's early style as finessed by Phillips was truly an innovative fusion of African American and rural white Southern genres. The blues or R&B part of Elvis's music was infused with a driving rhythm that derived from country-western music or mountain music, and the country part was given a hard beat that came from the blues. The combination grew out of Presley's eclectic personal tastes and his understanding of these regionally based sounds.

In combining country western, the music of the rural white South, with blues and R&B, the music of African Americans, Elvis and Phillips achieved a musical integration the same year that *Brown v. the Board of Education* (1954) forced the integration of schools in the South. This case would go on to spearhead the civil rights movement and the drive toward social integration. Elvis's first record is an example of cultural integration, which prefigured the social integration that became a big part of our sociopolitical history in the 1950s and early 1960s. And, it suggests the importance of popular culture in paralleling, reflecting, or influencing social change. It also suggests that in any study of an era's history or society, an assessment of popular culture is vital for fleshing out additional insights and nuances of the period.

Phillips and the group were excited about the single they cut and the innovative sound they produced, but they also were aware of the racial restrictions of their society. In an era when the city's white blue-collar workers were coerced into joining all-white unions, and Phillips received threats and put-downs for fostering the music of black artists, the four knew their efforts would be considered provocative.

## Releasing additional Sun Studio recordings

After Elvis's first record was such a local success (see the next section for more info on that success), Phillips began cutting additional single releases with his latest discovery in the fall of 1954. Like Elvis's first record, the other four Sun singles featured an R&B-flavored tune on one side and a country or pop song on the flip side, though Elvis rendered both tunes in his rockabilly style. As with "That's All Right" and "Blue Moon of Kentucky," Moore and Black backed Elvis on his other recordings.

Music historians with a purist view claim these recordings to be the high point of Elvis Presley's career, because they best reflect the raw rockabilly sound that proved so innovative and influential in the history of rock 'n' roll. Even though not everyone agrees with this assessment, the records are significant enough to be given their due. So in this section, I outline each of Elvis's follow-up Sun Studio recordings.

### "Good Rockin' Tonight" / "I Don't Care if the Sun Don't Shine"

The second single disc that Elvis recorded with Phillips was released in September 1954. The disc included the songs "Good Rockin' Tonight" and "I Don't Care if the Sun Don't Shine," and it sold 4,000 copies in the Memphis area in two-and-a-half weeks.

Though written and released by Roy Brown in 1947, "Good Rockin' Tonight" became better known the following year when R&B artist Wynonie Harris recorded the definitive version. Harris had speeded up the tempo compared to Brown's version, and Elvis speeded up Harris's interpretation even further. Scotty Moore's driving guitar rhythms emphasized the speed, and Bill Black's frenzied bass slapping drove home the beat to underscore the two distinctive features of rockabilly.

The song's first line, "Have you heard the news?" was originally derived from a phrase used during World War II to denote good news about the war: "Good evening, America, there's good news tonight." But, it has since been considered a metaphor to represent the shock of the news that surrounded Elvis's innovative sound.

Even though it had originally been written as a pop song for the animated Disney feature *Cinderella*, Elvis gave the flip side to his second single, "I Don't Care if the Sun Don't Shine," a rockabilly treatment as well. Still, it wasn't enough to overcome the bland pop lyrics, which lack the hipness of "Good Rockin' Tonight." Small wonder "Rockin'" has completely overshadowed it. The tune was more suited to the styles of pop singers Patti Page and Dean Martin, who recorded it in the early 1950s.

**Chapter 2: Walking a Mile in His Shoes: Examining Elvis's Early Years**

### "Milkcow Blues Boogie" / "You're a Heartbreaker"

The next single that Elvis recorded was released around the first week of January in 1955 and included "Milkcow Blues Boogie" and "You're a Heartbreaker." The single sold well locally, and both sides of the record received a lot of airplay on local radio. "You're a Heartbreaker" edges "Milkcow" out in terms of significance, because it became the first Elvis song for which sheet music was issued.

"Milkcow Blues Boogie" offers a good example of the way blues and country music exchanged influences. Blues singer Kokomo Arnold wrote and recorded the song in 1934, and then legendary bluesman Robert Johnson cut it in the mid-1930s. Texas swing singer Bob Wills, who may have heard Johnson's version because the bluesman recorded for a while in Dallas, released it a few years later in the country market. Elvis's version starts out slow like Johnson's interpretation, but then he rocks the rhythm and turns it into a rockabilly hit. As you can see, the historical lineage of the song tells the story here — from blues (Arnold and Johnson) to country (Wills) to rockabilly or rock 'n' roll (Elvis).

On the flip side of the disc is "You're a Heartbreaker," which could be classified as a sort-of retro-sounding country song. It has been dubbed the most country of all the songs Elvis recorded for Sun. Sam Phillips purchased the tune from amateur songwriter Jack Sallee, and it became the first Elvis song for which Phillips owned the publishing rights. This brought in more money for Phillips, because as publisher he got an additional cut for each disc sold. And, if another singer recorded it, he got a cut of that version, too.

### "I'm Left, You're Right, She's Gone"/ "Baby Let's Play House"

In April 1955, Elvis released a disc with the songs "I'm Left, You're Right, She's Gone" and "Baby Let's Play House."

The single's B side, "Baby Let's Play House," did so well that it became the first Elvis single to appear on a national chart. It climbed to number ten on the *Billboard* list of top-selling country songs. Many music historians cite this song as the epitome of the Sun Studio sound, partly because of the edgy syncopation of the word "Baby" at the beginning of the song and also because of the pure rockabilly rhythm. The provocative lyrics in which the singer declares to a girl that he "wants to play house" reveal the sexual overtones of the tune.

Elvis personalized the song by changing "religion" to "pink Cadillac" in the line, "You may get religion but don't you be nobody's fool." Elvis loved big cars, especially Cadillacs and Lincolns, and he was fond of having them custom colored. About a year after this song was released, Elvis bought his mother a brand-new pink Cadillac.

Bluesman Arthur Gunter wrote and originally recorded "Baby Let's Play House" in 1954, borrowing the title from the Eddy Arnold country song "I Want to Play House with You." Again, the origin of the tune reveals the back-and-forth influences between the different genres of Southern-based music. Elvis attacked this song with enthusiasm, humor, and a rush of adrenaline, making it his own.

Despite the witty title, "I'm Left, You're Right, She's Gone" features lyrics that are as banal as "Baby's" are provocative. Songwriters Stanley Kesler and Bill Taylor wrote the tune the year before based on an old Campbell's soup jingle. Country songs are notorious for using puns, twisting familiar phrases, and playing off common clichés, and this tune is a good example of that. The rockabilly treatment of this country song, as well as Elvis's enthusiastic performance, elevates the song above the content. But the song paled in comparison to "Baby Let's Play House." In fact, it didn't even chart.

### "Mystery Train"/ "I Forgot to Remember to Forget"

Elvis's single of "Mystery Train" and "I Forgot to Remember to Forget" was released in August 1955 and was his last single disc for Sun Records. "Mystery Train reached number 11 on the *Billboard* Country Disc Jockey chart, and "I Forgot to Remember to Forget" did even better, reaching number one on the *Billboard* jukebox chart and number one on its list of best-selling country songs.

"Mystery Train" has become one of Elvis's most emblematic songs, because the phrase "mystery train" has been appropriated by writers in referring to his music or career. The song previously had been recorded by another Sun Studio artist, Little Junior Parker, in 1953. Parker's version was inspired by the Carter Family's "Worried Man Blues." The song is a lament, but Elvis's pared-down, fast-paced interpretation is more haunting than mournful. The shuffling rhythm, which is the result of Scotty Moore's excellent guitar playing, is reminiscent of a train's locomotion.

According to Rolling Stones guitarist Keith Richards in an oft-repeated quote, "Everyone else wanted to be Elvis. After hearing ["Mystery Train"], I wanted to be Scotty Moore."

The flip side of the disc, "I Forgot to Remember to Forget," was more popular at the time of release. As a matter of fact, it remained on the country charts for 39 weeks, longer than any other Elvis single release on any *Billboard* chart. The song was written by Stanley Kesler and Charlie Feathers, with the latter singer-songwriter also under contract to Sun Records. One reason for the song's popularity may have been because it was recorded by several Sun artists. It was adaptable to any singer's style. In addition to Elvis, Johnny Cash released a version with piano accompaniment by Feathers in 1958. Jerry Lee Lewis cut it in 1961. Ironically, in retrospect, it has been forgotten, perhaps because of the elevation of "Mystery Train," because of its symbolic value in describing Elvis's life.

## Chapter 2: Walking a Mile in His Shoes: Examining Elvis's Early Years

# Making His Radio Debut with Deejay Dewey Phillips

Producer Sam Phillips knew he had something special in "That's All Right." So on July 7, 1954, he personally delivered a copy of the song to the hottest disc jockey in Memphis — Dewey Phillips (who was no relation to Sam). Dewey was an extremely colorful character, whose uninhibited personality was perfectly suited to his radio program in which he played the records of whatever singers he wanted to hear, including African American blues artists and R&B performers. Dewey did everything his own way. In fact, when he was reading a commercial over the airways, he often ad-libbed part of the copy, much to the chagrin of the sponsor, and usually concluded with, "Tell 'em Phillips sent ya."

Listeners knew Dewey was his own man, and they trusted his tastes and were influenced by his program. Phillips had known Dewey for several years, and they shared an interest in blues and R&B. For all those reasons, Dewey was the obvious choice to launch "That's All Right." (You can read more about Dewey in the nearby sidebar "Deejay Daddy-O-Dewey.")

Because he trusted Phillips, Dewey decided to spin "That's All Right" on his WHBQ program *Red Hot and Blue.* After listening to the record, he truly liked what he heard. When he introduced the single on his program the same night he received it, telephone requests poured in for the deejay to play it again. Dewey played the song over and over until he decided to put the unknown singer on his program that very night.

While his record was making its radio debut, Elvis was trying to relax at the movies. After Dewey phoned the Presley residence and asked for Elvis, Vernon and Gladys dashed to the Suzore #2 to retrieve him. They went up and down the aisles of the theater until they found him, and then the three raced to the station. Daddy-O-Dewey, as he called himself on the air, told the nervous young singer not to worry, because he would tell him when the on-air interview started. He asked Elvis several questions about his life and interests, trying to put him at ease. When Dewey thanked his guest for his time, Elvis asked whether he was going to be interviewed or not. The crafty deejay told him that he already had, because the mike had been open the entire time. According to Phillips, Elvis broke out into a panic sweat.

One of the questions that Dewey asked the novice singer was what high school he had attended, and Elvis replied, "Humes High." Though a harmless question on the surface, it revealed to listeners that Elvis was white, because Memphis was a segregated city and Humes was a white school. Because Elvis had recorded a blues tune written and previously released by a black man (Arthur "Big Boy" Crudup), and because Dewey often played the music of African American musicians, audiences could have assumed the singer was black without the deejay's polite revelation of Elvis's race.

Part I: From Rockabilly to Rock 'n' Roll

> ## Deejay Daddy-O-Dewey
>
> Born in the small town of Adamsville, Tennessee, Dewey Mills Phillips was just a small-town country boy until he came into his own on the airwaves of WHBQ in Memphis. Almost everything he did on his radio program was completely off the cuff. Part of the appeal of his program, *Red Hot and Blue,* was the music, but entertainment also came from his spontaneity, hip slang, and outrageous antics. He often referred to himself as Daddy-O-Dewey. Consideration of his career offers a window into the individualism that defined the 1950s deejays, who often had a significant impact on the music scene via their support of certain performers and genres of music.
>
> Prior to landing his job as a radio deejay, Phillips tried to hold regular jobs, but the same characteristics that made him a star on the radio made him virtually unemployable in the regular world. For example, he was fired from the Taystee Bread Bakery because he talked the bakers into stopping production in order to make little bread people. And as an employee at Grant's dime store, he got into trouble for talking like jive over the store's intercom. However, he eventually talked his way onto the staff of WHBQ, which was broadcast from the Hotel Chisca. Phillips took control of *Red Hot and Blue,* and despite having no formal training in radio, made the program a local hit.
>
> By the late 1950s, however, hard times befell Dewey Phillips. Top-40 programming had become the mainstay of popular radio, and real personalities like Phillips were shoved aside. In and out of work for the next dozen years, Phillips never regained the stature he enjoyed in the mid-1950s. In 1968, he died of pneumonia, and Elvis attended the service, never forgetting the first deejay to play one of his records.

After the buzz created by the *Red Hot and Blue* program, Sam Phillips sent "That's All Right" and "Blue Moon of Kentucky" to the factory to be pressed as both a 78 rpm single and a 45 rpm single. At this point, the phenomenal career of Elvis Presley was launched.

**TRIVIA** Thanks in part to Dewey Phillips's enthusiasm for Elvis Presley, "That's All Right" created a stir in Memphis, selling 6,300 copies in three weeks. The record climbed to number three on the local country-western charts, eventually selling 30,000 copies across the South.

## Performing in Public for the First Time

On July 30, 1954, Presley made his first public appearance at the Overton Park Shell. Accompanied by guitar player Scotty Moore and bass player Bill Black, Elvis sang his two new hits "That's All Right" and "Blue Moon of Kentucky."

# Chapter 2: Walking a Mile in His Shoes: Examining Elvis's Early Years

*TRIVIA*

Elvis was just one of several acts on the program at the Overton Park Shell that evening. The headliner was country yodeler Slim Whitman. Elvis was so new to the music scene that he was billed as "Ellis Presley" in ads for the event.

Like a tightly wound spring, the young singer moved all over the stage as he performed his two songs, partly because he had a case of stage fright. But stage fright aside, the young man was always full of nervous energy. Performing live gave him an outlet to release that pent-up energy. During the performance, he continually shook his leg while he sang, which caused some of the teenagers in the audience to scream. Backstage during a break, he asked Moore what the audience had been screaming at. Somewhat surprised at the audience reaction himself, Moore remarked that it was the way Elvis was shaking his leg.

*REMEMBER*

Exactly where or from whom Elvis derived his kinetic performing style has been hotly debated in biographies and music histories. The truth is that, like his musical sound, his performing style was an integration of influences, including singers and black and white gospel performers. It's a hybrid of various influences and is something unique to Elvis as an entertainer. In fact, it's something that differentiated him from later rockabilly singers. The following influences have been cited by various biographers as inspiring the performing style that forever branded "gyrating" a dirty word, but his live act is deceptively difficult to dissect, so I would caution drawing cause-and-effect conclusions:

- Lead singer Jake Hess of the colorfully dressed Statesmen was an expressive singer, while bass singer Jim Wetherington liked to wear wide-legged pants. When Wetherington shook his leg, his pants leg quivered. Elvis not only adopted an expressive singing style but he also had a fondness for wide-legged pants.

- Flamboyant Pentecostal preachers knew how to rile their congregations to emotional high points via their preachings. Elvis learned to drive his audiences to a sort of controlled hysteria.

- Blues musician Ukelele Ike, who played at the Gray Mule on Beale Street moved provocatively onstage as Elvis would do as his career progressed.

- Rhythm-and-blues singer Wynonie Harris also dressed colorfully.

Much later, Elvis's onstage movements, twitches, and gyrations would become controversial, making the singer notorious as well as famous. (See Chapter 5 for more information on the controversy over his performing style.)

# Chapter 3

# Touring As the Hillbilly Cat and the Blue Moon Boys

## In This Chapter

▶ Looking at life on the road with Elvis and his band

▶ Taking a closer look at Elvis's clothing preferences

▶ Understanding the importance of touring

After Elvis's first public appearance at the Overton Park Shell in 1954 (see Chapter 2 for more information on this performance), the inexperienced singer began performing at local Memphis clubs and venues with guitar player Scotty Moore and bass player Bill Black. After a few weeks, the bookings expanded to clubs and halls outside the city, including appearances at two of the most important venues in the South — The Grand Ole Opry and the Louisiana Hayride. The group was met with mixed results, but by 1955, Elvis and his band, who were dubbed the Hillbilly Cat and the Blue Moon Boys, began touring with established country performers.

For the next year and a half, Elvis and his band sharpened their skills and seasoned their act on the road, touring with some of the biggest names in country music. However their music didn't sound like the other acts on the bill. During that time, Elvis honed his singing style; adopted his trademark look of flashy clothes, long sideburns, and long ducktail haircut for his act; and developed his performing style from a series of tics, spontaneous bursts of energy, and jumpy steps to a deliberate set of moves calculated to elicit screams and excitement from the audience.

Most importantly, Elvis gained a following that included country fans, R&B fans, and African Americans. Eventually, his largest following became a vocal fan base of teenagers and young adults who responded to his expressive singing and sensual performing style with an enthusiasm that seemed like hysteria. Interestingly, throughout 1954 and 1955, when he toured in the South and was labeled a country singer, he received little complaint about his frenetic onstage movements or his atypical clothing and hair styles. The biggest complaints came from other country singers who disliked following Elvis and his high-powered act. He and his group whipped the young girls into a frenzy, leaving the traditional country acts in the dust.

**REMEMBER:** Elvis was heavily condemned for his music and performing style only after he became a nationally based recording artist in 1956 and his sound was called rock 'n' roll.

In this chapter, I turn back the clock to take a look at Elvis in the beginning, when he was a fresh talent with a new sound touring the back roads and the country venues of the South. I discuss his appearances on the *Grand Ole Opry* and the *Louisiana Hayride* radio program and examine how touring impacted his career. Finally, I point out the differences between Elvis and the other country acts that he toured with as well as the unique response of his audiences to his high-powered performances.

# Introducing the Blue Moon Boys

Elvis and his band toured as the Hillbilly Cat and the Blue Moon Boys. The name was inspired by the trio's first recording, "That's All Right," which was an old R&B tune by black musician Arthur "Big Boy" Crudup. At the time, local music aficionados and record buyers called R&B music "cat music," and Elvis was a rural white Southerner, or a "hillbilly" singer. Just like his music, Elvis's stage name integrated two styles of music. The name "Blue Moon Boys" was a nod to the flip side of the single disc "That's All Right," which was "Blue Moon of Kentucky."

**TRIVIA:** Producer Sam Phillips's secretary, Marion Keisker, may have been the person who coined Elvis's nickname, "the Hillbilly Cat" — at least according to a 1955 *Memphis Press-Scimitar* article.

Fellow Blue Moon Boys, Moore and Black, had initially been tapped by Phillips in 1954 to help whip Elvis into shape musically for recording. Phillips knew Moore as a local guitarist who was trying to single-handedly push his country group, the Starlite Wranglers, up the ladder of success. And Black, who also was an occasional member of the Wranglers, lived two doors down from Moore, so it was convenient for them both to show Elvis the ropes. Elvis also knew Black's younger brother, Johnny, because the family had lived in Lauderdale Courts at the same time as Elvis and his family.

**IN THEIR OWN WORDS:** According to Elvis biographer Peter Guralnik in *Last Train to Memphis,* Moore's impression of Elvis upon their first meeting was a humorous one: "He was as green as a gourd," Moore said. And here's Black's impression from the same meeting: "Well, he didn't impress me much. Snotty-nosed kid coming in here with those wild clothes and everything."

Moore, a respected guitar player around the Memphis music scene, gave Elvis's sound the driving rhythm that was its strength. Black played doghouse bass, which was the large, upright instrument popular in musical combos before the electric bass guitar took hold. With his bass, Black was in charge of the beat, often slapping the instrument so hard and fast that it looked painful.

## Attempting to describe Elvis's sound

When "That's All Right" was introduced, and Elvis was nervously stepping in front of an audience for the first time, the terms rockabilly and rock 'n' roll weren't commonly used. Descriptions of his music in ads and posters, trade magazines, newspapers, and country-western song books varied widely, indicating the problems that the industry had in categorizing it. The odd phrasings and unique terms that industry writers and music reviewers penned revealed the diverse regional genres that made up Elvis's music. The inability to pinpoint Elvis's music specifically suggests that no one realized that he had combined various regional sounds into an explosive new genre.

Writers groped for the right combination of familiar musical terms to convey what they heard. Many of them are downright amusing. Consider the following:

- On October 20, 1954, the *Memphis Press-Scimitar* referred to Elvis as a "promising young rural rhythm talent."

- The November 6 issue of *Billboard* identified Elvis's style as "both country and R&B, and he can appeal to pop."

- In a February 1955 article for the *Memphis Press-Scimitar*, reporter Robert Johnson described Elvis as "a white man's voice singing negro rhythms with a rural flavor." He referred to "That's All Right" as "the R&B idiom of negro field jazz."

- In the summer of 1955, the *American-Statesman* of Austin, Texas, speculated that Elvis had a "boppish approach to hillbilly music" — that is "half-bop, half-Western."

- *The Cowboy Sings* songbook (No. 44) offered this perceptive opinion: "The young artist has made both sides of the record ["That's All Right"/"Blue Moon of Kentucky"] acceptable to a much wider audience than the usual song which must be put into just one category."

Though Elvis would get all the glory because of his vocals, the contributions of Moore and Black to the rockabilly sound can't be underestimated.

After the trio recorded "That's All Right" and began appearing around Memphis night spots, Moore dropped out of the Starlite Wranglers, and he and Black hitched themselves to Elvis's star.

## Dressing As the Hillbilly Cat

When looking at photos of Elvis with the Blue Moon Boys, you immediately notice that the Hillbilly Cat stands out. Moore and Black often wore their western-style Starlite Wranglers costumes or white shirts with ties. Elvis, on the other hand, preferred the style of clothing that black rhythm-and-blues artists often wore. (See Figure 3-1.) Flashy, hip, bold, and urban, this type of clothing could be purchased on Beale Street, where the black night clubs and hot spots were located. Among the most respected shops on Beale Street was Lansky Brothers, which was operated by Guy and Bernard Lansky.

**Figure 3-1:** The Hillbilly Cat and the Blue Moon Boys dressed in opposing styles, but they had a love of music in common.

Elvis favored pleated pants with wide legs. These pants virtually vibrated when Elvis bounced on the balls of his feet while performing. He seemed to like trousers with stripes down the sides, because years later several people recalled seeing him in pink-striped and white-striped pants. Big baggy suit coats in white or black draped his thin body, while brightly colored ties in gaudy patterns rounded out the ensemble. However, sometimes he preferred tight, high-collared shirts in bright colors with the sleeves rolled up. Pink and black were his favorite colors, so, of course, he wore a pink and black suit for his first appearance on the *Louisiana Hayride*. But, he also was fond of his sea green bolero jacket, which he wore with a mariner's cap.

Elvis's wardrobe was certainly atypical of the western-style costumes associated with both male and female country artists at the time, which featured kerchiefs around the neck, Stetson hats, and shirts embroidered with patterns and trimmed with piping. However, some of these western costumes, such as those worn by Porter Wagoner and Hank Thompson, were actually quite gaudy with colored rhinestones and brightly colored patterns sewn onto the fronts, sleeves, and backs. So Elvis's Beale Street clothing wasn't any gaudier than that of typical country artists. Instead, he stood out because he dressed like African American R&B artists. Elvis dressed in his Beale Street attire both on stage and off, but he was fond of capping his look onstage with eye makeup and a carefully sculpted ducktail haircut.

Elvis's ducktail hairstyle took a long time to perfect and required three different hair products. He used a thick pomade to slick back the hair high on his head (though one carefully chosen strand always fell over his eyes while he performed). Another product slicked back the sides, and a third was used to form the central part that ran from the crown of the head to the nape of his neck. The effect resembled the rear end of a duck, so a less-polite name for this hairstyle developed: the duckass, or d.a.

**Chapter 3: Touring As the Hillbilly Cat and the Blue Moon Boys**

# *Hitting the Road on the Country-Western Circuit*

After the Overton Park Shell performance, Presley, Moore, and Black began to sing at tiny clubs around Memphis, such as the Eagles Nest, the Bel Air, and the Airport Inn. They also performed at the openings of shopping centers, using the back of a flatbed truck as a stage. Their public appearances were limited to high school auditoriums, small night clubs, and roadhouses in and around the Memphis area because all three musicians worked day jobs and couldn't afford to take time off from work in order to drive long distances to shows farther away. Elvis still worked for Crown Electric driving a delivery truck, Moore worked at his brother's dry cleaning service, and Black worked for a tire company. Because Moore had the most experience as a working musician, he served as the combo's manager and arranged the local bookings.

*TRIVIA*

The concert at the Overton Park Shell was Elvis's first public appearance as a professional singer, but he had sung onstage for the first time about two weeks prior to that performance. On July 17, 1954, he sang two songs with the Starlite Wranglers at the Bon Air nightclub in east Memphis. Moore, who played guitar for the Wranglers, set up the appearance to allow Elvis some much-needed practice in front of an audience.

As the owner-operator of a recording studio, producer Sam Phillips knew many promoters, deejays, and other members of the music industry, and he moved mountains to get Elvis and the Blue Moon Boys on the *Grand Ole Opry* and the *Louisiana Hayride.* The trio's infamous appearance on the *Opry* turned out to be a disaster, but their debut on the *Hayride* was a hit. After the success of the *Hayride,* Elvis and his band began touring in Arkansas, Louisiana, Texas, and other states where the *Hayride* broadcast reached. By late fall of 1954, all three band members had quit their day jobs. For better or worse, they were now professional musicians, and the road beckoned them.

In this section, I talk about the musical adventures and real-life exploits of the trio at the earliest point in their career together — a period often celebrated by biographers for the purity of the music and the anonymity of Elvis as a performer. From late 1954 to the end of 1955, the trio tore up the country-western circuit as the Hillbilly Cat and the Blue Moon Boys.

## *Failing at the Opry*

Overjoyed at the local success of "That's All Right," Phillips approached Jim Denny, the manager of the *Grand Ole Opry,* about booking the trio for the show. His argument was based solely on the strength of that first single and the idea that Elvis represented new blood, which heralded success among youth. Denny finally agreed to let the group sing one song for one performance on October 2, 1954, provided it was the country side to their single, "Blue Moon of Kentucky."

On the night of the show, Phillips drove the trio to Ryman Auditorium, home of the *Opry* radio show, in his four-door Cadillac, with Black's doghouse bass strapped to the roof. The Grand Ole Opry as an institution was — and still is — devoted to the most traditional style of country music. Popular performers sang live in front of a large audience, and the performance was then broadcast across the South every Saturday night by Nashville radio station WSM on a program called *The Grand Ole Opry.* The show was divided into segments, each with a different sponsor and headlining star. The performers who filled out the segments tended to vary from week to week based on whether they could fit an appearance in their schedules.

For the October 2 performance, Elvis was assigned to Hank Snow's segment sponsored by Royal Crown Cola. It probably wasn't a good sign when Opry regulars began to mumble about Elvis's eye makeup as he mingled backstage. As the Blue Moon Boys began the song, Elvis bounded onto the stage where many a country music legend had been born, but the reception by the audience and some of the personnel was cool. Given the traditional nature of the Opry, Elvis and his revved-up music just weren't suited for the show.

After the trio's one song was over, Denny told Phillips that Elvis wasn't a good fit for *The Grand Ole Opry.* The young singer was personally devastated by the negative reaction, because he and his family, like most rural Southerners, had been fans of the program much of their lives. Scotty and Bill also felt low, but Phillips felt he had scored a victory by simply getting one of his R&B-influenced rockabilly singers on the show.

## *Hopping aboard the Louisiana Hayride*

The Monday after the *Grand Ole Opry* appearance, Phillips booked the Hillbilly Cat and the Blue Moon Boys on the *Louisiana Hayride,* which was another live show broadcast over the radio. However, the *Hayride* was dedicated to showcasing new styles of country music and attracted a younger audience than the *Opry.* In its six years on the air, the program had featured Hank Williams when the folks behind the Grand Ole Opry had turned him away. The Hayride organization had also discovered Slim Whitman, Webb Pierce, Jim Reeves, and Faron Young. The new trio fit right in on the *Louisiana Hayride,* which was broadcast on KWKH from the Municipal Auditorium in Shreveport, Louisiana.

On October 16, Elvis and the Blue Moon Boys appeared on two segments of the *Louisiana Hayride* radio program. Each time, they performed both songs from their first single. Response to his first appearance was tepid, perhaps because the singer was still reeling from his Grand Ole Opry failure. By the second segment, however, a large group of college students had shown up,

## Chapter 3: Touring As the Hillbilly Cat and the Blue Moon Boys

and the reception was entirely different. The enthusiasm of the students lit up the room, making Elvis a bona fide hit on the program. The Louisiana Hayride organization contracted Elvis and the Blue Moon Boys to make 50 appearances, which they fulfilled more or less over the next year.

They began touring with the Louisiana Hayride road show, which featured a diverse bill of some of the program's most popular acts. The *Louisiana Hayride* live show paid Elvis only $18 for each Saturday appearance, with Moore and Black receiving only $12. However, hooking up with the organization meant that their act was broadcast over a network of 190 radio stations, which gave them exposure for their recordings and promotion for their concerts. More importantly, the Hayride tours across the South maximized their exposure for their latest records. In 1955, the Hillbilly Cat and the Blue Moon Boys made $430,000 in royalties for their Sun recordings. (You can read more about the group's Sun recordings in Chapter 2.)

## Adding a drummer: D.J. Fontana

Between the three of them, the Hillbilly Cat and the Blue Moon Boys made a ruckus onstage at the *Louisiana Hayride.* However, when they were backed by the house band during their performances, they saw the benefits of adding drums to their live sound. D.J. Fontana played as the regular house drummer for the program and whenever the trio performed on the *Hayride* radio program he backed them up. When the Hayride began booking the Hillbilly Cat and the Blue Moon Boys on tours with big-name country acts, Fontana went along as their drummer. Going on the road with specific acts wasn't uncommon for members of the Hayride house band, but by 1955, he was on board as a permanent Blue Moon Boy. When Elvis's contract was up with the Hayride, D.J. went with him.

Fontana's impression of Elvis was a positive one from the beginning. He recalled in an interview: "Elvis had this charisma about him. I don't think anybody could ever put their finger on what he did or how he did it . . . . Onstage he could feel the audience out in about five or ten minutes. He knew the songs they wanted to hear for some reason, and he could work that crowd to his benefit. He was really good."

## Acquiring a manager: Bob Neal

In November 1954, Presley, Moore, and Black took another important step toward establishing professional careers when they hired Bob Neal to be their official manager. Moore had been serving as their manager for small, local gigs, and Phillips had stepped in to secure the important *Grand Ole Opry* and *Louisiana Hayride* bookings. But, neither one could provide the service of a full-time manager who was dedicated to tracking down bookings, promoting the appearances, and placing print ads.

Neal, who had put together the Overton Park Shell show in July, was a disc jockey for country radio station WMPS and had a lot of connections in the local music business. Excited by Elvis's effect on his audiences and impressed with the young man's drive and ambition, Neal took on the role of manager, thinking he was getting in on the ground floor of something special. Sadly, any plans for helping Elvis make it to the national level didn't come to fruition for Neal. (See Chapter 4 for information on Neal and Colonel Tom Parker, Elvis's legendary manager.) For the time being, Neal pushed the group's records, booked tours across the South with big-name country acts, and handled all their business arrangements.

## Becoming a hard act to follow

By November, Elvis felt secure enough to quit his job at Crown Electric, and Moore and Black soon followed suit by leaving their day jobs. The following January, manager Neal began booking them on a series of tours that kept them on the road most of the month.

Throughout 1955, Elvis grew more popular with young audiences, who could be loud, disruptive, and demonstrative during the shows. His shows were so high energy that he riled the audience up, provoking them to want more of the same. Traditional country acts who followed Elvis on the bill seemed so tame in comparison that most dreaded going on after him. In fact, sometimes promoters had difficulty placing Elvis on the bill. If he closed the show, his young fans grew restless waiting for him. But, if he performed earlier in the program, the young crowds, who were ramped up by his act, were often rude to the remaining performers, or they simply left. As the year wore on, Elvis's high-energy shows caused complaints from the other performers and refusals to play on the same bill as the Hillbilly Cat.

However, not all country artists felt this way. Some, including younger singers such as Faron Young, Johnny Cash, Wanda Jackson, and the Carter Sisters, considered Elvis a kindred spirit, despite his crazy performing style and his tendency to dress in pink slacks, green bolero jackets, and fluffy shirts. When they toured on the same bill, Cash sometimes lampooned Elvis's act a bit by mimicking his moves. It was all in the spirit of fun, and the young performers enjoyed their time together on the road.

## Recognizing the Importance of Touring

Recording "That's All Right" may have made Elvis a professional singer, but touring made him a success. The way to create interest in a recording artist during the early 1950s was to introduce him or her through radio airplay and then create a live stage act to generate record sales (which in turn generated even more interest in the stage act).

## Touring with a who's who of country artists

Many overviews of Elvis's career make the mistake of downplaying his country music roots and overlooking the caliber of performer he toured with on the country circuits. Much of the Elvis lore and literature reveals a lack of interest and understanding of country music, preferring to overemphasize the R&B roots to "prove" that Elvis was the true social rebel he was painted to be. But, it's essential to recognize the country music context to understand the impact of his Southern background on his entire career.

Presley, Moore, and Black toured with traditionalists like Hank Thompson, the Wilburn Brothers, Webb Pierce, Hank Snow, and Jim Edward & Maxine Brown; crooners such as Carl Smith and Ferlin Huskey (later Husky); and contemporary country acts like Sonny James and Marty Robbins. All these performers became country music's biggest artists of the 1950s and 1960s and influenced the genre. Elvis was even on the same bill as comedian Andy Griffith, who became one of television's most beloved actors. Touring with these important figures suggests that Elvis was considered a hot act on the country-western circuit and underscores his Southern roots despite his different look and sound. Elvis had a lifelong love and respect for country music, which comes into play during the last phase of his career. Having watched these legendary artists perform close up surely made an impact on him, even if it wasn't immediate.

The two years that Elvis toured across the South with the Blue Moon Boys helped him accomplish several objectives that prepared him for national exposure. For one, touring with other country acts helped differentiate him from the pack, establishing him as a unique presence on the music scene. It also created a loyal following consisting of several age groups and types, who were eventually overshadowed by teenagers and young adults. Finally, it allowed him, and the Blue Moon Boys, to season the act, making it more deliberately provocative and exciting. During those two years, Elvis honed his performing style from a random set of tics and moves into a sophisticated "dance" in which a series of calculated movements — hip swiveling, leg shaking, finger pointing, chest heaving — elicited screams and squeals from his raucous audiences. This section details the impact of those two years on Elvis's career and act.

## *One in a million: Standing out from the crowd*

Elvis toured across the South with the biggest names in country-western music, from the legendary Mother Maybelle Carter, who was one of the first commercial performers in the genre, to yodeler Slim Whitman and country crooner Faron Young. He also shared bills with other prominent and diverse country entertainers who sang in a variety of styles; some were very traditional and others were more contemporary.

Country music is much more versatile and "elastic" than the mainstream media gives it credit for; the genre stretches to include many styles, forms, and specific regional sounds. While embracing traditional values, ideals, and sounds, country habitually absorbs influences from other popular genres, including pop, blues, and Tin Pan Alley.

Even though Elvis was easily accepted into the fold of country music, his full integration of regional musical styles made him sound quite different from the average act. Rockabilly, which fused the heavy beat of blues and rhythm and blues with a rocket-fueled country rhythm, was more than a new trend in country music; it was a forerunner to rock 'n' roll. The singer's limitless well of energy and his kinetic performing style also singled him out as different from standard country acts. And, if his sound and stage act weren't different enough, his Beale Street wardrobe closed the deal.

Touring on the country-western circuit served to contrast Elvis with the other acts on the bill. Elvis's unique qualities as an entertainer — particularly his singing and performing styles — were readily apparent to audiences, the press, record execs, and others in the music industry, because he stood out in comparison. His differences prepared audiences and industry folk to accept him outside the framework of the country-western scene when he took his career to the national level in 1956. (See Chapter 4 for more information on Elvis's breakthrough on the national music scene.)

## Establishing a diverse following

Elvis's fan base began to develop as soon as his first two recordings, "That's All Right" and "Blue Moon of Kentucky," hit the airwaves in Memphis. During his early career, Elvis's popularity spread among diverse groups, including African Americans, country fans, and young audiences. I discuss these fan bases in the following sections.

### Appealing to African Americans

Some of Elvis's early audience consisted of African American listeners, because "That's All Right" was played on black radio stations and on Dewey Phillips's program *Red Hot and Blue*. (Flip to Chapter 2 to find out more about the flamboyant Dewey Phillips.)

Stories abound that deejays didn't know whether Elvis was black or white when his career took off in the summer of 1954. Many of the stories were exaggerated and even romanticized by rock music historians, who tend to propagate Elvis's image as a rebel and focus on his ties to R&B music, but some of the stories are true. A deejay named Early Wright, for example, recalled that he regularly played Elvis's records at his Clarksdale, Mississippi, radio station. When he invited Elvis to make an appearance on

# Chapter 3: Touring As the Hillbilly Cat and the Blue Moon Boys

his radio program, Wright was surprised when a young white man showed up. Likewise some country stations refused to play his first single, because they thought Elvis was black.

Many African Americans remained fans after Elvis's race was widely known. In 1955, Sun Records repeatedly filled and refilled orders for Elvis's singles with R&B distributors across the South. The singer retained a following among R&B fans long after he signed with RCA in 1956. In a poll taken by *Cashbox* magazine of artists who dominated the R&B charts between 1949 and 1971, Elvis was ranked 19th. He was the only white performer on the list.

After Elvis died in 1977, his status among members of the mainstream entertainment press was at a low point. Outside of bona fide music historians and rock 'n' roll writers, few discussed his significance as a musical force in their musings over his death. In fact, when attempting to put his career into perspective, many claimed that he had stolen the music of black performers and watered it down in order to cash in on the burgeoning popularity of R&B with young white audiences. They speculated that black audiences and performers must have resented him; surely he was no "King" to them. These biased critics and cultural pundits didn't know of (or simply ignored) Elvis's popularity with black audiences during the 1950s, which has been well documented by Michael T. Bertrand in his book *Race, Rock, and Elvis* (University of Illinois Press).

## Attracting country fans and young audiences

After his appearances on the *Louisiana Hayride,* when he began touring the country circuits across the Deep South, Elvis was introduced to pure country audiences. He generally attracted the loyalty of country music fans who preferred the less traditional acts heard on the *Hayride,* but conservative country fans who turned out to see the other performers on the bill were often sufficiently amused by his raucous stage act.

As Elvis crisscrossed the South throughout 1955 on one tour after another, his fan base grew and became dominated by young audiences. He attracted teenage boys and girls and young adults for several reasons:

- The music, especially the beat
- Elvis's age, which was obvious from his hair and clothing style
- The excitement of his performing style, which was revealed only through touring

As the year went on, the young fans, who were sometimes loud and more raucous than typical country audiences, came only to see Elvis. However, that doesn't mean that others in his fan base who weren't as demonstrative, such as country fans or African Americans, stopped buying his records or listening to his music.

## Shakin' and gyratin': Honing a performing style

The young female fans became unglued when Elvis shook his legs and swiveled his hips. What started out as natural nervous movements to the beat of the music became a more calculated performing style as Elvis turned into a more seasoned performer. In this section, I offer some insights into Elvis's trademark gyrations.

### Refining his influential moves

By 1955, Elvis had begun to fine-tune his performing style, in which he moved his hips, shook his legs, and sometimes collapsed totally on the floor. He remembered the flamboyant movements of the gospel quartets he watched as a kid, the deep feeling of the blues performers, and the rhythm behind the R&B singers. He gradually combined all of these into a unique performing style, which, over the course of time, he used to work the audiences into a frenzy.

Bill Black also added entertainment to the show. He liked to dance and roll around on the floor with his huge bass fiddle. The group's performances were sometimes considered too wild in small towns, and a few country singers didn't like to perform after Elvis, because the crowd was too worked up after his act. (Flip to the earlier section "Becoming a hard act to follow" for more information.) However, in larger towns, they were a hit.

Traditional country singer Porter Wagoner, who also was a star on the *Louisiana Hayride,* recalled Black's contribution to the onstage shenanigans in an interview for the book *Elvis Up Close.* "[Bill Black] got as much applause as Elvis did because he done this mimickin' thing. Elvis would shake his leg and then Bill would just go crazy and shake his leg, ass, and everything else — really wild . . . Elvis would throw his guitar around his shoulder, and then Bill Black would try and do that with his big stand-up bass. It was real entertainin'. People would just tear the house down!"

According to Moore, Elvis's trademark stage moves began the night he played at the Overton Park Shell on July 30, 1954. And, those who write about Elvis can't help but emphasize his performing style at this time, detailing its effect on girls in the audience. In describing his stage act, most biographers and authors depend on the personal reminiscences of those who performed with Elvis, or those lucky enough to have seen him in 1954 or 1955. Some valuable sources of primary research are available, but you have to be careful of personal accounts, because they can be exaggerated, colored by emotion, or tainted by film footage and kinescopes of Elvis performing much later.

## On the edge of hysteria: One night in Jacksonville

On May 13, 1955, Elvis performed in a concert that has since become part of his legend. His performance is legendary not because of what happened onstage but because of what happened after it was over. Elvis was singing in Jacksonville, Florida, at the stadium where the Gator Bowl was played. Over 14,000 people attended, many of them teenagers and young fans who were there only to see Elvis.

That night someone accidentally left a backstage gate open and unlocked, and no one noticed that it was open enough for people to slip under. Elvis and the audience had really clicked during the performance, and so after he sang his last song, he jokingly remarked, "I'll see all you girls backstage." Moments later, when he was in the area marked off as his dressing room, about 50 screaming girls got in and began ripping his clothes off. They pulled off his suit jacket and ripped a ruffled pink shirt to pieces. Fearful of injury, Elvis began climbing a shower stall, only to have the girls pull his shoes and socks off. They were tugging at his pants when help arrived to rescue the stunned star.

The next day, the newspapers were filled with stories about girls ripping the clothes off the latest singing sensation. This story illustrates the effect Elvis had on the female fans in the audience. It also reveals what real hysteria was like. It was common at the time to refer to Elvis's screaming fans as "hysterical" and the atmosphere at his concerts as "hysteria," but most of the time Elvis controlled the reaction of the fans to a large extent. However, this incident revealed what could happen when fans crossed the line into true hysteria.

---

The impression left by these exaggerated accounts is that Elvis's performing style was so instinctive that it blossomed almost immediately. And, inevitably some variation of the word "hysteria" is used to describe the audiences, painting a picture of them as out of control. Elvis moved around onstage from the beginning, because he was naturally full of nervous energy and just plain anxious about performing before the public. However, it's doubtful that Elvis's performing style fully developed the moment he stepped onstage at Overton Park.

Instead, he most likely realized that his spontaneous tics and moves had an effect on the audience, and so he began to hone those moves in an effort to tease the audience and ramp up their reactions. Some of the onstage antics did turn raucous, and audiences did get out of control occasionally, but most likely the "hysteria" was more or less controlled by Elvis. Eventually, the interaction between audience and performer became part of the act — and part of the attraction of seeing Presley perform live.

### Using rare new footage to reevaluate Elvis's performing style

Recently, rare film footage of Elvis from 1955 surfaced, and it clearly supports the idea that his performing style evolved during the year and a half that he toured. It also showed that a Presley concert wasn't always defined by hysterical girls. The 8mm color footage is silent, but it shows a 20-year-old Elvis singing on an outdoor stage at Magnolia Gardens in Houston on April 24, 1955. The footage was shot by a pair of newlyweds who were eager to try out their new camera. The pair was close to the elevated stage and to the left of Elvis, so the angle clearly captures the singer as he moves about the stage.

Those familiar with Elvis's performing style will recognize some of his trademark moves in this footage: He continually bounces on the balls of his feet as he sings, and on occasion he stands back to swivel his hips. But, these movements lack the drama of his later television performances after he becomes a national sensation. Here, on this sunny day in Houston, Elvis spends most of his performance pacing from the back of the stage, where Moore is playing the guitar, to the front to sing into the microphone. While not much of the audience is visible, a couple of girls can be seen calmly sitting on the end of the stage looking out into the crowd; others stroll leisurely in front of the camera. The scene stands in marked contrast to his later concerts in the same way that his stage act lacks the calculation and interaction between performer and audience of his later shows. Available as an extra on the DVD collection *Elvis: The Ed Sullivan Shows* from Image Entertainment, the footage adds a new perspective on the development of Elvis's performing style.

This recently found footage makes another point: Elvis may be one of the most written about celebrities in the history of entertainment, but that doesn't mean that there isn't anything new to discover about him. New evidence can shed light on his music, his performing style, or his career; new perspectives can change the critical perception of him and his impact on American culture. With a cultural figure as significant as Elvis, the book is never closed.

# Chapter 4

# Shocking America: Elvis Becomes a National Sensation

*In This Chapter*

- ▶ Meeting Colonel Tom Parker
- ▶ Recording for RCA
- ▶ Examining Elvis's appearances on television

As Elvis rocked his way across the South in 1955, touring with big-name country stars, he attracted the attention of major record labels. Buzz about the crazy Hillbilly Cat and his very vocal fans suggested to many in the music industry that he was capable of breaking out of the regional market to become a national success.

Country-western promoter and ex-carnival operator Colonel Tom Parker began watching the young singer in the late winter, and before the year was out, he had become a part of Presley's team. He negotiated a contract with nationally based RCA Victor that included a buyout of Elvis's existing contract with Sun Records. Some execs at RCA didn't know what to make of the strangely dressed singer with the organic approach to recording, but his first singles for the company were instant hits. Part of the plan to launch their new property was to gain national exposure on the many television variety shows that dominated programming during the 1950s. To that end, they succeeded in ways that they could never have foreseen.

After debuting on Tommy and Jimmy Dorsey's *Stage Show,* Elvis created a national scandal when he performed on *The Milton Berle Show,* setting off a controversy that heated up throughout 1956 and culminated with his infamous appearance on *The Ed Sullivan Show* in which he was filmed only from the waist up. The controversy dogged him throughout the 1950s.

In this chapter, I chronicle the biggest year in Elvis Presley's life — 1956 — the year he launched his career on a national stage. Elvis was propelled into a level of fame that he would never escape, and American culture was changed forever.

# Meeting Colonel Tom Parker

Biographies of Elvis Presley penned by both professionals and personal acquaintances often paint Colonel Tom Parker as the villain in the story. Parker's background as a carnival barker when he was a young man in Florida made him easy to underestimate. Elitist writers often looked down on his persona as an old-time carny hustler who relied on unsophisticated promotional stunts, exploitation tactics, and the merchandising of cheap products to build his client's career. After Elvis died, the Colonel revealed his true identity, which showed that his exaggerated stories about himself and his outrageous persona allowed him to deflect attention from his real past.

Parker was the force behind Elvis's evolution from a regionally based country performer to a nationally known rock 'n' roll star. Parker first saw Presley in early 1955 and watched as he grew into a unique performer whose charisma attracted the most rabid fans. Parker eventually stepped in to become a part of the action.

The Colonel realized a recording contract from a major company was necessary to reach a mainstream audience, which meant the highest level of popularity and financial success. He had contacts at RCA Victor and connections with the William Morris Agency to facilitate Elvis's introduction to that level of show business. This section tells the story of how Parker became Elvis's manager and how he maneuvered his one and only client into the big time.

The "Colonel" in Parker's name doesn't refer to an official military rank. It comes from an old Southern custom of honoring a gentleman by bestowing the title of Colonel on him. The practice originated in colonial times when men of landed gentry were honored for financing the local militia, but eventually the title became a more generic tradition or custom. Usually the honor is specific to a particular state; in Parker's case, he was named Colonel by Governor Jimmie Davis of Louisiana in 1948.

## Uncovering the Colonel's true background

From the beginning of his career in the music industry — long before he met Elvis — Parker played the old carnival huckster to the hilt, especially for the press, Hollywood studio executives, or any others he felt were underestimating him. He delighted in telling his old carny stories, making impossible deals, haggling over the tiniest detail in a contract, and complicating standard contracts with unusual clauses and requirements. All these tactics were designed to give him an advantage in deal making, and they generally worked.

In truth, Parker's exaggerated carny image helped deflect any serious inquiries into his past. Parker always told reporters that he hailed from

Huntington, West Virginia, which was a difficult fact to verify because the West Virginia state courthouse burned down decades earlier, destroying all the records housed there. It turns out, however, that the Colonel wasn't Tom Parker at all. Instead, he was born in 1909 as Andreas Cornelis van Kuijk of Breda, Holland. Parker entered America illegally around 1929, perhaps by jumping from a Dutch ship docked in Florida. During the 1930s, he crisscrossed the American South on the carnival circuit, doing everything from selling cotton candy to working as a *barker* (the person who lures customers to entertainment acts by shouting out their attractions). Parker began two carnivals himself before giving up the carny life to become a dogcatcher and later a promoter of country-western acts. As a successful promoter and manager, he made important contacts in the music business that served him well when managing Elvis.

Parker's real identity didn't surface until 1981, four years after Elvis's death, when the Presley estate investigated the former manager for mismanaging Elvis during the last few years of his life. When the estate decided to sue the Colonel, he revealed his true identity. Ever the slippery carny, he tried to claim that he wasn't a U.S. citizen but a man without a country, which meant that he couldn't be sued. The case was eventually settled out of court, but the news about Parker's true past shocked the Elvis community.

## Waiting in the wings to sign Elvis

In 1954, Parker was working as a promoter under the name Jamboree Attractions when he signed a talent and booking partnership with country singer Hank Snow. Parker would be in charge of booking acts for his road shows and handling Hank Snow Enterprises, which included radio, TV, film, and recording commitments.

In early 1955, Elvis's manager Bob Neal signed Presley and his band to one of Snow's tours. He and the band shared the bill with Snow, Mother Maybelle and the Carter Sisters, the comedian known as the Duke of Paducah, and Jimmie Rodgers Snow (Hank's son). The Colonel took notice of Elvis, particularly his energetic and intense singing and performing styles. Parker then decided to keep a close eye on the kid with the high-powered act.

In May 1955, when Elvis was mobbed by girls backstage in Jacksonville, Florida, the Colonel saw the near riot as proof of the boy's star power. (See Chapter 3 for more information on this incident.) So Parker adopted a proprietary attitude toward Elvis but said nothing to anyone about managing him. Part of his interest, which others on the tour began to notice, took the form of introducing Elvis to RCA scouts and promotion experts and persuading them to send the boy's Sun singles to the executives in Nashville. He also began filling Elvis's head with promises about his future career.

## Making Elvis his sole client

In the summer of 1955, Sam Phillips of Sun Records leaked word to those in the business that he might be willing to sell Elvis's contract if the price was right. This led Bob Neal to begin fielding inquiries from independent and major labels who wanted to buy out Elvis's contract.

Selling Sun's hottest property may have seemed crazy, but Sam had good reasons for wanting to make a deal. Sun Records was too small to handle demand outside of the South, because it didn't have a distribution network capable of meeting the orders that a nationally based singer would generate. Plus the company was already strapped for cash in trying to meet the manufacturing demands of their success thus far. Sam knew he would have to sell sooner or later.

At this point, the Colonel stepped in, first as a special adviser to Elvis and later as his manager. Parker would be instrumental in working out a deal between RCA and Sam Phillips — the deal resulted in Elvis becoming a national recording artist.

### Becoming Elvis's special adviser

On August 2, Elvis's parents, Vernon and Gladys Presley, met with the Colonel about signing a contract naming him "special adviser" to Elvis and Bob Neal. Elvis's parents had to sign the contract because he was under 21 years of age. (You can read more about the Presleys in Chapter 2.) A second near riot in which fans ripped the clothes off Elvis's back had occurred in Jacksonville that month, and Gladys feared for the safety of her son. The Colonel reassured her that he didn't want a repeat of this type of behavior, but Gladys was still leery of Parker, so she and Vernon didn't sign. At about the same time, the Colonel was talking up an RCA deal with Phillips, and he, too, was put off by the former carny and didn't agree to the deal even though he knew it was inevitable.

By August 15, Elvis and the Colonel had worn down Gladys with the help of Hank Snow, whom Mrs. Presley admired. She, Vernon, and Elvis signed the contract naming Col. Thomas A. Parker as "special adviser to Elvis Presley ['artist'] and Bob Neal ['manager'] . . . to negotiate and assist in any way possible the build-up of Elvis Presley as an artist. . . ."

The Colonel began to edge out Neal almost immediately, and the country music deejay realized that his role had been diminished. One of the few tasks Neal did manage during this time was to put Elvis's fellow band members, Scotty Moore and Bill Black, on salary instead of giving them a percentage of the take, which had been the arrangement thus far. Moore and Black wouldn't necessarily make less money than they had up to that point, but they wouldn't get a chunk of the big money that would come in after Elvis broke big either. Though both musicians balked at this change in status, it was clear that the crowds were coming to see Elvis, not them. Plus, the Colonel was making noises about not using the two musicians at all. In the end, they accepted the deal, but the addition of Parker to the business dealings changed the dynamic of the group. Parker's lack of interest in the Blue Moon Boys was apparent from the start, and this drove a wedge between the musicians and Elvis. Black in particular disliked the situation — and the Colonel.

### Using the deal with RCA to become Elvis's manager

Parker spent most of the fall of 1955 working on landing a record deal with a nationally based recording company. He had connections at RCA, but he played them against executives from other companies in his efforts to get the best deal. Parker didn't formally ask Sam Phillips's permission to negotiate Elvis's contract, which angered Phillips to the extreme. Phillips finally confronted Parker and told him he would agree to sell for the outrageous asking price of $35,000, plus $5,000 for back royalties that he owed Elvis. The price was more than any company had ever paid for a recording star, and Phillips thought this would be more than Parker could handle.

By mid-November, the Colonel persuaded RCA to agree to this price because some of the execs knew Elvis was a hot property, and they were nervous about Parker's threats to go with another company. On November 21, the deal was signed in the little studio at Sun. In addition, the Colonel had brought in Hill and Range music publishers on a side deal in which Elvis and the music publisher shared the profits on all Hill and Range–owned songs that he recorded (see the later section "Considering the role of Hill and Range" for more details). Figure 4-1 shows Elvis, the Colonel, and the RCA execs after their deal was signed.

Parker's flamboyant personality comes through in many of the widely quoted remarks he made to the press, including this one: "When I first knew Elvis, he had a million dollars' worth of talent. Now he has a million dollars."

As part of his participation in the profits from the RCA deal, Neal agreed not to renew his contract with Elvis when it ran out in March 1956. Despite Gladys Presley's suspicions and Sam Phillips's reservations, the RCA coup, in effect, made Elvis Presley Parker's sole client.

Neal wasn't the only person edged out of Presley's career. Parker also left Hank Snow behind in the dust as well. The exact details of this maneuver aren't known, but many rumors, speculations, and half-truths exist. However it happened, in early 1956, Parker told Snow that he was concluding their business relationship, except for booking him for a few more dates. Snow was furious partly because he and Parker were partners in Jamboree Attractions and partly because the country music star felt he had helped land Presley a contract with RCA. Snow brought legal action against the Colonel, and the case dragged on for five years before it was settled in Parker's favor.

**Figure 4-1:** (From left) Steve Sholes of RCA, Sam Phillips of Sun, Coleman Tily of RCA, Elvis, and Colonel Parker make the deal for RCA Victor in late 1955.

# Finding a Home at RCA

In 1956, as Elvis began his new relationship with RCA thanks to the wheeling and dealing of Colonel Tom Parker (see the preceding section for more), changes were on the horizon. The Colonel and the execs at RCA decided to stop promoting Elvis Presley as only a country-western performer. Instead, they released his songs as pop music and promoted him on all three national charts — country western, pop, and R&B.

As odd as it may seem now, Parker and RCA didn't even consider promoting Elvis as a rock 'n' roll singer. Though rock 'n' roll music had been around for a couple of years, it wasn't considered a major genre of music. There were no rock 'n' roll charts — at least not for a couple more years. As the year progressed, Elvis and his music started to be associated with the rock 'n' roll phenomenon in the press until he and his raw, raucous sound epitomized the controversial new genre.

Elvis's first recordings for RCA extended the sound he had developed at Sun Records, but the executives also tweaked it enough to push his music away from raw rockabilly toward a fuller rock 'n' roll sound. In this section, I reveal Elvis's initial experiences with RCA and analyze his first recordings. Finally, I discuss Hill and Range's involvement in Elvis's recording contract.

## Working with Steve Sholes

Signing with a major label meant that a number of executives in RCA's front office became involved in handling aspects of Elvis's musical career. One of the most important in the early years was Steve Sholes, RCA's premier A&R

(artist and repertoire) man. Sholes oversaw the recording and promotion of the company's specialty singles, which included country western, gospel, and R&B, so he was closely involved with the details of Elvis's first RCA singles.

Sholes, who was in agreement with the Colonel, wanted to release Elvis's singles in the pop, country, and R&B markets. The idea was to promote Elvis as a pop singer — exposing him to audiences in the north, Midwest, and west — to increase his teenage fan base, while still releasing his records in the country and R&B markets in order to retain his existing audience.

Executives in RCA's New York office didn't always share the enthusiasm for Elvis that Sholes felt, and many were waiting for the veteran A&R man and his newest talent to fail. But Sholes and his battery of assistants and coordinators went to work promoting their new artist in the entertainment press and rereleasing Elvis's Sun singles on the RCA label. Hill and Range music publishers also released a songbook of his hits.

## Recording for RCA for the first time

Sholes assigned Chet Atkins, RCA's music coordinator in Nashville, to organize Elvis's recording sessions, which started on January 10, 1956 — two days after Elvis's 21st birthday. Atkins not only worked as a producer and coordinator for RCA, but he also was a talented guitarist who released award-winning instrumental records. Revered in the country music industry, Atkins knew a lot of talented sessions musicians. For Elvis's first recording session, he arranged this solid group of musicians and backup vocalists:

- **Scotty Moore and Bill Black:** The Blue Moon Boys (see Chapter 3), who had worked with Elvis since his first single record, were hired to offer consistency from the old days at Sun to his new home at RCA. Moore, who admired Atkins as a guitarist and musician, was both thrilled and nervous to be there.
- **D.J. Fontana:** Fontana, who had toured with Elvis on the road but had never recorded with him, checked in on drums.
- **Chet Atkins:** The big man himself played rhythm guitar.
- **Floyd Cramer:** Cramer, a talented pianist who had backed Elvis on the *Louisiana Hayride,* moved to Nashville to work on Elvis's RCA sessions. (Refer to Chapter 3 for more on Elvis's involvement in the *Louisiana Hayride.*) He became one of the city's most respected sessions musicians and went on to record his own instrumental albums.
- **Ben and Brock Speer:** The Speer Family gospel quartet had just been signed by RCA, and Atkins invited two of the members, Ben and Brock, to provide backup vocals on any ballads that Elvis might record.

- **Gordon Stoker:** Even though he was a member of the Jordanaires, a highly popular gospel quartet, Stoker provided vocal backup without the other members (RCA had just signed the Speer Family, and Atkins wanted to make use of all or any of them wherever possible). However, Elvis took to Stoker right away, and it would be the Jordanaires who became his regular backup vocalists.

### Session one: Nashville

A quick summary of the first RCA recording session in Nashville may be "Everybody's nervous, except Elvis." RCA's Nashville studios were huge and the atmosphere was highly professional. Plus an uncertain Steve Sholes was in the booth riding shotgun on the engineers, and renowned musicians were on hand to provide support. If Elvis was intimidated at this complete change of pace from Sun Records, he didn't show it — perhaps because he had sought Sam Phillips's advice before coming to Nashville.

In Peter Guralnik's *Last Train to Memphis,* Phillips recalled years later that he offered this advice to a nervous but excited Elvis after he signed with RCA: "Look, you know how to do it now, you go over there and don't let anybody tell you — they believe enough in you that they've laid some cold cash down, so you let them know what you feel what you want to do."

Elvis attacked his first song, Ray Charles's "I've Got a Woman," with everything he had. In effect, Elvis performed the song while he recorded it, which impressed the cool, calm Atkins so much that he called his wife to come down to the studio to see the exciting Elvis. Most singers with training hold back during recording and focus on capturing a technically well-crafted version of the song. Elvis, who wasn't a trained singer, sank his heart and soul into each recording, giving his records an extra dash of vitality and intensity.

Elvis cut "Heartbreak Hotel" and "Money Honey" the same day as "I've Got a Woman." The following day, Elvis recorded two ballads that Sholes had found for him — "I'm Counting on You" and "I Was the One." Despite Elvis's relaxed attitude and Atkins's excitement over his recording style, Sholes and the RCA executives in New York weren't entirely happy with the Nashville session. They were concerned about the following:

- **At first, Sholes was disconcerted by Elvis's organic, instinctual approach to recording.** He didn't like Elvis's approach because it could potentially take up time (and time is money in show business), and because the level of emotion with each take was unusual. Elvis's approach was to sing a take, play it back, discard it, and then sing another, repeating the process until he felt he had captured the tune.

  Elvis didn't read music, nor did he have any professional experience at arranging it. He just instinctively knew what he wanted to do and when. And, each time he sang a song for recording, he performed it, giving it

# Chapter 4: Shocking America: Elvis Becomes a National Sensation

the same level of emotion and expression as if he were singing it before an audience.

- **Sholes and other executives disliked the way Elvis warmed up before each session.** His warm-up consisted of singing a few gospel tunes with the Jordanaires or with other musicians who were there. The RCA execs thought it a waste of time, but the practice soothed Elvis's nerves and focused his attention.

- **RCA executives in New York were troubled with the sound of the Nashville session.** They wanted Elvis to sound just like he had on his Sun recordings, and between the larger scale sound produced by the supporting vocalists and musicians and the inclusion of ballads on the song list, the work from his first session didn't fit that bill.

"Heartbreak Hotel," the biggest hit to come out of these first sessions, was presented to Elvis in November 1955 at a disc jockeys' convention by songwriters Mae Boren Axton and Tommy Durden. Durden came up with the idea for the song after reading a newspaper article about the suicide of a young man who had left behind a bitter note that read: "I walk a lonely street." As recorded at RCA, the song exaggerates the echo effect that was associated with his Sun sound, creating an eerie, downright ghostly effect as Elvis sings the opening lines to each verse. His voice is penetrating and the sound is despondent, perfectly capturing the alienation of disaffected youth.

## Session two: New York

After recording for the first time in Nashville, a second recording session was arranged in New York for January 30 and February 3, because Elvis was in town to appear on television (see the later section "Taking Television by Storm"). During this session, Elvis covered Carl Perkins's "Blue Suede Shoes" and Little Richard's "Tutti Frutti." He also cut Arthur "Big Boy" Crudup's blues tune "My Baby Left Me," among other songs.

This time, instead of having a huge clan of accompanying musicians, Sholes lined up only piano player Shortly Long in addition to Moore, Black, and Fontana. Long was a good boogie-woogie piano player, and Sholes thought Long's style would work well with Elvis's music. The focus during this session was on explosive, fast-paced songs, because Sholes and RCA seemed to want something new and spectacular out of their latest singing sensation.

Exactly what RCA expected from Elvis during these first sessions isn't known, probably because Sholes and the execs didn't really know either. Sholes called Sam Phillips after the New York session and sought his advice about how to handle Elvis. Phillips basically told Sholes to leave Elvis alone and to respect the young singer's instincts for selecting songs and cutting them. And so Sholes did.

## Releasing an album: Elvis Presley

Eventually seven tracks from the Nashville and New York sessions were chosen for Elvis's first long-playing album, *Elvis Presley.* These tracks were combined with five songs that were previously recorded at Sun Records but never released. The album, which was released on March 13, 1956, sold more than 360,000 copies by the end of April. At $3.98 per copy, *Elvis Presley* became RCA's first million-dollar album by a single artist. It reached number one on the *Billboard* Top LPs chart, remaining there for ten weeks.

"Heartbreak Hotel" wasn't included on this first full-length album. Released as a single on January 27, 1956, "Heartbreak Hotel" became Elvis's first gold record and climbed to number one on the *Billboard* singles chart, where it stayed for eight weeks. The song also reached number one on the *Billboard* country chart and number three on the R&B chart. Given its quick success, the song might seem a natural to be included on the album. But, during this era, singles were much more important in advancing a singer's career than albums, because they received extensive exposure on the radio and jukeboxes in addition to selling in record stores. Often, a singer's strongest recordings were released to stand alone from an album.

RCA pushed Elvis hard the first year he was under contract. Later in 1956, RCA released a second long-playing album, *Elvis,* and an extended-play album, *Love Me Tender,* featuring music from Elvis's first film. (For more on Elvis's movies, check out the chapters in Part II.)

An *extended-play album* or, EP, is a multitrack record with approximately four to seven songs. Once a common tool in the music industry, EPs fell out of favor during the 1960s.

## Tweaking Elvis's sound

As Elvis recorded more material at RCA in New York and Nashville throughout 1956, he moved farther away from the pure rockabilly style of music that he played at Sun Records. He selected more ballads to record, and his up-tempo songs became fuller because of the number of musicians and vocalists backing him. The echo effect and reverberation, which were his trademarks at Sun, were discarded.

After Sam Phillips's advice to Steve Sholes was borne out by the financial success of the singles and first album, the execs at RCA stepped back and let Elvis select his songs and record them his way. Sholes and others made suggestions to Elvis about which tunes to cut, but he made the final selections — at least during this first year.

## Chapter 4: Shocking America: Elvis Becomes a National Sensation

By July 1956, when he stepped back into the RCA studios, Elvis seemed to be seeking a bigger, more explosive rock 'n' roll sound. During this session, he recorded two of his signature songs, "Hound Dog" and "Don't Be Cruel." The latter became one of his most successful singles. In fact, as of today, it boasts triple platinum status by the Recording Industry Association of America (RIAA).

### "Hound Dog"

In 1952, Jerry Leiber and Mike Stoller wrote "Hound Dog" — a song about a gigolo — for blues singer Willa Mae "Big Mama" Thornton, who growled the saucy lyrics to a hard-driving blues beat.

Other singers covered the infamous song shortly after Thornton, including country artists Tommy Duncan, Betsy Gay, Jack Turner, Billy Starr, and lounge act Freddie Bell and the Bellboys. Bell enlivened the tempo and tampered with the lyrics to add humor. He added the line of the chorus about the Hound Dog's inability to catch rabbits.

After Elvis performed a scandalous version of "Hound Dog" on *The Milton Berle Show* and a notorious interpretation on *The Steve Allen Show* (see the later section "Taking Television by Storm" for details), Sholes pressured the young singer to record the novelty tune. After more than 30 takes, Elvis eventually captured a rousing rock 'n' roll interpretation of the song, which he patterned after Bell's but made more aggressive.

### "Don't Be Cruel"

R&B singer-songwriter Otis Blackwell wrote "Don't Be Cruel" the previous year around Christmastime. The tune, which Elvis selected from a stack of demos, became the flip side of Elvis's hit single "Hound Dog." A relatively new tune, "Don't Be Cruel" hadn't been recorded by any singer prior to Elvis. Because the song wasn't associated with any singer's specific style, Elvis could make it entirely his own. The recording's easygoing but fast-paced rhythm, light tone, and harmonious backup vocals by the Jordanaires indicate how far Elvis had moved from his Sun sound.

Blackwell sold "Don't Be Cruel" to music publisher Shalimar Music for $25 on Christmas Eve in 1955. Elvis's parent publisher, Hill and Range (see the next section for details), acquired the tune, and the demo for the song was placed in the stack of potential material for Elvis to record. When Elvis wanted to record the song, Hill and Range told Blackwell that he would have to cut a deal and share the writer's credit with Elvis even though Elvis didn't contribute anything to the writing of the song. Blackwell was uneasy about the deal, but the talented yet down-on-his-luck songwriter realized he stood to make a lot of money from royalties — even at half credit — if Elvis recorded the song. He took the deal and later wrote additional songs for Elvis to record, including "All Shook Up," "Paralyzed," and "Return to Sender" (co-written with Winfield Scott).

Assigning half of the credit to Elvis smacks of unfairness to those who know little of the popular music industry, especially because Blackwell was African American. Many African Americans were cheated by record publishers and companies during this era, and Blackwell's deal with Hill and Range seems to be an example of this. However, this particular situation is more complicated than it seems on the surface. While not every popular singer took credit for writing the songs they recorded, the practice certainly wasn't invented by Colonel Tom Parker, Hill and Range, or RCA. It goes back to the 1920s when pop singer Al Jolson introduced it.

The practice derives from the fact that songs become hits because famous performers record them. After the song becomes a hit, other entertainers want to perform or record it, but the original singer responsible for its popularity gets nothing unless he or she was the songwriter. Elvis may not have written "Don't Be Cruel," but if he hadn't recorded, Blackwell wouldn't have made the money on it that he did. Blackwell understood this, and when interviewers later asked him about it, he wasn't critical of the practice.

Elvis never revealed what he thought of this practice. However, in a couple of interviews from the time, reporters asked him about his songwriting skills. Elvis always noted that he had never written a line in his life, and that his songwriting credit was only a business practice. Eventually, this practice of assigning partial credit to performers became passé in the recording industry, and Hill and Range abandoned it for Elvis.

## Considering the role of Hill and Range

The Colonel insisted that Elvis form two songwriting companies shortly after inking his deal with RCA. The singer called his companies Elvis Presley Music and Gladys Music (after his mother, Gladys Love Presley). Both of these companies were under the umbrella of Hill and Range, which was affiliated with RCA through connections among personnel for the two companies. Hill and Range received half the income generated by these two publishing companies, which were responsible for obtaining the rights to all the songs that Elvis recorded. The singer formed Elvis Presley Music and Gladys Music to handle only his songs so he could receive publishing royalties. No other singers were involved with these companies.

This setup with the two publishing companies was financially advantageous for Elvis because he received a publisher's royalty and a performer's royalty each time a song he recorded was broadcast. If he claimed partial songwriting credit for tunes he recorded, he could receive a songwriter's royalty as well. This setup represents how well Colonel Parker understood the music industry at this time and how he liked to finesse his deals to wring out every last advantage for his client. With these publishing companies, he arranged for his "boy" to get the maximum profit for each recording.

# Chapter 4: Shocking America: Elvis Becomes a National Sensation

Hill and Range employed songwriters to regularly write tunes for the company, which it kept on hand for the recording artists it had publishing deals with. Most of these artists were country singers, including Hank Snow, Lefty Frizzell, Ernest Tubb, and Eddie Arnold. The songwriters gave up most of their rights to these songs, which were published through the companies associated with Hill and Range, such as Elvis's two companies. The role of Hill and Range was to provide the songs for these subsidiary publishing companies and to administrate the rights and royalties. The songs were either written by the Hill and Range house songwriters, or they were obtained from freelance writers who recorded their tunes on demo discs in the hopes that Hill and Range would buy them.

Obviously, it was best for all parties financially if Elvis recorded only those songs published by his own companies. However, he wasn't prevented from recording other songs. Eventually this arrangement with Hill and Range would stifle Elvis's career, because the Colonel, RCA, and Hill and Range didn't want him to record the music of outside songwriters. See Chapter 8 for more information about Hill and Range later in Elvis's career.

## Taking Television by Storm

The Colonel's strategy for making Elvis a national star involved showcasing him on television, which became the most explosive part of his plan. It could be said that Elvis's career and the popularity of TV took off at about the same time. However, even the Colonel couldn't have anticipated what would happen to Elvis as a result of his television exposure over the next year.

Commercial television hadn't been widely developed until after World War II, and it didn't become popular with the public until the early 1950s, when coast-to-coast broadcasting became possible. By *coast-to-coast broadcasting* I mean that a program airing on the East Coast could be picked up and viewed on the West Coast at the same time. Throughout the 1950s, TV became increasingly popular, until it surpassed the movies as America's number-one form of entertainment.

In this section, I examine Elvis's television appearances throughout 1956, offering details of each performance and contrasting his act with typical television fare of the period. I also focus on the increased media attention he gained with each small-screen performance and the way Elvis was used as ratings pawn among the major television shows. I discuss the controversy created by his television performances in Chapter 5.

## Appearing on Stage Show

Colonel Tom Parker and Elvis signed a contract for the singer and his band to appear four times on a CBS television program called *Stage Show,* a variety show in which a selection of popular singers, dancers, and comedians performed each week in front of a live studio audience. The show was hosted by two musicians who had been popular in the 1940s, Tommy and Jimmy Dorsey. On January 28, 1956, Elvis made his national television debut on *Stage Show.* The reaction of the in-studio audience to Elvis's performance was strong enough for him to be signed to two additional appearances.

Elvis stood out like a sore thumb during his first *Stage Show* program, because the rest of the performers seemed tame in comparison. Ella Fitzgerald and Sarah Vaughan, who were well-known jazz singers, performed in evening gowns and sang in their established styles. Two comedians in nice suits did stand-up routines, while a troupe of acrobats, a young boy who played the organ, and other family-style performers appeared in other segments.

When it was Elvis's turn, he raced on stage like he was shot out of a cannon. As he sang "Shake, Rattle, and Roll" and "I Got a Woman," he constantly moved his body. During the instrumental break in each song, he stood back and shook his entire body to the beat of the music. A few girls in the audience screamed, which made the singer smile. In addition, his long, slicked-back hair came tumbling down over his face when he moved, and the eye shadow around his eyes gave him a sleepy, sexy look. And clearly his Beale Street clothes were simply too hip for the house. Compared to the smooth, polished performances of the other guests, Elvis seemed wild, raw, and alien.

Elvis improved his performances each time he appeared on *Stage Show.* By the last two shows in March, he was an old hand at getting the studio audience worked up when he sang. For his last appearance on March 24, he waltzed out on stage, dramatically strummed the opening chords to "Heartbreak Hotel," and then paused, waiting for the girls to scream. As he broke into song, he moved across the stage, shaking his shoulders and swinging his legs. Certain moves were obviously designed to elicit screams and yelps from the girls in the audience, and Elvis's smiles proved that he was delighted at this explosive effect on his female fans. He moved freely and loosely throughout the performance, making eye contact with the camera and the studio audience. He teased the women with his provocative moves; they screamed for more; he promised to go farther; sometimes he did. With each Presley appearance, *Stage Show* received higher ratings, but the show never surpassed its competition on other networks.

> ## "Corn liquor at a champagne party": A flop in Vegas
>
> Colonel Tom Parker didn't make many mistakes in guiding Presley's career. However, he did make an error in judgment in April 1956 when he booked his young singer into the New Frontier, a big Las Vegas hotel and nightclub. At that time, Las Vegas was an adult vacation spot, and the clubs preferred to book the big pop and jazz performers of the period, such as Frank Sinatra, Rosemary Clooney, and Louis Prima. The adult audiences at the New Frontier didn't understand Elvis's Southern-based rockabilly. After a few performances, he was bumped to being the second act, and comedian Shecky Greene took over as the top-billed act, with house-band leader Freddy Martin remaining as emcee. *Newsweek* magazine seemed thrilled that Elvis flopped, describing his act as "somewhat like a jug of corn liquor at a champagne party" (May 14, 1956).
>
> Some good did come out of the Vegas trip, however. While there, Elvis went to see other shows at the clubs and hotels, including a show by dramatic pop singer Johnnie Ray. He saw a rock 'n' roll group called "Freddy Bell and the Bellboys" in a small club. The group did an up-tempo version of Big Mama Thornton's blues tune "Hound Dog." Elvis liked their version of the song so much that he decided to add it to his repertoire.

## *Tearing up The Milton Berle Show*

In the spring of 1956, Elvis appeared on *The Milton Berle Show* for the first time. The show was broadcast from the USS *Hancock,* which was docked at the San Diego Naval Station. Despite the novel location, this television appearance is barely mentioned in biographies or other accounts of Elvis's career. That's because his second appearance on Berle's program completely overshadowed it.

All the rumors, criticism, and bad publicity surrounding Elvis and rock 'n' roll snowballed into a full-blown controversy on June 5, 1956, when he performed for the second time on *The Milton Berle Show.* The Berle program was a variety show similar to *Stage Show* in that it featured a number of entertainers who performed their latest songs, dances, or comedy routines in individual segments. But, *The Milton Berle Show* was one of the most popular programs of the 1950s, and it had a higher profile among the viewers and the media. In other words, more people paid attention to who was on it and what they did.

That evening, Presley sang "Hound Dog" for the first time on television. He had heard the song during his disastrous Las Vegas engagement (see the nearby sidebar "'Corn liquor at a champagne party': A flop in Vegas" for details) and decided to include a version of it in his act. Because he hadn't recorded it yet, no one knew what to expect. Elvis appeared without his customary guitar, so his hip movements, pelvic thrusts, and leg shakes were more obvious than usual. As he sang the first verses and moved freely about the stage, the live studio audience of girls and women responded appropriately with screams and yelps. This reaction encouraged Elvis to push his performance farther. He slowed down the final chorus to a blues tempo, grabbed the microphone stand, balanced on the balls of his feet, and then thrust his hips forward toward the mike stand. The effect was highly sensual, if not sexual. The studio audience screamed with excitement. Figure 4-2 illustrates Elvis's sensual performing style on the show that night.

**Figure 4-2:** Elvis performs provocatively on *The Milton Berle Show*.

Despite the positive reaction of the teens in the audience the previous night, the next day, newspaper articles expressed outrage over Elvis's sexy performance. Reviewers felt that he had gone too far. In fact, many compared his performing style to a striptease. John Crosby, a reviewer for the *New York Herald Tribune,* summed up what many believed when he called Elvis "unspeakably untalented and vulgar."

Elvis's performance on *The Milton Berle Show* gave the people who were critical of rock 'n' roll a specific example to rally around. Parents, the media, religious groups, and even the PTA (Parent Teacher Association) expressed concern about the negative influence of this type of music.

## Clowning around on *The Steve Allen Show*

Despite the criticism that Elvis received from his appearance on *The Milton Berle Show,* other television hosts were eager to have Presley on their shows. The controversy that Elvis created attracted viewers and increased ratings.

### Chapter 4: Shocking America: Elvis Becomes a National Sensation

A month after *The Milton Berle Show,* Elvis appeared on *The Steve Allen Show,* a variety series that focused on comedy skits. Steve Allen's program had just premiered in June, and it was on at the same time as *The Ed Sullivan Show.* Sullivan's program was considered the high point of variety programs, and Allen was determined to give Sullivan a run for his money. In the days before cable and syndicated television stations, competition for viewers among the networks was fierce. Allen knew that Elvis was a good choice to lure viewers away from Sullivan's program.

Allen was a clever man. He wanted Elvis on his show, but he didn't want the criticism. NBC-TV didn't want the headaches either, so they issued a press release stating, "Elvis Presley will not be allowed to bump and grind." Allen diffused the controversy over Presley by using comedy. Instead of having the hot, young entertainer perform in his usual provocative style, he asked Elvis to sing "Hound Dog" to a real basset hound. The dog sat on a pedestal while Elvis stood next to him in a tuxedo. The singer held the dog's long face in his hands, and then belted out the song. The studio audience giggled, the viewers at home got a glimpse of Elvis's sense of humor, and the TV critics had less to complain about. Elvis the Pelvis had been tamed — at least temporarily.

Later in the program, Elvis joined Allen, comedienne Imogene Coca, and fellow Southerner Andy Griffith in a comedy sketch that satirized country-western radio programs like the *Grand Ole Opry* and the *Louisiana Hayride.* Many of the jokes were condescending toward Southern culture. Elvis said little about the Allen show at the time, but his friends claimed that later he revealed how angry and humiliated he felt by Allen's manipulation of his act.

Fans were furious that their idol had been tamed, and they picketed NBC-TV studios the next morning with placards reading "We want the gyratin' Elvis." Elvis also was upset because he had been made to look ridiculous. Clearly Allen became the real winner that night, because his show beat *The Ed Sullivan Show* in the ratings, which was a major feat in the 1950s television wars. After those ratings were reported in the newspapers, Sullivan became the last variety-show host to ask Elvis to appear on his program.

## From the waist up: Tackling The Ed Sullivan Show

Ed Sullivan, who had established his reputation as a savvy showbiz columnist for a major New York newspaper, was a powerful figure in the television industry. An appearance on his show meant an act or entertainer had made the big time. It was like getting a seal of approval in mainstream show business.

The Colonel had tried to get Elvis on *The Ed Sullivan Show* earlier that year, but the showbiz legend didn't want to pay Parker's asking price of $5,000 for his client. Sullivan then publicly declared that he wouldn't allow Presley on his show, because he wasn't his "cup of tea." This comment was an obvious reference to and criticism of Elvis's sexy, hip-swiveling performing style, but ratings speak louder than personal taste.

After seeing the success that Elvis brought to *The Steve Allen Show,* Sullivan changed his mind. He wanted the good ratings that booking Elvis would bring, but Sullivan also knew that if he didn't have Presley on his show, his program's reputation as a showcase for the latest talent might suffer. So the Colonel signed Elvis to appear on *The Ed Sullivan Show* for an unprecedented fee of $50,000 for three performances. Elvis received a much higher fee than if Sullivan had signed him earlier.

Elvis appeared on the *The Ed Sullivan Show* on September 9 and October 28, 1956, and on January 8, 1957. For the first two performances, he sang and performed in his usual style, which went over very well with the audience, but the third performance became one of the most infamous in Elvis's history. I offer the lowdown on each performance in the following sections.

### *The first two appearances*

Sullivan himself wasn't there for Elvis's first appearance on September 9, because he was recuperating from a car accident. In Sullivan's place, actor Charles Laughton hosted the show. Elvis appeared via network hookup from California, where he was shooting his first film, *Love Me Tender.* (See Chapter 6 for more information on Elvis's first film.)

For his first set on the Sullivan show, Elvis sang "Don't Be Cruel," "Ready Teddy," and a shortened version of "Hound Dog." He bounced on the balls of his feet as he sang, and, as usual, the girls in the studio audience screamed. In his second set, he introduced the title song from *Love Me Tender* by declaring it to be "different from anything we've ever done." The audience screamed before and after the performance, but the sad nature of the ballad wasn't conducive to the game he and the audience played in which Elvis twitched and the girls screamed.

For the October appearance, Sullivan was on hand to introduce Elvis for his three sets. Elvis sang the same songs as in his first performance, except that he replaced "Ready Teddy" with the ballad "Love Me." As he always did during his songs, Elvis bounced on his feet, twitched his chest, pointed his finger, stretched out his arms, and generally teased the studio audience with his performing style. He smiled into the camera every time he made the girls shriek.

However, compared to his appearances on the *Stage Show* and *The Milton Berle Show,* this performance was relatively tame. It wasn't until his third set, in which he sang "Hound Dog," that he cut loose by swiveling his legs,

## Chapter 4: Shocking America: Elvis Becomes a National Sensation

bouncing on the balls of his feet, twitching his shoulders, walking with a jerky gate, and gyrating his hips. But, he did cut loose, causing the girls in the audience to scream throughout the entire performance. Elvis also let his sense of humor come through, lampooning his own performance by rolling his eyes during "Love Me Tender" and introducing "Hound Dog" as "one of the saddest songs we've ever heard."

### *The infamous appearance*

For his last appearance on *The Ed Sullivan Show* in January 1957, Elvis sang a medley of his biggest hits of the moment: "Don't Be Cruel," "When My Blue Moon Turns to Gold Again," and "Too Much." For his third and last set that evening, he and the Jordanaires concluded with an a cappella rendition of the gospel classic, "Peace in the Valley," which he dedicated to earthquake victims in Hungary. After the performance, Sullivan declared on camera to the whole television viewing audience that Elvis Presley was "a real decent, fine boy" and "a nice person." The statement was considered a validation of Elvis by Sullivan, and the singer appreciated the gesture.

Comedienne Carol Burnett made her national television debut the night Elvis made his third and final appearance on *The Ed Sullivan Show*. Oddly, few, if any, have asked Burnett her impressions of this infamous night in television history.

Of course, what was infamous about Elvis's final appearance, which has since gone down in pop culture history as a symbol of the clash between generations, was the censorship of the singer's performing style. Sullivan and the network censors at CBS decided that the cameras should film Presley only from the waist up so that his provocative hip movements couldn't be seen. In effect, however, the edict only served to focus attention on Elvis's movements. Dressed in one of his Beale Street specials, Elvis stepped in front of the camera, complete with eye makeup and proceeded to give the live audience his full array of trademark tics, moves, and gyrations, causing the audience to be even more vocal than usual. The audience at home could only imagine what he was doing with those hips; and their imagination was more effective than if they had actually seen him.

Much speculation exists on why Sullivan and CBS decided to censor Elvis's third appearance but not his first and second. Of course, the exact reason will never be known. The simplest explanations maintain that Sullivan was merely succumbing to the heated controversy that had swirled around Elvis for several months. However, quite possibly, the waist-up order was motivated by the provocative performance during the third set of Elvis's previous appearance. In looking back over the three Sullivan appearances, the legendary host and the censors most likely noticed that during his third set on the October 28 show, he swiveled and gyrated much more than he previously had. The eruptions from the audience were more vocal, and the performance was closer to his appearance on *The Milton Berle Show,* which was the lightning rod for the storm of controversy that year.

Other explanations for the censorship are much more colorful. In a taped interview on the DVD release *Elvis: The Ed Sullivan Shows,* Marlo Lewis, who was a producer on the Sullivan show from 1948 to 1959, claims that many on the Sullivan show heard a rumor that Elvis had placed a Coke bottle down his pants for that last set of his October 28 appearance. When he bounced and moved around, the Coke bottle gave an obscene impression through his pants. Based on that rumor Sullivan gave the waist-up order for the final appearance, but this story is little more than an urban legend. Other versions of the story insist that Elvis had placed an empty toilet paper roll down his pants to produce a similar impression.

Whatever the reasons for the decision, the incident has become part of the Elvis Presley legend. It's often used to illustrate how controversial the singer was in 1956. Some writers have exaggerated the incident by claiming he was censored on television on several occasions. But, the waist-up rule was applied to the singer only this one time.

# Chapter 5

# What's the Ruckus About: The Impact of Elvis the Pelvis

## In This Chapter
▶ Dissecting the red-hot controversy created over Elvis
▶ Understanding how the Colonel, Elvis, and Uncle Sam cooled the controversy
▶ Considering the two most important women in Elvis's life

In comparison to the music scene of our contemporary era, which has brought us Madonna, wardrobe malfunctions, and rappers with "unique" vocabularies, the controversy created by Elvis Presley and his hip-swiveling performing style seems tame. Yet, during the 1950s, the controversy generated a firestorm of criticism aimed at rock 'n' roll, teenagers and their tastes, Southern culture, and Elvis himself. Virtually every popular magazine, major newspaper, high-powered deejay, and self-righteous reporter in America weighed in on the trouble with Elvis Presley as though the moral fiber of the country depended on it. However, the intensity of the criticism — and the sheer mean-spiritedness of some of the comments — suggests that there was more behind the controversy than meets the eye.

In the 1950s, Elvis definitely had the country "all shook up," and this chapter tells you all about the controversy, its deeper significance, and the path that Elvis and his manager took to deflect it.

## Anatomy of a Controversy

Many attribute the controversy surrounding Elvis to a generation gap; in other words, teenagers fought with their parents over the adoration of their idol that the older generation didn't approve of. A clash of tastes between generations was indeed *part* of the reason for the hullabaloo, but other, more complex reasons were part of it as well, revealing deep-rooted issues in our society and culture.

The controversy focused on Elvis's raucous musical sound and his unique performing style. It wasn't only the provocative gyrations and sensual movements that were controversial, however. The impact these movements had on the girls in the audience was a concern as well. The controversy was ignited by Elvis's television appearances in 1956 (see Chapter 4 for details about these TV appearances) and fueled by the increasing criticism aimed at rock 'n' roll. As the controversy swirled around him, Elvis continued to tour around the country. Negative comments, false accusations, and rumors dogged him even in the South, where he had been touring since 1954.

In August 1956, Judge Marion Gooding in Jacksonville, Florida, ordered Elvis not to shake his legs and swivel his hips during a performance at the Florida Theater. He obliged, but when he wiggled his little finger on stage during "Hound Dog," the girls in the audience shrieked anyway. Elvis had appeared in Jacksonville in 1955 shaking his legs and swinging his hips in his usual style, but nothing was made of it. But he had been billed as a country singer back then. In 1956, when he was called a rock 'n' roller, that same performance style was suddenly considered too sexy and dangerous. Clearly the reputation that rock 'n' roll and Elvis Presley had earned by 1956 was much worse than the actual music or performances.

Obviously, there was more behind the backlash against Elvis than his sensual moves. In this section, I dissect the controversy to uncover why young girls and other teenagers gravitated toward Elvis's music to the dismay and disgust of older generations, how Elvis's music upset the conventions of the music industry, and how the mainstream public and press revealed their prejudices toward indigenous Southern cultures through their criticisms of Elvis.

The backlash against Elvis revealed a chasm in America between different groups and cultures: young versus old; black versus white; working class versus middle class; and Southern culture versus mainstream culture. The success of Elvis Presley and the popularity of his music proved that regionally based entertainers who appealed to specific groups and subcultures could challenge established entertainment institutions and undermine mainstream tastes. On a deeper level, Elvis and his success showed that beneath the complacency that was generally associated with the 1950s, certain groups — blacks, poor whites, teenagers — were dissatisfied with the norms represented by the status quo. Fearful of the challenge to the mainstream tastes and norms that Elvis, his music, and his in-your-face performing style represented, the status quo criticized, ridiculed, and attacked Elvis, his Southern culture, his ties to black rhythm and blues, and his youthful fans.

# Chapter 5: What's the Ruckus About: The Impact of Elvis the Pelvis

## Weighing the backlash: Generational conflict and sex

Rock 'n' roll had been in the public eye for about two years when Elvis signed his contract with RCA in 1955, and during that time, this new musical genre attracted the attention of young audiences. So-called authorities in music, psychology, education, and parenting feared that the raw sounds and "jungle beat" of rock 'n' roll led to juvenile delinquency and an increased desire to engage in sex. From April through October 1956, a wave of articles discussing the link between rock 'n' roll, sex, and juvenile crime was published in popular magazines, including *Time, Newsweek, Life, Look, Collier's,* and *America.*

During this same time frame, Elvis also was targeted by these magazines for his music, hair and sideburns, clothing style, and most of all, the effect of his performing style on teenage girls. It didn't take a great leap of imagination for journalists, reviewers, and other critics to relate Presley's personal appearance and performing style to the decadency of rock 'n' roll and the horrors of juvenile delinquency. The connection to Elvis's music was made even though the singer, his manager Colonel Tom Parker, and RCA exec Steve Sholes took pains never to specifically label his music. They did this because they wanted to avoid the connection with rock 'n' roll as much as possible and to promote his music in all markets.

Elvis's appearance and performing style, which were exposed on national television, were at the heart of the controversy and led to the singer's nickname "Elvis the Pelvis." In retrospect, this aspect of the controversy has received the most attention; in fact, most now attribute the uproar strictly to generational conflict. Given American society's prudishness regarding women and sex, seeing teenage girls act with complete abandon at Elvis's concerts became more than parents and authority figures could bear. Interestingly, no one seemed concerned that young boys were adversely affected by the hip-swinging walks of Marilyn Monroe, Jayne Mansfield, and the other sex symbols who were dominating the entertainment magazines of the time.

The following sections examine the way Elvis and rock 'n' roll were depicted in the press and how this depiction exaggerated the perception of Elvis as profane and vulgar.

### Linking Elvis with rock 'n' roll . . . and sex

A pattern emerged in the newspaper accounts and magazine articles of the mid-1950s in which the writers depicted Elvis as a threat to established norms of behavior and appearance. These writers continually harped about the following:

- The tastelessness of Elvis's hair and clothing
- The similarities of his performing style to a striptease or burlesque act

- His Southern accent
- The destructive or hysterical antics of his fans

Comparing Elvis's performing style to a striptease in mainstream magazines and newspapers gave it a lewd sexual connotation that alarmed the parents of teenage girls. Elvis's appearances on television in 1956, which showed close-up shots of his hip gyrations and exposed the way he deliberately incited the enthusiastic squeals of the girls, only reinforced the comments of the press.

A sampling of the type of comments made about Elvis reveals how he was painted as a threat to the purity of young girls. Consider the following quotes:

- *Look* magazine (August 7, 1956) warned America that Elvis "wiggles like a peep show dancer" and that "Onstage, his gyrations, his nose wiping, his leers are vulgar."
- *Illustrated* (September 7, 1957) noted that "his body, gangling and loose-jointed, contorts from the hips down as if a whole empire of ants had invaded his pants."
- *Life* (August 27, 1956) claimed that "He uses a bump and grind routine usually seen only in burlesque."
- *TV Scandals* (as quoted in *Elvis World* by Jane and Michael Stern) must have really frightened parents with the comment, "What's most appalling is the fans' unbridled obscenity, their gleeful wallowing in smut."

The sexual connotations of his performing style weren't the only accusations made against Elvis. Parents of teenage boys had cause to be just as nervous. Between April and August of 1956, these stories about the antics of teenage Elvis fans appeared in the media:

- An article in *Life* magazine titled "A Howling Hillbilly Success" (April 30, 1956) claimed that fans in Texas were compelled to kick through a plate-glass door to get to Elvis. The door was indeed broken, but there's no way to know whether fans did it intentionally.
- The *Newsweek* article titled "Hillbilly on a Pedestal" (May 5, 1956) repeated several outrageous rumors told to reporters by teenage fans who were enamored by their idol's rebel notoriety; they claimed that Elvis sold dope, had been in jail, and was dying of cancer.
- A report from Jacksonville, Florida, repeated in *Life* magazine (August 27, 1956), claimed that teens were soaking their Presley records in water to make his trademark hiccups and syncopated lyrics more pronounced.

### Identifying the youth culture

Few writers were perceptive enough to realize that the clash between parents and teenagers over Elvis and rock 'n' roll was mostly the result of a burgeoning youth culture. During the 1950s, America experienced an era of prosperity, and the benefits of the boom trickled down to teenagers. Many teens worked part-time jobs and others received allowances, giving them a disposable income. In the past, teens worked to contribute to their family's survival or well-being, but during the 1950s, middle-class teens were relieved of this responsibility by the economic prosperity. (Flip to Chapter 20 for a more detailed look at this burgeoning youth culture and Elvis's effect on it.)

One author from the era proved to be more perceptive than most. John Sharnik of *House and Garden* magazine wrote that Presley and rock 'n' roll shouldn't be feared because neither was more than "background music in the war between the generations." He rightly reasoned that adults were angered "that a distinctive [teen] audience exists at all, that within our own society there is a large, well-defined group whose standards of taste and conduct we find baffling and even terrifying." He summed up by noting, "Youth is almost a national cult." Little did he realize he was acknowledging what would be an American obsession for the next 50 years — youth.

During the 1950s, teens became a recognizable subculture, with their own clothing style, slang, social activities, and favorite movie and recording stars. The more their tastes were catered to by manufacturers, the entertainment industry, automobile companies, and others, the more they clashed with adults who represented the mainstream tastes of the status quo.

America's teens weren't the only young people to go crazy over Elvis Presley. In the Soviet Union, Russian teenagers who loved rock 'n' roll were called *stilyagis,* and they faced far more than angry parents for being Elvis fans. Communist authorities banned rock 'n' roll, forbade the sale of rock records, and condemned Elvis as a capitalist pawn. However, Elvis's music was available on bootleg records that were sold underground. The records were cut on discarded hospital X-ray plates and sold for about $12.50 each.

## Weighing the criticism: Rock 'n' Roll versus Tin Pan Alley

Part of the problem that the music industry had with Elvis's musical style was that it was based in regional sounds indigenous to the South. In addition, Elvis had broken through with a record produced by a regionally based company. His sound and music weren't like those associated with the mainstream pop music industry. The musical establishment resented the success of Elvis and those who followed in his wake, and the controversy surrounding Elvis the Pelvis in 1956 was undoubtedly exacerbated by this. This section explores the clash between Elvis's music and the smooth sounds and conventional styles of Tin Pan Alley.

### Touring Tin Pan Alley

The songs and sounds of Tin Pan Alley dominated the music industry from the late 19th century to the 1950s. Located along 28th Street between Fifth Avenue and Broadway in Manhattan, the original Tin Pan Alley consisted of several buildings and offices that housed the major music publishers of America. Music publishers, who had songwriters and promoters on their payrolls, kept their offices along this stretch of Broadway, and the sound of songwriters pounding out their tunes on worn-out pianos made for a noisy, cacophonous neighborhood — inspiring the name Tin Pan Alley.

Musicians, song writers, and song promoters (called *pluggers*) hurried in and out of these buildings, hustling the latest pop tunes to publishers who hoped the hottest band or pop singer would make everyone rich with a recording. Many of these publishers later moved and newer companies were established elsewhere, but the name "Tin Pan Alley" to represent the music publishing business stuck. Broadway and vaudeville theaters, nightclubs, and musical comedy venues thrived nearby, making New York a performing arts mecca. So, the state easily became the home of the mainstream music industry.

Many of the mainstream songwriters, composers, arrangers, and others associated with Tin Pan Alley were European immigrants or the offspring of immigrants, so a direct connection to European styles was part of mainstream music. Other influences on mainstream songwriters and singers included Broadway musicals, vaudeville and music hall entertainment, and later Hollywood composers and songwriters. Music publishers, songwriters, and arrangers absorbed influences of various genres and styles, such as ragtime, jazz, and even Hawaiian music, but the pop ballad remained the dominant song type associated with Tin Pan Alley and mainstream music.

### Clashing with Tin Pan Alley's style and traditions

Under the direction of Sam Phillips, Elvis's natural musical style fused R&B, blues, and country western. He was inspired by pop music and truly appreciated all styles, but those three genres represented the main threads of his sound. Not only were these genres indigenous to the South, but they also were hard sounding, beat driven, and emotionally raw — the opposite of the smooth-sounding pop ballad. (See Chapter 2 for more information on Elvis's unique style.)

Elvis first recorded at Phillips's tiny Sun Studio, where blues, R&B, and some country acts cut discs, hoping to develop a career in music. Elvis's singles were released through Sun Records, Phillips's small label that distributed throughout the South. In other words, every aspect of Elvis Presley and his music prior to signing with RCA was outside the perimeters of the mainstream music industry.

# Chapter 5: What's the Ruckus About: The Impact of Elvis the Pelvis

As soon as Elvis was signed to RCA Victor, a nationally based record label, in 1955, industry insiders began to snipe, revealing the prejudices against regional music and its makers. At a music industry convention in November 1955, rumors swirled over the signing of Elvis and what it meant to the industry. A Tin Pan Alley insider was overheard remarking that Sam Phillips recorded his artists in a closet, which was a snide comment referring to the tiny size of Sun Studio and Phillips's irregular methods of capturing unique sounds. The person surmised that RCA would never be able to duplicate that sound again, so he thought Elvis was sure to fail at his bid to become a big-time recording artist. This Tin Pan Alley insider must have surely eaten his words. As it turned out, Elvis became the most significant recording artist of the 20th century — and Tin Pan Alley disappeared by the early 1960s.

## Considering the demise of Tin Pan Alley

Elvis can be considered the vanguard of rock 'n' roll, and his large-scale success in changing the course of popular music spelled the beginning of the end for Tin Pan Alley.

Adding insult to injury, rock 'n' roll records were charted as pop music during the mid-1950s, because no chart existed specifically for rock 'n' roll. So rock records competed with mainstream pop recordings for space on the same charts. As Elvis's records consistently topped the pop charts in 1956, music industry veterans became more critical of this new genre and of Elvis himself.

Elvis's music wasn't the only music that bypassed Tin Pan Alley conventions and the dominance of the mainstream music industry. Other rockabilly performers, rock 'n' roll singers, and R&B artists, including Carl Perkins, Chuck Berry, and Bo Diddley, received national exposure through Northern-based disc jockeys who worked for huge radio stations in major cities. These deejays not only began playing regionally produced records, but they also organized rock 'n' roll shows in big-time venues to showcase nonmainstream styles of music. Elvis didn't invent rock 'n' roll, but his national exposure occurred at the same time that rock 'n' roll was gaining popularity and notoriety.

If Tin Pan Alley resented the financial success and growing popularity of Elvis and rock 'n' roll, then the entertainment press and mainstream reviewers, who were accustomed to the smooth tones of pop music, were openly hostile to it. Their comments were often cruel and demeaning, repeatedly referring to Elvis as a "hillbilly" in the most pejorative sense of the word, though they labeled his music rock 'n' roll. A good example is the comment made about Elvis and rock 'n' roll in *Newsweek* in an article titled "Hillbilly on a Pedestal" (May 5, 1956): "Alleged to be a new kind of music . . . rock 'n' roll is actually a coarsened version of what a "jump" band like Count Basie does with refinement."

## Weighing the subtext: It's the Civil War all over again

Generally, the war of generations between teens and their parents overshadows any other interpretation of the backlash against Elvis and his music. However, sometimes a music historian makes a case for racism as the reason behind the controversy. This argument claims that Elvis brought the music, culture, and uninhibited expression of African American R&B artists into the living rooms of mainstream America via national television. This pushed many folks of Middle America out of their collective comfort zones. Based on a few newspaper and magazine articles, this theory seems to be true in some parts of the South, but an extensive search of mainstream magazines and articles from the period discovers yet another cause for the ruckus.

The press and public were indeed "all shook up" over Elvis, but it had more to do with the singer's background as a poor working-class Southerner than his predilection for singing R&B music. The *subtext* — or deep-rooted meaning — beneath the surface of the controversy suggests that Elvis's "hillbilly" heritage was the basis for his alienation from the mainstream, and therefore part of the cause of the backlash. His "strange" accent, attire, music, and performing style, which were painted as "Southern," made him popular and appealing to teenagers. However, this popularity threatened the tastes and cultural values of the mainstream culture. Insulted that their values were being undermined and threatened by Elvis's and rock 'n' roll music's increasing appeal to young people, arbiters of middle-class tastes and values lashed out at Elvis with prejudiced comments and unfounded opinions.

In the following sections, I offer a provocative perspective on the role that Elvis's Southern heritage played in the attacks against him and his music by major publications that were located mostly in the North.

### Homing in on the word "hillbilly"

When nationally based magazines used the word "hillbilly" to describe Elvis Presley in 1956, they didn't intend it as a suggestion of quaint nostalgia. The word was — and still is — used to refer to rural white working-class Southerners. While rural Southerners may refer to themselves as hillbillies, it's most often used as a derogatory term outside the South, with connotations of ignorance, backwardness, and gullibility. In most instances, the articles directly or indirectly implied that Elvis's Southern background caused him to be outside the mainstream and therefore undesirable and even a threat. To the writers of these articles, Elvis's Southern "hillbilly" background indicated a lack of taste and sophistication.

Article titles, such as "A Howling Hillbilly Success" (*Life*) or "Hillbilly on a Pedestal" (*Newsweek*), insinuated an insult as did certain descriptions of his music, such as "a moronic lyric in a hillbilly idiom" (*Time*).

## Chapter 5: What's the Ruckus About: The Impact of Elvis the Pelvis

As far back as the 1920s, when the first country tunes were recorded by Northern-based companies for radio airplay, the term "hillbilly music" has been considered pejorative by singers who perform it. Music pioneer Ralph Peer, who first recorded authentic hill-country tunes and later became part of the recording industry, dubbed an early country act "Al Hopkins and the Hill Billies." When Hopkins protested because of the name's association with the negative stereotype of rural Southerners, Peer, who was from the North and didn't understand how often the term was used as a put-down, insisted they keep it. By the 1950s, *Billboard* magazine discontinued the use of the term "hillbilly music" because of its negative connotation, opting instead for "folk' and then later "country western."

### *Insulting the singer's accent*

Northern writers and reviewers seemed preoccupied with Elvis's accent and used it to ridicule his singing style by phonetically spelling out his pronunciation of lyrics to imply that he was an alien "other" (or, at the very least, an unworldly outsider). Throughout 1956, phonetically spelling out Elvis's accented speech became a norm for newspapers and magazines. The following are just three of the many examples that offer an idea of this demeaning inclination:

- A short article in *Time* (May 14, 1956) referenced Elvis's accent three times. A caption over a photo of Elvis in the recording studio read "Elvis Presley: 'Hi luh-huh-huh-huv yew-hew,'" to ridicule the singer's accent. The author also declared Elvis's diction to be poor and attempted to prove it by again spelling out how he pronounced lyrics, thereby equating poor diction with a Southern accent.

- An article in *Look* magazine (August 7, 1956) quoted Elvis responding to allegations that his music was vulgar. Every time Elvis said "I," the article spelled it "Ah" to refer to his Southern accent. Focusing on his accent in this way completely undermined Elvis's point.

- *Life* (August 27, 1956) got in on the joke when they also phonetically spelled out the way Elvis sang a ballad as "Ah wa-ha-hunt yew-who, Ah ne-eed yew-who, Ah luh-huv yew-who. . . ."

Much was made of Elvis's preference for sideburns, ducktail haircuts, and gaudy clothes. Because these criticisms of his personal appearance were made in the same space as the insults to his Southern accent, readers could infer that his lack of taste had to do with his background as a poor, working-class Southerner. These criticisms all were part of creating the impression that he was a "Rube from Rubeville," as the *Spokane Review* dubbed him on August 31, 1957. As a matter of fact, the media rarely mentioned Elvis without referencing that he was from the South, from Memphis, or from Tennessee.

### Rooting out the real meaning (and it's not pretty)

What were all the pundits really worried about? Well, the truth is that Elvis threatened the status quo, and the danger he really represented was the sexual threat embodied in his performing style. In the dark corners of the controversy over Elvis Presley lies the negative stereotype involving the "hillbilly" male full of animal magnetism who courts adolescent girls and takes one as his bride. In other words, the sight of a greasy-haired, strangely dressed Southern-born singer thrusting his pelvis into the television cameras while he sang "Baby, I wanna play house with you" to the willing teenage girls of Middle America was considered out of bounds by the status quo. And, the mainstream press and public reacted accordingly.

## Cooling the Controversy

Colonel Tom Parker realized relatively quickly that the bad publicity over Elvis's notorious rock 'n' roll image was driving away the very audience that he hoped to attract. So he embarked on a strategy designed to counter the accusations in the press that Elvis was a threat to American society or a dangerous influence on his fans.

This section offers an overview of the Colonel's strategy, which included charity work, a merchandising deal, and a Hollywood makeover. Other events not orchestrated by the Colonel also helped generate positive, or at least neutral, press, including Elvis's purchase of the mansion called Graceland located on the outskirts of Memphis. However, the event that really turned the tide in favor of Elvis was his induction into the army, which Parker exploited to "his boy's" advantage. All these maneuvers and strategies served to cool the red-hot controversy so Elvis and the Colonel could successfully court a mainstream audience.

### Countering the bad publicity

The Colonel fought Elvis's negative image and reputation with his own tactics. On July 1, 1956, shortly after Elvis's notorious performance on *The Milton Berle Show* (see Chapter 4 for more details), the young singer appeared on a TV interview program called *Hy Gardner Calling*. Each week, Gardner, a syndicated columnist, interviewed celebrities via telephone. The audiences saw the interviews via split screen.

Elvis's appearance on *Hy Gardner Calling* gave him an opportunity to dispel some of the outrageous rumors swirling around him, including one that claimed he smoked marijuana to reach the frenetic state necessary for his performing style and another that claimed he once shot his mother. Viewers saw a gentler, more vulnerable side to Elvis, who admitted confusion over the enormity of his success and expressed disbelief that critics could find his music to be a negative influence on anyone.

Parker also made sure that Elvis was photographed while donating to charities, such as the March of Dimes and the American Cancer Society. Part of this charity effort involved Elvis's dedication of the song "Peace in the Valley" to a Hungarian relief organization during his last appearance on *The Ed Sullivan Show.* (Check out Chapter 4 for more information on Elvis's *Sullivan Show* appearances.) In addition, Parker allowed local high-school kids access to Elvis so they could interview him for their school newspapers. He would have professional reporters and photographers on hand to record Elvis's generous gesture toward his young fans. Finally, stories about Elvis's close relationship with his parents began to appear in print. And, the singer was careful to include in interviews that he neither smoked cigarettes nor drank alcohol. And, at this time, Elvis neither smoked nor drank.

## Merchandizing Elvis like other pop culture figures

In September 1956, the Colonel signed a deal with merchandiser extraordinaire Hank Saperstein to put Elvis's image on a line of products. Saperstein had merchandised other trendy figures of the 1950s with much success, including Wyatt Earp, the Lone Ranger, Ding Dong School, and Lassie. All these figures were connected to popular television shows of the 1950s. Kids across the country could find these all-American heroes pictured on everything from lunch boxes to T-shirts. While most of Saperstein's Elvis-related products were aimed at teenagers, Parker wanted Elvis's likeness to be plastered on some kid-related items as well. He believed this merchandizing would not only generate a tidy income but also serve to connect his client with these other family-friendly characters.

If you were a teenager in 1956 who had just dropped by your local five-and-dime store, you may have found the following Elvis products to your liking:

- Elvis Presley lipstick in Hound Dog Orange, Tutti Frutti Red, and Heartbreak Hotel Pink at $1 per tube
- A faux white-marble bust of Elvis for $2
- A silver-plated charm bracelet and necklace with a heart-shaped pendant at $1 each
- Perfume with Elvis's picture on the label, which was priced according to the bottle size

- Elvis Presley clothing, including green-stitched black jeans, hats, sneakers, bobby socks, scarves, underwear, and T-shirts emblazoned with the titles of his biggest hits
- An Elvis Presley record player, record box, photo album, and autograph book in soft-pink faux leather

## Going Hollywood

On a much larger scale than merchandising, the one aspect of Elvis Presley's career that truly aided in overcoming his image as a dangerous rock 'n' roller was his starring roles in several Hollywood films. Between 1956 and 1958, Elvis appeared in four films. Three of those films were loosely based on Elvis's life and career, but they told fictional stories. While Elvis's fans loved seeing their idol on the big screen, the films also encouraged older audiences to accept him and his music. Flip to Chapters 6 and 7 for a full account of the way movies helped soften his image during the 1950s and then change it completely during the 1960s.

## Buying Graceland

By the end of 1956, Elvis had become so famous that he was forced to move from the small ranch-style house in Memphis that he had bought for himself and his family earlier that year. Fans had taken to hanging around the house, hoping to catch him at home. Any number of them could be found lingering in the driveway, picking blades of grass from the lawn, or even listening outside the walls in hopes of catching a word or two from their idol. The Presleys were extremely grateful to fans for Elvis's success, so they were tolerant of this behavior. However, neighbors weren't so welcoming and brought a lawsuit against the family for creating a public nuisance.

In the spring of 1957, at the age of 22, Elvis purchased a small mansion on the outskirts of Memphis. The house had been named Graceland by the previous owners, and so Elvis and his family kept the name. Gladys Presley had seen the house first, and because she liked it so much, Elvis bought it. You can see photos of Graceland in the color photo section of this book.

The mansion was christened Graceland by the original owners, Dr. Thomas and Ruth Moore. Mrs. Moore named the estate after her aunt, Grace Toof.

Not long after Elvis completed the purchase, the famous Music Gates were added to the front to keep out fans and visitors. The wrought-iron gates feature two stylized figures of a guitar player with musical notes bridging the space between them. Supposedly, the notes represent the opening bars of "Love Me Tender." Graceland would be Elvis's primary home for the rest of his life. Unlike other celebrities and movie stars, he didn't permanently relocate to Hollywood or New York. He preferred to stay in Memphis, the city he called his hometown. You can read more about Graceland and its many rooms in Chapter 19.

*REMEMBER:* Newspaper articles about Elvis's decision to live in the town where he grew up and the publicity surrounding his purchase of a big house for his family helped balance the bad press over his notorious rock image and the strange rumors about shooting his mother or taking drugs before his performances.

## Serving in the army now

Elvis didn't get to enjoy his new house for very long. At the end of 1957, he was drafted by the army. However, he was able to get a deferment for three months so he could finish making the movie *King Creole* (1958) before he was called up. (See Chapter 6 for more information about *King Creole*.)

On March 28, 1958, Elvis Aron Presley was inducted into the army. As an entertainer, Elvis could have joined special services, meaning he would have traveled around the world to entertain American soldiers wherever they were stationed. This tour of duty would have been much easier than what the average soldier went through. However, Elvis turned down the army's offer to join special services, choosing to serve his country just like any other American soldier — which, of course, is how the Colonel played it to the press.

The Colonel made sure that the press had access to almost every stage of the induction process, from the time Elvis showed up at the Memphis draft board until he was carried away by bus to Fort Chafee, Arkansas, where he was indoctrinated. Elvis was photographed in his underwear being weighed by army doctors, picking out his fatigues, climbing on the bus bound for Fort Chaffee, and most famously, sitting patiently while an army barber cut his hair into an army buzz and shaved off those sideburns. No photos could have been more significant to improving his image than those of a wistful Elvis in the barber's chair as the clippers peeled off inches of his hair. For two years, he had been dogged by constant criticism and mean-spirited attacks about his hair and sideburns. Not only did he willingly give up his personal look to serve his country in the army, but now he also looked like everyone else! Check out the color photo section to see Elvis in uniform.

*REMEMBER:* Nothing the Colonel or Elvis did to improve the singer's image came close to generating the level of positive publicity that joining the army did. And the proof was in the immediate change in attitude by the mainstream press. *Life* magazine, which had been highly critical of Elvis in 1956, featured three major articles from April through October 1958 about Presley's army service. Similarly, *Look* magazine, which also had been highly critical of Elvis in 1956, gave the army story a great deal of positive attention.

### Controlling the media's access to Elvis

From 1956 to 1958, Elvis freely and honestly answered any question asked of him by the press with no interference from the Colonel. Reading only a few of the interviews and articles offers a nice portrait of a naive kid having the time of his life on a wild ride.

However, Elvis did make some offhand remarks and candid admissions that inadvertently added to his bad press. For instance, Elvis was often asked whether he was going to marry any time soon, and the singer was fond of answering, "Why buy the cow when you can get the milk for free?" And during an interview with a female reporter in Texas, Elvis played with her hair and called her "Baby" throughout, which the reporter used against him in her critical article. These comments clearly didn't help his image at the time, but Parker was soon going to rein him in by maintaining stricter media access.

After Elvis's discharge from the army in 1960, Colonel Parker used the positive publicity over the singer's army service to spearhead a campaign to completely obliterate the Elvis the Pelvis image. Elvis would change his personal appearance, give up touring to focus on becoming a Hollywood actor, and alter his musical style to lean more toward pop than rock 'n' roll. Parker also would limit the media's access to Elvis to avoid putting the singer in a situation where he'd make comments that could damage his newly formed image.

Access to the press was limited to whatever publicity and promotion the Colonel and others in charge of Elvis's career wanted released. So, of course, this information didn't dwell on rock 'n' roll, his Southern background, or his candid comments. Parker preferred short-term press conferences in which several reporters were privy to the same information in an open forum rather than lengthy one-on-one interviews alone with Elvis. (You can read more information in Chapter 7 on the transformation of Elvis after the army.)

## Noting Two Touchstones in Elvis's Personal Life

As the saying goes, when one door shuts, another one opens. In Elvis's case, this adage applied to two major events that occurred while he was in the army. In 1958, his beloved mother, Gladys Love Presley, died, and toward the end of his tour of duty, he met Priscilla Beaulieu, who would later become his wife. This section offers a brief account of both life-altering experiences.

**Chapter 5: What's the Ruckus About: The Impact of Elvis the Pelvis**

> **REMEMBER:** Just as his service in the army did, both of these personal experiences — the death of his mother and his meeting Priscilla — matured Elvis. An older, more confident Presley emerged in 1960 ready to tackle the next phase of his career.

## Suffering a terrible loss: The death of Gladys Presley

On August 14, 1958, just five months after Elvis went into the army, Gladys Presley died, possibly from heart complications due to hepatitis. Elvis, who had always been close to his mother, was devastated by her death. He broke down many times in front of reporters, friends, and family in the days before her funeral. Gladys had loved her son very much, and she had been his biggest supporter. Her death was the worst event in his life up to that point, and in many ways, he never got over the loss.

At the funeral, the Blackwood Brothers, the gospel quartet that had attended the Presleys' church in Memphis before Elvis became famous, sang Gladys's favorite hymns. Gladys was buried at Forest Hill Cemetery in Memphis, but after Elvis died, her remains were moved to rest beside those of her son in Meditation Garden behind Graceland.

After his mother's funeral, Elvis was sent to Bad Nauheim, West Germany, to serve out his two years of military service in the 3rd Armored Division. The only concession the army made to Elvis's celebrity was to allow him to live off-base with his family so he could have a bit of privacy. Elvis was well known in Europe, so living separately was necessary to keep him from fans and reporters. His father, Vernon, and his grandmother, Minnie Mae, joined him shortly after he arrived in Germany. They were later joined by various friends and cousins, because Elvis wanted to be surrounded by family and friends. With the recent loss of his mother, who had been his major support system, Elvis needed the support of his family and friends as well as the distraction of a lot of company. As a matter of fact, he would rarely live without a houseful of friends and family again.

## Meeting Priscilla

Toward the end of his tour of duty, Elvis met a 14-year-old girl who impressed him very much. Priscilla Ann Beaulieu was the stepdaughter of Air Force Captain Joseph Paul Beaulieu, who also was stationed in Germany. Elvis had been stationed in Germany for quite some time before the Beaulieus arrived, and Priscilla remarked to her stepfather that she hoped she would run into the famous singer while they were there. Captain Beaulieu was none too keen on the idea, remarking that he wouldn't let her walk across the street to see Presley!

Elvis and Captain Beaulieu knew someone in common, U.S. Airman Currie Grant, who thought that Priscilla and Elvis would hit it off. He arranged the meeting between the famous singer and the pretty teen. He also vouched for Elvis with Priscilla's father, who was worried about his daughter becoming mixed up with a famous rock 'n' roller. Despite her young age, Elvis and Priscilla dated frequently during the last few weeks that he was stationed in Germany. However, they were seldom alone, partly because Elvis preferred not to leave his house (and his house was always full of people) and partly because promises were made to the Beaulieus that Priscilla would be well tended. However, Elvis and Priscilla did manage a few stolen hours together in his room.

Priscilla went to the airport to say goodbye when Elvis's tour of duty was over, and she was photographed by major magazines such as *Life* as she waved to him and cried. When he returned to the States, reporters asked him about her, but he downplayed their relationship, probably to protect her and her family from the press. Little did these reporters know that seven years later, Elvis Presley and Priscilla Beaulieu would marry. (See Chapter 7 for an account of Elvis and Priscilla's marriage.)

# Part II
# From Hot-Headed Rebel to Hollywood Leading Man

The 5th Wave — By Rich Tennant

"They told me my movie career would rely heavily on my background growing up in a two room house in hard scrapple Tupelo, Mississippi."

"What's your next film?"

"Blue Hawaii."

## In this part . . .

As far back as 1956, movies were used to make Elvis Presley more palatable to the mainstream public. Playing a version of himself in three of his first four movies appealed to his fans but also presented him as a sympathetic figure to the general audience, which helped temper the controversy surrounding his music and performing style.

After Elvis was discharged from the army, he and his management team made the deliberate decision to turn him into a mature, conventional-looking leading man to attract the broadest audience possible. He stopped performing in public and turned his attention entirely to the movies. Elvis supported this decision because he wanted to be an actor, but sadly his career in Hollywood didn't turn out the way he wanted.

As his movies became formulaic, Elvis grew increasingly disappointed with his Hollywood career. This is one of the reasons his films have such a horrible reputation that in many ways isn't deserved. In this part, I examine how Elvis's image and music were changed as a result of his film career. I also talk about his films — the formulaic musical comedies as well as those that don't follow the formula.

# Chapter 6

# Taming the Rebel: Elvis Goes to Hollywood

### In This Chapter

▶ Revealing Elvis's path to movie stardom

▶ Referencing Elvis's real-life experiences in the movies

▶ Reshaping Elvis's notorious rebel image through his movies

Elvis's career as a movie star began in 1956 during the heat of the controversy over his singing and provocative performing style. In fact, Elvis's entrance into Hollywood became a deliberate and important step in dealing with the controversy and expanding his audience beyond his teenage base. Elvis's management team launched a film career for the singer in order to keep the fans happy while broadening his appeal and diluting the controversy swirling around "Elvis the Pelvis" in the press. Elvis, on the other hand, had a loftier ambition: He intended to become a legitimate actor like so many singers before him. (See Chapter 5 to understand the significance of "Elvis the Pelvis.")

Many biographers and rock 'n' roll historians regret the impact that Elvis's film career had on his raw rockabilly sound and his uninhibited, sexually provocative performing style. They bemoan the way the movies instigated the process of taming Elvis. In this context, his films are presented in a negative light. Yet, you must remember that conforming for a mainstream audience was the desired goal of Elvis's management team. And, to some extent, that was Elvis's goal, too. The fact that his movies brought Elvis Presley into mainstream culture doesn't mean that all the films are without interest or merit. It's time to reevaluate his film career with more objectivity.

In this chapter, I discuss Elvis's movie contract with producer Hal Wallis. I also take you through the first four movies Elvis made, explaining how and why these films incorporated aspects of the singer's real life into the plots. Specifically, casting Elvis in *Loving You, Jailhouse Rock,* and *King Creole* served to create a mainstream figure out of a controversial star. This strategy became a model for later generations of rock 'n' roll stars and rap artists to follow. Finally, I tell you how Elvis's early movies helped reshape his controversial image and set the stage for his career as a leading man.

# Embarking upon a Movie Career

In 1956, Elvis was fortunate enough to attract the attention of Hal Wallis, one of Hollywood's most successful and talented producers. Wallis had a reputation for spotting talented new entertainers and turning them into stars. Elvis, a lifelong fan of the movies, embraced the idea of becoming an actor, and so he eagerly put himself in Wallis's hands. This section covers how Wallis came to sign Elvis to a contract and why the singer was so keen to shift gears in his career. It also details the importance of Elvis's first film, *Love Me Tender,* which wasn't produced by Wallis. The filmmaker lent his new star to another studio to make this Civil War drama, which in many ways is quite different from his other movies.

## Signing with Hal Wallis

While looking for something to watch on television one evening in the spring of 1956, Hal Wallis stumbled across Elvis Presley on Tommy and Jimmy Dorsey's *Stage Show* (see Chapter 4 for more information about *Stage Show*). Not only did Wallis find this hot new singer with the odd name "electrifying," but he also realized that the effect Elvis had on the audience spelled movie magic. He recognized Elvis's charisma as a performer, and he knew that Elvis could transfer that appeal to the big screen.

The next morning Wallis called Elvis's manager, Colonel Tom Parker (often referred to as simply "the Colonel"), and arranged a screen test. When the day for the screen test finally came, a nervous Elvis performed a scene from *The Rainmaker,* which Wallis was in the process of adapting from the Broadway stage to the big screen. Elvis's screen test was impressive enough for Wallis to offer him a three-film deal, with the option to renew. The contract wasn't exclusive, so Elvis was free to make films for other producers or studios.

Wallis was a veteran of old Hollywood. He had worked his way up through the ranks of Warner Bros. from the publicity department to producer, beginning in the 1920s. During the Golden Age of the 1930s and 1940s, Wallis produced some of the studio's best films, including *Casablanca, Sergeant York, King's Row,* and *Now, Voyager.* He formed his own production company in 1944, releasing his films through Paramount and later through Universal. Over the years, he signed several prominent entertainers to *personal contracts* (a contract with Wallis, not a studio), including the team of Jerry Lewis and Dean Martin, Shirley MacLaine, and Charlton Heston.

Wallis's talents as a producer included his ability to match a performer to material that would showcase the newcomer's unique qualities. To Wallis, this strategy was the sure path to stardom. His reputation reached back to his days at Warner Bros., when he cast stars such as Humphrey Bogart, Ingrid Bergman, and Bette Davis in their best roles. Not surprisingly, Wallis titled his autobiography *Starmaker*.

# Chapter 6: Taming the Rebel: Elvis Goes to Hollywood

With the approval of the Colonel and Elvis's William Morris agent, Abe Lastfogel, Wallis devised a series of films that attracted Elvis's fans but also appealed to other factions of moviegoers. The Colonel signed Elvis with William Morris, one of the largest talent agencies in America, in 1955 to help with bookings and mapping out his client's future. In general, Lastfogel proved particularly useful in negotiations with studios and producers.

## Following in the footsteps of Sinatra

Elvis loved the movies, but the key reason he embraced a movie contract at this explosive point in his recording career was because he personally believed that the most successful entertainers parlayed their recording triumphs into movie careers. He held singers such as Bing Crosby, Frank Sinatra, and Mario Lanza in high regard as role models because he admired the way they shifted from recording to acting. In interviews at the time, Elvis talked enthusiastically about how becoming an actor was a good career move. He noted that singers peaked quickly and then faded away, but good actors had long careers. He even speculated that he would make some films in which he didn't sing, much like Sinatra and Crosby had done.

Elvis's vision for his film career was to become a bona fide actor; his management team's goal was to eliminate the controversy surrounding the singer and broaden his audience. At first, Elvis's goal for his movie career didn't contradict the Colonel and Wallis's plan, but as time passed, his goal grew increasingly at odds with theirs. This difference in perception between Elvis and his management team helps to explain his utter disillusionment with Hollywood later on and why he turned his back on his movies, even his good ones. Flip to Chapter 8 to find out more about the clash.

## Evaluating Love Me Tender

Elvis signed his contract with Wallis in the spring of 1956, but the producer felt that he didn't have the right material at the time to showcase the singer to his best advantage. So Wallis allowed Presley to co-star in a film for another studio while he developed a *property* (a story or script owned by Wallis) especially for his new star. Elvis's first film became *Love Me Tender*.

Originally titled *The Reno Brothers*, *Love Me Tender* was produced by 20th Century Fox, with Elvis co-starring in a secondary role. The story involves four brothers whose lives are changed tragically by the Civil War. Elvis plays the youngest brother, Clint Reno, who stays home during the war to work on the family farm. Clint marries his older brother's sweetheart, because the family thinks that the brother (Vance) has been killed in battle. However, when Vance returns home unexpectedly, the family is torn apart by the marriage. After a series of bad decisions and mistakes in judgment, Clint is shot and killed.

### The first film versus the typical film

In some ways, Elvis's first film, *Love Me Tender,* released in the fall of 1956, is an anomaly in his career, because it doesn't follow the characteristics of any of his other films. *Love Me Tender* differs from most of Elvis's other films in the following ways:

- Elvis doesn't play the main male character.
- It's a period picture, taking place in the post–Civil War era.
- Elvis doesn't play a character written especially for him.
- It doesn't make use of Elvis's iconography (see the later section "Telling Elvis's Life Story: How His Movies Act As Autobiography" for more on how many of Elvis's first movies echoed his life).
- Elvis's character dies in the end.

Despite these differences, *Love Me Tender* set in motion a pattern that would typify the Elvis Presley picture. That pattern included the addition of songs to appeal to his fans and to exploit his participation. This pattern seems to make sense because Elvis was a singer, but it can be distracting in some genres. In *Love Me Tender,* for example, Elvis's contemporary singing style is at odds with the period in which the story is set and detracts from the drama. When his character cuts loose on the Reno front porch with a rousing rendition of "We're Gonna Move," it interrupts the story line instead of enhancing it.

Of the four songs added to the film, the ballad "Love Me Tender" is best suited to the story line. Songwriter Ken Darby reworked the Civil War song "Aura Lee" as "Love Me Tender," adding new lyrics but retaining the melody. The ballad was released with slightly different lyrics as a single, and it sold a million copies in advance, reaching the top of the *Billboard* Top 100 chart. The song's success persuaded the studio to change the title of the movie from *The Reno Brothers* to *Love Me Tender.*

### Elvis and his costars

The major stars of *Love Me Tender* included leading man Richard Egan and leading lady Debra Paget. Pairing Elvis with established actors helped him learn the ropes of film acting and masked his inexperience on screen. Egan mentored Elvis, who was working hard to construct a credible character.

With leading lady Debra Paget, Elvis established another type of "pattern" that would be consistent throughout his film career: He developed a crush on Paget, and he tried his best to win her affections. Elvis and Paget got along well on the set, but she didn't return his romantic feelings, largely because her mother had bigger plans for her daughter's career. Elvis would go on to make 30 more feature films, and during the production of many of them, he found someone in the cast to date, often his leading lady.

Chapter 6: Taming the Rebel: Elvis Goes to Hollywood    **105**

# Telling Elvis's Life Story: How His Movies Act As Autobiography

By the time Elvis had completed *Love Me Tender,* Hal Wallis had developed a suitable vehicle for Elvis to star in. A *vehicle* is a movie built specifically around a star's image. For example, a producer may tailor a script to showcase a performer's talents, or he may shape a character to suit a star's screen persona. Some vehicles are loosely adapted to the star's special characteristics; others are worked tightly around them. The star's appearance in the vehicle is the guiding force in the film, deliberately overshadowing plot and character development. Elvis's next three films, produced before he went into the army in 1958, were vehicles tightly shaped to his public persona.

Wallis ordered the scriptwriters to tailor *Loving You* and *King Creole* to Elvis's image and talents, and producer Pandro Berman of MGM developed *Jailhouse Rock* especially for the hot new star. The films' story lines borrowed heavily from the details of Elvis's life and career. The strategy behind featuring Elvis in such deliberate vehicles was to ensure the support of his built-in fan base. Fans would attend the movies because Elvis was the star, but after recognizing that certain elements in the films were parts of Presley's own story, they would return to watch the movies again as Elvis-related experiences.

A way to turn the scripts into vehicles for Elvis Presley was to make use of "the Elvis Presley iconography." This iconography is a set of personal characteristics and career events associated with the singer that fans were familiar with because of photographs, newspaper and magazine articles, fan magazines, interviews, and public performances. While these characteristics and events derived from Elvis's real life, they were simplified and codified into a blueprint for the scripts for his movies. When fans saw these characteristics, actions, or people in the films, they drew a connection between the fictional leading character and the real Elvis Presley. The Elvis Presley iconography included the following:

- **Hair and sideburns:** Elvis's long sideburns and ducktail haircut, which he kept in place with three different pomades, was ridiculed in the press, emulated by teenage boys, and beloved by adolescent girls. (See Chapter 4 for more information on the criticism of Elvis's personal appearance.)

- **Clothing:** Elvis's colorful Beale Street wardrobe was distinctive and unconventional. Plus, there was one consistent style feature associated with his clothing that others adopted, too — the turned-up collar. (See Chapter 3 for more information on Elvis's clothing style.)

- **A taste for Cadillacs:** As soon as Elvis began to earn some real money, he hit the local car dealer to buy Cadillacs and Lincolns, often in offbeat colors. The first Cadillac, which he bought for his mother, was pink; others were cream, baby blue, and purple.

> **TRIVIA**
> 
> On more than one occasion, fans discovered Elvis's car in a parking lot after a concert and destroyed the finish by writing their names and phone numbers in lipstick or etching them in with nail files.
> 
> ✔ **Band members:** Elvis's backup musicians included Scotty Moore, D.J. Fontana, and Bill Black, and fans recognized their faces from Presley's TV appearances. The Jordanaires also often provided background vocals, and they were known to the fans as well.
> 
> ✔ **Performing style:** Elvis's distinctive performing style, in which he gyrated his hips, shook all over, pointed his finger, and rocked on the balls of his feet, was the high point of a Presley performance.

The roles that echo Elvis's life events also fit an archetypal story line that moviegoers of all ages would recognize — the show business success tale (see the later section "Explaining the success myth" for more information). In this type of story, a talented performer with a new style battles personal demons in his struggle to make it to the top. By repeatedly casting Elvis in this type of story, the films effectively suggested to audiences that the singer's real-life career was no different than that of countless other singers. These films implied that even though Elvis's music was different and outrageous by some standards, there was really nothing new — or dangerous — about Elvis Presley the performer.

**REMEMBER**

The films were intended to imply that Elvis Presley was neither new nor dangerous. Elvis's management team sought to change public perception of the singer, but in real life, Presley was a threat because he changed the status quo. He influenced the tastes of a new generation, changed the direction of popular music, and brought the music of rural Southerners and African Americans into the mainstream.

The following sections discuss how each of these three films appropriated aspects of Elvis's real life and career and fit them into the mold of a show business success tale. The films are discussed in order of release.

## Looking at Loving You

Of all the Presley vehicles, the musical drama *Loving You* corresponds closest to Elvis's own life story. It wasn't intended to be a biography, however. Released in July 1957, *Loving You* tells the tale of Deke Rivers, a young, working-class Southerner with a "boogie-woogie" singing style that drives the girls wild. Music manager and public relations expert Glenda Markle, played by Lizabeth Scott, realizes that Deke can tap into the youth market that her country band, the Rough Ridin' Ramblers, can't. Deke is a naive kid who doesn't understand his effect on girls, but Glenda exploits his sensation and sensuality in publicity stunts that sometimes backfire. The press saddles Deke with a reputation as a troublemaker who incites teenagers to act out.

Deke becomes depressed and confesses to Glenda that his real name is Jimmy Tompkins and that he stole his name to cover up a tragic past. Glenda lands Deke a one-man show on television to prove that he's a legitimate talent who isn't just a bad influence on young people.

## Behind the scenes

To ensure that *Loving You* captured the flavor of Elvis's life as an entertainer and showed the excitement surrounding his performances, Wallis sent director/cowriter Hal Kanter to observe Elvis in his hometown of Memphis and as he made his final appearance on the *Louisiana Hayride* on December 16, 1956. (See Chapter 3 for more information on the *Hayride*.) Kanter was both shocked and amazed by this new singing sensation. He was amazed at what he called the "electric excitement" generated by Presley onstage, and he was shocked at the way the crowds forced the singer to live a sequestered, protected existence. Because of this firsthand experience, Kanter effectively captured both sides of Elvis's fame in the script for *Loving You*.

## Elvis as Deke Rivers

In *Loving You*, Deke's rise to fame as a young Southern-based singer with a new sound parallels the beginning of Elvis's own career, particularly the impact he had on the girls in his audience and the accusations that he incited acts of juvenile delinquency. The film also references Elvis's country music connection by showing Deke touring with a country band. (Refer to Chapter 3 for more information on Elvis's early career on the country-western circuit.) The movie even hints at Elvis's R&B connection when Deke belts out a wicked rendition of "Mean Woman Blues."

*Loving You* offers many obvious references to the Elvis iconography, which fans would have easily recognized. The following examples represent some of the most obvious:

- **Hair and sideburns:** A local troublemaker taunts Deke Rivers in a diner by calling him "Sideburns," echoing the criticism Elvis received for his own side whiskers. Several scenes draw the viewer's attention to Deke's hair as well. In one instance, he combs it while looking in a mirror. The scene is similar to a famous photo of Elvis by Albert Wertheimer; in another scene, Glenda runs her hands through Deke's hair.

- **A taste for Cadillacs:** Glenda buys Deke a white and red convertible as a publicity stunt. Near the end of the film, a shot of the car parked behind the theater shows fans writing messages on the car with lipstick. The shot is extraneous to the film's plot; no comment is made about this defacement and the incident is never referred to in the film. Thus, the shot isn't really part of Deke Rivers's fictional story; it's a depiction of an actual moment from Elvis's life used to manipulate the audience into seeing the two as one.

- **Band members:** Scotty Moore, Bill Black, and D.J. Fontana, who were Elvis's real-life band members, make up the band that back up Deke Rivers. While Moore and Fontana don't have character names in the film, Bill Black is listed as "Eddie" in the cast list. Most of their screen time finds the three of them playing onstage, but in one scene, they're sitting around backstage with Deke joined in a brief conversation.

- **Performing style:** Deke's sensual performing style, which is the same as Elvis's own personal performing style, stirs up the local girls in the scene that introduces Deke to Glenda and the viewing audience. During the musical numbers, the fictional character of Deke slides away almost completely because he's singing and performing exactly like Elvis Presley. At this point, viewers become aware that they're watching Elvis, not Deke. Indeed, that's the reason for seeing the film.

In the last sequence of the movie, Deke performs a concert that's broadcast on television. This concert is reminiscent of the TV variety programs so popular during the 1950s. Deke is presented singing before an enthusiastic live studio audience. Elvis's real-life parents, Gladys and Vernon Presley, are part of the audience and are clearly visible during a close-up.

During the production of *Loving You,* Elvis didn't date costar Dolores Hart, but he did date one of the actresses who had a bit part, Yvonne Lime.

## Exploring Jailhouse Rock

If *Loving You* exploits the well-mannered Southern boy that the Colonel touted as the real Elvis, *Jailhouse Rock* plays off the part of the singer's image that's associated with the tough rebel. Released in 1957, the film stars Elvis as Vince Everett, a working-class stiff sent to prison for manslaughter. Rude and ill-tempered, Vince learns to play the guitar from cellmate and former country-western star Hunk Houghton, played by Mickey Shaughnessy. After Vince is released from jail, he begins a career as a recording artist with the help of record industry veteran Peggy Van Alden, played by Judy Tyler. Peggy helps Vince develop a new sound, which begins to attract the attention of teenagers. Peggy and Vince fall in love, but Vince's hardened attitude and cynicism cause the two to split personally and professionally. A tragic accident results in Vince's change of heart, and the two are reunited.

### Behind the scenes

*Jailhouse Rock* was produced by Pandro Berman and released through MGM — not by Wallis through Paramount Pictures. Wallis's deal with Elvis wasn't exclusive, so the Colonel was able to make deals with other studios.

Chapter 6: Taming the Rebel: Elvis Goes to Hollywood

Berman followed Wallis's lead in rounding out the script by echoing parts of Elvis's real life so that *Jailhouse Rock* would qualify as a Presley vehicle. However, Berman didn't have a master plan in regard to Elvis's career, because he wasn't invested in it. Presley was tied to Wallis by a personal contract, whereas Berman was merely assigned to *Jailhouse Rock* by MGM. Berman never worked with Elvis again.

### Elvis as Vince Everett

Vince Everett's personal life had little to do with the real Elvis Presley, but the character's rise to fame from country-western singer to rock 'n' roll star to movie actor parallels Elvis's own career path. Plus, Vince's surly attitude and lack of respect for authority and convention posit him as a rebel, which was part of Elvis's image as a rock 'n' roll star. More importantly, Vince Everett radiates a sexuality that's instinctual, animalistic, and dangerous — much like Elvis did when he performed. You can see a photo of Elvis performing as Vince Everett in the color photo section of this book.

In one of the most famous scenes in any of Elvis's films, Vince grabs Peggy and kisses her hard on the mouth, but she's offended by his "cheap tactics." Vince, well aware of his effect on women, growls, "Them ain't tactics, honey. It's just the beast in me."

As you might imagine, *Jailhouse Rock* is far less sentimental than *Loving You*, and Vince Everett is a tougher character than Deke Rivers. However, both films include many of the same references to the Elvis iconography. The following list includes iconographic references from *Jailhouse Rock:*

- **Hair and sideburns:** The film refers to the importance of Presley's hair by using an ironic approach. Instead of giving the fans what they expect, the film offers a scene in which Vince's hair is cut short while in prison. Elvis, as Vince, is framed in a medium close-up as the clippers plow through the long, thick hair. This scene must have been shocking to fans.

  Even though fans didn't know it at the time, the hair that was being butchered so unceremoniously on Elvis's head was actually a wig.

- **A taste for Cadillacs:** When Vince brags about making his first million, he asks Peggy what color Cadillac he should buy. Later, after Vince's first hit record, Vince's lawyer reveals while dictating a contract to a dictating machine that the color is white.

- **Clothing style:** Like Elvis's trademark turned-up collars, Vince wears his collars straight up throughout most of the film. Also, Vince's liking for oversized pants, plaid or print shirts with rolled-up sleeves, and sports jackets that don't quite complement the printed fabric of his shirts is very close to Elvis's personal tastes in clothing.

- **Band members:** Elvis's real-life band mates Scotty Moore, Bill Black, and D.J. Fontana play three of the musicians who back up Vince when he records "Don't Leave Me Now." None of them have character names, but they're Elvis's musicians playing Vince's musicians.

- **Performing style:** In some of the film's musical numbers, including "Baby, I Don't Care," the fictional character of Vince Everett virtually disappears because the singing and performing styles are that of Elvis Presley. Again, the purpose is to collapse the character into Elvis's star image to satisfy the audience's desire to see Presley.

## Turning King Creole into an Elvis vehicle

*King Creole,* a musical melodrama released in 1958, is set in New Orleans. Elvis stars as 19-year-old Danny Fisher, who lives in a poor neighborhood with his sister and weak-willed father. Danny works in the clubs in the French Quarter as a busboy to earn money for the family, but his father is repeatedly disappointed in him, especially after Danny is prevented from graduating high school because of his bad attitude. When a club owner hears him sing, Danny lands a job as a regular performer at the King Creole nightclub. The singer's life is complicated by his father's disapproval of his profession of choice and by his involvement with local racketeer Maxie Fields, played by Walter Matthau, and Maxie's girlfriend, played by Carolyn Jones.

### Behind the scenes

*King Creole* was based on the novel *A Stone for Danny Fisher* by Harold Robbins. In the novel, Danny lives in New York and is an aspiring boxer. The original script followed the novel more closely, and at that time, newcomer Ben Gazzara was tapped to play Danny Fisher. When that deal fell through, Hal Wallis had the script rewritten as a vehicle for Elvis. The locale was changed to musical New Orleans, and Danny's desired profession became singing. Veteran director Michael Curtiz helmed the musical drama, rendering a tightly crafted narrative in expressive black-and-white cinematography. Curtiz's craftsmanship is why this film is often touted as Elvis's best.

Dolores Hart, who played opposite Elvis in *Loving You,* co-starred as the love interest in *King Creole.* Rumors to the contrary, Hart and Elvis didn't date during the production of this film. Hart, who was another of Hal Wallis's discoveries, enjoyed a successful career as an ingénue actress. Later she turned her back on Hollywood to become a nun. She's currently the Prioress at the Benedictine Regina Laudis Abbey in Connecticut.

### Elvis as Danny Fisher

*King Creole* may be the most far removed from Elvis's personal life and career path, but it still uses the Presley iconography so fans can make the connection between Danny and Elvis. Consider the included elements:

- **Hair and sideburns:** Danny's long hair comes tumbling over his face in two types of scenes: when he fights and when he sings, giving his coiffure a dangerous and threatening connotation. When Elvis sang in concert, he used a certain pomade for the front of his hair to make it fall down in front of his eyes, which often made the girls scream.
- **A taste for Cadillacs:** During an argument between Danny and his father over Danny's decision to sing at the King Creole nightclub, a frustrated Mr. Fisher asks him what it is that he wants out of life. Danny sharply retorts, "A pink Cadillac," which is a reference to the legendary pink automobile that Elvis purchased for his mother.
- **Band members:** Elvis's favorite backup vocal group — the Jordanaires — and his regular musicians — Scotty Moore, D.J. Fontana, Bill Black — back Danny at the King Creole nightclub. Again, they're Elvis's musicians playing Danny's musicians.
- **Performing style:** As expected, Danny's performing style doesn't differ at all from Elvis's. In fact, Danny's sensuality is alluded to comically by one of the strippers at the King Creole. A colorful character named Forty Nina complains that no one needs to come see her act anymore, implying that Danny's onstage performance is hotter. The joke recalls the many times that columnists and TV reviewers compared Elvis's act to a striptease or burlesque.

# Using Elvis's Movies to Spin His Image

Each of the three Elvis Presley vehicles released in 1957 and 1958 (*Loving You*, *Jailhouse Rock*, and *King Creole*) follow a similar plotline: A talented entertainer faces outside obstacles and inner demons on his way to show business success. The story is an archetypal tale in the entertainment industry that's often dubbed the *show business success myth*. This tale has been used throughout movie history.

This section explains the importance of this archetypal tale in Elvis Presley's movie career, and shows how his association with it was used to reshape his image. The purpose was to make Elvis Presley seem less threatening, more familiar, and therefore more acceptable to a mainstream audience.

## Explaining the success myth

The Hollywood industry embraces the *show business success myth* — a subgenre of the biographical drama or biopic — because it touts the star system as a fundamental part of the entertainment industry. The show business success story involves a talented performer who overcomes personal and professional obstacles to become a star embraced by audiences. Achieving stardom is a personal and professional triumph. The subgenre is at least as old as the 1927 film *The Jazz Singer* starring Al Jolson and as recent as the 2002 rap musical *8 Mile* with Eminem.

This archetypal tale not only supplies the plots to *Loving You, Jailhouse Rock,* and *King Creole,* but after the release of these films, it could be seen as the paradigm to Elvis's real-life career.

Because fans and audiences recognized that these three films borrowed extensively from Elvis's own life in the story lines and characterizations, his life story became intertwined with the elements of the show business success myth. After these three films and the publicity and promotion surrounding them, it would be difficult not to see Elvis himself as the embodiment of the show business success story. Remarkably, these films effectively recast Elvis Presley's life story and star image from that of an unrepentant, Southern-based rebel who seemed threatening to the norms of society to a paradigm of the show business success myth, which was much more familiar and acceptable to mainstream audiences. Though nothing about Elvis or his life had changed, the movies reshaped his image and the story of his life in an effort to change public perception.

## Seeing the characters of Deke, Vince, and Danny as Elvis and vice versa

In their respective films, Deke Rivers, Vince Everett, and Danny Fisher are socially alienated youths who have problems with authority. They fulfill the roles of the rebel, strutting and stomping their way through scenes of angst and alienation while fighting their inner demons. The story lines eventually explain the sources of their discontent; in doing so, the story lines offer a reason for the youths' rebellious behaviors. In other words, Deke, Vince, and Danny are really just misunderstood. After they deal with the underlying trauma of their personal issues, they're presented as understood and, more importantly, accepted back into mainstream society, usually through the love of the leading lady.

If so much of Elvis Presley can be found in Deke, Vince, and Danny, he, too, must be alienated and misunderstood and, therefore, capable of redemption by mainstream society. By recasting Elvis's real life into the fictional stories of these three characters, the films undermined the controversy over Elvis Presley's hip-gyrating performing style and countered accusations that it leads to juvenile delinquency.

The controversy surrounding Elvis didn't completely die away until he went into the army in 1958. (See Chapters 5 and 7 for more about the effect of army service on his career.) The controversy tended to heat up whenever he toured the country in a series of live performances, which resulted in bad publicity from newspapers. However, the box office success of his films, his association with such Hollywood veterans as Wallis, and the positive publicity generated in some movie *fanzines* (movie-fan magazines) offered an alternative view of Elvis as a success story. This countered or at least complicated the effect of the bad publicity. The films had an impact on the depiction of Elvis in the press, and thus his public perception, but it's impossible to measure the success of the efforts to mainstream Elvis's image.

## Shaping Elvis's music and performing style into Hollywood production numbers

*Loving You, Jailhouse Rock,* and *King Creole* served to redefine the music of Elvis Presley, or at least put it in a context that made it less threatening and less alien to mainstream society. The singing styles of Deke, Vince, and Danny are described in the films as new, modern, and targeted toward the kids or teenagers, but they never have the connotation of being threatening or lurid. Issues of influence and inappropriate behavior are addressed in *Loving You,* but adults eventually come to the conclusion that rock 'n' roll music is simply a new sound for a new era, much like jazz or big-band music had been in other times.

Even more effective in handling the controversy was the way Elvis is depicted when performing in the films. The depiction contains or controls his movements. In other words, each film normalizes Elvis's music or performing style, but it's still recognizable as his. Consider how Elvis's performances are depicted in each of his vehicles:

- In *Loving You,* Elvis is part of a country-western show; in *King Creole,* he performs in the nightclubs of Bourbon Street. Both venues would be familiar to adult audiences. Also, the conventional way that the musical numbers are filmed in these movies (with Elvis center frame while the musicians perform in the background) standardizes the presentation. Elvis gyrates, snaps his fingers, shakes all over, and moves in the manner to which he's accustomed, but his mobility is limited by the range of the camera. The familiar venues and the limited movements contain his performances, making them less wild and threatening. Thus, he also seems less threatening.

- The title song of *Jailhouse Rock* offers the most interesting example of how producers contained Elvis's explosive performing style. For this legendary production number, featuring Elvis as a jailbird dancing alongside his fellow inmates, his trademark moves were reworked into a controlled choreography, robbing them of spontaneity, unpredictability, and sensuality. The idea of uncontrolled sexuality was removed from his performance, making it suitable for a mainstream audience.

For decades, biographers stated that choreographer Alex Romero allowed Elvis to choreograph the "Jailhouse Rock" number himself, but that's untrue. Romero tried to teach Elvis some traditional dance steps and moves for the occasion, but the singer couldn't conquer them. So, instead, Romero ditched the original plan and based the number's moves and steps on Elvis's established performing style.

## Co-starring with some well-known actors

The producers cast recognizable adult actors and stars alongside the young singer in order to attract a broad range of ages to the singer's films, which was typical of the era. Here are some of the costars that Elvis worked with in his first three vehicles:

- *Loving You* co-starred Hal Wallis's discovery Lizabeth Scott as music manager Glenda Markle. Popular character actor Wendell Corey acted as the bandleader of the country-western group.

- *Jailhouse Rock* featured Mickey Shaughnessy as Hunk Houghton who teaches Vince about music and life, and Judy Tyler of *The Howdy Doody Show* played love-interest Peggy.

- *King Creole* featured the best cast of any of Elvis's films, with Walter Matthau as gangster Maxie Fields, Carolyn Jones as the troubled Ronnie, Vic Morrow as local troublemaker Shark, and veteran actor Dean Jagger as Danny's father.

# Chapter 7

# Reinventing His Image: Elvis Becomes the Leading Man

## In This Chapter

▶ Understanding Elvis's service in the army as a turning point
▶ Establishing the formula for the typical Elvis Presley movie
▶ Looking at Elvis's transformation into a Hollywood leading man
▶ Exploring the pop sounds of Elvis's movie music
▶ Examining Elvis's marriage to Priscilla Beaulieu

*E*lvis's tour of duty in the army, which lasted from 1958 to 1960, marked the most obvious and profound turning point of his career, because it signaled the end of the controversy generated by his regionally tinged rock 'n' roll music and his provocative performing style. Elvis emerged from the army a confident and mature entertainer, with a new look, a changed sound, and a different direction for his career. This new direction led Elvis straight back to Hollywood, where his transformation into a smooth, pop-singing leading man was complete by the early 1960s.

Elvis devoted himself to his movie career, which successfully matured his image in the eyes of the public. He starred as a handsome yet conventional leading man in so many lighthearted musical comedies that Elvis the Pelvis (the nickname he earned from his sensual hip-swiveling performing style and notorious rock 'n' roll image) was obliterated in the minds of the press and public. Also helpful was the fact that the soundtracks to these movies featured a vocally confident Elvis singing in a smooth pop-rock style that bore only a passing resemblance to the raw Southern-based rockabilly music that began his career in the 1950s.

In this chapter, I examine the steps Elvis's management team took in order to reinvent him in a way that would encourage the mainstream public to embrace the former hip-gyrating sensation. Because much of Elvis's new image was manufactured through his musical comedies, I break down the formula behind those vehicles, detailing each characteristic. I also mark the changes in his musical style, particularly in the soundtrack music. Finally, nothing matures a pop idol like marriage, and no discussion of Elvis's maturation would be complete without a consideration of his marriage to Priscilla Beaulieu.

# Returning to Hollywood to Rebuild a Career

The folks who handled Elvis's career, including his manager Colonel Tom Parker (also known as simply "the Colonel"), film producer Hal Wallis, and to a minor extent his William Morris agent Abe Lastfogel, capitalized on the positive publicity generated throughout the singer's army service. Doing so successfully disassociated Elvis from the notoriety of rock 'n' roll. This strategy was a big step in constructing a new image for Elvis as a Hollywood leading man with broad appeal to all audiences.

The reconstruction process started with interviews and press conferences reiterating that Elvis served in the army without the benefit of special privileges. Photos of Elvis wearing his uniform flooded newspapers and magazines. Within a few weeks of his discharge, Elvis even co-starred in a television special with Frank Sinatra and Sammy Davis, Jr., which aligned him with entertainers who epitomized mainstream show business.

Next, Wallis cast Elvis in his first post-army film, *G.I. Blues,* which is a musical comedy that became the prototype for the Presley movie of the 1960s. As with Elvis's pre-army films (see Chapter 6), Wallis constructed a vehicle that not only showcased Presley's singing talent but also referenced his real life as a way to shape public perception.

In this section, I detail the steps that the Colonel, Elvis, and Wallis took just after the singer's discharge to take advantage of the goodwill generated over his army service. I show you exactly how these steps charted the course for the next stage of Elvis's career.

## Using the army as a turning point

Cooling of the controversy over Elvis the Pelvis actually began in 1956, when Presley signed a movie contract with Hal Wallis. The series of semiautobiographical films he made with Wallis prior to joining the army in 1958 went some distance in taming Elvis's rebellious image, but nothing changed the hearts and minds of his critics like serving his country. (Flip to Chapters 5 and 6 for a complete discussion of the controversy and how his pre-army films helped tone it down.)

# Chapter 7: Reinventing His Image: Elvis Becomes the Leading Man

## He's in the army now

According to *The Elvis Encyclopedia* by Adam Victor, Elvis noted this about his impending army service in 1958: "The army can do anything it wants with me. Millions of other guys have been drafted, and I don't want to be different from anyone else." In many ways, Elvis *was* like everyone else in the army. He performed his regular duties in Company D of the 3rd Armored Tank Division, which included driving a jeep, went on maneuvers, and participated in war games just like all the other soldiers. But, his fame also set him apart from the other men. To protect his privacy, Elvis was permitted to live in a house with his family off base, while the other soldiers lived in barracks on base. This prevented him from bonding with the rest of his unit, though he did make a few close friends, including Joe Esposito and Charlie Hodge (see the appendix for more on these two men). Whenever he got a pass or leave, Elvis stayed at his house surrounded by family and friends. He did very little sightseeing for the same reasons he didn't go out much at home: He always seemed to draw an unwanted crowd. The exception was a trip to Paris in 1959. Because Elvis kept to himself, and because army service is repetitive by nature, not a lot of meaningful information is available about his army stint.

Back on March 24, 1958, when Elvis reported to his draft board, took his physical, and moved on to Fort Chaffee, the Colonel made sure photographers recorded every stage of the process. He reiterated to the press that Elvis was going into the regular army and wouldn't take advantage of the military's offer of serving his time in Special Services. For the next two years, any time Elvis was on the cover of a fanzine, he was decked out in uniform, reminding the public he was doing his duty for the country. (Check out the color photo section to see Elvis in uniform.)

On the day Elvis returned home after his tour of duty, photographers and reporters were on hand in both Germany, where he was stationed, and the United States. At the press conference at McGuire Air Force base near Fort Dix, New Jersey, where Elvis landed on March 2, 1960, his commanding officer awarded him a 3rd Armored Division Certificate of Achievement for faithful and efficient performance of duty. The Colonel, Nancy Sinatra, and executives from RCA were on hand to welcome him home as well. Nancy was there representing her father, Frank Sinatra, who would soon host Elvis on one of his television specials.

The newspapers were flooded with stories about Elvis's return home, his commendations, his new sense of maturity, and his willingness to serve his country. Newspapers sought out comments and quotes from the men who served alongside him, his sergeant, and even notable celebrities. Politicians, columnists, and others who condemned Elvis in 1956 did an about-face, praising his patriotism, humility, and sense of duty. Elvis's two-year stint in the army granted him a clean slate, wiping away his previous negative public opinion and replacing it with a fresh, positive perspective.

In March 1960, Senator Estes Kefauver of Tennessee was quoted in papers throughout the country as saying, "To his great credit this young American became just another G.I. Joe . . . I for one would like to say to him yours was a job well done, Soldier."

## The King meets the Voice

On March 26, 1960, Elvis taped a guest appearance on Frank Sinatra's television special, *The Timex Special* (also known as *The Frank Sinatra Show, Elvis Is Back,* and *Frank Sinatra's Welcome Home Party for Elvis*). Colonel Tom Parker made the deal with the show's producers months before Elvis was released from active duty. He thought that appearing with Sinatra would showcase Elvis to a wide audience made up of adults and pop-music enthusiasts as well as to his original fan base.

Never one to take chances, the Colonel made sure that during the taping at the Grand Ballroom at the Fontainebleau Hotel Elvis would receive an enthusiastic response from the studio audience. He guaranteed this response by packing in 400 members of one of Elvis's biggest fan clubs.

The show was subtitled "Welcome Home Elvis," and in the opening segment, Elvis walked out in his army uniform. Later in the show, he performed both sides of his latest single: "Stuck on You" and "Fame and Fortune." Sinatra then joined him onstage for a short duet. Presley sang Sinatra's "Witchcraft," while Sinatra crooned Elvis's "Love Me Tender."

The setup for Elvis's segment looked very different from his last TV appearances on *The Ed Sullivan Show*. (Head to Chapter 4 for more information about these appearances.) This time around:

- Elvis snapped his fingers and swayed in time to the smooth-sounding orchestrations, suggesting fluid movement without "gyrating" his hips.
- He performed without his guitar to strum, thump, or use as a prop.
- His look was much different. He wore a stylish, conservative tuxedo; his hair was shorter on the sides and back; and his sideburns were gone.

Sammy Davis, Jr., Peter Lawford, and Joey Bishop appeared on the television special as well as Sinatra's daughter, Nancy. Davis, Lawford, and Bishop were members of Sinatra's famed "Rat Pack," the name given to the singer's longtime cronies who represented the elite of show business, especially in Las Vegas.

Elvis's conservative clothing, short hair, subdued performing style, and appearance alongside the Rat Pack clearly signaled that Elvis was courting a mainstream, adult audience. Sinatra, known as "the Voice," had been the idol of teenage girls during the 1940s. He matured to expand his audience, eventually becoming the biggest name in show business. Similarly, Elvis, who was called "the King," had been the idol of teenage girls during the 1950s. Appearing with Sinatra suggested that Elvis was following the same career path and was therefore the natural heir to the Voice.

While Elvis was in the army, his original fan base also had matured, which perhaps helped them accept his new direction. But, most likely, they simply were excited to see him perform after a two-year absence from the scene.

## Singing the G.I. Blues

*G.I. Blues,* which was released in 1960, was the third and final film under Elvis's original contract with Hal Wallis. So as soon as Elvis and the Colonel set foot in Hollywood in the spring of 1960, Parker negotiated another three-picture deal with the producer.

### Seeing success from fans and critics alike

*G.I. Blues* was enormously successful; it ranked 14th in box-office receipts for 1960. The soundtrack album, which included the rousing title song and the gentle ballad "Wooden Heart," remained on the charts longer than any other Elvis Presley album. Film reviewers applauded the new Elvis. They were glad his sideburns were gone, and they thought he would find plenty of new fans among adult audiences.

Sadly, Elvis didn't appear to share critics' enthusiasm for *G.I. Blues.* He felt that the film had too many musical numbers, and he believed that some of the numbers made no sense within the plot. He also was concerned that the quality of many of these songs wasn't as good as the music from his earlier films. In addition, he was eager to attempt more demanding and serious roles.

### Weaving Elvis's life into the plot

The movie's story line revolves around singer Tulsa McLean who's finishing his tour of duty in the army. Just as he had done with *Loving You* and *King Creole,* Wallis instructed the scriptwriters to take details from Elvis's own life to flesh out the script. (See Chapter 6 for more information on Wallis and his strategies.) As a result, in *G.I. Blues* Tulsa is not only stationed in Germany, but he's also a member of a tank division just as Elvis had been.

Using details of Elvis's life to flesh out the character suggested to audiences that the character was more Elvis than Tulsa; and because fans hadn't seen their idol in two years, they were eager to watch Elvis on the big screen. Wallis's strategy guaranteed fan support at the box office. Also, by building Elvis's recent military service into the character description, the producer capitalized on the positive publicity flooding the newspapers and magazines. Elvis had never been more popular, and he was getting massive amounts of free publicity; if this popularity and attention didn't attract a wide audience to his movies, then Wallis couldn't imagine what would.

### Setting the movie apart

*G.I. Blues* may have been autobiographical like most of Elvis's pre-army films, but it exhibited little else in common with his previous movies. Here are some of the differences:

- *G.I. Blues* is a musical comedy rather than a musical drama.
- The plot line revolves around the complications of love, with Elvis's character reluctant to settle down, and the leading lady adamant about it. *Love Me Tender* aside, Elvis's pre-army films were examples of the show business success tale.
- During the musical numbers, Elvis no longer gyrates in a provocative, sensual way. He still moves freely when he sings, but a troupe of long-legged female dancers placed in the background does most of the hip swiveling.
- Elvis's character is a mature, cool, confident ladies' man who isn't a threat to the status quo like his characters were in the pre-army films. He's decidedly clean cut, with short hair and no sideburns.
- To further show that Elvis's character offers no threat, he's shown singing a Bavarian-style folk tune to children at a puppet show, and then he baby-sits an adorable infant.
- Many of the songs in *G.I. Blues* are fast paced, but they don't have the hard-driving sound, gritty vocal delivery, and regional flavor of Elvis's 1950s music.

These characteristics helped mainstream Elvis by eliminating the controversial elements — the music, the sensual performing style, the youthful angst, and even the hair and sideburns. (See Chapter 5 for a rundown of characteristics that created the controversy surrounding Elvis.)

Elvis's hair is not only short and in a conventional style in *G.I. Blues;* it's also a different color. After *Loving You* was released in 1957, Elvis started to dye his hair jet-black, which was the color of his mother's hair. Elvis' natural hair color was dark blond or light brown, but it usually looked darker because of the pomade that Elvis used to slick down his flamboyant ducktail haircut. The two films that Elvis made after *Loving You* are black and white, so the change in his hair color wasn't obvious. *G.I. Blues* and most of his other films during the 1960s were shot in color, and so the rich tones of Elvis's blue-black hair were more noticeable. No one knows exactly why Elvis chose to change his hair color. Some speculate that it was because his mother dyed her hair black; others suggest it was inspired by one of his favorite actors, Tony Curtis.

## Calculating a Successful Movie Formula

After *G.I. Blues,* Elvis appeared in two serious films for 20th Century Fox that challenged him as an actor — *Flaming Star* and *Wild in the Country.* Unfortunately, neither film matched the box-office success of *G.I. Blues.* The Colonel attributed the disappointment to their lack of songs. (See Chapter 9 for more information about *Flaming Star* and *Wild in the Country.*)

When Elvis returned to star in his next film for Hal Wallis, the Colonel and Wallis were determined to make it a financial success. To that end, Wallis developed *Blue Hawaii* as another musical comedy vehicle for Elvis. This way he could take full advantage of Presley's singing talent.

In this section, I examine the characteristics of *Blue Hawaii* that were considered instrumental in its success. These characteristics would be repeated in subsequent Presley films, establishing the formula for the musical comedy that dominated his film career. (See Chapter 9 for a thorough discussion of those films that didn't follow the formula.)

### Establishing the Presley formula

Wallis and the production team loaded *Blue Hawaii* (1961) with 14 songs — the most of any Presley picture. With a running time of approximately 102 minutes, the film averages a musical interlude every 7 to 8 minutes. Wallis didn't use many biographical details from Elvis's life for this film — save for the fact that his character, Chad Gates, is just out of the army. Instead, he relied on the many musical numbers to pull in the Presley audience, which was beginning to expand beyond the teenage demographic.

*Blue Hawaii* provided Elvis with one of his signature songs, "Can't Help Falling in Love." During the 1970s, Elvis closed his concerts with this song — one of the few movie tunes that he deemed worthy of singing in concert.

Chad Gates, the son of a wealthy pineapple-plantation owner, is nothing like the angst-ridden working-class characters Elvis had played in his pre-army films. Instead, the plot involves Chad's reluctance to trade in his Hawaiian shirt for a business suit. Even though he's being pressured by his parents to join his father in running the plantation, Chad prefers playing music on the beach with his Hawaiian friends. To his parents' dismay, he lands a dream job as a tour guide for the agency that his girlfriend, Maile, works for, allowing him to enjoy the beautiful Hawaiian landscape and perfect weather. Maile hopes for something permanent with Chad, but he prefers being chased by female tourists of all ages.

### Elvis's favorite director

Norman Taurog directed 9 of Elvis's 31 features, partly because Elvis favored the veteran director, who was good-hearted and without the ego often found in Hollywood. After particularly difficult scenes, the fatherly director liked to pass out candy bars to cast and crew.

Taurog was known primarily for directing lighthearted star vehicles and comedies, a specialty that dated back to the silent era when he worked with silent comedian Larry Semon. He was the consummate studio craftsman, working with many major stars in more than 70 films across six decades. He won an Academy Award in 1931 for *Skippy,* a vehicle for child star Jackie Cooper. He was nominated again in 1938 for the Spencer Tracy classic *Boys Town.* In an oft-quoted statement, Taurog, who died in 1981, said of Elvis: "I was always proud of his work, even if I wasn't proud of the scripts. I always felt he never reached his peak" (*The Elvis Encyclopedia* by Adam Victor).

---

*Blue Hawaii* was shot on location in America's newest state, which had joined the union in 1959. Scenes were filmed at Waikiki Beach, Hanauma Bay, and Ala Moana Park. The exotic location became a principal element in the promotion of the film. The tropical landscape was not only beautiful, but it also made the perfect backdrop for romance. Promotion for *Blue Hawaii* promised "Exciting Romance . . . Music in the World's Lushest Paradise of Song!" Another slogan for the film was "Elvis Presley Guides You Through a Paradise of Song."

The promotion for and publicity surrounding *Blue Hawaii* reduced the film to the following four elements:

- Music
- An exotic paradise
- Romance
- Elvis

These four elements, which were pushed in publicity and promotion, became the essence of the formula for the Presley vehicle.

*Blue Hawaii* was released during the Thanksgiving and Christmas holidays in 1961. It quickly grossed almost $5 million, and the soundtrack album was the fastest selling album of that year. Unfortunately for Elvis, however, the success of *Blue Hawaii* restricted him to acting in musical comedies. The Colonel, Wallis, and some of the execs at RCA used the tremendous box-office

## Chapter 7: Reinventing His Image: Elvis Becomes the Leading Man

figures to convince a disappointed Elvis that this was exactly the kind of movie his fan base — which had expanded to include all age groups, families, and fans of movie musicals — wanted to see.

After *Blue Hawaii,* Elvis made 23 more fictional features, many of which were financial and popular successes. Even though Elvis failed to become the serious actor that he desired to be, he did become a successful movie star for much of the 1960s. And, while none of his films were award contenders, several were highly entertaining and well crafted.

### Crediting Hal Wallis as the father of the Elvis musical

Hal Wallis's strategy as a producer was to tailor film projects to the talents of his stars. He had a nose for discovering entertainers or actors who had star quality and then building scripts around their strengths. (See Chapter 6 for more information on Wallis.) From his first film with Elvis, Wallis preferred to develop specific vehicles exploiting his star's singing talent and public image.

Wallis's strategy was based on his experiences from working at Warner Bros. during the Golden Age of Hollywood, when stars were under exclusive contracts to studios that cast them according to their images and strengths. Later as an independent producer releasing through Paramount, Wallis honed this strategy to a special skill.

With his eye for talent, Wallis discovered Elvis and began making tons of films with him. In fact, Elvis made more films with the veteran producer than with any other industry executive or studio. Wallis, more than anyone, shaped Elvis's film career by continually casting him in musical vehicles. Elvis wasn't exclusively under contract with Wallis, so he was free to sign with other studios and producers as long as he fulfilled his obligations. Some studios and producers, such as MGM and Sam Katzman, followed Wallis's lead and cast Elvis in formulaic musical comedies, while others, such as 20th Century Fox and United Artists, tried another strategy. (Flip to Chapter 9 for insight into his films for Fox and United Artists.)

Often, in Presley biographies and career overviews, the Colonel gets the blame for the formulaic musical comedies. However, that accusation is inaccurate, because the Colonel had little experience in the creative side of the film industry. He could no more develop a film vehicle than Presley's pet chimp, Scatter. However, the films certainly suited the Colonel's preference for fan-targeted movies jammed full of songs. Instead, the father of the Presley vehicle was Hal Wallis.

## Making an Elvis film: Add these ingredients and stir

There's no denying that many of Elvis Presley's films had lots of similarities — even those with excellent production values, good directors, and charming costars. According to Wallis, to make an Elvis musical comedy, you followed this set of characteristics:

- **Exciting or stimulating jobs:** Elvis's characters always worked at professions that most people only dream of. They were never trapped in the workaday world of businessmen or other professionals. They never went to an office and never sat behind a desk. Instead, his characters held stimulating jobs that allowed him to work outdoors or that were dangerous and adventurous. For example, he played

    - A race car driver in *Viva Las Vegas, Spinout,* and *Speedway*
    - A small-aircraft pilot in *It Happened at the World's Fair* and *Paradise, Hawaiian Style*
    - A boat skipper in *Clambake* and *Girls, Girls, Girls*
    - A rodeo performer in *Stay Away, Joe* and *Tickle Me*
    - A carnival worker in *Roustabout*
    - A trapeze artist turned lifeguard in *Fun in Acapulco*
    - A Navy frogman in *Easy Come, Easy Go*
    - An entertainer in *Harum Scarum* and *Girl Happy*

- **Lots of music:** No matter what job Elvis's character held, he could also sing. Presley's characters averaged nine musical numbers per film.

- **Exotic locations or well-known vacation spots:** The settings for *Viva, Las Vegas* and *It Happened at the World's Fair* are self-explanatory. Hawaii provided the setting for *Blue Hawaii; Girls, Girls, Girls;* and *Paradise, Hawaiian Style. Easy Come, Easy Go* and *Clambake* were set in Florida. *Fun in Acapulco* was set in Mexico, while *Tickle Me* had Elvis taking up refuge at a dude ranch. *Double Trouble* landed the singer in London and Antwerp. Transitory settings include the carnival backdrop of *Roustabout;* the Indian reservation in *Stay Away, Joe;* a turn-of-the-century riverboat in *Frankie and Johnny;* and the racing milieu of *Speedway* and *Spinout.*

- **Romance:** The plots of Elvis's films continually focused on the rocky road of romance between his lady-killer character, who was loathe to settle down, and the leading lady, who had her heart set on landing Elvis.

- **A touch of heart:** Elvis's characters may have been ladies' men, but in each film, he sang at least one song to a child or someone's mother to soften his character and prove he was good husband material underneath his cocky exterior.

✓ **Casts of colorful characters:** Elvis musicals always boasted a supporting cast of colorful characters. These characters, played by veteran actors, provided most of the comedy.

After the success of *Blue Hawaii* at the box office, the Colonel convinced Elvis that his fans didn't want to see him as part of an ensemble cast in serious films with little music. Elvis agreed to star in the formulaic musicals, though he personally didn't care for the genre. He began to derisively refer to them as the Presley Travelogues, because of the way his carefree characters drifted from one vacation locale to another.

## Listing the best of the Travelogues

The Presley Travelogues never won any awards, but many of them are well-crafted Hollywood musical comedies with good casts, colorful characters, and solid production values. (See Chapter 10 for a detailed discussion of the major directors, famous stars, and solid character actors that graced Elvis's films.) Besides *G.I. Blues* and *Blue Hawaii,* which I discuss earlier in this chapter, the best of the Travelogues include those in the following sections.

### Viva Las Vegas (1964)

The chemistry between Ann-Margret and Elvis highlights *Viva Las Vegas.* This dynamic musical is filled with excellent songs such as the title tune by Doc Pomus and Mort Shuman, a well-respected rock 'n' roll songwriting team. Because Ann-Margret and Elvis were famous for their moves, the production numbers by rock 'n' roll choreographer David Winters accentuate dance, energy, and movement. You can see Elvis and Ann-Margret dancing in Figure 7-1.

*Viva Las Vegas* became Elvis's highest-grossing film at the box office.

Figure 7-1: In *Viva Las Vegas,* Ann-Margret matched Elvis's energy and charisma.

## Doin' the Clam and Slicin' Sand

David Winters, a hip, young choreographer who worked well with rock 'n' roll music, designed the production numbers for several Elvis films. In 1965, the producers of *Girl Happy* asked him to invent a dance for the film. Winters came up with the Clam, which was introduced with the song "Do the Clam." Unfortunately, the Clam didn't catch on like other 1960s dance crazes such as the Pony, the Monkey, or the Jerk.

The Clam wasn't the only dance to be spotlighted in an Elvis Presley film. The Forte Four sing the song "The Climb" in *Viva Las Vegas*, with Elvis, Ann-Margret, and a group of teens performing the dance steps (also choreographed by Winters) that went with the song. In *Blue Hawaii*, Elvis introduced a dance called Slicin' Sand with a song by the same name, but like the Clam, the dance didn't catch on.

### *Roustabout (1964)*

Legendary star Barbara Stanwyck, a good friend of Wallis, co-stars with Elvis in this colorful story with a carnival backdrop. Elvis plays sullen, selfish Charlie Rogers who finds his calling as a carny and in the process learns compassion, humility, and how to care about others. Stanwyck's participation seemed to raise the level of acting across the board.

### *Girl Happy (1965)*

A version of the Ft. Lauderdale Spring Break story, this film exudes the youthful spirit that the Lauderdale experience thrived on. Much of the appeal is the cast of costars, cohorts, and comrades. Pert, affable Shelley Fabares, who appeared in three Presley Travelogues, exhibits a nice chemistry with Elvis. Similarly, Gary Crosby, Joby Baker, and Jimmy Hawkins make great comic sidekicks for the star.

### *Speedway (1968)*

This race car romance lacks the spark of the other films I mention, but it co-stars Nancy Sinatra, a long-time friend of Elvis's. Sinatra was on a roll after a series of popular singles, including her signature "These Boots Are Made for Walking." She gives this film a '60s vibe that's charming in retrospect. The movie's highlight is the set design for the local club called the Hangout. Customers sit in brightly colored car bodies, which stand in for tables and chairs.

*TRIVIA*

The set design from *Speedway* was undoubtedly part of the inspiration for the club Jack Rabbit Slim's in Quentin Tarantino's *Pulp Fiction* (1994).

# Playing a Leading Man Off-Screen

By the time *Blue Hawaii* was cleaning up at the box office from 1961 to 1962, Elvis's image had altered into the mature Hollywood leading man — handsome, confident, conventional looking, and part of the mainstream of show business. No hint existed of his pre-army image as a rebellious and misunderstood boy who was notorious for his controversial music and provocative performing style that appealed to the teenage demographic.

In this section, I talk about the off-screen Elvis Presley during the time of his transformation into a mature leading man. I not only analyze the Elvis that was presented to the press and public, but I also consider what was going on with Presley behind the scenes. I let you in on information that no one outside his inner circle knew about.

## Handling the press

Constructing and maintaining Elvis's new image required more than just starring in roles as older, mature characters. To show that Elvis himself had changed off-screen as well, the Colonel controlled the publicity and promotion surrounding the personal life of his one and only client. The publicity departments for the studios for which Elvis made movies also generated press that underscored the changes.

This controlled publicity had been standard practice for the star system during the Golden Age of Hollywood when the studios had stars under long-term contracts and deliberately guided their careers to control them. Elvis, who was under contract to Wallis, was experiencing the tail end of that star system.

To a large extent, the publicity and promotion that was generated for Elvis countered those characteristics about his image that seemed to set critics off during the 1950s. Much care was taken to show that the new Elvis

- Looked and dressed like other Hollywood leading men
- Was as much a man of Hollywood as he was of the South
- Was a responsible member of society

Elvis's exposure to the media was limited to press conferences, group interviews, and the occasional one-on-one with journalists who had always been Presley friendly, such as Lloyd Shearer of *Parade* magazine. Luckily, Elvis had become media savvy since his pre-army days, when he used to blurt out comments that were then taken out of context. Now, his responses were pat answers to questions that reporters asked frequently. Interviews were never conducted at any of Elvis's residences; instead they almost always took place on the sets of his movies between takes. Often the studios or the Colonel simply issued press releases peppered with a lot of "quotes" by Elvis, and these were used as the basis of articles by the media.

## Dressing like a movie star

So much space was devoted to Elvis's coiffure, sideburns, eye makeup, and flashy clothing from 1956 to 1958 that it must have amounted to a national obsession. (See Chapters 4 and 5 for a thorough account of Elvis's personal appearance and how it was treated in the press.) When he returned from the army, it wasn't an accident that Elvis showed up for press conferences and interviews in his uniform and then later in conventional street clothes. Reporters, columnists, reviewers, and fanzine writers duly noted the change in appearance.

The epitome of the publicity over Elvis's manner of dress occurred in late 1963 during the production of *It Happened at the World's Fair*. MGM issued press releases detailing the extensive wardrobe of suits and sports jackets designed for Elvis for the movie, which were duly noted in columns and articles around the world: 10 suits, 4 sports coats, 30 specially designed shirts, 15 pairs of slacks, and 6 dozen ties. Considering that Elvis played a self-employed airline pilot trying to earn money to fix his plane, the wardrobe obviously wasn't intended to match his on-screen character. Instead, the details about his wardrobe for the film highlighted the fact that he was now a leading man of taste and distinction. To see a photo of Elvis donning a suit from his new wardrobe, check out Figure 7-2.

**Figure 7-2:** Elvis looks downright dapper in *It Happened at the World's Fair*.

# Chapter 7: Reinventing His Image: Elvis Becomes the Leading Man

The strategy to eliminate any vestiges of the old hip-swiveling kid with a unique wardrobe is obvious in an interview printed in *Australasian Post*. In the interview, Elvis supposedly claimed, "I could hardly believe that I had actually ever worn some of the gaudy shirts and sports jackets . . . They're kid stuff. Fine for a schoolboy. But I'm not a schoolboy anymore. I'm 28 years old, and I've met enough well dressed people in the past few years to know that I looked like a hick for too long a time." Even though the quote is attributed to Elvis in the article, it reeks of press-agent speak, in which writers for studio publicity departments provided stock interviews to fanzines and newspapers upon the release of each film. The movie stars were rarely involved in these tactics; instead, their interviews usually were ghostwritten for them.

## Taking the South out of the boy

The quote that was attributed to Elvis in the *Australasian Post* (see the preceding section) reflects another characteristic of the post-army publicity campaign — subtly eliminating his Southern identity from his image.

During the 1950s, critics of Elvis's music, performing style, and personal appearance often attributed his so-called lack of taste and inhibition to his rural Southern background, perpetuating an unflattering stereotype of the ignorant hillbilly. (Check out Chapter 5 for more information on the anti-Southern prejudice against him.) However, in the studio-controlled publicity of the 1960s, efforts were made to "bury" his roots so deep that the public and the press would forget them.

With the exception of *Blue Hawaii* and *Kissin' Cousins,* in which his characters or his family were from the South, Elvis's film alter egos no longer hailed from the South after his transformation as they had in his pre-army musical dramas. As a matter of fact, his characters' hometowns are rarely mentioned at all, because many of them are footloose wanderers who breeze into resort towns looking for love and adventure.

## Hanging with the Memphis Mafia

The entourage of close friends, bodyguards, relatives, and employees that accompanied Elvis everywhere he went was dubbed the "Memphis Mafia" by the entertainment press during the 1960s. Traveling with his friends had become a habit during the 1950s when Elvis was touring, but after his discharge from the service, the singer gathered his own "army" of cohorts to help him with daily chores, vehicle maintenance, scheduling, and security.

Most of all, however, the Memphis Mafia provided Elvis with round-the-clock company, entertainment, and even girls. As the years sailed by and Elvis grew older, having an entourage of buddies who had little ambition of their own seemed to keep the singer in a state of arrested development. Members of the Memphis Mafia came and went, but long-time members included Red West, Sonny West, Joe Esposito, George Klein, Charlie Hodge, Marty Lacker, Alan Fortas, and Lamar Fike. (See the appendix for more information on each of these individuals.)

Considering that the entourage consisted of at least a half dozen young men at any given time, it would have been odd if the press hadn't noticed them. They accompanied Elvis to the set, on location, and to the recording studio. Most of the time his companions remained in the background, but the boredom of downtime between scenes often resulted in on-set high jinks, games, and practical jokes. Directors often resented the intrusion of the Memphis Mafia on the set, but nothing was ever reported in the press, because the press accepted Elvis's explanation for the group's presence — they were friends and family members who helped him out with the daily grind of fame and fans.

## Dating his leading ladies

From the beginning of his Hollywood career, Elvis developed a reputation for dating his costars while a movie was in production. And if Elvis didn't date his leading lady, he often found someone in the cast or behind the scenes to bond with romantically for the duration of the shoot. Rumors about Elvis's crushes on actresses were circulated in fanzines, columns, and newspaper articles. Much of what was said was manufactured for its publicity value, but some of the rumors were true.

While on-set romances between costars aren't unheard of in Hollywood, the fact that Elvis did this on virtually every film is a bit unusual. The reasons behind his hot pursuit of his costars can only be guessed at, but Elvis had always loved the girls, and they loved him back — it was part of his personality.

Of all his relationships with costars, his romance with Ann-Margret turned out to be the most serious. During the production of *Viva Las Vegas,* Elvis and the red-headed dynamo set the publicity mill grinding when they showed up at restaurants and clubs around Las Vegas. The romance was a dream come true for the MGM publicity department, who made the most of it in their promotion. Even though their relationship didn't last for the long term, the two remained friends for the rest of Elvis's life.

Elvis also enjoyed the company of these beautiful and talented actresses:

- Yvonne Lime during the production of *Loving You*
- Anne Neyland during *Jailhouse Rock*
- Juliet Prowse shortly after *G.I. Blues*
- Tuesday Weld during *Wild in the Country*

- Joan Blackman who co-starred in both *Blue Hawaii* and *Kid Galahad*
- Yvonne Craig during *Kissin' Cousins*
- Deborah Walley during *Spinout*
- Mary Ann Mobley who appeared in both *Girl Happy* and *Harum Scarum*

*TRIVIA*

Donna Douglas, who enjoyed fame as Elly May Clampett on *The Beverly Hillbillies,* is one costar who didn't have a fling with Elvis. The deeply religious Douglas recalled that she and Elvis spent hours on the set of *Frankie and Johnny* talking about spirituality and religion.

# Trading Rock 'n' Roll for Pop

To accompany his new image as a mainstream leading man, Elvis shifted his musical style from rock 'n' roll to a pop-influenced sound. Smooth, polished, and refined compared to the raw rockabilly or the R&B-influenced music of the 1950s, Elvis's new style was suited to the soundtrack recordings that dominated the 1960s. In the following sections, I offer an overview of Elvis's music during his movie era.

## Living in a pop-music world

Elvis's 1960s music can be described as a rocking pop style. It was often fast paced and rhythmic, like rock 'n' roll, but it was smooth, effortless, and easy to listen to, like pop. It wasn't revolutionary like his 1950s rockabilly sound, nor was it dramatic and intense like his 1970s music.

*REMEMBER*

Elvis changed his style of music for several reasons, including the following:

- **Personal taste:** Elvis liked many styles and genres of music, and he didn't think it unusual to include pop and rock 'n' roll on the same album. However, he didn't think it odd to break into a gospel classic at a concert where his fans were expecting rock 'n' roll either.

  Elvis admired several pop singers just as he admired singers in all genres of music. Among the pop stylists that he respected and listened to were Dean Martin, Mario Lanza, the Ink Spots, and Herb Alpert.

- **Current trends:** Because a smoother style of music made a comeback among new young singers during the early 1960s, Elvis's style and song selection became more pop oriented. The hard-driving rhythms of Chuck Berry, Jerry Lee Lewis, and Little Richard — who had become popular in the wake of early Elvis — were no longer as big as they had been. Instead, clean-cut, well-dressed male singers, such as Bobby Darin, Fabian, and Frankie Avalon, crooned snappy love songs or slow ballads in an easygoing, melodic style.

- **Changing image:** The new direction of Elvis's music was intended to help audiences forget the controversy of his earlier music and hip-swiveling performing style and to expand his fan base to older audiences.

## Recording in the studio again

Just days after his discharge from the army in March 1960, Elvis drove to the RCA studio in Nashville for his first recording session in almost two years. During the first few days of recording, Elvis cut the rock 'n' roll tune "Stuck on You," which became his first post-army single. A couple weeks later, Elvis returned to Nashville to record the tracks needed to make an entire album. By the end of April, *Elvis Is Back* was released. In less than two months, RCA had cut and pressed a new Presley album, and it was playing on the radio.

The songs selected for the album were a mix of the familiar and the new. They included his usual mix of rock 'n' roll, country, and R&B tunes, but a few of the numbers were mellow and smooth like pop music, including "Fever," which Peggy Lee had made famous two years earlier.

Not all the songs that Elvis recorded in April were included on the album. Two songs from the pop genre were held back for later release, and they became two of the biggest hits of his career. I discuss these songs in the following sections.

### "Are You Lonesome Tonight?"

Al Jolson had introduced this sad ballad in the 1920s, but Elvis was probably more familiar with a 1959 version of the song that had been recorded by pop singer Jaye P. Morgan. Despite its history as a pop song, "Are You Lonesome Tonight?" released in November 1960, did well on the country music charts for Elvis. However, he wouldn't record another song that hit the country charts until 1968 — a signal that his music was taking a different direction.

A unique feature of "Are You Lonesome Tonight?" is the talking bridge. Well into the song, Elvis stops singing and begins to speak as though he's the person that the song is about. He tells the story of his broken heart and the girl who left him behind before launching into the final chorus. Songs with talking bridges were quite popular in the 1920s, when "Lonesome" was introduced. And, in general, they weren't uncommon in country-western music. But, talking bridges weren't associated with rock 'n' roll or R&B.

### "It's Now or Never"

"It's Now or Never," one of Elvis's shortest pop tunes, was based on a well-known Italian song titled "O Sole Mio," which pop singer Tony Martin had recorded in 1949. Elvis liked the Martin rendition, but he wanted new lyrics and a new arrangement before he was willing to record it. Elvis's version of the Martin tune became one of his signature songs when it was released in July 1960.

# Chapter 7: Reinventing His Image: Elvis Becomes the Leading Man

---

## Elvis's music is never out of style

In recent years, Elvis's movie music was given a second life after several songs ended up as part of the soundtracks for contemporary movies. For example, "Devil in Disguise" became the closing song for a 1989 comedy called *She-Devil*. And, the entire soundtrack for the 1992 comedy *Honeymoon in Vegas* consisted of Elvis Presley tunes recorded by a variety of modern-day singers.

Likewise, some of his movie music was reworked by contemporary performers, who updated it and gave it a different spin. "A Little Less Conversation" from *Live a Little, Love a Little* was remixed by a Dutch deejay act called Junkie XL in 2002. After the song played behind a Nike World Cup commercial, it was released as a dance-mix single. Thus, almost 25 years after his death, Elvis had a single in the top ten again.

---

The song's basis in "O Sole Mio" pleased Elvis because the old Italian tune had been associated with both Enrico Caruso and Mario Lanza, who were two opera singers that he admired. Lanza had died about the time that Elvis commissioned the new lyrics, and it's likely that he was influenced to record the song because of his appreciation of Lanza.

"It's Now or Never" was Elvis's biggest selling single during his lifetime. Estimates claim that the tune sold around 30 million copies. After its long run as a single, the song was released on the extended-play album *Elvis by Request* in 1961.

## *Savoring the soundtrack tunes*

Most of the films that Elvis starred in during the 1960s were musicals, and soundtrack albums were released for each of them. After 1964, the Colonel suggested that Elvis record only soundtracks. The Colonel considered Elvis's movies to be promotion for the accompanying soundtrack albums, and the albums were reminders to fans that they should see the movies again. In Parker's scheme, a film without a soundtrack, or album without an accompanying film, was a wasted opportunity.

Elvis recorded dozens of songs for the soundtrack albums throughout the 1960s, so they represent a considerable percentage of his musical output. Sheer volume aside, the soundtrack music is difficult to assess because it's so erratic in quality. Doing a thorough investigation requires wading through a lot of mediocre and poor-quality music. However, buried among the lower-quality songs are a surprising number of high-quality Elvis tunes from the 1960s.

For example, many of the tunes from *Viva, Las Vegas* are in the hard-driving style of his pre-army music, including "C'mon Everybody" and "What'd I Say." Other excellent songs from this period include the following:

- "Return to Sender" from *Girls! Girls! Girls!*
- "Little Egypt" from *Roustabout*
- "Rubberneckin'" from *Change of Habit*
- "Wolf Call" from *Girl Happy*
- "Can't Help Falling in Love" from *Blue Hawaii*

### Saying goodbye to live performances

On March 25, 1961, Elvis performed live at the Bloch Arena in Pearl Harbor, Hawaii, as a benefit for the U.S.S. *Arizona* memorial fund. After this concert, Elvis didn't give another live performance until 1969, and he made no television appearances from 1960 to December 1968. Throughout most of the 1960s, anyone who wanted to see Elvis Presley had to go to the movies.

The U.S.S. *Arizona* was a battleship that had been sunk on Pearl Harbor Day on December 7, 1941. The fund was trying to raise money to build a memorial to the sailors of the *Arizona* who had been killed in battle. Ticket prices for Elvis's performance ranged from $3 to $10, with 100 ringside seats reserved for people who donated $100. Elvis and the Colonel bought 50 special seats and donated them to patients from Tripler Hospital in Hawaii. Elvis's benefit raised more than $62,000 for the memorial fund. On March 30, the House of Representatives of the Hawaiian legislature passed special resolution #105 to thank Elvis and the Colonel. The memorial was completed the following year and officially opened on Memorial Day in 1962.

There's no doubt that getting involved in the benefit for the U.S.S. *Arizona* memorial made Elvis seem more acceptable to the adult audience that shunned him when he was a rock 'n' roll rebel. But his career wasn't the only reason that Elvis wanted to help. He had a sensitive, generous nature, and throughout his entire life, Elvis gave freely to charities and other worthy causes, whether he received publicity for it or not.

## Marrying Priscilla and Settling Down . . . At Least for a While

On May 1, 1967, Elvis Presley married Priscilla Beaulieu, surprising the press and public because so little was known about the petite brunette who had won the affections of the King of Rock 'n' Roll.

## Chapter 7: Reinventing His Image: Elvis Becomes the Leading Man

The lack of a press profile for Priscilla is a testament to the Colonel's talent for controlling the information about Elvis that was released to the media. Elvis had met Priscilla while he was in the army, and then she moved to Memphis to finish high school during the early 1960s, when she was barely 16 years old and Elvis was in his mid-20s. Though the plan had been for her to live with Elvis's father and stepmother, the truth was that she lived at Graceland in Memphis, where she attended a private high school. If the press had uncovered this information, the scandal would have destroyed the mainstream image that the Colonel, Wallis, and Elvis had so carefully constructed.

All the stories about Elvis's on-set romances helped deflect attention from the home front in Memphis, where Priscilla spent most of her time. She patiently waited for Elvis to return home between films, enduring the rumors about flings with his costars. While Elvis denied the rumors, many of them were based on truth. Priscilla was determined to outlast the rumors and the flings, because Elvis had always talked about marriage to her.

Priscilla became Elvis's best-kept secret — she was someone outside the film industry who devoted her entire life to him. For Elvis, coming home to Priscilla was a respite from the Hollywood movies that he hated, and her innocence was an antidote to the scheming of Hollywood insiders. Elvis groomed her to be his biggest support and the woman he wanted as a wife, but she was never really an influence on his career or a partner in his decision making.

Elvis and Priscilla were married at the Aladdin Hotel in Las Vegas and honeymooned in Palm Springs, California. The ceremony lasted just eight minutes, and only a few of Elvis's buddy-bodyguards were asked to witness the event. It was a surprisingly private affair for such a public figure. (To see Elvis and Priscilla on their wedding day, flip to the color photo section.) On February 1, 1968 — exactly nine months from the day they were married — the couple's only child, Lisa Marie Presley, was born in Memphis.

Elvis never expressed his views about his marriage to the press or public. He always kept his private opinions and personal feelings about Priscilla to himself. However, several friends and costars recalled that Elvis was content and happy after his marriage. He was thinner than he had been in years and seemed to have settled down. The years of Elvis's marriage (1967–1972) were also the years of his last extended period of creativity.

# Chapter 8

# Sinking to a Low Point in Hollywood

### In This Chapter
▶ Taking a look at the Presley Travelogues
▶ Seeing how the Colonel's wheeling and dealing affected the quality of Elvis's movies
▶ Working with producer Sam Katzman
▶ Considering the worst of Elvis's movie music
▶ Factoring in the fans

Although Elvis made some dismal movies during the mid- to late-1960s, this stage of his career is often negatively exaggerated by biographers and film historians who lack an understanding of film history and production practices from that time period. Too often, this part of Elvis's movie career unfairly overshadows his entire filmography. Some biographers and writers even propagate inaccuracies and misrepresentations.

In this chapter, I chronicle the decline of Elvis's movies during the middle of the 1960s by discussing his manager's handling of the movie deals and the effect of the low budgets on the films themselves. I also talk about the accompanying soundtrack albums, the reasons for their mediocre quality, why Elvis continued to make both low-budget vehicles and poor-quality albums, and the fans' reactions. (You can read more about *vehicles,* or movies built around a star's image, in Chapter 6.) Professionally, the films and soundtrack albums made money until the very end of the decade. Personally, however, Elvis found himself in a rut that left him depressed and alienated.

## Examining the Change in Approach to Making an Elvis Movie

In 1964, the moviegoing public was treated to two *Presley Travelogues* (the term Elvis coined to describe his movies; see Chapter 7) that mark a definitive point in Elvis's career — *Viva Las Vegas* and *Kissin' Cousins*. The former represents the best of the Presley Travelogues, while the latter has been called one of the worst.

*Viva Las Vegas* co-stars the dynamic Ann-Margret, who at the time was about to break big as a major star of the 1960s. The film also benefits from location shooting in Las Vegas, contains some of Elvis's best movie music, and was directed by a veteran of musical comedies, George Sidney. *Kissin' Cousins,* on the other hand, lacks a dynamic female costar, was shot mainly on one set at California's Big Bear Lake, and suffers from a soundtrack of mostly lackluster, if not ludicrous, songs.

Impressed with *Viva Las Vegas,* reviewers praised Ann-Margret for what she brought to the film and were pleased with the producers for not showcasing Elvis in every sequence. *Viva Las Vegas* made a good showing at the box office, grossing almost $5,000,000. Unfortunately it had cost at least half that amount — maybe even more, because it went over budget. *Kissin' Cousins,* however, cost a flat $800,000, and not only was Elvis in every scene, but he was playing two characters (see the later section "Kissin' Cousins" for more on Elvis's dual roles in this film). The two films represented two approaches to the Presley Travelogues: allotting a decent budget to ensure good production values versus cutting costs to maximize profits no matter the consequences.

Elvis's manager, Colonel Tom Parker (also known as "the Colonel"), assessed the productions of both films and decided that the better value had been *Kissin' Cousins.* So, after that, he actively sought out multiple-film deals in which production costs were kept to a minimum, soundtrack costs were slashed, and shooting schedules were short. The king of cost cutters was producer Sam Katzman, who produced two of Elvis's worst films — *Kissin' Cousins* and *Harum Scarum.* You can read more about these movies in the later section "Introducing Sam Katzman: King of the Quickies."

The Colonel's decision to lower budgets didn't cause a definitive clean break between big-scale Elvis films and low-budget ones. Luckily, Elvis was still under contract to people like Hal Wallis, who didn't low-ball production values on the order of someone like Katzman. (Flip to Chapter 6 to read more about Elvis's relationship with Wallis.) But, the Colonel's decision resulted in several poorly crafted films that affected the perception of the Presley Travelogues as a whole. It also meant that Elvis was forced to record quickie soundtrack albums with dozens of mediocre songs. These albums left Elvis a forgotten presence in the music industry.

# Dealing with the Devil: Considering the Colonel's New Movie Deals

Because the Colonel thrived on making deals, throughout the mid-1960s he complicated Elvis's film career with an ever-expanding array of negotiation ploys, promotions, and side projects. Parker spent his time, energies, and expertise on negotiating deals, caring little about the worthiness of the scripts, the level of production values, the caliber of the acting, or the quality of the soundtracks.

After the frustration he felt over the big budget and long shooting schedule of *Viva Las Vegas* (see the preceding section for details), the Colonel jumped into a frenzy of deal making that engaged Elvis in simultaneous movie contracts with a variety of studios until 1968. It was an exhausting schedule of three films per year for Elvis, but it made him the highest-paid actor in Hollywood in the mid-1960s.

Hal Wallis's widely quoted comment on the Colonel is only a slightly exaggerated one: "I'd rather try and close a deal with the Devil."

If the devil is in the details, then in this section, I detail the Colonel's deals, offering insight into the impact of his strategies on the quality of Elvis's movies from the mid-1960s onward.

## Let's make a deal

The Colonel's standard deal called for a big salary for Elvis upfront, along with a percentage of the profits, which generally kicked in after the film recouped its initial budget. The Colonel received 25 percent of Elvis's monies. The cheaper the production costs, the smaller the budget, and the faster Elvis's profit participation kicked in. So it's no small wonder that Parker pushed for smaller budgets, faster shooting schedules, and lower production costs. Beginning with *Kissin' Cousins,* he even pursued deals with hotels, motels, transportation companies, and resorts to reduce production costs whenever Elvis's films were shot on location.

Parker prided himself on wearing down the other party in a negotiation until he got what he wanted for "his boy." One of his primary tactics was to negotiate improved conditions for his client at every opportunity, not just at the conclusion of contracts. Much to everyone's frustration, the Colonel resigned new multifilm deals with Wallis and the execs at MGM before the old deals were close to being up, creating hard feelings among the participating parties. He also repeatedly asked for bonuses, clothing fees, consulting fees for either him or Elvis, promotion expenses, and any other costs he could think of. Often he was successful in obtaining these added incomes, because producers and studio execs grew exhausted from his constant harassment.

Parker also took charge of the films' major promotion schemes and publicity campaigns, for which he used the old-fashioned carny term "exploitation." He liked to boast about the many marketing ploys he came up with to bring in audiences. For this service, he made side deals with the studios in which they paid Parker an additional fee for his marketing ideas. For example, upon a film's release, Parker offered fan club members free promotional merchandise related to the movie to ensure their loyalty. He also suggested publicity stunts to major theater chains that were showing an Elvis movie, such as hosting dance contests to promote *Viva Las Vegas*. Parker was an old hand at luring audiences to a show. And while some of his marketing schemes were effective, others weren't. He proved most effective at keeping Elvis's fans loyal by offering them freebies, publicity photos, and other incentives.

## Let's make a movie — fast and cheap

Throughout the mid-1960s, Parker pushed to shorten shooting schedules, because shorter time frames lowered production costs and therefore budgets. He even talked Hal Wallis into shaving off two weeks from the shooting schedules for his movies with Elvis, beginning with *Roustabout* in 1964.

When not working with Wallis or MGM, Parker sought out small production companies, because they proved more willing to offer big upfront salaries for Elvis while keeping the shooting schedules short.

The short shooting schedules, in addition to the other cost-cutting measures, began to cause a decline in the production values of the Presley Travelogues. Cost-cutting tactics caused the following negative effects:

- The acting in the movies suffered because the schedule left little time for rehearsal and limited time for retakes.

- Shooting on actual locations was abandoned in favor of shooting in the studio, on preexisting outdoor sets, and via rear-screen projection. The Presley Travelogues were set in exotic or unusual locales and would have benefited from location shooting to underscore the beauty or exoticism of the setting and the feeling of escapism that was central to the films' sense of fun and adventure.

- Shot selection was kept to a minimum, because fewer shot setups can shorten the shooting schedule. However, minimum shot selection can adversely affect a film. Scenes are routinely divided into long shots, medium shots, and close-ups. The variety of shots makes the film more visually interesting to the viewer, directing his gaze and sustaining his attention. More shots also keep the pace of the film lively. Unless the film is in the hands of a stylish director, limiting the shot selection can be less stimulating for the viewer and result in lackluster pacing.

- Little time and care were spent on the soundtrack albums. In fact, the musicians would record the instrumentals one day and Elvis would record his vocals on another, depending on his mood. (Read more about the poor quality of the soundtrack albums in the upcoming section, "Considering the Movie Music.")

Some of the Presley Travelogues suffered more than others. Those from the small studios without the veteran crews and talented producers fared much worse, including *Tickle Me, Frankie and Johnny,* and *Clambake.* The musicals made for Wallis, such as *Roustabout,* tended to exhibit bigger costars and higher production values. Most of the production companies and studios followed the formula for the Presley Travelogue until the tail end of Elvis's career. (See Chapter 7 for an explanation of the formula for the Presley Travelogue; see Chapter 9 for more information on Elvis's last four films, which don't follow the Travelogue formula.)

Despite these conditions, Elvis's films continued to make money at the box office, and the studios were still eager to make deals with "the Devil." One of Parker's most successful deals — for all parties — was with the small production company Allied Artists for the movie *Tickle Me,* which was released in 1965. Elvis was paid $750,000 upfront, which was more than half of the film's budget, and he was set to receive 50 percent in profit participation. Allied Artists was in financial difficulties when it made the deal, but it was counting on Presley's popularity to pull the company out of the red. To see Elvis in *Tickle Me,* check out Figure 8-1.

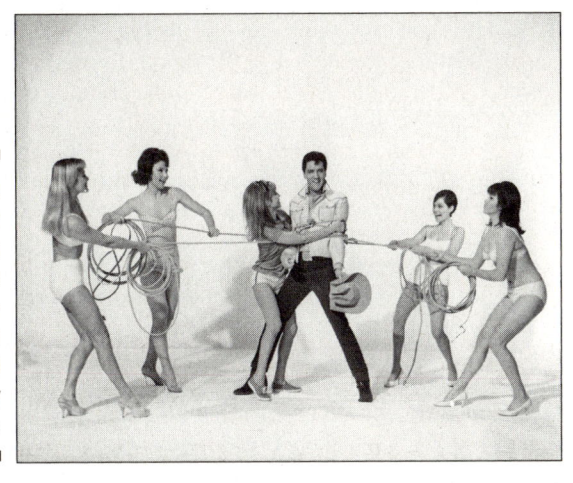

**Figure 8-1:** Costar Jocelyn Lane ropes Elvis on-screen literally and figuratively in *Tickle Me.*

To cut costs down to the bone, the Colonel suggested that the soundtrack album for *Tickle Me* consist of no new recordings. Instead, Parker dug up over 20 songs that Elvis had recorded previously for other albums or occasions. He asked Elvis to select 10 or 12 to be worked into the film's script. Because the songs had been previously arranged and recorded, Allied Artists saved on the cost of recording a soundtrack. In the end, Elvis came through for the production company, because *Tickle Me* turned out to be the third highest-grossing film in its history.

> ### Saying goodbye to Hal Wallis
>
> In 1967, after a ten-year relationship with Elvis, producer Hal Wallis opted not to renew his contract with the singer. Diminishing profits and the Colonel's continued harassment for more money and renegotiations convinced Wallis that the Presley pictures were no longer worth it. Elvis resented Wallis for saddling him with the Presley Travelogue, so he wasn't sorry to leave the veteran producer. Plus, Elvis was irritated because Wallis ordered director John Rich to accelerate production on *Easy Come, Easy Go* (1967), relegating it to the same lackluster treatment as other studios were giving Elvis's movies. You can read more about Hal Wallis and his relationship with Elvis in Chapter 6.

# Introducing Sam Katzman: King of the Quickies

In the mid-1960s, Parker signed a deal with producer Sam Katzman to make two films, *Harum Scarum* and *Kissin' Cousins*. Katzman had earned the nickname "King of the Quickies," because he made films quickly and for little money by cutting corners. During the 1950s, most of Katzman's movies were low-budget rock 'n' roll flicks aimed at teenagers. Many of them retain an innocent charm and are notable for starring up-and-coming actors such as John Savage. However, by the 1960s, Katzman's films were a mixed bag of badly crafted biker movies and silly sci-fi features.

Parker and Katzman shared similar views on cutting costs to maximize profits. In that way, they were a match made in heaven. For tough-talking Katzman, the two most important factors in making a movie were keeping to the short schedule and staying on budget. Unfortunately, he had little talent for storytelling, and no interest in visual style. In this section, I describe Katzman's approach to making movies, and I discuss what may arguably be Elvis's two worst films.

Katzman once produced a film with an eight-and-a-half-day shooting schedule. As a point of comparison, Elvis's film *King Creole* took about two months to shoot, which was about average during the 1950s and early 1960s.

## Kissin' Cousins

When Katzman was producing *Kissin' Cousins* (1964) he gave it a meager 15-day shooting schedule. When director Gene Nelson ran two days over that schedule, tensions escalated on the set between him and the producer. Elvis found it difficult to work under the stress, so he offered to call in sick to give Nelson a break. The experience was nerve racking for everyone, and the resulting film was a wreck.

The story in *Kissin' Cousins* features Elvis in a dual role — two Elvises for the price of one, which delighted the Colonel. His first role is as an Air Force officer who tries to persuade the Tatums, a Tennessee mountain family, to allow a missile base to be built on their land. He also plays the backwoods son of the Tatum clan. As Officer Josh Morgan, Elvis appears with black hair; as Jodie Tatum, he wears a dark-blonde wig, which was closer to his natural hair color. Refer to Figure 8-2 to see Elvis in his dual role.

**Figure 8-2:** Elvis played both Josh Morgan and Jodie Tatum in the 1964 film *Kissin' Cousins*.

The other characters in the film are stereotypical Southerners, including barefoot hillbillies, moonshiners, lazy hound dogs, man-chasing mountain girls, and pipe-smoking mountain mamas. Considering Elvis's Southern heritage, the story line and character depiction are downright insulting. For that reason, *Kissin' Cousins* is often considered Elvis's career low point.

## Harum Scarum

In *Harum Scarum* (1965), the second Katzman-produced musical, Elvis stars as movie star Johnny Tyrone, who's kidnapped while making a public appearance in the Middle East. He escapes and joins a troupe of pickpockets and rogues, which provides ample opportunity for Elvis to sing.

*Harum Scarum* had an 18-day shooting schedule, but the extra time in comparison to *Kissin' Cousins* did little to improve it. Poorly plotted, the film was a confusing hodgepodge of characters who all seemed to be acting in a different movie. Even the Colonel knew the film was a complete disaster; he advised MGM to release it quickly and quietly.

**TRIVIA:** In an attempt to "fix" the movie, the Colonel suggested to MGM that they record a voice-over from the perspective of a talking camel. The movie was so far-fetched that Parker thought a talking camel might make it seem like an intentional spoof. Needless to say, MGM declined the suggestion.

**REMEMBER:** After viewing *Harum Scarum,* the Colonel may have realized that Katzman's tactics were too extreme, because they never worked together again. The Colonel still pushed studios to decrease shooting schedules, but they were never again as short as Katzman's.

## Considering the Movie Music

The lack of care in the production of the Presley Travelogues even trickled down to Elvis's soundtrack albums. During the production of the *G.I. Blues* and *Blue Hawaii* soundtracks in the early 1960s, Elvis had worried that the songs weren't of the same quality as those he recorded in his pre-army movies. (See Chapter 6 for more on these soundtracks.) A couple of years later, he knew for sure that his soundtrack albums had deteriorated, and he grew bored with them.

By the time of *Kissin' Cousins* in 1964, he was so disgusted with the soundtrack situation that he no longer recorded his vocals with the musicians who played the instrumental tracks. The musicians recorded in the studio on the assigned booking date, and Elvis recorded his vocals when he felt like it.

Not all of Elvis's movie music was poor, but because he had recorded dozens and dozens of soundtrack tunes, the good songs are lost among the mediocre ones. The result is that any good music is overshadowed by the plethora of lackluster material. (Check out Chapter 7 for more information on the movie music that stands the test of time.)

**REMEMBER:** As listening albums, the soundtracks seemed repetitive, unmemorable, and lackluster. However, the songs were designed to work within the context of a narrative movie. So they advanced the story, helped build the characters, and successfully expressed the emotion of a scene. In fact, within the context of the films, many of the songs did benefit the material.

Still, there's no escaping the fact that Elvis recorded some forgettable songs during his Hollywood career. His music all but disappeared from the charts from 1963 to 1968. Consider the following:

- Between 1960 and 1968, Elvis didn't score a song on the country charts.
- After 1963, his music never appeared on the R&B charts again.
- In 1965, he had only one top-ten single, "Crying in the Chapel," which he had actually recorded in 1960.

- In 1966, only one of his songs, "Love Letters," made it into the top 20.
- Surprisingly, many of his albums — even the forgettable ones — made the top-ten album charts in the mid-1960s, but just barely. By 1967, none of his music charted anywhere near the top 20.

## Considering the role of the songwriters

Many of the songs for Elvis's films were written by songwriters who were associated with RCA's publishing house, Hill and Range. These writers churned out tune after tune, with little interest in expressing themselves or penning original-sounding material. Plus, they were willing to give up royalties to Elvis's publishing companies set up through Hill and Range, a sure sign that they considered songwriting a day job, not a form of artistic expression. (See Chapter 4 for more information on Elvis's publishing companies.) These writers were capable of stringing together tunes for movies, but their work wasn't the same caliber as those writers who composed songs for Elvis's non-soundtrack albums.

Even though most of the songwriters for the soundtrack albums worked for Hill and Range, some songwriters seemed to come out of nowhere. This latter group included Dolores Fuller, who penned "Rock-a-Hula Baby" for *Blue Hawaii*, "Do the Clam" for *Girl Happy*, and "Barefoot Ballad" for *Kissin' Cousins*. Fuller was the girlfriend of Ed Wood, who's a cult director of such notoriously bad movies as *Plan 9 from Outer Space*. She appeared in a couple of Wood's movies before making a career change into the popular music industry.

## Factoring in poor marketing practices

In addition to the lackluster material from mediocre writers, RCA didn't market or package Elvis's albums wisely. His soundtrack albums were a hodgepodge of songs that lacked unity and consistency. And to top it off, the Colonel and the execs at RCA were determined to saturate the market by releasing material at an extremely rapid rate. RCA often released one Presley soundtrack while an earlier one was still on the charts. The standard practice was for a performer to get as much mileage as possible from an album before releasing the next one.

RCA and the Colonel released the albums this way in part because they were soundtrack albums, which had to follow the release dates of the movies. The Colonel in particular preferred this strategy, because he felt the soundtrack album advertised the film, which in turn reminded fans to buy the album. How effective this strategy was in selling Elvis's albums is open to debate.

## Focusing on the Fans

The question arises as to why Elvis's films and albums from this era continued to make money. Clearly, some of the audience grew weary of the Presley Travelogues, because the later films didn't gross on the same level as *Blue Hawaii* and *Viva Las Vegas*. Yet, they still made a substantial return on their investment.

The key to their success was the core of original fans, whom Parker courted with his promotional items, premiere privileges, and other gimmicks. Both Elvis and the Colonel held these fans in high regard and treated them with respect. Parker correctly estimated the power of this group of fans when he told a scriptwriter that a quarter of a million die-hard Elvis Presley fans were willing to see each movie three times. The fans believed Elvis's charisma transcended any mediocre material. When the lines formed at the box office, the people in those lines came to see Elvis and nothing else.

## Reflecting on Elvis's Movie Career

Despite the dissatisfaction and malaise that Elvis felt by the mid-1960s, he continued to make movies and record soundtrack albums. He really had no choice in the matter, considering he was contractually obligated to continue. In fact, by 1964 the Colonel had Elvis tied up with film deals until 1968. (See Chapters 9 and 10 for information on the end of Elvis's film career.)

Presley knew that he had lost his edge as a singer — mostly because the material was so dull — but no one was interested in making it more dynamic. After all, the albums sold well enough on their own, and the material worked more or less within the context of the films' narratives. Also, the albums promoted the movies, and the movies served to remind people to buy the albums. The system worked to everyone's financial advantage. From a business standpoint, investing money to change the system was senseless.

Elvis didn't reveal his distaste and profound dissatisfaction for his movies until he changed the course of his career at the end of the decade and completed his movie obligations. By that time, the movies had become less lucrative and a new career direction looked both creatively and financially promising for him. (You can read more about Elvis's career comeback in Chapter 11.)

# Chapter 9

# Looking Beyond the Presley Travelogue

### In This Chapter
▶ Considering the Elvis movies that didn't follow the Presley Travelogue formula
▶ Examining Elvis's movies from the early '60s
▶ Shedding light on the last films of Elvis's Hollywood career

The Presley Travelogue generally gets all the attention in discussions of Elvis's film career, though much of the commentary is negative. (See Chapter 7 for a thorough discussion of the Presley Travelogue, the nickname that Elvis himself bestowed on his formulaic musical comedies.) But a look at his complete filmography of 31 narrative features reveals that a third of them don't fit the formula for the typical Presley vehicle. No consideration of Elvis's Hollywood career can be complete — or accurate — without these films that break out of the mold.

Elvis starred in movies from a variety of genres, including musical dramas, westerns, melodramas, and farces, yet few Presley biographers examine these films at length. The glossing over of these films is perhaps because they complicate the standard view of Elvis's movies as repetitive, formulaic, and therefore, without merit.

In this chapter, I deviate from the norm to shine a spotlight on Elvis's non-formulaic films, noting important details about their production, offering insight into their strengths, and provoking thought about their importance. Interestingly, these films reflect aspects of American social history, giving them an interest beyond Elvis's career.

## Breaking the Travelogue Mold

If the typical Presley Travelogue film can be summarized as a musical comedy in an exotic setting that revolves around the romance of Elvis's cocky, adventure-loving character with the leading lady, then several of his films fall short of this description. His first four films released during the 1950s don't follow this formula, and biographers tend to treat these pre-army films with respect because they star the young Elvis. (Refer to Chapter 6 for a complete discussion of Elvis's musical dramas of the 1950s.) However, several films from the 1960s also deviate from the norm, yet these films are brushed over as anomalies, considered casualties of a squandered career, or simply ignored. In the following sections, I show you how these films differed from the standard Elvis movie.

## Delving into the genres and story lines

Elvis's non-Travelogue movies include westerns, a melodrama, satires/farces, a period comedy, and musical dramas. Some of these films feature serious themes that reflect the social issues and problems of the era, a characteristic generally not associated with Elvis movies. Others were based on best-selling novels and respectable literary sources. These latter films challenge the prevailing notion that his movies were mindless.

## Exploring Elvis's roles

In these non-Travelogue films, Elvis plays characters who live in tough, hard worlds where they must endure and survive personal and family hardships. The characters aren't carbon copies of each other, nor are they in keeping with his typical role. The variety of characters he played in these films exhibit a broader range of emotions than the typical Presley role. This emotional range pushed Elvis to stretch himself as an actor, especially early on.

## Clashing over the music

As odd as it may sound, Elvis longed to star in a film in which he didn't sing. To him, a non-singing role meant that he was an authentic actor, not a singer-turned-actor. However, Elvis's manager Colonel Tom Parker (also known as "the Colonel") held the opposite view. In regard to Elvis's films, Parker was completely uninterested in aesthetics, style, or selecting material that enhanced his client's acting prowess.

Instead, Parker believed that fans came to see Elvis's films in order to hear him sing. So, of course, Parker was adamant that songs be included. He also knew that the addition of songs meant a soundtrack album, which added more income to the coffers. When initial scripts didn't feature production numbers or songs, the Colonel persuaded the studios or the producers to include them.

**Remember:** Privately, Elvis was always disappointed when a film project was turned into a Presley vehicle by the inclusion of songs. However, he rarely questioned Parker's decisions or authority. (Flip to Chapter 4 for a thorough discussion of the dynamics between Parker and Presley.) At the time, Elvis realized that his acting career goals didn't match those of the Colonel or others involved in his films.

## Considering Four Films from the Early '60s

In this section, I examine four films from the early 1960s as a showcase for Elvis's acting ambitions. Even though he had high expectations for himself, he failed to become the accomplished actor he strived to be. However, these films did feature themes and ideas that spoke to important issues of the era, giving them an added depth and significance. Elvis made four films for these two different studios:

- **20th Century Fox:** This studio launched Elvis's career as an actor in 1956 with *Love Me Tender*. Then in 1960, the Colonel made a two-picture deal with Fox. Fox chose not to use Presley in the same way as producer Hal Wallis, who preferred to star Elvis in formulaic musical vehicles that exploited his existing image and popular singing style. (See Chapters 6 and 7 for a thorough examination of Wallis's strategy regarding Elvis's film career and his role as the "author" of the Presley Travelogue.) Instead, the folks at Fox cast Elvis in serious roles in dramatic films based on acclaimed novels. They placed him in an ensemble cast of several strong leading actors and venerable character actors, who were handled by renowned directors and veteran producers.

- **United Artists:** In 1962, Elvis signed a two-picture deal with the Mirisch brothers, who were producers with their own independent production company that released through United Artists. For the Mirisches, Elvis starred in *Follow That Dream* and *Kid Galahad,* which were both released in 1962. The Mirisches didn't strategize on the same level as 20th Century Fox, but like Fox, they didn't follow the formula for the Presley Travelogue.

**Trivia:** The average Presley Travelogue featured about a dozen songs, while 20th Century Fox had minimized the number of songs to two for *Flaming Star* and four for *Wild in the Country*. United Artists, on the other hand, offered a compromise at six for *Follow That Dream* and six for *Kid Galahad,* which was enough to satisfy the Colonel.

In the following sections, I discuss each of Elvis's four early films with Fox and United Artists, including plot details, differences between these films and the Travelogues, and a bit about what went on behind the scenes.

## Shooting a western: Flaming Star

*Flaming Star,* which was released in December 1960 by 20th Century Fox, gave Elvis the chance to prove himself as a serious actor. In this tragic western, Elvis plays Pacer Burton, the young son of a white settler and a Kiowa Indian. A Kiowa uprising forces Pacer to choose sides between the white settlers and his mother's people. The character endures prejudice, feels his first pangs of love, and suffers an identity crisis — a set of events that represented a broad range of emotions for Elvis to play. See Figure 9-1 for a look at Elvis in this role.

**Figure 9-1:** Elvis worked hard to be a serious actor in *Flaming Star* (1960).

*Flaming Star* touts a socially progressive story line that depicts the prejudice Pacer experiences because of his half-caste status. The plot may take place in the Old West of the 1870s, but the theme was relevant to race relations in the 1960s as well. The important story line certainly elevates the significance of *Flaming Star.*

### Feeling the pressure on the set

Unfortunately, Elvis's efforts to give a dynamic performance in *Flaming Star* fell short. A sense of unease developed between Elvis and director Don Siegel. Siegel wasn't thrilled that producer David Weisbart had hired Presley, but he accepted the situation. However, Elvis still felt the director's disapproval on the set.

Later, Siegel claimed that the singer's entourage of friends, assistants, and bodyguards were constantly on set. Elvis and his gang practiced karate, played touch football, and chased girls, and the director thought it interfered with communication between him and Elvis. The tension undoubtedly affected Elvis's performance, which was superficial and erratic compared to the other actors in the ensemble. He lacked control over his line delivery, especially during emotional scenes when he tended to blurt out his dialogue too rapidly.

**TRIVIA**

Elvis sang two songs in *Flaming Star:* the title song and "A Cane and a High-Starched Collar." A four-song print had been shown to a preview audience, but it was never released. Siegel may have thought that so many songs would detract from the movie's serious tone. Siegel may have been correct from an artistic point of view. After all, the movie received lots of good reviews. However, it was a box-office disappointment compared to *G.I. Blues,* and the Colonel blamed it on the lack of songs.

### Recognizing the strength of the cast

**REMEMBER**

Despite any shortcomings in Elvis's performance, *Flaming Star* remains a well-crafted, highly watchable western. Its success is due to the efforts of the cast and crew. Consider some of the high-profile industry personnel Fox gathered to produce the film:

- The ensemble included veteran character actor John McIntire, legendary Mexican movie star Dolores Del Rio, and respected actors Steve Forrest, Barbara Eden, and Richard Jaeckel. The advantage of an ensemble cast is that solid performances by the whole can balance the weaknesses of the individuals.

- Director Siegel, who later won critical acclaim for the original *Dirty Harry,* was a master of tightly directed action scenes, and his skills are evident in *Flaming Star.*

- The script was based on a popular novel by Clair Huffaker. Nunnally Johnson, a long-time Hollywood producer and screenwriter famous for scripting *The Grapes of Wrath,* cowrote the film with Huffaker.

- Established composer Cyril Mockridge produced the background music.

## Milking the melodrama: Wild in the Country

After *Flaming Star,* Elvis got another chance at serious acting in *Wild in the Country,* which was released in 1961 by 20th Century Fox. In this Southern melodrama, he stars as a young hothead named Glenn Tyler, whose anger and frustration are the result of his underprivileged background. After serving time in a juvenile hall, he's put under the care of a female psychiatrist, played by Hope Lange, who wants him to try college and become a writer. Two other women, played by Tuesday Weld and Millie Perkins, also play important roles in Glenn's life. He evolves from sullen to sensitive as the story line progresses, giving Elvis an opportunity to stretch himself as an actor. Elvis's performance is better in this film than in *Flaming Star,* and he exhibited some undeniable chemistry with spitfire Tuesday Weld, but he still has problems with rushing his line delivery and building a character with depth.

*Wild in the Country,* which was scripted by the legendary left-wing playwright Clifford Odets and directed by socially conscious scriptwriter Philip Dunne, exhibits a class consciousness that points out the disparities between the advantaged middle classes and the permanent underprivileged. Glenn's lack of opportunities, such as access to college, are presented as the reason for his violent tendencies; likewise, the lack of opportunity and class prejudice that Tuesday Weld's character experiences result in her promiscuous behavior. The characters embody progressive liberal ideas on poverty, class, and crime. The effort of Odets and Dunne to imbue a conventional melodrama with important themes makes this film a respectable addition to Elvis's filmography.

No songs were included in the original script for *Wild in the Country,* but when *Flaming Star* didn't perform to expectations at the box office, six musical numbers were added. Four made the final cut, including the title song, "I Slipped, I Stumbled, and I Fell," "In My Way," and "Husky Dusky Day." The film still failed to meet box-office expectations, and the Colonel again blamed the lack of songs. But his assessment wasn't necessarily accurate.

## Tackling satire: Follow That Dream

Elvis gives one of his most successful performances as Toby Kwimper in the lighthearted social satire *Follow That Dream,* which was released in 1962 by United Artists. In the film, Toby and his backwoods family claim squatters' rights on an empty stretch of beach in sunny Florida, and then build a homestead there out of salvaged materials, much to the chagrin of local officials. Stuffy bureaucrats try to get rid of the honest, down-home Kwimpers, who don't care for the complexities of the modern world but whose approach to life is the essence of true family values.

On the surface Toby appears to be a dumb rube, because he speaks with an accent, displays no interest in material things, and sees the world in a simple way. A lustful female psychiatrist and two shady gamblers try to take advantage of Toby, but he foils them. Elvis's layered performance as Toby required him to portray a character who the people in the film believe to be simple and incapable, but who audiences know to be clever and resourceful, without altering the nature of the performance. The rube who isn't as dumb as sophisticated urban dwellers believe him to be is a staple character in Southern culture. So, because of his own Southern roots, Elvis undoubtedly understood the nature of this character. Elvis also exhibited a flair for real character comedy in this film, a talent he would rarely have the opportunity to showcase again.

*Follow That Dream* featured a half-dozen songs. Most of them were serviceable tunes in that they fleshed out the characters or plot, but the title song was above average. Like most well-made musical comedies, the solid cast of character actors added a lot of fun and charm to the film. Comedy veterans Arthur O'Connell, who played the head of the Kwimper clan, and Roland Winters, who played the judge, were particularly effective.

*TRIVIA*

As based on the acclaimed novel *Pioneer, Go Home* by Richard Powell, *Follow That Dream* is a clever satire on the frustrations of our fast-paced, modern society, whose members have forgotten the simple pleasures of life.

## Making a musical drama: Kid Galahad

*Kid Galahad,* a remake of a Depression-era Warner Bros. film, tells the story of a naive boxer, played by Elvis, who's manipulated by a hungry manager eager to make the big time. The original film from 1937 benefited from the gritty, low-budget Warner Bros. style, but this United Artist remake produced by the Mirisch Brothers in 1962 lacks an effective visual style to re-create a boxing milieu.

In this film, Elvis holds his own in a cast that includes such noteworthy stars as Gig Young, Charles Bronson, Ed Asner, and Lola Albright. Perhaps he was improving as an actor through the experience of working in several films of different genres, or maybe he simply was more relaxed on the United Artists sets than on the Fox sets, where expectations were greater and the directors more demanding.

The film featured conventional movie-musical songs, but they didn't help the film at the box office. The film made a respectable $2 million upon its initial release, but it paled in comparison to *Blue Hawaii*.

## Factoring in the Final Films

Elvis's last four movies differed from the formulaic Presley Travelogue, but they were produced from 1967 to 1968, a period of transition for the singer. During this time, Elvis had become completely disillusioned with Hollywood, and he was in the process of making some important career changes. He didn't seem to care that he had finally broken free of the Travelogue formula, and he also didn't use these roles to turn around his film career.

From all accounts, Elvis simply wanted to finish his existing film contracts and get them out of the way. By the time his last film, *Change of Habit,* was in production, Elvis was experiencing a comeback to the music scene, and his talents and creative focus were directed toward honing a new musical style and returning to live performances. (See Chapter 11 for a full discussion of

Elvis's comeback to musical prominence.) Despite his musical comeback, the tunes in these films don't reflect the new direction of his music. With a couple of notable exceptions, the songs remain standard movie-musical fare.

*REMEMBER*

Elvis's last four films, made for a variety of studios and producers, recouped their investment money at the box office. However, even though they didn't flop, they made very little over their investment costs. In the eyes of the Colonel and some of Elvis's contracting studios, this meager return signaled an end to his success in the movies. Studios and producers who had worked with Elvis for years, including MGM and Hal Wallis, didn't renegotiate contracts after 1967.

In dealing with these final films, biographers, music historians, and other writers take their cue from Elvis's lack of interest. Most of them barely mention the last four films, often erroneously grouping them with the typical Presley Travelogues. Like Elvis, they were in a hurry to move on to another chapter of his life and didn't take these films seriously. The films lack the craftsmanship and production values of the movies mentioned earlier in the chapter, but they represent an aspect of Presley's film career that deserves consideration.

*REMEMBER*

The key difference between Elvis's later films and his earlier musical comedies is the attempt to adapt to changing times both in the film industry and in the country in general. A criticism aimed at Elvis's Hollywood is how old fashioned the films had become by the late 1960s. However, in sweeping his later films under the rug, biographers and historians ignore the ways in which his movies actually did reflect the changing times.

In the following sections, besides discussing how these films differ from the Travelogue formula, I also focus on the way Elvis's last films reflect the changing times in Hollywood and across the country. I put them in the context of the times to point out some interesting qualities and surprising strengths. As you read through the sections, consider the following topics:

- **Sex:** Despite the romance that was part and parcel of the Presley Travelogues, Elvis's characters did little more than kiss the leading ladies. By the late 1960s, however, attitudes toward the depiction of romance and sex on the big screen had loosened. Surprisingly, Elvis's film *Live a Little, Love a Little* wrestles with the new attitudes toward sexual mores, making this film more adult in tone.

- **Violence:** The loosening of censorship guidelines in the industry made graphic violence more common in the new Hollywood, a factor that becomes relevant to Elvis's western *Charro!*

- **Politics:** The politics and social consciousness of the 1960s made an impact on the story lines of *Change of Habit* and *The Trouble with Girls*. Both films include scenes dealing with prejudice, and the former draws attention to the poverty and lack of opportunity in the nation's inner cities.

## Sleeping with the girl (finally): Live a Little, Love a Little

*Live a Little, Love a Little,* released in 1968, became the first Presley film to include premarital sex. In the story line, Elvis's character Greg Nolan, a slick photographer who works for a *Playboy*-type magazine called *Classic Cat,* has an accident on the beach and recuperates in the beach house of a kooky '60s girl. In the course of their unconventional relationship, they share a night of passion, even though the audience doesn't actually see it. In addition to really getting the girl, Greg enjoys another 1960s-style episode when he experiences a psychedelic dream sequence complete with go-go dancers and a man dressed in a dog suit.

An offbeat comedy about sex and romance, *Live a Little, Love a Little* exhibits a screwball quality that's refreshingly hip compared to the formulaic Presley Travelogues. Despite its refreshing quality, however, the film's characterization and plotting are weak. The movie didn't fare well at the box office, and the studio felt it too lackluster for a release in the United Kingdom, despite Elvis's fan base there.

Considering that Elvis's films were targeted to fans, who were now older, and marketed to mainstream audiences, including families, the addition of premarital sex and nonconformist characters reflect how tastes and social standards loosened during the course of the swinging '60s. The film also reveals the industry's attempt to reinvent familiar genres — like the romantic comedy — to stay relevant to the times.

Only four songs made up the soundtrack to this film. Of those, "A Little Less Conversation" proved to be the best, though at the time, it was cast aside with the other tunes. It wasn't released until 1973 when it appeared on the album *Almost in Love.* However, the lively tune was remixed and revised in 2002, when it topped the charts in the United Kingdom. It was released on the 2002 hit compilation *ELVIS 30 #1 Hits.*

## Reminiscing with a period piece: The Trouble with Girls

Elvis's 1969 period comedy *The Trouble with Girls* exhibits no signs of updating the material with contemporary themes, even though it was released by MGM, the same studio that produced *Live a Little, Love a Little.* (Refer to the preceding section, "Sleeping with the girl (finally): Live a Little, Love a Little," for more on this movie.)

In *The Trouble with Girls,* Elvis stars as Walter Hale, the manager of a 1920s Chautauqua, which was a traveling tent show that provided education as well as entertainment. Walter is relatively new to his job, and he's trying to prove himself with the former manager. Sometimes he reverts to less-than-scrupulous methods, but he leads the show to great success in the end. The film offered a slice of Americana from the past. A few of the subplots didn't involve Elvis, so he wasn't the focus of every scene. The period setting and the reduction in screen time for Elvis's character weren't typical of his movies. By this time, Elvis's films weren't performing to anyone's expectations; in the case of *Trouble,* the Colonel was reluctant to gather and report the box-office statistics.

Six songs were included to round out the story line, but none of them are memorable. Indeed, a couple of them represent low points even for the soundtrack recordings, including "The Whiffenpoof Song."

## Breaking into the Italian western genre: Charro!

In 1969, Elvis finally starred in a film in which his character didn't sing even one song — the western *Charro!* Elvis crooned the title song over the credits, but his character, Jess Wade, never once broke into tuneful reverie. Elvis had longed for a role that pushed his musician side to the background for some time. Unfortunately, it was too late, and he was no longer interested in his film career.

The script for *Charro!* indicated that this gritty western was to be in the mold of Clint Eastwood's Italian westerns, which were enormously popular in the late 1960s. Italian westerns featured violent, scruffy-looking cowboys who frequently double-crossed each other. Even the good guys weren't heroic in the traditional sense. Presley's character, Jess Wade, is a former bad guy who comes up against his old gang, which is terrorizing a small Mexican town. Jess uses a lot of gun powder and violence to stop them.

At first, Elvis expressed enthusiasm for this film, because the original script kept closely to the explicit sex and graphic violence associated with the Italian western. To Elvis, this signified that the film was targeted to a serious adult audience. Unfortunately, by the time he showed up on the set, the violent gunfights and seedy brothel scenes had been toned down considerably and replaced by conventional barroom brawls and unhappy saloon girls. In addition to the watered-down script, the film's director, Charles Marquis Warren, lacked the talent or insight to effectively re-create the unique style of the Italian western. Disillusioned once again, Elvis went through the paces, anxious to get the film over with.

The budget for *Charro!* was $1.5 million, and the film made little profit. The Colonel no longer kept or released statistics, perhaps because the films weren't doing as well, or perhaps because both Elvis and the Colonel's interests lay elsewhere.

Composer Hugo Montenegro, who had done the music for some Italian westerns, wrote and arranged the background music for *Charro!*

## Getting dramatic: Change of Habit

In his final big-screen appearance, Elvis starred as Dr. John Carpenter, a doctor who practices in an inner-city slum. A social drama with a strong cast, *Change of Habit* (1969) co-stars Mary Tyler Moore as one of three nurses who are sent to help the inner-city doctor. However, Elvis's character doesn't realize that these nurses are also nuns, and he falls in love with Moore's character. The story was very loosely based on the real life of a nun who had worked with children who had speech handicaps.

The film would have benefited from being shot on location in an inner-city neighborhood, because the Universal back lot where it was shot looks artificial and less than authentic. Also, the idealistic resolution the film offers to deep-seated social issues is trite. Nonetheless, the events in the story line reflect the social turmoil and violent trauma that major cities were facing in the late 1960s, including the inequalities of healthcare in the ghettos, the disenfranchisement of minorities, and the breakdown of and need for a change in social institutions, such as law and order and the church.

The director of *Change of Habit,* a young man named Billy Graham, used improvisations and other acting exercises to help his actors understand the motivations of their characters. These tactics became common and accepted among a new generation of directors and actors. Elvis would have benefited from them earlier in his career. According to Graham, Elvis did very well in these exercises when he was interested, but he wasn't always willing to make the effort. His lack of interest was perhaps due to his disillusionment with Hollywood.

Only four songs were used in the film. One of them, "Rubberneckin'" is a decent pop-rock tune, which was recorded in Memphis at American Sound Studio during Elvis's sessions with talented producer Chips Moman. (See Chapter 11 for more on these sessions.)

*Change of Habit* was probably the kind of film Elvis would have preferred to star in for most of his acting career, but never had the opportunity. Unfortunately, it was too little, too late. By the time *Change of Habit* went into production, Elvis had decided against acting in any more films.

# Chapter 10

# Defending Elvis's Movies: They're Not That Bad

### In This Chapter

- Understanding the criticism of Elvis's movies
- Taking a look at the teen musical
- Seeing Elvis's career as a model that other singers followed

Finding value, entertainment, and meaning in Elvis's movies is definitely the minority viewpoint. A look at many of the Presley biographies, memoirs, and career overviews reveals that the prevailing opinion of Elvis's movies is a negative one. The low opinion began with Elvis himself, who became so disillusioned with the direction that his film career took that he eventually dismissed his entire Hollywood experience. (Glance at Chapter 8 for more on Elvis's perspective on his movies.) The viewpoint was continued by biographers who looked down on his film career because it changed Elvis from a notorious rock 'n' roller to a conventional movie star, making him less exciting and less innovative in their eyes.

However, the reasoning behind the prevailing view doesn't really hold up under close scrutiny. Elvis had personal reasons for turning his back on his movies, so he didn't see them in an objective light. And, those writers who criticize Elvis's movies often fail to put his Hollywood career in context of the film industry. When considered in context, Elvis's movies actually fit neatly into a kind of musical comedy that, at the time, was popular with youth audiences and lucrative at the box office. In these films, young pop singers, like Elvis, were tapped to star in lighthearted romantic tales with themes, plotlines, character types, and music relevant to a new generation but still appealing to a wide range of ages. As a matter of fact, Elvis's contributions to this subgenre were better crafted and acted than most.

Not only were Elvis's films in this subgenre financially successful, but they also turned the singer into a movie star, which meant he was accepted and popular with the mainstream audiences in a way he certainly hadn't been in the 1950s. Falling into mainstream popularity was his management team's objective from the beginning. Elvis's career path from controversial rock 'n' roller popular with a niche audience to successful pop-singing movie star accepted by the mainstream serves as a model for contemporary hip-hop, rap, and other performers hoping for a lengthy career in show business.

In this chapter, I explain the shortcomings of the common critical perception of Elvis's film career and explain why it has become the prevailing view. I also offer an alternative understanding of the movies based on the subgenre to which they belong. In addition, I talk about the movie music in relation to its specific purpose within the films, which allows you to appreciate it or at least tolerate it. I round out this chapter by comparing Elvis's career path to those of contemporary stars seeking mainstream acceptance.

# Understanding Why the Movies Need to Be Defended

Elvis's Hollywood career needs a solid defense, because few writers have ever considered it within the context of the period or within the framework of the film industry. Therefore, few have discussed it with authority. Biographers, music historians, and others who criticize Elvis's movies tend to consider the films in retrospect of his entire career.

In comparing his movie-era work to the innovative sound and cultural significance of his 1950s music, the sweet pop sound and clean-cut image don't measure up. From the perspective of these writers, Hollywood robbed Elvis of everything that was unique about his music and performing style. This view not only taints their discussion of the movies but also results in a narrow discourse on this entire phase of his career. And, many writers use the fact that Elvis saw his film career as a failure as further validation of their low opinion.

In this section, I tell you about Elvis's disappointment in his career and the initial criticism of his films. I also tell you why this criticism is misplaced.

## Factoring in Elvis's dissatisfaction

Elvis himself made fun of his movies in his later life, and he often remarked bitterly that he was disillusioned with his film career. Because Elvis thought his tenure in Hollywood was a disappointment, it was easy for everyone else to pick up on his cues and declare his film career a failure. To set the record straight, I reflect here on some of the reasons behind Elvis's dissatisfaction with his Hollywood career.

# Chapter 10: Defending Elvis's Movies: They're Not That Bad

In the August 11, 1969, issue of *Newsweek* magazine, Elvis announced that his film career was over, remarking, "I got tired of playing a guy who gets into a fight, then starts singing to the guy he's just beat up." This declaration is often quoted in biographies and career overviews to "prove" that Elvis's film career wasted his talents. After all, even he found his movies to be ridiculous.

Part of Elvis's opinion was based on his profound dislike of the musical comedy genre. He didn't like the type of movie in which the characters randomly burst into song, because he felt it was unrealistic. This type of musical is clearly an acquired taste. Some viewers can suspend disbelief and accept this fanciful convention of the genre; others can't. Elvis fell into the latter camp, and unfortunately, the musical comedy was the type of movie he was most associated with.

However, the main reason for his resentment was his failure to be taken seriously as an actor. From his first weeks in Hollywood, Elvis dreamed of becoming a serious actor in dramatic roles, but these desires didn't pan out. He grew more bitter and disappointed with each movie he made. (See Chapters 6 for a complete understanding of Elvis's goals in his film career.) His suspicions that his movie career wouldn't pan out like he had dreamed turned into a bitter realization with a specific incident involving film producer Hal Wallis.

Here's what happened: In April 1964, during the last days of shooting on Elvis's film *Roustabout* (1964), a story appeared in the entertainment press regarding Wallis's upcoming film *Becket* (1964), starring two of the most respected actors of the time, Peter O'Toole and Richard Burton. The article described how Wallis financed *Becket* based on the projected revenue for *Roustabout,* because Wallis's Presley features always made money. The article was condescending toward Elvis's movies, suggesting how ironic it was that such a prestigious film starring "two brilliant Shakespearean-trained actors" was dependent on "Sir Swivel Hips." *Becket* went on to win acclaim and an Academy Award for best adapted screenplay, while *Roustabout* was treated as just another fluffy musical comedy.

This article made Elvis realize that Wallis was never going to star him in a film of the caliber of *Becket.* He discovered that the producer's plan was to make money from his musical comedies in order to finance the kind of film that Elvis had always wanted to act in. Elvis felt used — and then eventually used up.

In an oft-quoted statement, Wallis once declared, "A Presley picture is the only sure thing in Hollywood."

## Examining the standard view of Elvis's movies

As soon as Elvis's last Hollywood feature film was released in 1969, the singer felt free to express his poor opinion of his movie career. In public, his criticism took the form of the occasional joke about the lightweight nature of his movies, but in private conversations, his view was considerably more bitter. After Elvis died, biographers took up his negative viewpoint and even expanded on it. Unfortunately, the biographers tended to be music critics or historians, which colored their perspectives and didn't prepare them for understanding how the film industry worked.

Two main criticisms of Elvis's movie career emerged from the first wave of biographies published after his death, and these two ideas have been repeated by subsequent authors until they have become clichés. The first criticism maintains that Elvis could have been a successful serious actor if he hadn't been tied down by the formulaic musical comedies. The other criticism blames the movies for a "decline" in his music as he changed from rock 'n' roll to the softer pop-rock sound of the movie soundtracks. Upon examination, neither of these critical assumptions is an accurate assessment of what happened with Elvis's movie career.

In this section, I take a general look at the first Elvis biographers and why their specific backgrounds and expertise colored their interpretations of Presley's film career. Then I examine their criticisms, looking at them from a film history perspective, to point out their shortcomings.

### Considering the biographers

Throughout most of his career, Elvis's manager Colonel Tom Parker (also often referred to as simply "the Colonel") controlled the access to his client by the media or other writers. Subsequently, Elvis left behind no definitive interview or lengthy discussion in which he defended, analyzed, or explained his music or career choices. So after his death, biographers depended on secondary sources, such as friends, associates, and family members, for information on the private Elvis. Some of these interviewees had faulty memories, and some had their own agendas, making their remembrances suspect. Also, these biographers were freer to speculate about the Colonel's handling of Elvis's career, because neither Elvis nor Parker was on record explaining their strategies and opinions in detail.

The first serious writers to put Elvis's career and contributions into any kind of cultural perspective after the singer died were rock-music historians, including Dave Marsh and Greil Marcus. These two writers had honed their craft and perspective as writers for *Rolling Stone* magazine, and it showed in their assessment of Presley's Hollywood career. Their views were critical and derisive, because the movies had spelled the end of Elvis the notorious rock 'n' roller. And, of course, that was the part of Elvis's career these writers were most interested in. They also believed that Elvis's movie career weakened his musical output during the 1960s by forcing him to record softer pop-influenced material, so they disliked most — if not all — of the movie music. Other biographers who approached Elvis's life from a music perspective wrote similarly of his Hollywood career. The formulaic nature of movie vehicles added to the criticism heaped on the films by biographers who were rock 'n' roll reviewers or music historians.

Though wonderful writers and perceptive music critics, writers like Marsh and Marcus lacked insight into the history and inner workings of Hollywood, making their opinions about Elvis's movies just that — opinion. Instead of understanding the Presley Travelogues as musical vehicles deliberately constructed by Wallis to show off Elvis's premiere talent — singing — they tended to simplistically blame the Colonel for exploiting Presley and squandering his talents. Later writers simply repeated the perspective of these first serious biographers, propagating the criticism of the Hollywood movies and their music. However, these critics tended to praise those pre-army movies in which a hard-rockin' Elvis sang and looked like . . . well, a hard-rockin' Elvis.

These biographers and music historians tend to regard Elvis's films in isolation, without relating them to other movies that were popular at the time or to the era that produced them. Like all popular arts, movies reflect the times that produce them, and they're subject to a variety of influences that surround them. To consider Elvis's films without a discussion of the era, the influences, or the industry is to leave out much of the story. (Flip to the later section "Appreciating Elvis's Movies As Part of the Teen Musical Subgenre" for more information on how to best compare Elvis's movies to those produced during the same time period.)

### Disputing the claim that Elvis should have been a serious actor

One of the oft-repeated criticisms about Elvis's movie career claims that he could have been a serious actor if only he had been allowed to appear in big-budget, high-profile projects. But, there's no guarantee that he would have been successful. Throughout the history of Hollywood, scores of performers from other arenas of entertainment have attempted serious acting careers, and many of them have been successful. But, some have experienced only limited success in movies. Some even failed completely.

During the 1960s, the film industry was in a period of transition and more unpredictable than usual. Achieving stardom was even a riskier toss of the dice. Several pop singers embarked on Hollywood careers during that period just like Elvis had, and many of them co-starred in serious films by major directors. Yet, they experienced only limited success as legitimate actors. If Elvis had abandoned the musical vehicles that his audiences preferred, he might have fizzled out as a serious actor like pop singers Pat Boone, Tommy Sands, Ricky Nelson, Fabian, and Frankie Avalon had when they tried to reach beyond their natural charisma and singing talents.

A variation on the argument that Elvis could have been a great actor purports that Elvis should have followed in the acting footsteps of rebels James Dean and Marlon Brando by appearing in serious dramas in which he played rebels, outsiders, antiheroes, or mavericks. He had started down that path with *Jailhouse Rock* and *King Creole,* and he returned to that sort of character in *Wild in the Country,* but the musical comedies pushed him in a different direction.

However, both Dean and Brando had seriously studied the Method approach to acting at the prestigious Actors Studio in New York City. The Method is an internal approach to acting in which the actor attempts to step into the emotional and mental shoes of his character. The actor uses personal memories and experiences to realistically portray intense emotions. The Method requires study and practice to accomplish well. Elvis, on the other hand, was never trained. During Elvis's heyday in Hollywood, the new wave of legitimate actors who were gaining attention in the film industry had studied acting as a craft in college or in acting schools. How far Elvis's natural charm and charisma would have taken him in serious drama is unknown. Without training, Elvis had no guarantee that he could have handled complex, serious roles in the long term.

When looking at the state of the industry during the time frame of Elvis's career, and considering his lack of formal training, it's clear that his chances of becoming a James Dean, a Marlon Brando, or any other serious actor weren't good. The biographers that suggest otherwise fail to consider film history.

### Disputing the criticism that the movies hurt his music

Some say that Elvis's Hollywood career weakened his music and squandered his musical and creative talents. But, this argument indirectly proposes several assumptions about his movie career, including the suggestion that Elvis would have continued to be a rock 'n' roll innovator if not for his "going Hollywood." Whether Elvis would have continued as a musical innovator if he hadn't pursued a Hollywood career is speculative at best, but most likely he would have still abandoned his regionally flavored rock 'n' roll style for several reasons.

When Elvis returned from the army in 1960, he was faced with a new music scene. Ballad singers and pop stylists had increased in popularity during the late 1950s, softening rock 'n' roll as a genre until the mid-1960s. At that point, the British Invasion spearheaded by The Beatles changed the direction of rock once again. The early 1960s were dominated by the smooth sounds of singers such as Frankie Avalon, Pat Boone, Fabian, Paul Anka, Connie Francis, Bobby Darin, and Tommy Sands. The trend represented a shift from the doo-wop, rhythm-and-blues, and Southern-flavored rockabilly that rocked the radio airwaves and shocked the industry pundits in the mid-1950s. So Elvis's pop-rock music of the 1960s fit nicely into the pop sounds of the era.

**Chapter 10: Defending Elvis's Movies: They're Not That Bad**

REMEMBER: Perhaps one of the reasons critics of his pop sound and mature image dismiss his music during this era is because Elvis set trends during the 1950s, but he seemed to merely follow them in the 1960s.

One of the most compelling reasons that Elvis wouldn't have continued singing his regionally flavored rock 'n' roll involved the nasty scandals surrounding this style of music. In addition to the accusations that the music incited juvenile delinquency and riots, several specific rock 'n' roll pioneers got into trouble while Elvis was in the army.

In 1958, for example, the press discovered that Elvis's fellow Sun Studio recording artist Jerry Lee Lewis had married his 13-year-old cousin while still married to his first wife. Lewis was virtually blackballed in the industry. Radio stations refused to play his records and many of his tour bookings were cancelled. The year before, flamboyant entertainer Little Richard turned his back on rock 'n' roll when he found God. The singer walked away from the music industry during a major tour, causing huge losses for booking agents and tour promoters. Later, when he wanted to return to show business, his earlier actions made agents and promoters leery of booking him. In 1960, "Johnny B. Good" singer Chuck Berry was charged with a Mann Act violation when he drove an underage girl across state lines. He was convicted and went to prison for almost three years.

During the 1950s, many in the media felt that Elvis was headed for scandals such as these because of his provocative performing style. However, his stint in the army had cooled the controversy and paved the way for a different career path — one that wisely steered him away from the notoriety of rockabilly and rock 'n' roll. (See Chapter 7 for more information on the effect of Elvis's army service on his career.)

## *Appreciating Elvis's Movies As Part of the Teen Musical Subgenre*

Elvis wasn't the only pop or rock 'n' roll singer to star in lighthearted musical comedies or the occasional youth-oriented melodrama during the 1960s. From Elvis and Frankie Avalon to Herman's Hermits, many of the decade's chart-topping singers and bands found themselves in vehicles developed around their signature sounds or styles. These films share enough characteristics to be identifiable as a specific *subgenre,* or subcategory, of the musical comedy. Elvis's films are part of this subgenre known as *teen musicals.*

In this section, I describe the characteristics of the teen musical and put the subgenre in context of the times to show how it reflects the issues, preoccupations, and culture of the young. I also show you how Elvis's films fit neatly into this group. When comparing the Presley Travelogues to other films in the same subgenre, the success of his movies makes sense — and their fluffiness seems less objectionable.

## *The typical teen musical*

Teen musicals evolved from the low-budget, black-and-white rock 'n' roll movies pioneered by the King of the Quickies, Sam Katzman, in the 1950s. (See Chapter 8 for information on how Katzman crossed paths with Elvis.) Like Katzman's quickies, later teen musicals appealed to a youthful demographic by showcasing the music of performers that young people idolized as well as the slang and fashion fads of the day. Unlike Katzman's movies, teen musicals of the 1960s were shot in Technicolor, making them candy-colored romantic fantasies for the young — or the young at heart.

The success of the teen musical, including the Presley Travelogues, began with the music, which was the bait to draw in the target audience. The teen musical's appeal also depended on capturing the sense of fun and optimism that goes with being young, while at the same time underpinning it with the accepted ideals and values of mainstream culture. So, Elvis's singing, girl-chasing characters breeze into town looking for the big score, a new adventure, or the next race, but what they find instead is the right girl and the potential for a happy family.

Consider how the following elements fit into the teen musical:

- **Music:** Teen musicals cram as many songs or musical acts as possible into running times. During Elvis's era, some of the musicals featured pop-flavored songs that sounded more like a Hollywood executive's idea of what rock music should be. Others included performances by actual rock 'n' roll bands of the era.

- **Plot:** Plots of teen musicals revolve around the romantic complications of teens and young adults, who are depicted as living in a world of their own. Adults are outsiders to this world, so they are relegated to comic relief or uptight authority figures. The audiences' identification with the troubles, trends, music, and slang of this youth-oriented world is a key to a teen musical's success.

- **Setting:** Stories for teen musicals are often set in locations popular with teens. During Elvis's day, these included vacation resorts, Ft. Lauderdale, and other beachlike spots. The films capture the pleasures of youthful pastimes, which in Elvis's day included car racing, surfing, playing sports, nightclub hopping, or meeting at the local hangout.

✓ **Conflict:** Teen musicals also reflect serious youth-oriented dilemmas, particularly those involving individuality versus peer pressure; freedom versus responsibility; romance versus sex; and youth versus maturity. While the story lines are lighthearted and some of the characters comical and fun loving, it's the themes that audiences relate to because these are serious issues that most young people struggle with.

The teen musicals from the 1960s that were set at the beach remain the most well-known examples, because they have become an icon of American pop culture. The best-remembered beach movies, which starred Annette Funicello and Frankie Avalon, were produced quickly by low-budget champions American International Pictures (AIP). The series started with *Beach Party* (1963) and followed with several additional movies using the same formula. In each film, Funicello played DeeDee, who spent most of the plot trying to keep Frankie, played by Avalon, in check. As the series continued, the subplots became zanier, adding bikers, mermaids, and evil twins to the mix.

When the beach began to look too familiar, the party moved to the ski slopes. A whole new subseries was born after producer Gene Corman at AIP decided to use a ski resort as the setting for *Ski Party*. Not to be outdone in the wacky department, *Ski Party* featured a talking, skiing polar bear. This sort of zany, unrealistic detail is not unusual in the teen musical, so the exaggerated characters and plot events of Elvis's *Kissin' Cousins* and *Harum Scarum* are in keeping with the subgenre. (See Chapter 8 for a more information on these two films.)

Some of the British rock groups that invaded American shores in the mid-1960s also were packaged into musical vehicles to showcase their mod fashions, long hair, discothèque hangouts, and specific style of rock music. Peter Noone's band, Herman's Hermits, made a splash with their feature film *Hold On!* (1966) while the Dave Clark Five muddled through *Catch Us If You Can* (1965).

## The Presley Travelogues

Elvis's vehicles make sense when considered within the context of the teen musical (described in the preceding section). The formulaic plots, endless songs, and wacky moments that stretch believability aren't so much weaknesses in his films, because they're typical of the subgenre. In the following sections, I compare and contrast Elvis's movies in this subgenre with the typical teen musical.

> ## Elvis's best costars
>
> The following list includes some names you probably recognize. Each actor or actress here is respected within the film industry, and their talents contributed to the production values of the Presley Travelogues.
>
> - Walter Matthau, Carolyn Jones, and Dean Jagger in *King Creole* (1958)
> - Juliet Prowse in *G.I. Blues* (1960)
> - Dolores Del Rio and John McIntire in *Flaming Star* (1960)
> - Angela Lansbury in *Blue Hawaii* (1961)
> - Gig Young in *Kid Galahad* (1962)
> - Tuesday Weld, Hope Lange, and Millie Perkins in *Wild in the Country* (1961)
> - Arthur O'Connell in *Follow That Dream* (1962) and *Kissin' Cousins* (1964)
> - Ann-Margret in *Viva Las Vegas* (1964)
> - Barbara Stanwyck and Leif Erickson in *Roustabout* (1964)
> - Joan Blondell in *Stay Away, Joe* (1968)
> - Mary Tyler Moore and Jane Elliot in *Change of Habit* (1969)

### Comparing the similarities

In general, the Presley Travelogues adapted many of the conventions of the teen musical. Consider these characteristics, which mirror the conventions listed in the preceding section:

- **Music:** The Travelogues averaged 10 to 12 songs per film.
- **Plot:** Like other teen musicals, the plots focused on romance while the characters worked to achieve a recognizable goal, such as winning a race, finding a job, or earning money.
- **Setting:** The Travelogues were set in exotic locales or vacation spots, such as Las Vegas, Acapulco, the World's Fair, Ft. Lauderdale, or simply the race track or beach.
- **Conflict:** Elvis's character generally matured from a footloose and fancy-free race car driver, pilot, or charter-boat skipper to responsible husband material by the end of the movie, reflecting a key theme. Elvis's movies contrasted the fun of staying young and chasing girls with the responsibility of being in a mature relationship.

In addition to following the conventions of the teen musical subgenre in general, some of Elvis's movies also were directly influenced by specific films. Here are some examples:

- After spring break in Ft. Lauderdale and other resort areas became a popular subject (with the films *Where the Boys Are* [1960] and *Palm Springs Weekend* [1963]), Elvis starred in his own Lauderdale adventure, which was titled *Girl Happy* (1965).

- When the mod scene in England and Europe was all the rage, as in *Catch Us If You Can* (1965), Elvis appeared in *Double Trouble* (1967), which featured the swinging discothèques of London and Amsterdam.
- The considerable number of Presley Travelogues set near tropical beaches, including *Blue Hawaii* (1961), *Paradise, Hawaiian Style* (1966), and *Clambake* (1967), reflected the popularity of the Frankie and Annette beach movies.

Many of the costars in Elvis's films also appeared in the other teen musicals. An entire troupe of actors became instantly recognizable for their association with this subgenre. Nancy Sinatra, Yvonne Craig, Shelley Fabares, Gary Crosby, Pam Austin, Joby Baker, and Chris Noel crossed over from one teen musical to another. And no matter how much they aged, they were always welcome at the party.

### *Contrasting the differences*

The Presley Travelogues differ from the teen musicals because they were intended for a mainstream audience of older adults, children, and families in addition to the audience of teens and young adults. Unlike the typical teen musical, Elvis's films include children and senior citizens, and it wasn't unusual for his character to become attached to a child as part of his maturing process (as in *It Happened at the World's Fair* [1963] and *Paradise, Hawaiian Style* [1966]). In both instances, Elvis's character is forced into a situation in which he has to look out for a child's safety, which reveals his maturity and responsibility. Likewise, Elvis's characters sometimes sang to older people, such as the leading lady's grandmother, which helped Elvis appeal to the age group least familiar with teen musicals.

Unlike many of the teen musicals, Elvis's films are surprisingly multicultural. In *Blue Hawaii,* his character dates a native Hawaiian against his mother's wishes, and he easily adopts aspects of her culture, symbolized by his final musical number, "Hawaiian Wedding Song." In *Girls! Girls! Girls!* he's close friends with a Chinese family, and he sings to their young daughters. In *Paradise, Hawaiian Style,* his character works with a Japanese partner, played by Japanese actor James Shigeta.

Elvis's films also stand out from the crowd because many of them boast high-quality production values, especially those produced by Hal Wallis. By *production values,* I mean the craftsmanship of a film and how well basic filmmaking techniques are used to enhance the material, no matter how slight that material might be. Wallis employed veteran Hollywood directors, cinematographers, and editors to ensure that his films had the highest level of craftsmanship. He took advantage of shooting on location to showcase the exotic scenery or to capture a sense of authenticity, and he hired some of Hollywood's best scene-stealing character actors to elevate the level of acting. Better budgets accounted in part for the high production values but they also were the result of Wallis's talents and experience. One need only compare *Blue Hawaii* to *Beach Party* to see the difference between Elvis's teen musicals and the typical example of the genre. Both are fun to watch, but the Wallis-produced *Blue Hawaii* exhibits higher production values.

A review of *Easy Come, Easy Go* (1967) from *Variety* commented on the quality of Elvis's movies: "Anyone who has seen similar films recognizes the superior quality of Presley's films; the story makes sense; the songs are better, and better motivated; cast and direction are stronger; production values are first-rate."

Part of the quality of Elvis's films comes from his fellow actors. He worked with some of the best in the business, past and present. Some of his colleagues were movie stars, some starlets, some character actors, and some veterans from another era, but all of them raised the level of the acting in the films, causing the films to stand out from the average teen musical. See the nearby sidebar "Elvis's best costars" for a list of the most notable actors and actresses he worked with during this period.

## Revealing how the movie music works

Those who criticize the movie music in Elvis's vehicles tend to overlook the songs' critical functions in helping tell the story. This lack of understanding sheds a different light on the songs, which may work well within the context of the story but seem silly outside of the movies. To truly evaluate Elvis's movie music, you have to take into consideration the way movie music works.

Most of Elvis's films were *integrated musicals*. In these musicals, the songs and production numbers were integrated into the story lines. This is the type of musical in which characters randomly break out into song — while they're driving, working, arguing, or going about some other daily activity. In contrast are *backstage musicals*, which are nonintegrated. In backstage story lines, the musical numbers are part of a show that the characters are staging.

Integrated musicals are more fanciful and require a greater suspension of disbelief, while backstage musicals are more grounded in reality. Most of the Presley Travelogues and even some of Elvis's other movies, such as *Follow That Dream* (1962) and *Kid Galahad* (1962), are examples of integrated musicals. His pre-army musical dramas, such as *Jailhouse Rock* and *King Creole*, are considered backstage musicals.

In the integrated musicals, the songs play a part in the story line. They advance the plot, relate something about a character, or create the mood for a scene. The lyrics and sometimes just a few bars of the melody can take the place of scripted dialogue to communicate important information. Yet, outside the film, these songs are often too specific to the story to stand on their own. Unfortunately, many critics of his movie music do just that — discuss them out of context.

The conclusion of *Blue Hawaii* (1961) provides an excellent example of how production numbers or songs function in an integrated musical. Like most of the Presley Travelogues, the plot revolves around a goal or quest that Elvis's character is hoping to achieve, and the pursuit of the leading lady parallels that goal or quest. The completion of the goal is indicated by the union of Elvis with his leading lady, and their union is revealed by the closing production number.

Elvis's character's success in the tourist industry in *Blue Hawaii* isn't announced through dialogue. Instead, it's revealed by his elaborate wedding to the woman who helped him get his start as a tour guide. In the movie, Elvis's character states that he wouldn't marry the leading lady until he proved himself. So the wedding represents both personal and professional triumph. The wedding itself isn't a traditional ceremony with spoken vows; it's depicted as the closing production number titled "Hawaiian Wedding Song." It is this musical number — and only this musical number — that trumpets the union of Elvis with his leading lady as well as his professional success.

## Following in Elvis's Footsteps

Elvis and his management team of the Colonel, Abe Lastfogel of the William Morris talent agency, and producer Hal Wallis weren't the first to plot a client's career path from one arena of entertainment to another. The strategy had been around since the silent era, when vaudeville performers successfully launched careers in Hollywood by tailoring movies to their specific talents. But Elvis's career represents one of the most successful examples, because he conquered so many arenas of entertainment and reinvented himself more than once. As such, his career — all of it — should be examined and given its due.

Singers, rap artists, comedians, and even sports figures hoping to build a long-term career continually break into movies in vehicles constructed around their talents and star images. For instance, many alumni from *Saturday Night Live* — from John Belushi to Will Ferrell — have broadened their appeal by courting a mass audience through the movies. Similarly, controversial rap artists, such as Ice-T and Ice Cube, have become successful actors in family programs and movies by charting a path similar to Elvis's. Even rebellious and unpredictable rapper Eminem starred in *8 Mile* (2002), a movie about a talented but troubled rap artist based on events in his own life. Much like *Loving You* did for Elvis Presley in 1957, *8 Mile* brought mainstream recognition to Eminem, at least for awhile, resulting in his Academy Award win for best song.

Academy Award nominee Eddie Murphy, who became a star through his stint as a cast member on *Saturday Night Live,* was a King-size Elvis fan when he was a teenager. Yet, Murphy wasn't influenced by Elvis's singing style. Instead, he was enamored with Presley's magnitude as a star. The fact that Elvis conquered more than one arena of show business — recording, live performance, television, and films — inspired the young comedian, who wanted to parlay his own television success into other areas. Murphy became a stand-up comic in major venues, recorded an album, and then became a popular movie star in a series of comedy vehicles designed around his talent. When Murphy proclaimed Elvis to be the greatest entertainer of all time, the focus was on the word "entertainer," alluding to his well-rounded stardom.

All these examples, especially Murphy's, validate Elvis's career path, including his much-maligned movie career. The Presley Travelogues may not be inspiring in and of themselves, but the decision by the Colonel and others to change the course of Elvis's career by broadening his audience has proven to be influential.

# Part III
# From the Las Vegas Stage to the End of the Road

## The 5th Wave     By Rich Tennant

"A jumpsuit, huh?"

## In this part . . .

Elvis's decision to become a Hollywood leading man clearly worked too well, because throughout the 1960s audiences had forgotten his rockabilly roots. Fortunately, he revitalized his career with *The '68 Comeback Special,* which reminded America of his power and charisma as a performer. The success of the special encouraged Elvis to return to the stage. In 1969, he opened at the International Hotel in Las Vegas to sold-out audiences, which jump-started the last stage of his career. This last phase was dominated by nonstop concerts and touring.

The rigors of the road, personal disappointments, and other problems took their toll on Elvis Presley, and his career began to decline in the mid-1970s. But not before he accomplished several one-of-a-kind achievements, including his stint at Madison Square Garden in 1972 and his *Aloha from Hawaii* television special in 1973. This part examines the last stage of Elvis's career, which is the phase most associated with the singer because of his preferred costume, the jumpsuit. This part ends with the sad news of Elvis Presley's death on August 16, 1977.

Elvis Presley strikes a pose on the set of *Jailhouse Rock* (1957). See Chapter 6 for more on this film, which was developed exclusively for the star and borrowed many details from his life and career.

Elvis's newly shorn hair, which made the fans flip, is evident in this army photo. Check out Chapter 5 for details about Elvis's stint in the army.

The change in Elvis's image from young rebel to mature leading man is evident in this publicity shot from the early 1960s. Part II tells you everything you need to know about Elvis's career as a movie star.

On May 1, 1967, Elvis Presley married Priscilla Beaulieu. Check out Chapter 7 for additional wedding details.

Elvis bought Graceland, this small mansion on the outskirts of Memphis, in 1957 (see Chapter 5). Today it serves as a legendary tourist destination.

A Vegas-era Elvis performs in one of his iconic jumpsuits and capes, the Black Conquistador (also known as the Conquistador). See Chapter 13 for details about Elvis's costume of choice throughout the 1970s.

This Awards Exhibit, which showcases Elvis's many accolades and his best jumpsuits, is located in the racquetball building at Graceland. Chapter 19 has more information on this and other notable stops on the tour of Graceland.

Elvis woos his audience during a live segment in *The '68 Comeback Special*. Head to Chapter 11 for more information about the televised special that changed the course of the King's career.

Elvis had the sunroom at Graceland converted into this striking gold and white music room. See Chapter 19 for more about this room and other notable Elvis tourist destinations.

Elvis sings "The Lady Loves Me" poolside at the Flamingo Hotel in *Viva Las Vegas* (1964).

Check out the stained-glass peacocks displayed in the living room at Graceland. For more details about this room, see Chapter 19.

Elvis poses with wife Priscilla and daughter Lisa Marie. The Appendix tells you more about these two important women in Elvis's life.

Elvis's flamboyant den was later called the Jungle Room by Graceland's many visitors. In this room, Elvis recorded the material for the final albums released before his death (see Chapter 15).

Elvis starred in 31 feature films during his 13-year movie career. Although many of these films fit into what Elvis called the "Presley Travelogue" formula, Chapter 9 gives you the lowdown on the films that broke the mold, including *Flaming Star* (1960).

Elvis made a habit of engaging in high jinks on the sets of his movies and of dating his costars. During *Blue Hawaii*, rumors flew about Elvis and Joan Blackman (left of Elvis). Chapter 7 gives you more behind-the-scenes information.

This black leather suit has become an icon of *The '68 Comeback Special* (shown here), which in itself is symbolic of Elvis's career comeback and his return to live performing in Las Vegas (see Chapter 12).

Elvis sings "No More" on location in *Blue Hawaii* (1961). Chapter 7 tells you more about this film, which provided Elvis with one of his signature songs, "Can't Help Falling in Love."

*Elvis: Aloha from Hawaii* was the first worldwide live satellite broadcast (1973). See Chapter 14 for more on this and other career highlights.

Elvis Presley's grave (along with the graves of his parents and grandmother) rests behind Graceland in the peaceful Meditation Garden. See Chapter 19 for more about the final resting spot and Chapter 15 for more about the tragic death of a legend.

Despite his death in 1977, Elvis — dressed here in the Blue Nail jumpsuit (aka the Powder Blue) — is often the year's highest-grossing celebrity. See Chapters 18 and 20 for more about Elvis as a significant figure in today's culture.

# Chapter 11

# Making the Comeback of a Lifetime

### In This Chapter

▶ Finding new collaborators

▶ Making *The '68 Comeback Special*

▶ Rejuvenating Elvis's career with a new album

Despite being financially lucrative — and, therefore, a success in the eyes of his manager Colonel Tom Parker — Elvis's movie career left him disappointed, depressed, and downhearted. By the mid-1960s, he was no longer challenged by the movies he made or the soundtrack albums he recorded. Changes in the music scene during the 1960s — particularly after The Beatles spearheaded the British Invasion — rendered Elvis Presley old hat in the eyes of the youth market that he helped create and define.

The dejected Elvis didn't realize his significance to the music scene at the time, but fortunately others did. In the late 1960s, several people outside Elvis's immediate circle challenged and influenced him to change the course of his career. For Elvis to completely remold his image for the public and then deliver some of the finest music of his career represents a comeback of mythic proportions. That this phase of his career would come to a tragic end doesn't detract from the magic of the moment when the King of Rock 'n' Roll returned from a long respite to reclaim his throne.

In this chapter, I discuss music producer Felton Jarvis, who inspired Elvis to record something other than movie soundtracks; Steve Binder, who produced and directed *Elvis — The '68 Comeback Special;* and Chips Moman, who produced *From Elvis in Memphis,* one of the best albums of the singer's career. The success of these ventures, especially *The Comeback Special,* rejuvenated Elvis's career, setting the stage — literally — for his return to live performances.

# Getting Back on Track with a New Producer

In 1967, Elvis recorded his most well-known gospel album, *How Great Thou Art*. The album effectively boosted Elvis's career, because it sold well, charted significantly, and won awards. Most importantly, cutting the album improved Elvis's morale and rekindled his passion for recording. Felton Jarvis not only produced an exceptional album, but he also inspired Elvis to select material he believed in, which was something the singer had not done in a while. This section examines Jarvis's working relationship with Elvis, explores the music they made together, and discusses the role the music played in the singer's comeback.

## Working with producer Felton Jarvis

In May 1966, Felton Jarvis, who was on staff at RCA, agreed to produce Elvis's next album. Jarvis felt that the quality of Elvis's music had slipped during the 1960s, and he wanted to improve the sound of the recordings and the selection of the material. Elvis and Jarvis immediately hit it off, with the young producer grasping right away what Elvis wanted in a sound mix.

Jarvis replaced legendary country guitarist Chet Atkins, who had produced several of Elvis's non-soundtrack albums. In fact, Atkins suggested that Jarvis take over producing Elvis's albums, because he thought that Jarvis was more suited to the singer's working methods, which grew out of Elvis's unconventional lifestyle.

For example, the low-key Atkins wasn't inclined to push Elvis to record, so few recordings were made in the mid-1960s that weren't related to movie soundtracks. Atkins also disapproved of the singer's unstructured approach to cutting an album. Elvis liked to book a few days to record and then cut the album in long, marathon sessions that often lasted through the night. Elvis was accustomed to odd hours, and he thought nothing of working until dawn. But Atkins detested this approach. To Elvis, a song was finished when it felt right to him. If that meant he had to record the song 40 times to get it to that place, he stayed until the job was done.

Like Elvis, Jarvis was a man with eclectic musical tastes who was accustomed to late hours and the unconventional lifestyle of creative people. He also was a true fan who credited Elvis for inspiring him to pursue a job in the music industry. Plus Jarvis's enthusiastic personality was infectious and often influenced the atmosphere of recording sessions, which encouraged Elvis to push himself. With so much in common, Jarvis thought of himself and Elvis as true musical allies. No wonder they made beautiful music together.

With Jarvis as producer, Elvis cut an award-winning gospel album and recorded at least two important singles, "Guitar Man" and "U.S. Male," which foreshadowed his musical rebound. Jarvis remained Elvis's primary producer until the singer's death in 1977.

## Perfecting Elvis's songs and their sound

The music Elvis made with Jarvis was better than a lot of the music he made in the '60s for two important reasons: Elvis had a better selection of material to choose from, and Jarvis improved the sound of the recordings themselves. Together Elvis and Jarvis improved the songs and the sound.

### Advancing mediocre material

Jarvis had discovered that Elvis's two music publishing companies — Gladys Music and Elvis Presley Music — required songwriters to fork over partial publishing credit and a percentage of their royalties in order to have their songs recorded by Elvis. Most decent songwriters refused to accept this deal. As a result, Elvis's publishing companies usually had to acquire songs from mediocre writers. Because the Colonel and RCA executives preferred that Elvis record tunes only from his publishing companies because of the financial advantages, it was small wonder that the singer was drowning in bad material. (See Chapter 4 for more information on Elvis's publishing companies and how they operated.)

So Jarvis went to work improving Elvis's material. He knew several young, talented songwriters whose work was perfect for Elvis, and he exposed Presley to their songs. "Big Boss Man" by Al Smith and Luther Dixon and "Guitar Man" by up-and-coming country artist Jerry Reed became two recordings that proved important for Elvis, because they would later be included in *The '68 Comeback Special*. It was always a struggle to get the Colonel and RCA execs to agree to let Elvis record the work of outside talent, and to let those songwriters keep the publishing rights, but Jarvis was instrumental in changing hearts and minds enough to allow for the possibility.

### Developing a high-quality sound

After collecting a better selection of material for Elvis to choose from, Jarvis improved the sound quality of Elvis's recordings. He did so by basically "undoing" what the producers of his soundtrack albums had been doing for years. Beginning in the early 1960s, Elvis noticed that his albums were mixed so that the sound of the musicians and the voices of the background singers were turned way down, which made his voice too prominent. The music, background vocals, and Elvis's vocals didn't work as an integrated whole, and the recordings lacked energy and excitement. However, RCA executives, the Colonel, and the movie studios didn't care, because making good records was secondary to exploiting their star. Flip to Chapter 8 for an example of Elvis being overexposed through the movies and their accompanying soundtrack albums.

Elvis told his new producer that he wanted a big sound, increased levels on the background vocals, and heartier instrumentation, and Jarvis agreed. Much of the singer's pop-flavored music of the 1960s had been sent to New York to be mixed by engineers and producers who knew little of Elvis's strengths and talents. Jarvis thought their mixing inadequate for someone of the stature of Elvis Presley. So he improved the sound enormously by personally supervising the mixing of Elvis's recordings.

## Spreading the Gospel

Elvis and Jarvis's musical collaboration paid off on the gospel album *How Great Thou Art,* which reveals the producer's efforts to improve the sound and quality of Presley's work.

As a child of the South, Elvis was steeped in gospel music, and he loved the four-part harmony style sung by male gospel quartets such as his frequent backup singers, the Jordanaires. So Elvis was thrilled when Jarvis hired his long-time favorite quartet, the Imperials, whose lead singer was the colorful Jake Hess, to back him on *How Great Thou Art.* In addition, the Jordanaires were on board as usual, along with a female vocal group that added a wider range to the sound. A high point of the album, at least for Elvis, occurred when Elvis and Hess sang a duet on "If the Lord Wasn't Walking by My Side."

On *How Great Thou Art,* Jarvis brought out certain aspects of Elvis's voice that were seldom used, including reaching into the falsetto range and using a vibrato technique. Unaccustomed to pushing himself with these techniques, Elvis worked hard to perfect them. The new techniques forced him to sing parts over and over, but with Jarvis's patience and enthusiasm, Elvis succeeded. Songs such as the title track and "Stand by Me" feature some of Elvis's most expressive interpretations of any songs he recorded in his entire career. However, after a few days of recording, Elvis grew weary (which wasn't unusual behavior for him), and the gospel sessions ended abruptly.

In September 1967, more sessions with Jarvis were arranged because RCA wanted a follow-up album to *How Great Thou Art.* During this time, "Guitar Man" and "U.S. Male" were cut, but tensions over securing material from outside songwriters resulted in arguments in the studio, particularly when those in Elvis's camp pushed Jerry Reed to let go of the publishing rights to "Guitar Man." Reed refused to cave, and eventually he was able to retain the rights. Because of these troubles, Elvis again lost his enthusiasm for these recording sessions, and the second album was delayed because the team lacked material.

## Chapter 11: Making the Comeback of a Lifetime

### Savoring the success of How Great Thou Art

*How Great Thou Art* effectively boosted Elvis's career, a fact borne out by the statistics. The album reaped over $1 million in record sales, earning a gold record. It reached number 18 on the *Billboard* list of Top LPs, and it remained on the charts for 29 weeks. The soundtrack albums Elvis recorded, which sometimes numbered three a year, hadn't performed this well since the early 1960s.

The album also brought Elvis his first Grammy Award. Elvis won only three Grammys during his lifetime — all of them for gospel recordings. *How Great Thou Art* won Best Sacred Performance in 1967, the album *He Touched Me* won Best Inspirational Performance in 1972, and a live version of the hymn "How Great Thou Art" won Best Inspirational Performance in 1974.

Elvis felt a kinship with Jarvis and looked forward to working with him again. It's certainly fitting that Elvis and Jarvis created a gospel album at a time when the singer was at a creative and spiritual low. He was discouraged by his movie career and uninterested in the soundtrack music he was forced to record. In the past, gospel had inspired his interest in music, and it had calmed his nerves before recording sessions and performances. And then during 1966 and 1967, it soothed his soul and reminded him of his breadth and range as a singer, encouraging him to record material that he believed in. As they say in the South, it called him back home. Recording *How Great Thou Art* with Felton Jarvis proved to be a step on the path to a comeback — not only because of the quality and success of the album but also because of its effect on Elvis's morale.

## Creating a Hit: The '68 Comeback Special

*The '68 Comeback Special,* a highly innovative television program, represents a turning point in Elvis's career because it inspired him to return to live performances. However, if the Colonel would have had his way during the production of the special, it may not have turned out so well. This section details the production of the special — from its conception by the creative team to its perception by the public.

*The '68 Comeback Special* was originally titled *Elvis,* but *Singer Presents Elvis* was printed on some of the promotional materials (because of its affiliation with Singer Sewing Machines). However, because the program was instrumental in revitalizing Elvis's music and career, it has since become known as

*The '68 Comeback Special.* The name has become so pervasive that only the most die-hard of Elvis's fans remember the original title, and many books refer to the program only as *The '68 Comeback Special,* or simply *The Comeback Special.*

## Shaping the special

In early 1968, Colonel Tom Parker closed a deal with NBC and Singer Sewing Machines for Elvis to appear in his own television Christmas special. The special would be broadcast on NBC and sponsored entirely by Singer. The show eventually aired on December 3, 1968, but it was actually produced during the summer months.

When Parker made the deal with NBC for a television special starring his one and only client, Elvis Presley, he wanted a program that could be quickly produced with the least amount of effort — and for a rock-bottom price. His vision for an Elvis Presley Christmas special was to have "his boy" stand in front of a festive holiday set with a decorated tree, sing familiar carols for an hour, and then wish everyone a Merry Christmas. Fade out.

The creative personnel behind the special completely disagreed with the Colonel's idea. They wanted to use the special to capture what they felt was Elvis's genius — his music. They wanted to prove that the singer's original music had been essential to the development of rock 'n' roll and that Elvis wasn't some relic from the past. And the Colonel's idea had "relic" written all over it.

With their innovative approach to the special, the creative team — led by producer-director Steve Binder — got Elvis on their side, and in one of the few times in his career, the singer defied his manager. He told the Colonel in no uncertain terms that he wanted to do the special Binder's way.

The creative team behind the special had plenty of experience showcasing modern music for a mainstream audience, so Elvis was in good hands as you can see from the following list of key players:

- **Producer-director Steve Binder** had earned a reputation for capturing the high-powered energy of rock music on film with the legendary *T.A.M.I. Show,* a 1964 concert movie featuring the biggest acts of the time, including The Rolling Stones and James Brown. He also directed several episodes of NBC's prime-time rock-music variety show, *Hullabaloo.*

- **Executive producer Bob Finkel,** one of four executive producers under exclusive contract to NBC, specialized in variety shows. The prolific producer was responsible for *The Andy Williams Show,* for which he won three Emmys, *The Perry Como Show, The Dinah Shore Show,* and *The Jerry Lewis Show,* among others. He earned the prestigious Peabody Award for *The Julie Andrews Show.* Well respected in the industry, Finkel was later elected president of the Producer's Guild of America.

- **Musical engineer Bones Howe** was a recording engineer who became a top independent music producer during the 1960s, producing hit records for The Turtles, The Association, and Jerry Lee Lewis, among others. The year after *The '68 Comeback Special,* Howe won a Grammy for his production of the Record of the Year, "Aquarius/Let the Sunshine In" by the 5th Dimension. Later, he became a pioneer in promoting the use of pop and rock music in motion pictures, which led him to a career in music supervision for films.

Binder completely cast aside the Colonel's idea for the show, and he and Howe reshaped the special to fit their vision of Elvis Presley. They envisioned the special as a series of high-energy production numbers that showcased the musical influences on Elvis's sound and illustrated how he integrated those influences into his own style. After work on the special began, they added two informal segments in which Elvis was recorded live singing before a small studio audience.

Of all the numbers in the special, the informal segments have earned the most acclaim, and yet they originated from such a simple idea. Binder was inspired to create this part of the special when he watched Elvis, his long-time friends and companions, and some of the musicians sit around the baby grand piano in the singer's dressing room on Stage 4 and jam for hours.

Elvis enjoyed this type of informal musical play, which helped him loosen up before and after recordings and decrease tension in any professional or personal situation. Each day after rehearsals, Binder watched as the group sang their hearts out. Elvis played the piano while others drummed on chairs, kept time on the piano top, or brought in the occasional tambourine. Someone would start to sing or play a song, and then the others would join in. The informal group tried all genres, but there was always an emphasis on Southern-based music.

Binder began taking notes about the types of songs they played, and then he snuck a pocket tape recorder into the dressing room to record the sessions. As he watched and listened, he understood that he was witnessing "the real Elvis" — a natural-born musician who could integrate musical genres into a style that was all his own. And, this inherent love and appreciation of all music deeply inspired the other musicians who joined in. Eventually, Binder went to Elvis with the idea of including a version of these jam sessions into the show.

## Looking closely at the completed special

Despite the creative conflicts between the Colonel and Binder, the idea for *The '68 Comeback Special* was conceived and put into motion. (See the preceding section to find out more on the conflicts.) The special ended up with four production numbers and two informal segments in which Elvis sang live before a small studio audience — and no Christmas carols. In this section, I describe the production numbers and live segments, explaining their meanings and impacts.

"Guitar Man," the song by Jerry Reed that Elvis recorded with Felton Jarvis (see the earlier section "Getting Back on Track with a New Producer" for details), became a musical link that loosely tied the special together. The song tells the story of a singing guitar player who leaves home to seek his fame and fortune in the honky-tonks and nightclubs of the South; Binder and Howe used this song as a leitmotif throughout the special. At times, a line or two from the song's chorus pops up in a production number, and Elvis often appears with a guitar strapped to his back to remind us that he's the Guitar Man. Most importantly, the song provided the story line for the special's third production number.

### The production numbers

The polished production numbers in the special combined orchestrated music with choreographed routines from the Claude Thompson Dancers. Even though these numbers weren't atypical for the era, they were exceptional examples in their use of rock 'n' roll music, which stripped away any sentiment or silliness that sometimes plagued musical specials on the small screen. Also, none of the numbers featured spoken dialogue or introductions; instead they relied on song and dance to make their points.

Each of the following four production numbers showcased a different aspect of Elvis's sound:

- **Trouble:** In this number, a dynamic Elvis Presley reminds America that he's still sexy, surly, and downright provocative as he opens the special with a bluesy rendition of "Trouble," from his 1958 film *King Creole*. The atmosphere is electric as a brooding Elvis looks into the camera and growls out the opening line, "If you're looking for trouble/You came to the right place." The camera then pulls back to reveal a background reminiscent of the iconic set from the title tune of *Jailhouse Rock*, Elvis's 1957 film. (You can read more about *King Creole* and *Jailhouse Rock* in Chapter 6.) The entire number purposefully recalls the singer's past, particularly the controversy surrounding Elvis the Pelvis and his gyrating hips. Check out Chapter 5 to find out more about this controversy.

- **Gospel medley:** A dancer interpreting the spiritual "Sometimes I Feel Like a Motherless Child" opens a production number devoted to gospel music, which inspired Elvis personally and influenced his sound musically. Elvis performs a moving version of "Where Could I Go But to the Lord" and "Up Above My Head," backed by the female vocal trio the Blossoms. Then he, the Blossoms, and the Claude Thompson Dancers conclude the segment with the rhythm-and-blues-inspired "Saved." Without a word of dialogue or narration, this production number suggests the evolution of popular music from black spirituals to rhythm and blues (R&B) to the music of Elvis Presley.

- **Guitar Man:** "Guitar Man" pays homage to the secular influences on Elvis's sound, specifically honky-tonk country music. Expanding the special's leitmotif into a musical story, this number features Elvis as the Guitar Man, who sings parts of four songs. He begins his journey by singing "Nothingville" to suggest he's busted and broke. With only his guitar strapped to his back, he roams the honky-tonk bars and carnival midways across the South looking for a chance to sing. He encounters carny toughs while singing "Big Boss Man" and is tempted by women during "Little Egypt." At the end of the number, the Guitar Man walks off into a promising future on a road lined with lights while singing a new verse to his theme song, which reveals a new maturity achieved through experience.

- **If I Can Dream:** "If I Can Dream" was the closing number of the special. The song was written by musical director W. Earl Brown, who penned the song as a response to the assassinations of Martin Luther King, Jr., and Robert Kennedy, which had occurred that year (1968). Brown intended for the song to be a heartfelt plea for understanding and a statement of hope for the future, so Elvis performed the song with great conviction and passion. The large scale of the song, with its reference to King's "I Have a Dream" speech" and its monumental ending, foreshadows Elvis's music of the 1970s. If "Trouble" celebrated Elvis's past, "If I Can Dream" pointed him toward his future.

### *The live segments*

Two segments in which Elvis sang live before a small studio audience turned *The '68 Comeback Special* into a showcase for the singer's strengths. Binder interspersed the two live segments, sometimes called the "sit-down segments," among the special's formal production numbers. The two segments were cut together from four live shows that Elvis performed in an intimate setting to four different audiences. These segments weren't scripted, and they had no specific plan.

In these segments, Elvis and four musicians, including original Blue Moon Boys Scotty Moore and D.J. Fontana, sit on a small stage in the round surrounded by an audience of mostly female fans. (See Chapter 3 for information on Moore and Fontana.) During a medley of his past hits, Elvis prowls the stage like a large cat as he belts out "Hound Dog," "Blue Suede Shoes," "All Shook Up," and more. New arrangements, plus Elvis's lower vocal range, add new life to these old tunes, so the effect is electrifying rather than nostalgic. True to the eclectic nature of his repertoire, Elvis also sang R&B tunes, including a blistering rendition of "Tiger Man" and "Memories," a beautiful new pop ballad that would become one of his signature songs.

> ### Elvis's iconic black leather suit
>
> Costume designer Bill Belew, a member of Steve Binder's production team on past television specials, designed the iconic black leather suit that Elvis wore for the live segments. The suit is reminiscent of Elvis's 1950s image as a rebel, but it doesn't duplicate any costume or look that Elvis ever adopted. In other words, it recalls the past but doesn't emulate it. This was an important distinction for the creators of *The '68 Comeback Special.*
>
> In the years since the performance, the suit has become an icon representing Elvis's rebirth as a musical force to be reckoned with. Refer to the color photo section to see Elvis wearing his leather suit during the special.

## Understanding how the special redefined Elvis Presley

*The '68 Comeback Special* captured 42 percent of the total viewing audience, meaning that 42 percent of the people watching television on December 3, 1968, were watching Elvis Presley. The special was NBC's biggest ratings victory for the entire year, and it was the 1968–1969 television season's highest-rated prime-time show.

More importantly, the special challenged Elvis to interpret and record some of the best music of his career, and it reminded him that he was a singer who loved to perform for an audience. In fact, after the success of the special, Elvis and the Colonel made the decision to return to live performances. The special also reminded audiences that the real Elvis Presley wasn't the guy in an endless string of lightweight musical comedies; he was a unique musical talent who had changed the course of popular music.

Several rock critics and music historians have weighed in on *The '68 Comeback Special.* Perhaps the words of Greil Marcus, who always writes with great passion and expression, are the most famous. In his 1975 book *Mystery Train*, Marcus writes, "It was the finest music of his life. If ever there was music that bleeds, this was it." Also awestruck was critic Jon Landau, whose oft-repeated remark summarized the viewpoint of many: "There is something special about watching a man who has lost himself find his way back home."

## Recording From Elvis in Memphis

On the heels of the tremendous ratings of *The '68 Comeback Special*, Elvis recorded *From Elvis in Memphis*. It was one of the pivotal albums of his career, because it solidified his comeback as a singer who could still shake up the music industry. It also announced his new musical style — a large-scale sound that defined his career through the rest of his life. In this section, I show you the importance of Elvis recording the album in Memphis, the development of his new sound, and the people who contributed to it.

## Rediscovering Memphis as a recording center

Shortly after *The '68 Comeback Special* aired, Elvis returned to Tennessee to record new material. Instead of using RCA's facilities in Nashville, where Elvis had recorded most of his non-soundtrack music since 1956, he opted to cut his new material in his hometown of Memphis. He hadn't made a record there since his days at Sun Studio in 1955 (see Chapter 2 for information on Elvis's early days recording in Memphis).

Elvis was persuaded by members of his inner circle to try Memphis's American Sound Studio, which was operated and co-owned by producer/engineer Chips Moman. Moman, who was in the midst of the most successful period of his career, had a reputation for knowing how to tailor a song to the singer.

Recording in his hometown proved to be about more than just geography, however. Just as it had in the mid-1950s, Elvis's new sound was shaped once more by the musical influences and history that pervaded Memphis (see Chapter 2 for more information on Memphis's music scene). The blues, R&B, and soul music that made the city famous permeated the atmosphere at the American Sound Studio, influencing Moman and his house musicians. Their eclectic tastes and edgier playing styles stood in marked contrast to the conservative nature of Nashville's producers and sessions musicians. All of this made a definite impact on *From Elvis in Memphis* and on Elvis's new musical direction.

## Establishing a musical direction with his latest album

*From Elvis in Memphis* became Elvis's biggest critical and financial success since 1960. It charted for 24 weeks on the *Billboard* list of Top LPs and peaked at number 13. In the United Kingdom, the LP actually topped the charts. But, more importantly, the high-profile album capped his comeback and established a new musical direction that signaled Elvis's break from the pop-rock music associated with his film image.

Elvis accomplished the break from pop rock in part by focusing on a type of music loosely referred to as *blue-eyed soul* or *swamp pop*. This music was a soulful style of country music tinged with a little R&B, and it integrated Southern-based styles and sounds that attracted Elvis. Eager to pursue a different musical direction, Elvis embraced this sound and then expanded it into something larger and fuller to call his own.

Also helpful was the fact that Elvis felt a kinship with the musicians who were part of the American Sound Studio house band. The band consisted of young, hip Southern musicians who were steeped in blues and R&B and who also had been inspired by Presley's rockabilly in the 1950s. The house musicians rocked a harder sound than the sessions musicians at RCA in Nashville, partly because of the seasoned rhythm section, and this suited Elvis's musical preferences.

Elvis also had personal connections with some of the band members, including guitarist Reggie Young and organist Bobby Emmons, who had played with Bill Black's Combo in the 1960s (see Chapters 2 and 3 for more information on Bill Black). He also knew drummer Gene Christman, who had worked in Jerry Lee Lewis's band. Knowing the musicians in the house band and having musical tastes in common with them made it easier for Elvis and Moman to achieve the results they wanted.

The album's sound was rich and full, with Elvis offering emotionally stirring interpretations of such songs as "After Loving You" and "True Love Travels on a Gravel Road." Moman wrung the emotion and expression from Elvis throughout the sessions, enhancing the drama and power of the songs. However, he didn't allow Elvis to record the way he was accustomed to at RCA, where Presley was recorded singing "live" in the studio while the musicians backed him. In other words, everything was recorded on the same track. Instead, Moman recorded Elvis, the backup singers, and the musicians on separate tracks, and then overdubbed them later. This technique resulted in a tightly produced, technically proficient album, and it enhanced the full, large-scale sound.

The sessions at the American Sound Studio — and the albums and singles that resulted — launched the musical direction that defined the last phase of Elvis's career. The large-scale sound, expressive vocals, and sheer drama became an essential part of Elvis's new style, which proved to be perfect for live performance.

Categorizing Elvis's musical style from this phase of his career is difficult. Like his original sound, this new direction was at once a combination of influences, yet somehow unique to him as a performer. The diversity of Elvis's song selection also made categorizing and analyzing his music difficult for journalists and reviewers who wrote about him. It wasn't country or rock 'n' roll, nor was it R&B. Yet, it was all three of those genres at once. Eventually, folks stopped trying to label it. It became simply "Elvis's music."

## Selecting the songs for the American Sound recording sessions

The songs recorded during the three sessions at the American Sound Studio represented the following styles of music:

- Contemporary rhythm and blues as in the song "Only the Strong Survive"
- Classic country in "From a Jack to a King"
- A fusion of country and R&B with "In the Ghetto"

Elvis was obligated to record some tunes provided by RCA per his contract (see Chapter 4 for more on Elvis's relationship with RCA). But after he got those out of the way, he focused on some of the new compositions offered to him by a young generation of country music songwriters, such as Jerry Reed, Mac Davis, and Eddie Rabbitt. Like the members of the American Sound Studio house band, these songwriters had been liberated and influenced by Elvis's 1950s rockabilly music. Though diverse in genre, the songs were unified by their arrangements, which emphasized the large-scale, fully integrated sound that Elvis and Moman had perfected. (See the earlier section "Establishing a musical direction with his latest album" for more on Elvis's new sound.)

The three sessions at the American Sound Studio totaled about 14 days. Many of the songs recorded in the sessions ended up on *From Elvis in Memphis,* which was released in May 1969. A few cuts were released as top-selling singles during the summer, including "Suspicious Minds." Later, the leftover cuts were combined with several recordings of Elvis onstage to become the double album *From Memphis to Vegas/From Vegas to Memphis,* released in October 1969. The American Sound Studio sessions produced some of the best recordings of Elvis's career and also some of his biggest hits, including the following:

- **"Suspicious Minds":** This song became Elvis's first number-one single since 1962 — and the last number-one single of his career on the pop charts. It was inducted into the Grammy Hall of Fame in 1999. Written by Mark James, this song provides a good example of Elvis's music from the last phase of his career. It's incredibly fast paced and has a hard-driving base line that blends a thundering sound of horns, strings, and drums with the voices of Presley and a choir of female backup singers. As the song reaches its conclusion, all the elements are propelled forward at breakneck speed, rising to seemingly endless crescendo.

- **"In the Ghetto":** This 1969 single sold 1.2 million copies and reached number three on the *Billboard* singles chart and number one in the United Kingdom. Country singer and actor Mac Davis wrote the song, which offers a message about the endless cycle of poverty and crime.

Elvis and his family had been dirt poor in the country and poverty stricken in the city, so he could relate firsthand to the lyrics. Though initially nervous about the sociopolitical content, Elvis grew excited about the prospect, especially after Moman mentioned offering the song to another singer. Elvis recorded "In the Ghetto" against the objections of the Colonel, who disliked message songs.

- **"Kentucky Rain":** Though less well known in retrospect, this song was Elvis's 50th gold record. Country singer Eddie Rabbitt wrote the song with Dick Heard; the end result was a pop-inspired composition somewhere between a ballad and a country tune.

In 2007, Elvis's daughter, Lisa Marie, remixed "In the Ghetto," blending her voice with that of her father's. The song was recorded for download to raise money for the homeless victims of Hurricane Katrina, which blasted the Southern states in 2005.

# Chapter 12

# Viva Las Vegas: Returning to Live Performances

### In This Chapter

▶ Performing at the Las Vegas International Hotel in 1969
▶ Hitting the road again

The year 1969 became a seminal year for Elvis Presley in the same ways that 1956 and 1960 had. Just as the events in those years determined a career course and a specific image for Elvis, so did the events of 1969. This year again pointed Elvis toward a new image and a new career direction. His dynamic recordings from the first half of that year helped steer him toward that goal (see Chapter 11 for more information), but it was his smash engagement that summer in Las Vegas at the International Hotel that determined the last phase of his career and changed his image. The engagement at the International proved so successful that Colonel Tom Parker, Elvis's manager, inked a long-term deal with the hotel for Elvis to perform there twice a year.

Bolstered by his Las Vegas success, Elvis wanted to return to touring so he could perform for those who couldn't get to Vegas to see him. Shortly after an engagement in Vegas in February 1970, Elvis appeared at the Texas Livestock Show in the Houston Astrodome. The success of this series of record-breaking shows convinced Elvis that he could tour regularly.

The high-profile, critically acclaimed Vegas engagements of 1969 and early 1970, combined with his return to touring, completely changed Elvis's image. A year earlier, he had been a movie star associated with family-oriented musical comedies; now he was touted as a rock 'n' roll legend who was the hottest concert ticket in the country. For the first few years, Elvis enjoyed his new career and reveled in his new image, but repetition, depression, and boredom eventually wore him down. Four years later, he was in decline personally and professionally; he was in a downward spiral with no escape.

> ### Letting Streisand work out the kinks
>
> The International Hotel was still under construction when owner Kirk Kerkorian asked Elvis to open his new hotel — the largest in Las Vegas at the time. It featured 1,519 rooms, a 9-acre open-air leisure area on the roof, and the world's largest casino. The showroom seated 2,200 people. Staging Elvis's comeback as International's first engagement would have been the perfect monumental event to bring attention to the new hotel. However, Parker knew that the brand-new showroom would have unforeseen problems because it had never been tested. He also knew that Elvis's return to the stage was going to be covered extensively in the press and that any technical problems would have detracted from the impact of his return. So the Colonel and Elvis turned down Kerkorian.
>
> Barbra Streisand, who had achieved stardom the previous year after she won an Academy Award for her role in *Funny Girl* (1968), agreed to open the room. Just as Parker predicted, a number of problems popped up, including kinks in the sound system, which had to be completely reorganized. So Parker and Presley's decision to turn down Kerkorian's offer to open the hotel clearly worked in their favor.

But, in this chapter, I step back in time to the years before the decline to capture the excitement of Elvis Presley experiencing a career high point. Throughout 1969 and 1970, a happy, healthy Elvis enjoyed his comeback to live performances as fans and nonfans alike scrambled to see his concerts. And, the press — for once — appreciated the larger-than-life talent and charisma of the King of Rock 'n' Roll.

## Conquering Las Vegas

After Elvis felt the excitement of singing in front of an audience during the live segments of *The '68 Comeback Special,* he was motivated to return to performing in concert. (See Chapter 11 for more information on this special.) In February 1969, Elvis was invited to open the brand-new International Hotel in July, but he declined, preferring an engagement during the month of August. (See the nearby sidebar, "Letting Streisand work out the kinks," to find out why Elvis chose not to open the International.) Reports on the exact amount of his salary for this gig vary widely, but Elvis was supposedly paid a half-million dollars for four weeks. The marquis at the International read simply "ELVIS." This section offers a detailed account of Elvis's return to performing, one of the most important events in his life and career.

## Preparing for the first concert performance in eight years

Elvis hadn't appeared before a live audience since 1961, a year when his music had been much simpler. For his return to live performing, Elvis chose not to re-create his earlier image or sound. Instead, he planned his act on a broad scale by including a large number of backup vocalists and musicians to accompany him onstage at the International.

Joining Elvis onstage were the gospel-singing Imperials, the female vocal group the Sweet Inspirations, a rock band, and an orchestra. The members of his rock band included well-known guitarist James Burton, drummer Ronnie Tutt, bassist Jerry Scheff, keyboard player Larry Muhoberac, and guitarists/vocalists John Wilkinson and Charlie Hodge. (Hodge had been part of the Memphis Mafia since the days when he and Elvis were in the army together.) Part of the reason for such an extensive musical backing was undoubtedly due to the large room Elvis was to perform in at the International, but the enormous sound created by Elvis and his musical entourage seemed fitting for the return of a King.

Elvis was frightfully nervous about staging his comeback to live performances in Las Vegas, because he had bombed there when he appeared at the New Frontier Hotel in April 1956. The sting of his failure hadn't diminished with the passing years. (See Chapter 4 for more information on Elvis's Vegas flop in 1956.) He had time for several rehearsals before his engagement at the International, but he had no opportunity to iron out kinks before a live audience, which added to his anxiety.

The list of celebrities who were set to attend Elvis's opening included Cary Grant, Pat Boone, Fats Domino, Wayne Newton, Dick Clark, Ann-Margret, George Hamilton, Angie Dickinson, and Henry Mancini. Elvis also personally invited Sam Phillips, the man who had helped him develop his raw talent into a unique musical style, and Phillips was proud to attend.

## Opening night: July 31, 1969

To the hard-pounding strains of "Blue Suede Shoes," Elvis walked on stage at the International on the evening of July 31, 1969. No emcee was there to introduce him. Instead, he introduced himself with his signature moves: He grabbed the microphone, struck a familiar pose from the past, and snapped his leg back and forth. The crowd jumped from their chairs to give him a standing ovation before he sang one note. The sold-out audience began to whistle, applaud furiously, and pound on the tables. Singer Petula Clark, who had a hit single in the mid-1960s with "Downtown," stood on her chair screaming and applauding. When the ovation began to subside, Elvis launched into "Blue Suede Shoes" with such a fury that ten years of being a movie star melted away.

Elvis looked unbelievably handsome that night. He was dressed in a modified karate suit made especially for him out of black mohair by Bill Belew, who had created his leather costume for *The '68 Comeback Special*.

Onstage, Elvis's sense of humor came through as he clowned around with the audience. Visibly nervous, he poked fun at himself, joking, "This is my first show in nine [sic] years. It could by my last." He also joked with the crowd about the old days and the old songs. At one point, he decided to dedicate his next number to the audience and staff at the International: "This is the only song I could think of that really expresses my feeling toward the audience," he said in all earnestness, before breaking into "Hound Dog." This type of self-deprecating humor would become part of his act.

The high-powered show featured mostly rock 'n' roll tunes, and Elvis continually surprised the audience with his energy and diversity of songs. In addition to singing his old songs from the 1950s, he performed The Beatles hits "Yesterday" and "Hey Jude." When he launched into a six-minute version of "Suspicious Minds," the excitement was palpable. A single of the song wasn't released until mid-August, so on July 31 most of the audience hadn't yet heard it. When he finally finished the song, the audience gave him another standing ovation. Elvis closed his act with "What'd I Say" from *Viva Las Vegas* (1964), and again the sold-out crowd gave him a standing ovation. Even TV producer Jack Good, a celebrity in the audience that night, was seen dancing on top of his table. Elvis came back for an encore and sang "Can't Help Falling in Love," which became the song that he closed every show with for the rest of his career.

The lengthy show of close to 90 minutes included a playlist of fast-paced rock 'n' roll tunes and intensely expressive ballads. Later in the years, Elvis's playlist featured more pop and country songs, which changed the flavor of the act. But, on his opening night, he intended to move his audience, and he did.

## Congratulating Elvis after the show

Backstage after the performance, many celebrities and well-wishers, including Cary Grant, were on hand to congratulate Elvis on his triumphant return to live performance. In her biography *Elvis and Me*, Priscilla Beaulieu Presley reveals a touching story about Colonel Parker. At this moment of great personal and professional triumph for his one and only client, the Colonel pushed his way backstage. Everyone could see that tears were welling up in his eyes. Where was "his boy" he wanted to know. As Elvis emerged from his dressing room, the two men embraced, too overcome with emotion to say anything. People have told countless stories about Colonel Tom Parker over the years, many of them illustrating his shrewdness, his greed, his mistakes, or his ruthlessness. Yet no story reveals the complexity of the relationship between Elvis and the Colonel like this one.

## Respectful rivals: Elvis and The Beatles

Ever since The Beatles became a pop-culture sensation in the early 1960s, the press presented Elvis and The Beatles as rivals, but their professional relationship wasn't that simple. The Beatles had long acknowledged the importance of Elvis as an influence, and Presley and the Colonel graciously sent a famous congratulatory telegram to The Beatles on the night of their first appearance on *The Ed Sullivan Show.*

On August 27, 1965, The Beatles visited Elvis at his home in California. Several of Elvis's friends and companions were there, and each of them has told a different version of the interaction between Elvis and the Fab Four. Whatever happened, Elvis truly appreciated their talents despite any stories to the contrary. He sang two of their songs, "Yesterday" and "Hey Jude," in his 1969 show at the International Hotel. (The section "Conquering Las Vegas" gives you a rundown of this infamous show.) In an article in *Newsweek,* which originated from the press conference Elvis gave after his opening night at the International, Presley freely discusses the talent of The Beatles: "There are a lot of new records out now that have the same sound I started. But they're better. I mean you can't compare a song like 'Yesterday' with 'Hound Dog,' can you?"

The period that marked his comeback, which was roughly late 1968 to 1970, garnered Elvis some of the best press of his career, with the exception of *The New York Times,* which had never had a positive word for Elvis. This very brief time period is the only time he consistently got good reviews that recognized the magnitude of his talent. Consider this quotation from the *New Yorker* as representative of that period of time: "Then Presley came on, and immediately shook up all my expectations and preconceived categories. There was a new man out there."

## Signing the tablecloth deal

In the wee hours of the morning after the opening, the Colonel sat down with the general manager of the International Hotel to discuss the enormous success of the performance. There in one of the hotel's cafes, the hotel manager offered Elvis a five-year contract to play two months a year — February and August — at a salary of $1 million per year. In his typical flamboyant style, the Colonel took out a pen and began scribbling specific terms on the pink tablecloth. When he finished, he asked the general manager to sign the cloth to close the deal. Four days later, a more formal document was drawn up — and on paper this time.

In addition to the performance contract, Elvis was granted access to the hotel's presidential or royal suite any time he wanted it whether he was performing at the hotel or not. Colonel Parker also was granted access to a room, which he used frequently because he had an appetite for gambling.

## Breaking records

For the rest of August 1969, Elvis continued to thrill audiences with the same level of energy and enthusiasm during his two shows every night. His engagement at the International Hotel broke all existing attendance records for all of Las Vegas, selling over 100,000 tickets and grossing more than $1.5 million. In addition, the hotel's income from other operations doubled during that month.

The International presented Elvis with a spectacular gift after his record-breaking engagement — a huge gold belt with a belt buckle that read "World's Championship Attendance Record, Las Vegas, Nevada, International Hotel." The belt was made of gold over sterling silver, and it featured animal designs reminiscent of the signs of the zodiac. Elvis later added gems and precious stones to the belt and wore it regularly in concerts and during press conferences.

## Returning to Las Vegas

On January 26, 1970, Elvis returned to the International for another month of sold-out performances. Dean Martin attended the opening night of Elvis's second Las Vegas engagement. Elvis sang "Everybody Loves Somebody Sometime" as a tribute to Martin, the pop singer he had always admired. (Chapter 2 discusses more on Elvis's initial influences.)

Elvis altered his repertoire for this engagement by emphasizing his current recordings and including some contemporary country and rock ballads. He limited the use of his older material to a few key places during the show, or he covered it in a medley-style arrangement. Elvis was determined not to rest on his laurels, so he focused his act on his new material and his new sound, which he had developed with the help of Chips Moman at the American Sound Studio. (Read more about his recordings with Moman in Chapter 11.)

The show was shortened this time around to half the time of his 1969 shows — about 40 minutes. Many people claim that the hotel requested Elvis to shorten the show because high rollers and other gamblers spent less time at the gaming tables whenever he was in town, but no evidence exists to support this. More likely, Elvis suffered from a condition known as "Vegas throat," which is a sore throat caused by the dry desert air. Many entertainers contend with this condition when performing in Vegas, and Elvis probably shortened his act to ensure that his voice would last until the end of the engagement.

During this second engagement, Elvis wore a white jumpsuit for the first time on stage. Designed by Bill Belew, the costume was slashed down the front to reveal Elvis's chest, fitted closely at the waist, and belled out at the legs, which was the fashion of the day. The costume's high collar was inset with semiprecious jewels, and Elvis wore gold and diamond rings on the fingers of both hands. A macramé karate belt made of gold- and pearl-colored strands accentuated his slender waist. Throughout the rest of his career, Elvis most often wore variations of the jumpsuit, though they weren't always white.

Elvis wasn't merely a nostalgia act during his time in Vegas, but the success of his comeback was probably enhanced by the revival of 1950s music that began in the late 1960s. Many performers who had helped develop the rock 'n' roll sound and attitude reaped the benefits of this renewed interest in the roots of rock music. Bill Haley and the Comets, Chuck Berry, and Jerry Lee Lewis all were touring again and attracting large crowds. Elvis's success at this time not only benefited from the rock-nostalgia craze but undoubtedly influenced it. Yet, Elvis was careful to keep his material new and varied. He didn't identify himself with the rock 'n' roll revival, and his show was never considered to be merely an oldies act. In fact, even when he sang his hits from the 1950s, he used new arrangements to make them sound contemporary.

## Taking His Show on the Road

Following his success in Las Vegas, Elvis took his act on tour. The singer realized that he had missed all facets of a music career. He missed the satisfaction of recording material he believed in, and he missed the excitement of performing before a live audience. He wanted to perform for more than the two months he was engaged in Las Vegas, and he also wanted to reach out to fans who couldn't make it to the desert city to see him. With a newfound purpose, Elvis asked the Colonel to book additional engagements.

### Playing the Astrodome

For Elvis's first show on the road, Colonel Parker arranged for him to appear in the Houston Astrodome in conjunction with the Texas Livestock Show, which ran from February 27 to March 1, 1970. The Colonel's logic behind choosing this huge venue was simple: The livestock show would generate an audience regardless of whether Elvis was there or not, so they were guaranteed a built-in audience in case he didn't draw the numbers he had in Vegas. But, in the end, the Colonel need not have worried, because all the Houston Astrodome shows were sold out.

Texas had always been good to Elvis. In 1955, East Texas had been the scene of a great surge of Elvis-mania, which helped boost his early career. To return this kindness (and perhaps to ensure a sellout), tickets for Elvis's engagement at the Astrodome were greatly reduced in price, with some seats selling for as little as a dollar.

Despite the boost in confidence from his Vegas victories, Elvis was overwhelmed by the size of the Astrodome and the thought of having to please thousands of people. Referring to the Astrodome as an "ocean," he worried about losing some of his energy and dynamism in such a vast arena. Again his fears proved unfounded because the Astrodome sold out each night of his engagement, and the local music critics raved about his personal charisma and exciting act.

Elvis's evening show on Saturday, February 28, set a new record for the Astrodome with an audience of 43,614.

After the last of the six shows, Elvis held a press conference at AstroWorld, a Texas amusement park that closed in 2005 after 37 years in business. He answered questions from a horde of about 100 journalists. At the end of the press conference, he was awarded five gold records from RCA for material released in 1969, making him the only artist to date to win so many gold discs in one year.

The success in Houston inspired Elvis to continue touring, and his touring schedule quickly became grueling. By 1971, Elvis was on the road more than most other acts in show business. He would tour for three weeks at a time, taking no days off and doing two shows on Saturday and Sunday. He would rest for a few weeks and then repeat the cycle. Elvis usually played one-night stands, meaning every performance was scheduled for a different arena. Often Elvis and his entourage would arrive in a city and depart again in less than 24 hours. Elvis's concerts during this time were almost always sold out.

## Going through a divorce

Elvis's return to concert performing probably contributed to the disintegration of his marriage to Priscilla. Gone from Graceland much of the time while touring in concert, Elvis saw less of Priscilla and his daughter, Lisa Marie, as his career and lifestyle took a different direction. The horrendous pace of performing in a different city every night made traveling together difficult, and Elvis enforced a no-wives rule while on the road, which applied to himself and all members of the Memphis Mafia. In addition, like any rock act on tour, Elvis and his entourage didn't always behave like mature family men.

Priscilla left Elvis in early 1972, and Elvis sued for divorce in August of that same year. Elvis's lawyer succinctly summed up the problem when he released this statement: "Elvis has been spending six months a year on the road, which put a tremendous strain on the marriage." In October 1973, the couple was officially divorced, but it was an amicable split. They held hands during the divorce proceedings and walked out of the courtroom arm in arm. Their complex feelings for each other are evident in the fact that neither of them ever married again.

# Chapter 13

# Savoring Elvis in Concert

### In This Chapter

▶ Presenting the musicians and vocalists in Elvis's show

▶ Reviewing Elvis's 1970s concert hits

▶ Looking at the King's costume of choice: the jumpsuit

▶ Considering the concert rituals between fans and performer

Elvis's 1970s show was a far cry from his act in 1956 (see Chapter 3 for more information about Elvis's 1956 act). Rather than a three-man combo, Elvis was backed by a rock band, an orchestra, a female vocal group, a soprano, and a gospel quartet. The scale of the sound befitted the nickname that the Colonel gave him: the World's Greatest Entertainer.

Elvis rotated songs in and out of the act, but the grueling pace of his yearly schedule prohibited an extensive reworking of the show. By 1972, his act had settled into a series of patterns and rituals that was comforting and familiar to audiences. From the music to the costumes to the onstage routines, the Elvis Presley concert became a predictable and enjoyable experience. For most of the concert years, fans preferred the predictability, because they wanted to participate in concert rituals they knew were part of the show. Several of these routines were associated with key songs in the act and gave the illusion of intimacy between Elvis and his audience.

The interactive nature of the concerts in which gifts were bestowed, kisses exchanged, and emotions expressed can be compared to the rituals of romance. In effect, Elvis was romancing the female fans in the audience, and they were responding. Small wonder that Elvis's fans are so loyal.

This chapter offers a detailed overview of the typical 1970s Elvis concert, including the musicians and singers, the music, the jumpsuits, and the fan interaction so those who never saw Elvis in concert can know what it was like and those who did see him can remember with nostalgia.

## Introducing the Musicians Who Joined Elvis in Concert

For his return to concert performing, Elvis chose not to re-create his past by simply singing his old songs in a nostalgia-based act. He wanted a new sound for this new phase of his career. Elvis opted for a large-scale sound that required the contributions of a variety of musicians and singers, including a rock band, an orchestra, a gospel quartet, a soprano, and a soulful female vocal group. Each represents an important part of Elvis's 1970s sound, which was a mixture of rock, pop, country and gospel, and soul or rhythm and blues. Once again his musical style represented an integration of genres, but his sound was still very different from his 1950s music.

In this section, Elvis's extensive musical entourage takes center stage. Many had been influenced by Presley and in turn contributed to his later style and sound, reflecting the complexities of his music from this period.

### Rock 'n' rollers: The TCB Band

Formed in 1969 for Elvis's comeback engagement at the International Hotel, the TCB Band backed the singer until he died. TCB stood for "Takin' Care of Business," which was Elvis's motto, but this rock group was established before the phrase came about. Band leader James Burton assembled the group after Elvis called him personally in 1969 to ask for his help.

After Elvis died, the band recorded material for its own album, but it was never released. Then the band members went their separate ways until 1997, when the Elvis Presley Estate organized a tour called "Elvis: The Concert," which consisted of film footage of Elvis performing onstage backed by the members of the TCB Band who played live. The tour was so successful that it has been remounted several times.

The core members of the TCB Band include some of the best musicians in rock 'n' roll history. In the following sections, I honor these largely unsung musicians.

#### Lead guitarist James Burton

An accomplished and respected lead guitarist, James Burton got his professional start on the *Louisiana Hayride* as part of the staff band when he was only 14 years old. His stint on the *Hayride* came after Elvis's tenure, so their paths didn't cross. A few years later, Burton caught a break when he began playing lead guitar for Ricky Nelson. He backed Nelson on his major hits from 1958 to 1965. During the 1960s, Burton did session work for several West

Coast musical acts, including the Beach Boys and Sonny & Cher, while also working as the lead guitarist in the house band for *Shindig,* a rock 'n' roll television variety series.

Burton is still considered a rock 'n' roll guitarist with considerable range, but his background in Southern sounds and styles made him a perfect choice as Elvis's lead guitarist in the TCB Band. A hallmark of Elvis's live shows occurred when he turned to James during the bridges of certain songs and said, "Play it, James," and then Burton would solo.

Elvis was notorious for his humorous introductions of his band members and vocalists, once introducing Burton as "one of the funkiest chicken-pickin' son-of-a-guns you ever met in your life."

After Elvis died, Burton was a much sought-after musician, backing Merle Haggard, Gram Parsons, and Emmylou Harris, among others. His last major musical relationship was with John Denver, whom he backed off and on for 16 years. Glen D. Hardin and Jerry Scheff, two other Elvis Presley band members, also joined Denver's band. Burton was elected to the Rock 'n' Roll Hall of Fame in 2001. Today, he still serves the King by touring with "Elvis: The Concert."

An unsubstantiated anecdote regarding Elvis and Burton reveals Presley's regard for his lead guitarist. In 1974, Elvis met guitar legend Eric Clapton. In some versions of the story, Presley is unaware of the full extent of Clapton's reputation as a "guitar god." But, he offered to introduce Clapton to Burton so Eric could learn a thing or two about guitar playing.

### Pianist Glen D. Hardin

Glen D. Hardin didn't audition in 1969 to be one of the original band members for the International Hotel engagement. Instead, he replaced Larry Muhoberac as pianist in January 1970, playing on recordings and in concert with Elvis and the TCB Band until 1976.

A Texas native, Hardin first saw Elvis rocking the house in Lubbock in 1955. After his Navy service, Hardin joined the house band at the legendary Palomino Club in Hollywood, which specialized in West Coast country music. Buck Owens, Hoyt Axton, Willie Nelson, and Merle Haggard frequently played the club. He also toured with the Crickets, Buddy Holly's old band, and then was hired as the piano player on *Shindig,* where he met James Burton and Jerry Scheff. He also worked as a session pianist for singers from Bing Crosby to Roy Orbison. Hardin also could arrange music, and he arranged several of Elvis's large-scale numbers, including "Bridge Over Troubled Water" and "The Wonder of You." Hardin left the show in 1976 to join Emmylou Harris, perhaps recognizing Elvis's decline. Hardin's diverse career is impressive. Most recently, he has played piano for outlaw country singer Travis Tritt.

**TRIVIA**

As part of the house band on the television series *Shindig,* Hardin was in good company with many musicians who became an important part of the 1960s music scene, including Glen Campbell, Billy Preston, Delaney Bramlett, and Leon Russell. The band was first called the Shin-diggers, and then the name changed to the Shindogs.

### Bass player Jerry Scheff

Jerry Scheff didn't share the Southern background of many of the other TCB Band members. Instead the San Francisco–born bass player was steeped in West Coast jazz, and he actually began his career by playing the tuba. But, he did love the blues. He met guitarist James Burton when they were part of the *Shindig* house band together, and in 1966, he was a session musician on the soundtracks for Elvis's movies *Double Trouble* and *Easy Come, Easy Go.*

During the 1960s, Scheff played on the recordings of Sammy Davis, Jr., Linda Ronstadt, Barbra Streisand, Pat Boone, Neil Diamond, and Dionne Warwick. When he was invited to audition to be Elvis Presley's bass player, he wasn't sure if he wanted the position until he met Elvis and the two jammed through a blues session. Except for a year or two, Scheff stayed with the TCB Band until Elvis died. When his time with Elvis was all over in 1977, he toured with several high-profile rock and pop acts, including Bette Midler, Bob Dylan, John Denver, and Elvis Costello.

### Drummer Ronnie Tutt

Back in 1955, when Elvis was still a regionally based performer touring the country-western circuits across the South, a young Ronnie Tutt played on the same bill as the hip-swinging sensation. Tutt was a member of a western swing band, and his group opened for Elvis in the drummer's hometown of Dallas. Little did he know that 14 years later he would audition to be part of Elvis's comeback to live performances. Tutt claims that he won the audition over better-known drummers because he kept eye contact with Elvis while he sang. Though Tutt occasionally missed a tour or two, he remained the primary drummer of the TCB Band until Elvis died.

After playing for Elvis, Tutt worked for a number of singers and acts who represent a variety of musical styles, including Barbra Streisand, Johnny Cash, the Carpenters, the Beach Boys, Billy Joel, and Neil Diamond. Tutt has worked with Diamond for over two decades, remaining his primary drummer today.

**IN THEIR OWN WORDS**

In *The Elvis Encyclopedia* by Adam Victor, Ronnie Tutt recalls his approach to backing Elvis, "I emulated and accented everything that he did just instinctively. Every move, almost like a glorified stripper! And he loved that."

### Rhythm guitarist John Wilkinson

As a child growing up in Missouri, rhythm guitarist John Wilkinson was an Elvis fan and a music prodigy. Like Ronnie Tutt and Glen D. Hardin, Wilkinson experienced a minor brush with Elvis when the singer played in his hometown in 1956. The 11-year-old boy spoke with Elvis backstage and brashly boasted he could play guitar better than the singer. He played a few licks for Elvis, who predicted that the two would cross paths again.

Actually, their paths crossed several times, because during the mid-1960s, Wilkinson worked as a session musician for RCA. He also was part of the folk-rock scene at the time, performing as one of the Kingston Trio and doing session work with Gordon Lightfoot and Peter, Paul and Mary. In 1969, Elvis himself called Wilkinson to join the TCB Band. After Elvis's death, Wilkinson changed careers to work in the defense industry before a bout with bad health pushed him back into performing again on a small scale.

In 2006, Wilkinson wrote a book with friend and Tennessee author Nick Moretti titled *My Life Before, During and After Elvis Presley*.

## Gospel singers J.D. Sumner and the Stamps Quartet

J.D. Sumner and the Stamps Quartet joined Elvis's onstage act in November 1971, replacing the Imperials. Elvis loved the harmonies of gospel groups and had employed a quartet to provide backing vocals since 1956 when he asked the Jordanaires to support him in concert and on his recordings. His continued use of a touch of gospel in his music throughout his career reveals the impact of this genre on his entire musical output.

Elvis had known Sumner since he was a teenager, because the gospel giant was a member of the Blackwood Brothers Quartet. The actual brothers in the quartet belonged to the same church as the Presleys. The members of the Blackwood Brothers Quartet were local Memphis heroes and frequently sang at the all-night gospel shows at Ellis Auditorium; Elvis was known to attend these shows (see Chapter 2 for details). According to Sumner, he often let Elvis in the back door for free, and when Elvis became famous in 1956, he let Sumner into his shows for free. Sumner and James Blackwood did a lot for gospel music, establishing the Gospel Music Association and the National Quartet Convention, which established the Dove Awards, one of the highest honors in the field.

Bass singer Sumner was inspired to go into the gospel field by the legendary Frank Stamps, and in 1965, he left the Blackwood Brothers to purchase the Stamps Quartet name. He and the Stamps sang with Elvis from 1971 to 1977. In 1978, J.D. Sumner and the Stamps Quartet released an album as a tribute to Elvis, which was titled *Elvis's Favorite Gospel Songs*. He further paid tribute to his friend and associate in his book *Elvis: His Love for Gospel Music*, which was published in 1991.

> ### Seeing Elvis in concert today
>
> Produced by Stig Edgren, "Elvis: The Concert" uses modern technology to wed film footage of Elvis singing onstage while his backup musicians and vocalists perform live. The purpose is to re-create as closely as possible the experience of Elvis in concert. The footage was selected from *Elvis — That's the Way It Is, Aloha from Hawaii,* and *Elvis on Tour.* (See Chapter 14 for more on these documentaries and programs.) Edgren removed all the music from the footage except for Elvis's voice. During the concert, three large digital video screens project the footage of Elvis singing, while the TCB Band, an orchestra, the Stamps Quartet, and the Sweet Inspirations perform live. The middle and largest screen shows Elvis and the band members from the original footage. The side screens show the band members and vocalists playing and singing in the present. To make the experience seem more immediate, Elvis "interacts" with the band members in the present day. For example, Elvis introduces a band member in the 1970s and that person is shown on one screen as a young man and on another screen taking a bow in the present.

After Elvis's death, Sumner disbanded the Stamps to sing in a gospel supergroup called the Masters V with another of Elvis's idols, Jake Hess. He re-formed the Stamps in 1988, and the group often performed at Elvis-related events. Sumner died in 1998, and the Stamps name was passed on to one of his associates. The quartet still performs albeit in a different configuration than during the Elvis days.

*TRIVIA* Elvis loved Sumner's deep rich bass and often commented or joked about it onstage. Sumner once held the world's record for the lowest recorded note, which was a double low C during the song "Blessed Assurance," which is featured on the albums *Thank God for Kids* and *The Wait Is Over.*

## *Female vocal group, the Sweet Inspirations*

The beginnings of the Sweet Inspirations go back to the 1960s at Atlantic Records when its members served as the label's house vocalists, singing backup on songs by Aretha Franklin, Dionne Warwick, Wilson Pickett, Gene Pitney, and Van Morrison. Known simply as the Group, the original members included Cissy Houston, Doris Troy, and Dee Dee Warwick.

*TRIVIA* Cissy Houston is the mother of Grammy-winning singer Whitney Houston. Dee Dee Warwick is Cissy's niece and younger sister of singer Dionne Warwick.

By 1968, they were calling themselves the Sweet Inspirations after their most famous song, "Sweet Inspiration." At that time, the group included Houston, Sylvia Shemwell, Myrna Smith, and Estelle Brown. The group joined Elvis's act in 1969 when he hired them sight unseen after hearing their signature song. In 1970, Houston left the group and was replaced by Ann Williams. The Sweets, as they were nicknamed, stayed with Elvis until the end. In recent years, the Sweet Inspirations have reunited to join "Elvis: The Concert."

Interviewed for *Elvis Up Close* by Rose Clayton and Dick Heard, Smith believed that Elvis added their group to his act "because he wanted the spice of soul, but he didn't want it to be overbearing," which could be said of all the parts of his 1970s musical style.

## Soprano Kathy Westmoreland

Westmoreland represented the opposite end of the musical scale from bass singer J.D. Sumner, because she was a soprano with an extremely high range. She joined Elvis's act in 1970, replacing the previous soprano after she left unexpectedly during the middle of the Vegas engagement. Westmoreland thought she would be onboard for only two weeks, but she ended up staying with the show until Elvis died. She was a classically trained opera singer who had little experience with rock 'n' roll. Of course, that changed when she joined Elvis's musical entourage. Westmoreland sang backup with the rest of the singers on some songs, but she was added to the mix for certain ballads in which she sang a brief solo between Elvis's verses. During the show, if the audience seemed to be restless, Elvis often asked Westmoreland to sing a solo. Her angelic voice soothed the audience and helped to settle them down. After Elvis died, Westmoreland continued to perform but without the success of some of the other members of Elvis's onstage entourage.

Westmoreland, who had a personal relationship with Elvis at one time, wrote a book defending his final years. Titled *Elvis and Kathy,* the book was published in 1987.

## Orchestra director Joe Guercio

Joe Guercio, the director of the orchestra at the International Hotel, impressed Elvis when the singer performed there in 1970. So Colonel Parker made an arrangement with the hotel to have Guercio travel with Elvis on the road, along with an orchestra made up of more than 20 musicians. Guercio developed the orchestral arrangements for Elvis's songs, and he also arranged the singer's dramatic entrance onstage to the strains of the theme song from the 1968 film *2001: A Space Odyssey.* The orchestra added depth and scale to Elvis's music and provided a smoothness for the ballads and pop tunes that were an integral part of the act.

Loyal to the end, Guercio arranged and conducted the music for Elvis's funeral. (Refer to Chapter 15 for more details on Elvis's funeral.)

# Examining the Music: Uniquely Elvis

In early 1969, Elvis recorded a critically acclaimed album, *From Elvis in Memphis,* which revealed a new, vibrant style. Drowning in mediocre soundtrack albums, he had lost his cache in the music industry, but this new album reminded everyone that he was still a powerful interpreter of popular music. The songs from that album plus other material recorded around the same time yielded several singles that charted well. (You can read more information on *From Elvis in Memphis* in Chapter 11.)

The material for the album and singles was written by a new generation of Southern songwriters and musicians who had grown up listening to Elvis and rock 'n' roll during the 1950s. Their style wasn't traditional country nor did it sound like the West Coast rock that was dominating the charts. Sometimes called "swamp rock," this regional-tinged style influenced Elvis's sound during the 1970s, as did the music of African American R&B singers, called "soul music" at the time.

However, Elvis's music during the final phase of his career consisted of much more than just these Southern-based influences. His taste had always been eclectic, even when he was a young man, and this still proved true during the 1970s. For his live act, his song selection included contemporary rock 'n' roll, contemporary country rock, traditional country and gospel, R&B, and pop. More importantly, his sound seemed to fuse these styles together into something that was completely unique to Elvis. In other words, while it's easy to hear the influences of all these musical genres in Elvis's sound, you also can immediately recognize that sound as his style. Presley's song selection for his live act combined new material that he had recorded himself with standards or contemporary songs associated with a variety of other singers.

Elvis's sound was intense, hard driving, and large scale, and when he performed his music onstage, he was dramatic and theatrical. On the surface, his sound and performing style seem nothing like the Elvis Presley of the 1950s on the surface, but similarities do exist. For instance, during the 1970s, Elvis sang a unique blend of musical styles and genres, and he performed onstage with much flair and drama — a fair description of his 1950s music and performing style.

Using a sampling of songs from his 1970s concerts, this section explores Elvis's music from this highly recognizable but often maligned phase of his career.

## Revamping old favorites

In his concerts, Elvis sang several of his hits from the 1950s and a few tunes from his films in the 1960s, but unlike other pioneering rock 'n' rollers from the era, he didn't ride the nostalgia train. Instead, he used different arrangements for his past hits, or he relegated these songs to specific parts of the show to give them different connotations.

Elvis was an excellent judge of what his audience wanted to hear, and he knew they would want to hear his hits. After all, his 1950s tunes changed the course of music history. But Elvis also loved music too much not to want to update his style and sound. It wasn't part of his nature to rest on the laurels of his past. Here are some examples of how he used his old songs:

- "Love Me Tender" became a valentine to the fans.
- "Teddy Bear" became an opportunity for Elvis to throw souvenirs into the audience.
- "Can't Help Falling in Love" was a signal that the show had come to an end.
- "Hound Dog," "Heartbreak Hotel," "Don't Be Cruel," "Love Me," and other rock 'n' roll classics were generally sung as a medley with different arrangements than the originals.

## Performing the new singles

Between 1969 and 1972, Elvis released several successful singles that charted well. This magnitude of success hadn't occurred for the singer since the early 1960s. Some of these new tunes had been recorded at American Sound Studio in early 1969, a session that had produced the critically acclaimed album *From Elvis in Memphis*. (Refer to Chapter 11 for more information on the songs recorded at American Sound.)

Elvis's successful singles from this period, which became an essential part of his act, include the following:

- **"If I Can Dream"** was specially written to close *The '68 Comeback Special*. It was a song close to Elvis's heart, and he sang it with great conviction and emotion. The song was released as a single in November 1968 and reached number 12 on the *Billboard* Hot 100 chart. (I discuss *The '68 Comeback Special* in more detail in Chapter 11.)
- **"In the Ghetto,"** which was recorded at American Sound Studio on January 20, 1969, was released in April 1969 and charted at number three. The song was part of his playlist when he debuted at the International Hotel in the summer of 1969, and it remains an audience favorite.
- **"Suspicious Minds,"** like "In the Ghetto," was recorded at American Sound in January 1969, and it formed the centerpiece of his concert act. The song was released as a single in August 1969 and topped the charts at number one.

- **"Burning Love,"** which was recorded in Hollywood at RCA's Studio C in 1972, has always been a fan favorite, though Elvis supposedly didn't like the song. It reached number two on the *Billboard* Hot 100 chart.

## Move over Paul Simon: "Bridge Over Troubled Water"

Elvis recorded Paul Simon's chart-topping hit, "Bridge Over Troubled Water" in 1970, the same year that the singing duo Simon and Garfunkel released it. The song features a spiritual tone that appealed to Elvis, and it became another number that he performed with conviction when he sang it live. He performed the song regularly between 1970 and 1974, and then he sang it only occasionally after that.

Like many of Elvis's songs, "Bridge Over Troubled Water" starts slow and quiet and then builds to a dramatic conclusion. Elvis liked the melodrama of ballads and the theatricality of ending on a grand scale. He also had a way of making someone else's song his own, because he selected material that he had an emotional connection to. Simon had written and arranged the song to start slow and build, but Art Garfunkel's high voice is smooth and cool in comparison to Elvis's vocals, which are filled with passion and pain.

In 1986, Simon released an album that featured an eclectic mix of American rock, zydeco, and Tex-Mex with South African sounds, including the music of Ladysmith Black Mambazo. Inspired by his visit to Elvis's home, Simon titled the album *Graceland*. Besides its title, the fusion of genres and sounds of white and black music on the album also is reminiscent of Elvis's music.

## Remembering swamp rock: "Polk Salad Annie"

Elvis's version of "Polk Salad Annie," which was originally written by Southern rocker Tony Joe White, was recorded while he was performing onstage at the International in February 1970. Funky, sexy, and low down, the song was the epitome of *swamp rock*, a Southern-style rock 'n' roll.

The song was filled with Southern slang and cultural references that must have made mainstream audiences curious. The title made reference to an herb known in the South as pokeweed, poke, pokebush, pokeberry, pokeroot, polk salad, or polk sallet. Polk salad grows from one to ten feet tall in the wild and features single alternative leaves with crinkled edges. The stems are generally red, the flowers white, and the berries purple. The berries are poisonous, but the leaves can be cooked and served as greens. In the song, the singer claims he needs a "mess of it," meaning he desires a serving of it for a meal.

Later in the song, listeners hear a reference to "stealing watermelons from a truck patch," which is a small, rudimentary garden filled with vegetables and crops for a family's personal consumption (as opposed to a floral garden or a garden of produce to sell). Elsewhere the lyrics include "tote" to mean carry and "tote sack" to refer to a bag to hold valuables and possessions.

"Polk Salad Annie" allowed Elvis to revel in his Southern heritage, and he enjoyed performing it live, especially the musical exchanges with his band and the Sweet Inspirations.

## Singin' a song about the Southland: "An American Trilogy"

In 1971, country songwriter Mickey Newbury put together a unique arrangement of three 19th century songs, which he recorded and released as "An American Trilogy." Elvis heard the record and immediately incorporated the trilogy into his act for 1972. The piece has become so associated with Elvis Presley that it's difficult to imagine anyone else performing it with the same showstopping fervor that Elvis always did.

A combination of the Southern anthem "Dixie," Julia Ward Howe's abolitionist song "The Battle Hymn of the Republic," and the spiritual "All My Trials," the medley reflects Elvis's deep-felt patriotism, his religious convictions, and his deep affection for and innate understanding of his native South.

Backed with "The First Time Ever I Saw Your Face," "An American Trilogy" was released as a single in April 1972 at Elvis's insistence, but it struggled to sell even 100,000 copies. And, it never climbed higher than number 66 on the *Billboard* charts. But, the song is a perfect example of the difference between Elvis's live performances and his recordings. The song became a high point of the show when he performed it in concert with passion and conviction, but the record lacks the same level of expression.

Critics from the North and some music historians have failed to understand the significance of "An American Trilogy," which expressed the complexities of the South. Unable to accept the medley's overt sentiment, they speculate that Newbury had intended the piece to be ironic, or that Elvis, who was politically conservative, was simplistically patriotic. Many of these commentators fail to research the origins of the three songs that make up the trilogy. For Elvis, whose music symbolized the very essence of racial integration, the medley was a heartfelt expression of the history of his native South. Anyone who has heard his melancholy interpretation of "Dixie" and the dramatic grandeur of the trilogy's conclusion with "Battle Hymn" knows that it wasn't intended to be ironic or an expression of conservative values.

## Pondering the Priscilla Songs

Elvis and Priscilla separated in 1972, and they were divorced the following year. Even though they remained close and both moved on to different romantic interests, it proved to be a difficult time for Elvis. When Elvis and Priscilla began to grow apart, he included several songs about the trials and tribulations of life and love into his act:

- "Always on My Mind"
- "Separate Ways"
- "Funny How Time Slips Away"
- "You Gave Me a Mountain"

These new additions began around the spring of 1972, when he recorded "Separate Ways," "You Gave Me a Mountain," and "Always on My Mind." Fans interpreted these songs as a reflection of his marital woes, and they referred to them as the "Priscilla Songs." Even though he had been singing "Always on My Mind" since his return to live performances, in context with these other ballads, it took on the connotation of a Priscilla Song. More ballads about broken hearts and lost love would follow over the next couple of years; these songs, too, would be dubbed Priscilla Songs by fans.

During the Vegas engagement in 1972, as well as on the tours, Elvis didn't joke between numbers as he had in previous years, and the contact with the audience was kept to a minimum. The reason was undoubtedly Elvis's marital problems and subsequent breakup with Priscilla. The Vegas engagement, which ran from January 26 through February 23, suffered the most because Priscilla and Lisa Marie left Graceland and moved to Los Angeles on the last day of the engagement. Just after that, Elvis was admitted to the hospital for exhaustion.

Elvis never wrote a song, but his artistry and autobiography came through in his selection of material. Even though it's too simplistic to draw a cause-and-effect conclusion between Elvis's song selection in 1972 and his separation from Priscilla, his choice of material over the years is indirectly reflective of moods and feelings he was unable to vocalize any other way.

## Singing it his way

Elvis began singing "My Way" onstage in the summer of 1972. Singer-songwriter Paul Anka had penned the lyrics for this powerful song, which is about a man reflecting on his life as death draws near. Anka adapted "My Way" from a French love song called "Come d'Habitude," which he had heard on a visit to

Paris in 1969. He gave the song to Frank Sinatra when the singer asked Anka if he had any new material to record. Sinatra enjoyed a huge hit with the song, selling more than a million copies of the single.

The song became a personal anthem for Elvis — one that seemed to explain his eccentric lifestyle and larger-than-life image. A single release of this song by Elvis wasn't distributed until June 1977 — two months before he died.

## Appreciating the Significance of All the King's Jumpsuits

More than anything else, the white bejeweled jumpsuit has come to represent the Vegas era of Elvis's career. No more powerful icon exists in the world of Elvis; this single image at once connotes magnificent grandeur and gaudy excess — depending on whether you like this period of Elvis's career. To some, a jumpsuit-clad Elvis symbolizes the large-scale sound, theatrics, larger-than-life gestures, and dramatic performance style associated with this era; to others, it suggests a phony Vegas performer defined by his excesses — too many rhinestones, too much food, and too many drugs.

So much myth and misinformation and so many preconceived ideas surround the jumpsuits that it's difficult for many to read about them with an open mind. Yet Elvis's fans have long been fascinated by the jumpsuits, particularly the designs, which are not only intricate but also iconographic. Some of the designs represent Elvis's interests, values, personal tastes, and even moods. Elvis asked costumer Bill Belew to come up with a new jumpsuit design for every major tour, or at least for every year, so when looking at concert footage or photos, fans can estimate the year based on the jumpsuit and interpret the iconography to discover something new about him.

Elvis left behind no autobiography or definitive interview. Indeed, his personal life, values, and beliefs were hidden from the press and public at the Colonel's suggestion. Much that has been written about him has been through the point of view or personal perspective of others, leaving fans to search for creative ways to uncover Elvis's true feelings and beliefs. Considering his song selection at certain points in his life, as mentioned earlier in the chapter, and interpreting the designs of the jumpsuits offer a tiny window in the life of the man in the jumpsuit.

In this section, I discuss the origin of Elvis's jumpsuit and cover some insights into the iconography of the most famous of the King's costumes.

## Designing the first jumpsuit

Just before his second engagement at the International Hotel in January and February of 1970, Elvis asked costume designer Bill Belew to design a comfortable onstage ensemble that would allow him to move freely onstage. Belew had designed the black leather outfit the singer wore for the live segments of *The '68 Comeback Special,* and both Elvis and Priscilla admired his work, so it was natural that Elvis would work with the designer again. (I describe the karate suit costume that Elvis wore for the first engagement in Chapter 11.)

For the Vegas engagement, Belew designed a white wool gabardine jumpsuit that was slashed down the front, fitted tight at the waist, and belled out at the legs, which was the fashion of the day. The costume's high Napoleonic collar was inset with semiprecious jewels, and a macramé karate belt made of gold- and pearl-colored strands accentuated the singer's slender waist.

Compared with the later costumes that Belew designed for Elvis's Las Vegas appearances and tours, this first jumpsuit was modest. As the years passed and Elvis's stage show grew in scope and scale, his costumes became more and more elaborate, even flamboyant. The jumpsuits were often accompanied by waist-length or even floor-length capes lined with brightly colored silk.

According to friends and family, the gems and gold chains and rivets that decorated these costumes were real and could make the jumpsuit weigh as much as 30 pounds. Simply standing up in such a heavy costume could be physically exhausting, but Elvis generally didn't stand still. Instead, he moved quickly and gracefully across the stage under hot lights, causing him to perspire and wear out quickly. As the act became more theatrical, and the jumpsuits more elaborate and thus heavier, the show became shorter in length.

## Considering the jumpsuits as autobiography

Elvis's costumes, particularly the belts, were often emblazoned with symbols that had personal significance to Elvis. These motifs include eagles, karate symbols, peacocks, tigers, and sundials. The singer's fans refer to his costumes by name: the Mexican Sundial, the King of Spades, the Rainbow Swirl, the American Eagle, the Red Flower, the Gypsy, or the Dragon. While not every jumpsuit is rife with personal iconography, many of them do reveal something of interest about Elvis. I explain the meanings behind some of his most famous costumes in the following sections.

### The Burning Love

Elvis wore a bright red jumpsuit onstage during the fall of 1972, which the fans dubbed the Burning Love jumpsuit, partly because of its color and partly because Elvis incorporated the song "Burning Love" into his act that year.

The all-red jumpsuit may be the boldest color of all Elvis's costumes, and he elected to wear it during a particularly emotional time when his marriage was falling apart. Drawing cause-and-effect conclusions are too simplistic, and I will refrain from doing that in this case, but it is a curious color even by Elvis's standards.

Some confusion exists over the Burning Love jumpsuit because another of Elvis's costumes was also given the same name. Elvis wore a white costume and cape for one of the shows during the Madison Square Garden engagement, and a photo of him in this ensemble appeared on the front of the album *Burning Love, and Hits from His Movies, Volume 2,* which is the reason the white-and-gold ensemble was christened with that name. But over time, the red suit usurped the nickname.

Elvis donated the red suit to the National Cerebral Palsy Telethon in 1972. In 1995, the suit resurfaced at a Las Vegas auction and sold for $107,000.

### Aloha from Hawaii (also known as the Aloha Eagle)

The landmark television special *Elvis: Aloha from Hawaii* was telecast live to several countries via satellite on January 14, 1973. (See Chapter 14 for more information.) Elvis was amazed at the satellite technology that allowed him to sing before so many foreign countries at the same time, and he attributed it to American ingenuity. So, because he was proud of his country, Elvis wanted a costume that shouted "America" to the worldwide audiences.

For this show, Belew produced a white jumpsuit with an American eagle patterned in red, gold, and blue gems. The costume's spectacular calf-length cape proved too cumbersome in rehearsals, so Elvis asked Belew to modify it to a hip-length cape. A belt decorated with gold American eagles accented the ensemble.

Aside from the iconography that revealed Elvis's passion for his country, this costume has become legendary because in a burst of excitement over the crowd's enthusiasm, Elvis threw both the belt and the cape into the cheering audience near the end of the show. He ordered a second belt and cape to replace those so he could continue using the costume that year. The cape surfaced in a private collection during the 1990s.

By the end of 1974, Elvis stopped wearing capes onstage. Not only were they heavy, but members of the audience began grabbing the corners of the capes while he was performing, and he was in danger of falling offstage.

### The Memphis

This white jumpsuit with an abstract design was named the Memphis in honor of Elvis's hometown. He wore the suit when he opened his 1974 tour in Memphis, marking the first time Elvis performed in his hometown since 1961. Oddly, Elvis had worn this suit during his August 1973 Las Vegas engagement, so it wasn't new to the 1974 tour. However, it is a reminder of how much Elvis loved Memphis, the only place he could truly escape the pressures of his enormous stardom. The suit is also called the King by fans.

### The Tiger

Elvis wore the Tiger jumpsuit, also called the Mad Tiger, around 1973 or 1974. This white jumpsuit with a high collar sported an open V-neck, flared sleeves, and belled pant legs. The dominant design was a jumping tiger, which wrapped around the front of the suit from the bottom left to the top right. The suit was accented with tiger stripes down the sides of the legs, on the collar, and on the belt buckle.

*TRIVIA*

Karate, which he picked up when he was in the army, became an important hobby to Elvis. He dabbled in the sport for 20 years, and his karate name was the Tiger.

### The Peacock

Elvis wore the Peacock, which became one of his favorite jumpsuits, during a 1974 tour. A white jumpsuit with a V-neck and high collar, the Peacock features a large blue and gold bird rendered in a stylized design on the front and back. The birds were hand embroidered with gold thread. Blue stylized peacock feathers fell down the sides of the pant legs, and the belt included gold medallions that alternated with motifs that resembled the eye of a peacock feather.

A religious person, Elvis believed in an afterlife, and he knew that in some cultures, the peacock symbolizes eternal life. For that reason, he was captivated by the birds for a while. At one time he even kept a few live peacocks around Graceland. Inside the house, a peacock design can be found on the stained-glass windows that separate the living room from the music room. (To read more about the rooms of Graceland, flip to Chapter 19.)

*TRIVIA*

The Peacock was the most expensive jumpsuit ever made for Elvis, costing the singer more than $10,000. In recent years, the Peacock sold at auction for $300,000.

### The Bear Claw

Also known as the Sabre Tooth, this navy-colored jumpsuit offers a variation on the V-neck, flared-sleeve design. The Bear Claw features a scoop neck and baby blue puffy sleeves. The suit is decorated with designs similar to those found in Native American arts. The dominant motif is the bear's claw.

Simulated bear claws encircle the neck like a necklace and adorn the front of the suit as well as the flared area of the pant legs. Elvis wore this suit on tour in 1975 and 1976.

### Other jumpsuits

The following list of jumpsuits reveals a variety of colors and designs, belying the stereotype that Elvis wore only white jumpsuits:

- Green Cisco Kid (1971)
- The Blue Swirl (1972)
- The Adonis (1972)
- The Tiffany (1972)
- The Black Conquistador (1974)
- The Dragon (1974)
- The Blue Rainbow (1974)
- American Eagle (1974, not to be confused with the Aloha from Hawaii jumpsuit)
- The Black Phoenix (1975)
- The Red Phoenix (1975 and 1976)
- Indian Feather (1975)
- The Sun Dial (1976 and 1977)
- The Gypsy (1976)

Check out the color photo section in this book for a look at the Black Conquistador and other jumpsuits.

Costume designer Bill Belew revealed that just before Elvis died, the two of them had come up with a new twist on the old jumpsuits. Belew recalls in *Elvis Up Close* by Rose Clayton and Dick Heard, "There was a new look in development for Elvis. We had literally gone as far as we could with the jewels and the embroidery work, and I was working on this new idea: It was a costume with lasers. Between the spotlights hitting the jewels and the lasers coming from the suit, it would have really been spectacular."

## Ritualizing the Experience

The typical Presley concert of the 1970s was more like a series of rituals and ceremonies than a performance by a mere entertainer. Elvis engaged in dramatic actions and gestures throughout the concert, which were emotive, expressive, and therefore exciting to the audiences. Similarly, specific songs signaled certain behaviors that fans looked forward to, especially those involving interaction between the singer and the audience.

The interaction between Elvis and audience members while he was onstage gave the illusion of intimacy, which is the key to the Presley concert experience. Treating the concert and its routines like a ceremony created a close bond among audience members, even if there were thousands of them. And engaging in the rituals with Elvis cemented a connection between fan and performer that has lasted decades. Sometimes, his rapport with his audiences was like a conversation among a gathering of old friends; other times, it took the form of romantic flirtation. In this section, I discuss the interactions, routines, and rituals associated with the typical 1970s Elvis concert.

When Elvis played the International, which became the Las Vegas Hilton in 1971, most fans didn't come for only one performance; they booked rooms for a week or even two and attended both shows every night for the duration of their stay. Every one of Elvis's Vegas engagements was sold out far in advance, and the International made about $1.5 million per engagement. Waiters and maitre d's were tipped heavily for the best seats in the house, which was money they split among themselves. During Elvis's engagement, the tip amount was never less than $10,000 per night. No other Vegas entertainer commanded that level of fan devotion.

## Making an entrance

The Elvis experience began with the singer's grand entrance onstage. Early on, from about 1969 to 1971, his entrance was modest as he strolled briskly onto the stage and then ripped into "All Shook Up" or "That's All Right" for his first song.

But, as his act became more grandiose, he needed a more flamboyant entrance. So, in 1971, he created a new entrance: As Joe Guercio's orchestra played Richard Strauss's *Also Sprach Zarathustra,* popularly known as the "Theme from 2001," Elvis charged into the spotlight as though propelled by some supernatural force. He then launched into the first song, which was permanently changed to "See See Rider" in 1972. This entrance and opening song remained unchanged for the rest of his career.

## Exchanging gifts and tossing underwear

Much of the interaction that occurred between audience members and Elvis while he was onstage was comparable to exchanging "gifts." Elvis threw towels, scarves, and flowers into the audience; fans returned the gesture by throwing teddy bears, bouquets of roses, and other mementos.

The most intriguing part of this ritual was performed by members of the audience. Each time Elvis played Las Vegas, the hotel stocked fresh undergarments in the restrooms because the women liked to throw them onto the stage while he was performing. Occasionally, they threw the keys to their hotel rooms as well.

More peculiar parts of Elvis's act included him wiping the sweat from his brow and throwing the scarf or towel into the audience. As the years passed, this gesture became such a popular ritual that dozens of white towels were kept on hand so Elvis could throw them into the audience at frequent intervals. Charlie Hodge, one of Elvis's closest friends who played rhythm guitar onstage, was in charge of placing new scarves or towels around his neck. Fans coveted these scarves because they were actually worn by Elvis, even if only for a few seconds.

Elvis occasionally got carried away with the ritualized exchange of gifts and tossed expensive rings or his jewel-encrusted belts into audience. At least once, he threw his cape into the crowd (see the earlier section "Aloha from Hawaii" for details).

## Romancing his audience

Elvis resurrected his 1956 hit "Love Me Tender" for his 1970s act. Eventually, the song became a sort of valentine to the fans in that Elvis kissed, hugged, and held hands with many of the women in the audience while he sang the song. As soon as the audience heard the opening notes to this ballad, they lined up just below the stage like a receiving line for royalty, waiting to be blessed by the King's touch. In effect, Elvis was courting the women in the audience with the illusion of physical affection and tokens of his esteem.

This type of interaction can be traced back to Elvis's early career, when audiences became hysterical at his gyrations and performing style. Even then, Elvis exhibited an uncanny instinct for knowing what the fans wanted to see and hear; however, during the 1950s, the effect was akin to sexual attraction rather than romance. He teased them with a few hip and leg movements, they responded, and then he cut loose, singling out specific members of the audience to interact with. This phenomenon was also reciprocal in nature, forming a strong bond between performer and audience. If Elvis's fans were unusually loyal and demonstrative throughout his career, this interactive aspect of his act — from the beginning of his career to the end — was partially responsible.

Elvis said this about performing live: "A live concert to me is exciting because of all the electricity that is generated in the crowd and onstage. It's my favorite part of the business — live concerts."

### Dramatizing his act

When Elvis was particularly caught up in the music during a concert, he incorporated karate kicks and tai chi arabesques as well as other dramatic gestures, stances, and moves into his performance. During the years he wore a cape onstage, he was fond of taking the ends of the cape in both hands and lifting it into the air, spreading the cape like angel wings. Sometimes he even dropped to one knee. Elvis liked the effect because it was quite theatrical and stirred the audience. At other times, he shook his body in time to the music, raised his hands in striking poses, and prowled back and forth across the stage. See Figure 13-1 for a shot of Elvis performing during this time.

From his first moments onstage Elvis had always moved dramatically, partly because of his nervous energy and partly because it roused the audience. During the 1950s, his constant need to move took the form of his controversial hip and leg gyrations, which were sexual and sensual. Looking back at those moves, they were no less dramatic than the karate kicks, hand gestures, and body quivers of the 1970s. Some movements and mannerisms stayed consistent from the 1950s to the 1970s, particularly the way he shook his leg to keep time to the pulsing, fast-paced music.

Figure 13-1: Elvis got caught up in the music while performing, moving dramatically and constantly onstage.

### Leaving the building

During the 1970s, a Vegas-style comedian always opened Elvis's concerts. Rock music aficionados were appalled by the old-fashioned routines and stale jokes of these stand-up comics, particularly because they saw the rise of a new, more hip generation of comedians with socially relevant material. But, even when he was on the cutting edge of rock 'n' roll in 1956 and 1957,

## Chapter 13: Savoring Elvis in Concert

Elvis always toured with an oddball assortment of vaudeville-flavored acts dug up by his manager, Colonel Parker. It seems only natural that the Colonel would hire this type of opening act when Elvis returned to live performances in the 1970s. Elvis and the Colonel were accustomed to this kind of show business act, and the humor went over well in Vegas. Sammy Shore opened for Elvis in the early 1970s, and Jackie Kahane did the honors after 1972.

*REMEMBER*

Kahane's responsibilities as the comic relief included letting the audience know when it was time to leave the auditorium. Elvis rarely performed an encore, though many times the audience remained behind after the final number hoping Elvis would respond to the thunderous applause and return for one last song. However, to avoid any problems with overzealous fans, Elvis always ran backstage immediately after the last song, often while the band was still playing, and dashed into a car waiting at the stage door. Kahane then let the audience know that it was truly time to leave. Little did Elvis, Kahane, or anyone else connected with the Presley show realize that this closing moment would become one of pop culture's most infamous catch phrases: "Ladies and gentlemen, Elvis has left the building."

# Chapter 14
# Enjoying a Professional Peak

### In This Chapter
▶ Accepting an honor from the Jaycees
▶ Conquering New Yorkers at Madison Square Garden
▶ Broadcasting his music to the world in *Elvis: Aloha from Hawaii*
▶ Spreading his music throughout the country with documentaries
▶ Inspiring change in Las Vegas

After Elvis returned to live performances in 1969, he enjoyed several unique career highlights. From about 1970 to 1973, his return to the stage resulted in a stretch of sold-out crowds in Las Vegas, successful tours, and singular achievements unsurpassed by other entertainers. His accolades and accomplishments ranged from awards for his charitable donations to unprecedented engagements and one-of-a-kind performance venues.

Beyond these achievements, Elvis was respected by everyone from other Vegas entertainers to contemporary rock 'n' rollers. His successful return to Vegas influenced the style of entertainment that audiences expected to see in America's fun capital. Once dominated by smooth pop crooners, Las Vegas venues saw the rise of a different breed of singer with a large-scale, rock-influenced sound, a sexier performance style, and a more glitzy presence.

In retrospect, Elvis's years on tour and in concert in Vegas have taken on a negative connotation associated with his drug use, weight problems, health issues, and lifestyle of excess. Many assume that throughout the 1970s Elvis was considered an overweight, jumpsuited Vegas performer who appealed only to an unhip crowd of older women and working-class families. (See Chapter 17 for details about how this connotation evolved.) But, from 1970 to 1973, this wasn't true. A few bad notices aside, Elvis was considered a successful and respected entertainer in his public life throughout much of the 1970s, and this chapter details the highlights of this phase of his career.

> ## And the nominees are . . .
>
> Elvis was in good company the year he was honored with the distinction of being one of the Jaycees' Outstanding Young Men of America. The other recipients from 1970 included the following men:
>
> - **Thomas Atkins,** an African American councilman from Boston who worked as a civil rights activist during that city's tense racial problems of the late 1960s.
> - **Captain William Bucha,** a Medal of Honor winner who became an expert on the Middle East. Bucha later went on to serve as a foreign policy advisor to President Barack Obama's 2008 campaign.
> - **Dr. Mario Capecchi,** a molecular geneticist who later was the cowinner of the 2007 Nobel Prize in Physiology or Medicine.
> - **Harry Cherry,** a prominent businessman.
> - **Edward Thomas Coll,** a humanitarian who committed his life to volunteer service.
> - **James B. Goetz,** a radio broadcaster and regional media mogul who later became lieutenant governor of Minnesota.
> - **Walter Humann,** a business leader who later held key positions in major corporations, including chairman of Memorex-Telex and CEO of WJH Corporation.
> - **Dr. George Todaro,** a medical researcher who later worked with the National Cancer Institute.
> - **Ron Ziegler,** the White House Press Secretary during President Richard Nixon's administration, from 1969 to 1974.

## Becoming an Outstanding Young Man

In January 1971, Elvis was officially named one of the Ten Outstanding Young Men of America of 1970 by the Junior Chamber of Commerce (otherwise known as the Jaycees). This honor touched him deeply, especially because the ceremony was scheduled to take place in Memphis that year. The Jaycees are a nationally based community group devoted to civic duty. Each year, the Jaycees consider several young men for this honor, usually under the age of 40, who are prominent in their fields. Each name is suggested by a respected member of the community, and then a panel of distinguished judges makes the final decision. Memphis Sheriff Bill Morris, a friend of Elvis's since his Tupelo days, sponsored his nomination. The judges in 1970, who included former President Lyndon B. Johnson, chose Elvis not simply because he was a famous entertainer but because of his many acts of philanthropy.

An awards ceremony was held at Ellis Auditorium in Memphis on January 15, which included a prayer breakfast, a luncheon, a press conference, and an evening ceremony. At the ceremony, George H.W. Bush, later President of the United States, served as the keynote speaker. Then each honoree gave a speech while accepting his award statue.

> ### A generous gift: Elvis shows his true colors
>
> After being honored by the Jaycees, Elvis and Priscilla hosted a cocktail party for all the Outstanding Young Men of America honorees. At the party, he generously presented each honoree with a Mathey-Tissot watch as they came through the door. A tasteful-looking man's watch that displayed the date, the timepiece featured the name "Elvis Presley" on the beveled edge that encircled the face. Elvis generally gave these watches as a gesture of fellowship to friends and acquaintances; in this case, he wanted to show his respect for the other honorees. (For more on Elvis's penchant for giving jewelry as gifts, flip to Chapter 15.)
>
> A mix-up that revealed something of Elvis's nature occurred with the giving of these gifts. One of the watches was accidentally handed to an assistant transportation chairman for the Jaycees, who was thrilled to be singled out by Elvis Presley for a gift. Elvis didn't ask the Jaycee to give the watch back, because he didn't want to hurt the man's feelings. Instead Elvis ordered an additional watch for the ninth honoree.

Elvis agonized over his acceptance speech. His lack of formal education compared to most of the other honorees must have made him feel intimidated. But his inspiring speech was not only eloquent; it also was one of his few public statements that offered a glimpse of the real Elvis Presley. He based part of the speech on a song by soul singer Roy Hamilton, who was one of Elvis's favorites. Here's part of his moving speech, which was printed in the *Commercial Appeal* on January 17, 1971: "When I was a child, ladies and gentlemen, I was a dreamer. I read comic books, and I was the hero of the comic book. I saw movies, and I was the hero in the movie. So every dream that I've dreamed has come true a hundred times . . . I'd like to say that I learned very early in life that, 'Without a song the day would never end, Without a song a man ain't got a friend, Without a song the road would never bend, Without a song.' So I keep singing a song."

Elvis was extremely proud of the Jaycees award, which was the only honor he ever accepted at a public ceremony. Today the statue, which is often on display at Graceland, is nicked and scratched, giving the impression that perhaps it was neglected or discarded. In fact, the opposite was true: Elvis was so touched by this accolade that he carried the award with him on every tour, which accounts for its worn appearance.

# Went to a Garden Party: Elvis Performs in New York City

Perhaps it was because it was the home of Tin Pan Alley, or perhaps it was because of the city's harsh critics who had always barked at his heels, but Elvis had never performed in concert in New York City. Finally in June

1972, Colonel Tom Parker, Elvis's manager, arranged for him to play three shows at the famed Madison Square Garden. On the day the tickets went on sale, almost 2,000 people mobbed the ticket office before dawn. The shows sold out so quickly that a fourth show was added, and it sold out as well. Elvis became the first entertainer to sell out four consecutive shows in the Garden.

Despite the enthusiasm of the public, Elvis and the Colonel were intimidated by the big-city New York critics, so they courted them in a press conference before the engagement. A good-natured Elvis joked with the critics and poked a bit of fun at himself, hoping to win them over with charm.

At the Madison Square Garden press conference, Elvis made one of his most famous and revealing statements. When a reporter asked him about his image, Elvis grew serious for a moment and then quietly remarked, "An image is one thing and a human being is another . . . It is very hard to live up to an image."

Even though Elvis wore more than one jumpsuit during the engagement, the one most photographed was a white jumpsuit with a gold-lined cape. He accented the costume with the gigantic belt given to him by the International Hotel. The belt said "The World Champion Entertainer" — just in case the critics forgot who was performing. (You can read more about Elvis's jumpsuits in Chapter 13.) Elvis appeared to be in top physical condition during the engagement, which was attended by 80,000 people, including the cream of contemporary rock artists such as John Lennon, Bob Dylan, and Elton John.

RCA recorded all four shows at the Garden for an album called *Elvis as Recorded at Madison Square Garden.* To take advantage of the good press and enthusiasm generated over the engagement, the record company mixed the songs, pressed the records, and had the albums in stores in less than two weeks. The hasty release even beat the bootleggers to the punch! The successful album reached number eight on the Top LPs, remaining on the charts for 34 weeks.

Most of the New York reviewers and critics begrudgingly offered positive notices, though some of them didn't quite understand Elvis Presley and his music. Two separate but equally condescending reviews in the *New Yorker,* for example, seemed completely perplexed by "American Trilogy" and what it could possibly mean (see Chapter 13 for more information on this medley). However, *Variety,* the venerable show business trade magazine, summed up the experience perfectly, noting, "He stood there at the end, his arms stretched out, the great gold cloak giving him wings, a champion, the only one in his class."

# Performing for the World: Aloha from Hawaii

About a month after the Madison Square Garden engagement, Colonel Parker announced that Elvis would be participating in the first worldwide live satellite broadcast, because, according to the Colonel, "It is the intention of Elvis to please all of his fans throughout the world."

REMEMBER

Despite having a worldwide following, including the Far East, Elvis never played outside the United States and Canada. He had always wanted to, but the Colonel never arranged it. This satellite broadcast was the closest Elvis ever came to performing for people outside the States.

In January 1973, Elvis gave a benefit performance at the Honolulu International Center Arena in Hawaii for the Kuiokalani Lee Cancer Fund, which was the concert chosen to be broadcast to more than 40 countries via the Globecam Intelstat IV satellite. Titled *Elvis: Aloha from Hawaii*, the program was the first worldwide television broadcast, and more than a billion people eventually watched this one performance — roughly a third of the world's population at the time. Satellite transmission was still relatively new, so only an entertainer of Elvis's magnitude could interest the participants in pulling off this costly event. Figure 14-1 shows Elvis posing by an advertisement of his program.

In this section, the *Aloha from Hawaii* concert is reviewed in detail to capture this one-of-a-kind experience.

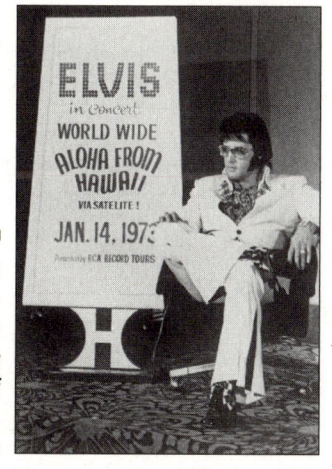

**Figure 14-1:** Elvis promotes the *Aloha from Hawaii* concert.

Because of the international audience, the sheer number of people who watched, and the fact that no one had used satellite capabilities for an entertainment program like this before, *Elvis: Aloha from Hawaii* is considered by some to be the high point of Presley's career. In *The Elvis Encyclopedia* by Adam Victor, Memphis Mafia member Sonny West said, "It was the pinnacle of his career; he never looked as good again."

## Achieving a career pinnacle

Taking advantage of advances in global communications, *Elvis: Aloha from Hawaii* was beamed by the Globecam Intelsat IV satellite on January 14, 1973, from Honolulu International Center Arena. Producer-director Marty Pasetta conceived a simple but effective stage setting for the special. A backdrop featuring Elvis's name in different languages reminded viewers that this special was for an international audience, and a runway jutting into the audience allowed the singer to safely walk out into the crowd without actually being a part of it. Elvis periodically walked the runway, leaning over to receive flower leis from audience members. To see Elvis performing in the concert, check out the color photo section.

Elvis sang a variety of songs throughout the concert special, including the following:

- Current hits, such as "Burning Love" and "Suspicious Minds"
- Past hits "Hound Dog," "Love Me," and "A Big Hunk o' Love"
- Pop and rock tunes like "My Way" and "Steamroller Blues"
- The moving Hank Williams classic "I'm So Lonesome I Could Cry"

The song selection was a fair approximation of his stage show from around that time.

After the audience left the arena, the production crew filmed Elvis singing five more songs, which were added to the U.S. version of the televised concert in order to lengthen it to a standard 90-minute television time slot.

Both this show and the dress rehearsal (which took place two days earlier) benefited the Kuiokalani Lee Cancer Fund. Lee was a Hawaiian composer who had died of cancer, and Elvis performed Lee's song "I'll Remember You" in his honor. About $75,000 was raised for the fund through ticket sales and additional contributions. The program cost the participating production companies and networks about $2.5 million, but they made their money back through advertising and fees.

## Broadcasting to the world

Broadcast at 12:30 a.m. Hawaii-Aleutian Time, *Elvis: Aloha from Hawaii* was seen in Australia, New Zealand, South Korea, Thailand, South Vietnam, the Philippine Islands, Japan, and the Far East. Even parts of Communist China supposedly tuned in. The next day, the show was rebroadcast to 28 European countries, except for the United Kingdom. Despite Elvis's enormous popularity in England and Ireland, the BBC didn't want to pay the asking price to participate. These broadcasts of the special consisted of a concert performance by Elvis in front of a live audience. NBC broadcast the program on April 4 for the U.S. audience, and used four of the additional five songs Elvis recorded after the live show (see the preceding section for details).

The American broadcast of the special received a *57 share,* meaning more than half of the people watching television tuned into *Elvis: Aloha from Hawaii.* More people watched this special than the first walk on the moon. In Japan, 37.8 percent of people watching television were tuned into Elvis, and in the Philippines, an amazing 92 percent of the television viewing public watched the special.

## Tossing the cape

Elvis performed a full dress rehearsal before an audience on January 12, which was recorded but not televised. Elvis wore a white jumpsuit that featured an American eagle on the front and back; this costume also came with a cape. For the finale of the rehearsal, Elvis donned the cape and sang his usual closing number "Can't Help Falling in Love," which he had first crooned in the 1961 film *Blue Hawaii.* Usually, he concluded this song by dropping to one knee and grabbing the ends of his cape in his hands, spreading the garment above him like angel wings — a grandiose gesture befitting the King. On this night, he added an extra touch by throwing the cape into the crowd. Earlier in the performance he had thrown his belt, so it was only fitting to toss his cape as well. (You can read more on this jumpsuit, cape, and belt in Chapter 13.)

After the rehearsal, Elvis's foreman, Joe Esposito, called costume designer Bill Belew in a panic to tell him that the singer had just thrown his cape and belt into the crowd. Belew and his crew worked overtime to make another cape, complete with jewels and hand embroidery. Belew's assistant flew with the new cape and belt to ensure that the accessories arrived on time and in top condition. After he delivered them, he stayed for the concert. When it was over, the assistant reluctantly called Belew to tell him that Elvis had thrown the second cape into the audience. Now a part of Elvis lore, the cape story has been told and retold in countless books and memoirs, with the details often confused. The episode deserves its legendary status because it offers a larger-than-life ending to a once-in-a-lifetime event.

## Reliving the concert over and over with the Aloha albums

Those fans who missed the concert didn't have long to wait for the album. RCA employed two record-pressing plants and worked them overtime to quickly get out an album. One month later, a double-LP titled *Aloha from Hawaii via Satellite* was released simultaneously around the world. The album became Elvis's first number one LP in eight years, and as it turned out, it was the last chart-topping album of his career, at least on the pop charts. Within two weeks, the album sold half a million copies before eventually reaching multi-platinum status.

Since then, RCA and the Elvis Presley Estate have issued many versions of this historic special and album, making it difficult to separate the original from the additional footage. Here are some of the many versions:

- In 1988, the music from the dress rehearsal was released as *The Alternate Aloha*.
- In 1992 and 1998, the album *Aloha from Hawaii via Satellite* was rereleased with the additional tracks recorded after the show.
- In 2000, a DVD of *Aloha from Hawaii* with both the special and the dress rehearsal was released.
- In 2004, another edition, also called *Aloha From Hawaii,* was issued that included the special, the dress rehearsal, the extra songs recorded for the American broadcast, and footage of Elvis interacting with fans at the Honolulu airport.

# Capturing the Concert Years on Film

Some claim that the best movies starring Elvis Presley are two documentaries that he made during the concert years — *Elvis: That's the Way It Is* and *Elvis on Tour*. Well crafted by prominent filmmakers, both documentaries received critical acclaim. As decades pass and memories fade, these documentaries not only chronicle his music and performing style but remind younger generations of his impact on audiences. This section offers the highlights of these two well-crafted documentaries.

## Elvis: That's the Way It Is

*Elvis: That's the Way It Is* focuses on Presley's 1970 summer appearance at the International Hotel, beginning with rehearsals in Hollywood, though addi-

## Chapter 14: Enjoying a Professional Peak

tional material is also included. Elvis began rehearsals July 5 at the MGM studios, where he's shown whipping his band into shape and mastering new material for the act. Elvis and the band rehearsed 60 songs altogether, but most of them didn't make it into the show. (Chapter 13 introduces the band he performed with at the International.)

Shots of the massive promotional buildup in Las Vegas are intercut with the rehearsal footage. A film crew was even sent to Luxembourg to record an Elvis Presley convention to illustrate the excitement of fans over Elvis's return to public performances. The film is structured so that the rehearsals, the scenes of preparation, and the shots of enthusiastic fans build anticipation and excitement for the main event.

The International show opened August 10, and the cameras recorded not only opening night but also several performances throughout the engagement. Plus, one segment in which Elvis sings "Mystery Train" and "Tiger Man" was filmed at a concert at Veterans Memorial Coliseum in Phoenix, Arizona. When edited together, the concert footage builds to an exciting, fast-paced climax of Elvis performing his best material. Dressed in a simple, white jumpsuit, accented with fringe instead of rhinestones and gems, Elvis is clearly at the top of his game.

*Elvis: That's the Way It Is* was directed by Denis Sanders, who won an Academy Award for Best Documentary for his film *Czechoslovakia 1968*. Award-winning cinematographer Lucien Ballard, one of the most respected in Hollywood, caught the excitement of Elvis's performance on stage with eight Panavision cameras.

One of Ballard's most acclaimed films is *The Wild Bunch* (1969), directed by Sam Peckinpah. This groundbreaking violent western is justifiably famous for its fast-paced editing in a montage style. This style of editing consists of a barrage of brief shots to depict an action, making the editing more obvious and the action more stimulating. Ballard and director Sanders employed a similar technique in *Elvis: That's the Way It Is* to capture the excitement of Elvis and his dramatic music. When Colonel Parker saw the film during a rough cut, he didn't care for the editing style, but when Elvis saw the final version of the film, he was pleased.

*Elvis: That's the Way It Is* was released on November 11, 1970, to good reviews. It reached number 22 on the *Variety* weekly box office report, which is a fair showing for a documentary. The *Hollywood Reporter* remarked that Elvis probably was the only entertainer alive who could draw enough people into a theater to make a documentary profitable at the box office. The film also introduced Elvis as a live performer to an audience who was too young to remember him from the 1950s and knew Elvis only from his movies.

## Elvis on Tour

The second documentary to capture Elvis in performance focused on his road show. *Elvis on Tour* chronicled the singer's short but grueling 15-city tour in the spring of 1972. The tour started in Buffalo, New York, and came to a rousing conclusion in Albuquerque, New Mexico. Filmmakers Pierre Adidge and Robert Abel succeeded in capturing the hectic pace of Elvis's touring schedule through a montage sequence of cities the singer visited during the tour.

One of the most telling scenes is not one in which Elvis sings onstage. Just before the show is about to start, Elvis, members of the TCB Band, the Sweet Inspirations, and the Stamps are shown waiting to go on. (Check out Chapter 13 for more on these groups that Elvis performed with.) A bit nervous, Elvis begins to sing the gospel song "Bosom of Abraham" to break the tension, and the others quickly join in. Obviously, everyone knows the song as they break into it spontaneously. Not only is gospel music key to Elvis's sound, but it's also the thread that binds together the seemingly diverse musical elements of his act — the rock band, the African American backup singers, and the country gospel quartet.

Costing $600,000 to produce (not counting Elvis's fee of $1 million), *Elvis on Tour* recouped its production costs after just three days in theaters. Documentaries are rarely major box-office draws, but this film was a financial success. Critically acclaimed as well, *Elvis on Tour* won a Golden Globe as the Best Documentary of 1972.

Again, the creative success of the film was due to its effective editing style, which relied on a split-screen technique to capture the excitement of Elvis in concert. Multiple images of Elvis performing were shown on the screen simultaneously, a technique that had been used in the 1970 documentary *Woodstock*.

The series of scenes from Elvis's movies plus the succession of clips of the different cities visited on the tour also depended on precise editing for its visual impact. In charge of these montage sequences was a young filmmaker named Martin Scorsese.

## Influencing Las Vegas Entertainment

One of the remarkable characteristics of Elvis's music, performing style, and career is that those three elements worked together to make Presley a wholly unique entertainer. And yet he also inspired others to follow his musical choices, his flair, and his performing style. During his concert years, Elvis seemed to be a show business genre unto himself, but other entertainers were clearly influenced by him, especially in Las Vegas. Elvis had a profound impact on Las Vegas entertainment, and only recently have his concert years been considered in that regard. This section offers some observations and comments on Elvis's impact on the city that sparked his comeback.

## A therapeutic shot in the arm for Las Vegas

The generation of pop singers that dominated the Vegas Strip prior to Elvis sang or crooned with conviction and personal style, but that style — epitomized by the members of the Rat Pack — was low key, relaxed, and simple. Standing in front of the audience in their suits, they sang the way pop singers had sung for decades. Even though they spoke to the audience, introduced songs, and joked onstage, a distance stood between the performer on the stage and the people in the audience. Audiences who grew up with rock 'n' roll couldn't relate to the conventions and music of previous generations, and they looked upon Vegas as a destination for members of their parents' crowd. So Las Vegas began to lose tourists, and the hotels often lost money on their entertainment.

Elvis's high-energy, large-scale, interactive show added excitement and sex appeal to Vegas entertainment, which attracted young adult audiences to the city. The jumpsuits and theatrics may have seemed like good old-fashioned show business, but Elvis combined them with a soulful, expressive singing style and a rock 'n' roll sensibility. His show became a template for future Vegas acts. (See the following section for details on acts that followed in Elvis's footsteps.)

Nancy Sinatra, who not only knew Elvis but also knew something of Las Vegas through her famous father, reflected in the ABC television special *Elvis: Viva Las Vegas,* "Las Vegas needed a shot in the arm, and Elvis was the potion. He got the young people in. And the young people helped to build a new Vegas."

## Establishing the Vegas-style performance template

Singers Tom Jones and Engelbert Humperdinck were among the first to follow in Elvis's footsteps in Vegas. Though Tom Jones played Las Vegas before Elvis, he ramped up the energy and sex appeal of his act after seeing Presley perform at the International in August 1969. Engelbert Humperdinck also frequented Elvis's shows during the 1970s.

Decades later, Elvis's combination of sex appeal and showbiz glitz with a rock 'n' roll beat can still be found in the acts of Vegas stalwarts Celine Dion, Cher, Prince, and Elton John. In addition, Elvis's long-term contract with the International and his month-long engagements prefigured the current Vegas *residency contracts* in which entertainers perform at the same hotel for several months. Even Elvis's entourage, consisting of the Memphis Mafia, and his penchant for gaudy jewelry — rings on every finger, long pendants, huge sunglasses — seem oddly contemporary.

In *The Elvis Encyclopedia* by Adam Victor, Engelbert Humperdinck said this of Elvis: "I learned about humility, charm, and how to work an audience from watching Elvis in concert. If you're going to steal — and every performer does it from someone at some time — then steal from the best, which was Elvis."

# Chapter 15

# Fading Away

### In This Chapter

- Understanding Elvis's unconventional lifestyle and how it affected him
- Watching Elvis lose interest in his work
- Mourning the King

The timing of Elvis's separation and divorce from Priscilla makes it virtually impossible not to find connections between his professional life and his personal life. The couple was separated in July 1972, a month after the Madison Square Garden engagement, and the divorce was final in October 1973. The *Elvis: Aloha from Hawaii* special, which was broadcast in January 1973, capped his succession of career high points. Those who were closest to Elvis, including friends and family members, noted that he and his career were never the same after the disintegration of his marriage.

Elvis's cousin Billy Smith noticed a change in Presley's behavior after Priscilla left for good, remarking in *The Elvis Encyclopedia* by Adam Victor, "Elvis changed a lot after he was married and after Lisa was born. But I think he changed the most after the divorce."

However, other factors contributed to Elvis's personal and professional decline, including his secluded existence and a number of self-destructive habits. Elvis also indulged in unhealthy eating habits and drugs over the years, which caused or aggravated health problems. Around 1973, the self-destructive habits accelerated, and by 1974, the effects had become noticeable in public. Ironically, the nonstop touring and month-long Vegas engagements that invigorated Elvis in 1970 had become a trap of repetition and routine by 1973. Caught in a cycle of disappointment, self-indulgence, and monotony, Elvis was no longer challenged by his career, and his drug use increased. Eventually, his excessive lifestyle led to the inevitable: Elvis Aron Presley died on August 16, 1977.

This chapter chronicles the singer's sad decline, going inside the gates of Graceland for a glimpse at the dark side of celebrity. It also offers a look at the final studio albums that Elvis recorded, suggesting that the songs he selected to record reflected his sadness and despair. The chapter concludes with a description of his funeral.

## Caught in a Trap: Discovering the Downside of Fame

When Elvis first became a national singing sensation in 1956, he enjoyed the adoring fans who followed him around or waited for him in front of his house. He flirted with them, joked around, and freely gave autographs. (See Chapters 3 and 4 for more on fan behavior during his early career.)

It wasn't long before Elvis's fans became too much for him to manage. If adoring fans caught up with him after a concert, they mobbed him, pushed him down, and sometimes stripped him bare. Elvis began to ponder the price of fame when he was shooting *King Creole* on location in New Orleans in 1958. The singer discovered he couldn't sightsee, eat in the city's magnificent restaurants, or enjoy the night life without his fans besieging him. So after his stint in the army, Elvis and his entourage grew accustomed to secluding themselves behind the gates of Graceland or behind the iron fence of his Hollywood home to protect the singer's privacy.

While relaxing at home in Memphis, Elvis and his entourage, who were called the Memphis Mafia, occasionally ventured into town to seek entertainment. Sometimes they rode their motorcycles late at night when they were sure that most people were asleep. Because Elvis's persistent fans prevented him from going out during normal hours, he often rented movie theaters (either the Malco or the Memphian) from midnight to dawn. Elvis also rented amusement parks or roller skating rinks after hours for himself and his friends. Buying sprees of furniture or jewelry, dental appointments, and other business transactions generally occurred after business hours as well. The after-hours lifestyle made it easier to avoid mobs of fans, but it also led to a Neverland-type of existence in which normal social conventions didn't apply.

This isolation from the norms of real life, coupled with his boredom when he was between projects and the privileges that came with stardom, eventually led Elvis to indulge in several destructive habits, including overeating, drugs, and expensive shopping sprees.

## Traveling the Road of Excess

Elvis's profession as an entertainer meant he lived without the constraints of the normal, nine-to-five world. And, because of his celebrity, he could get what he wanted when he wanted it. Elvis's talents paid the bills, so few members of his family or entourage dared to tell him "no." Most of his entourage indulged in everything he did, whether it be taking drugs, chasing women, or eating food at any hour. If Elvis found a new hobby, vehicle, or pastime that provided fun and entertainment, he purchased what he needed for himself and for the closest members of his entourage no matter the cost. This section details some of the behaviors of Elvis and the Memphis Mafia that provide context for understanding the dark side of too much privilege and enormous celebrity.

## Living in a state of arrested development

Elvis's daily life, even while resting at Graceland, was so far removed from a conventional lifestyle that he had lost touch with the norms of the everyday world. He slept all day and stayed up all night and surrounded himself with an entourage of buddies even while he was married. The fraternity-house atmosphere interfered with his emotional maturity and his marriage. When together, he and the Memphis Mafia could raise the roof with their antics, even causing trouble on the sets of his movies on occasion.

### Surrounding himself with an entourage: The Memphis Mafia

From the beginning of his success, Elvis liked to surround himself with friends and family members who served as bodyguards or who helped him with the details of travel. The entertainment press called this group of close friends, business associates, and employees "the Memphis Mafia." They not only worked for Elvis, but they also kept him entertained and indulged in the same habits and pastimes that he did. (Check out Chapter 7 and the appendix for more information on the members of Elvis's clan.)

No one will ever know for certain why Elvis surrounded himself with so many buddy-bodyguards for so long, but a hint can be found in a comment he made to *Tropic* magazine on April 28, 1968. Elvis revealed, "The trouble is, when a fellow is by himself and starts thinking, the bad things are always stronger in his memory than the happy things."

Elvis, Colonel Tom Parker (his long-time manager), and Vernon Presley (his father) never paid the members of the Mafia high wages, but Elvis loaned the men money for down payments on houses and gave them automobiles, motorcycles, trucks, jewelry, guns, and other expensive gifts. Most of the Memphis Mafia worked for Elvis out of friendship and not for the money. In fact, many of the men were so close to him that they lived at Graceland from time to time. But, living in a fraternity-like environment during adulthood isn't conducive to emotional maturity, and it didn't encourage Elvis to assess his bizarre lifestyle or give up his self-destructive habits.

Over the years, the faces in the Memphis Mafia changed, but a few men remained with Elvis for much of his career. The most prominent members of the group include Red and Sonny West (who were cousins), Marty Lacker, Joe Esposito, George Klein, Jerry Schilling, Charlie Hodge, Gene Smith (Elvis's cousin), Lamar Fike, and Alan Fortas. Some members of the Memphis Mafia had careers of their own and therefore didn't work for Elvis exclusively. George Klein, for example, was a disc jockey in and around Memphis for most of his life, and Red West, who started hanging out with Elvis around 1955, worked as a stuntman in Hollywood.

> ## Takin' care of business
>
> Elvis and the Memphis Mafia had their own symbol — a lightning bolt combined with the initials TCB. Elvis designed the insignia to symbolize the code of honor he wanted his entourage to live by; it signified a take-charge attitude toward life. TCB stands for "Taking Care of Business," and the lightning bolt represents speed, so Elvis's coat of arms means "taking care of business in a flash." He had charms produced with this insignia for each member of the Memphis Mafia, and many of the men wore them on chains around their necks. Elvis also had TLC, or "tender, loving care" charms designed for the wives and girlfriends of his favorite companions.

### Engaging in antics: Boys will be boys

During the 1960s, when Elvis devoted his career to making movies, members of the Memphis Mafia joined Elvis on location or on set at the studio. Some of the men had bit parts and some had jobs assisting Elvis, but their main function was to keep their boss company.

On a movie set, Elvis and his friends liked to pull practical jokes. After Elvis lost respect for the movies he was making, his kidding around seemed to take precedence over his acting. Pie fights were common, and on the set of *Easy Come, Easy Go* (1967), director John Rich often argued with Elvis about his constant practical jokes. During one scene, Elvis kept bursting into laughter every time he looked at Red or Sonny West. He blew his lines take after take. Rich lost his temper and ordered everyone off the set, but Elvis stepped in and set Rich straight. "We're doing these movies because it's supposed to be fun, nothing more," he told his director. "When they cease to be fun, then we'll cease to do them." But during the filming of *Clambake* (1967), Elvis's gang caused so much confusion on the set that when production on his next movie *Stay Away, Joe* (1968) began, a memo came down from the MGM executive offices warning Elvis and the Memphis Mafia that their usual behavior wouldn't be tolerated.

Other stories reinforce the idea that when together, Elvis and the Memphis Mafia could act like adolescents. Whenever Elvis was working in Hollywood, he and his entourage lived together in a Bel Air mansion that had once belonged to the Shah of Iran. (You can read more about this mansion in Chapter 19.) The house was the scene of many late-night parties, which often were attended by a host of Hollywood party girls, extras, and starlets. The constant parade of girls over the years made focusing on relationships impossible for all the Memphis Mafia members. The whole group remained in a state of arrested emotional development.

When Elvis first came to Hollywood, the high jinks weren't as sordid or adolescent as they would later become. In the early days, he organized a football team to relieve the tedium of movie production. Elvis and his buddies were joined on the football field by young actors such as Kent McCord, Ty Hardin, Pat Boone, Robert Conrad, Gary Lockwood, and Ricky Nelson.

Toward the end of his Hollywood career, after Elvis had become bored with making movies, his behavior and antics became wilder and more erratic. He took up more-expensive hobbies and less-constructive pastimes to fill his time in Hollywood. On one shopping spree while he was making *Tickle Me* in 1965, Elvis bought all of his friends motorcycles so they could go riding together. Another time, Elvis had his buddies go to several photography shops and buy all their flashbulbs. They dumped the flashbulbs into the swimming pool and shot them with BB guns. When a bulb was hit, it exploded and sunk. After three nights of shooting, it took a man two days to clean the pool.

## Struggling with a drug problem

Elvis's most destructive behavior was probably his use and abuse of prescription drugs, which eventually altered his behavior and personality. According to members of the Memphis Mafia, Elvis began to regularly use amphetamines and diet pills in the 1960s; the drugs were intended to help Elvis keep his weight down and stay awake for long hours. Some accounts claim that Elvis was introduced to amphetamines while in the army as a means to stay awake and alert during long hours on duty. To counteract the amphetamines, Elvis and his buddy-bodyguards, who indulged in whatever Elvis did, began taking sedatives and tranquilizers.

By the early 1970s, when he was touring on a debilitating schedule of one-nighters, Elvis was taking more medication than ever. The year 1973 seemed a watershed for increased drug use, and he began regularly taking such extreme narcotics as Dilaudid and Demerol. These drugs eventually left him in a state of mental limbo, and the affects of their use were apparent when he was performing — something that hadn't happened before.

At times, Elvis cut back on the drugs and attempted to detox during hospital stays, but the efforts didn't last. Given the nature of these heavy-duty narcotics, it seems clear that Elvis was looking to escape something. Whether it was career disappointment, boredom, spiritual loss, failed relationships, or a combination of factors is unknown and clouded by the highly subjective memoirs and personal accounts of friends and family members.

> ## No one could help
>
> In many of the memoirs by members of the Memphis Mafia, several claimed they wanted to get Elvis to realize his drug use was out of control. But, Elvis was a superstar who dictated what the group did not only because they worked for him but also because they spent their leisure time together. He signed their paychecks, bought cars and houses for them, and took them on vacation. The nature of the relationship between Elvis and his buddy-bodyguards made it unlikely that he would listen to them. As many of them have said, no one could tell Elvis what to do. Plus, some of the group did drugs with him, so they were in no shape to help him.
>
> According to the "bodyguard book," *Elvis: What Happened?*, Red West did have a heart-to-heart conversation with his long-time friend and employer when Elvis called to attempt to stop the publication of the book. Not surprisingly, he was unsuccessful in getting Elvis to listen. (See Chapter 17 for more about the bodyguard book.)

Even though Elvis clearly used his celebrity to obtain massive amounts of drugs, the context of the times needs to be taken into account in order to get the full picture. Elvis's substance abuse problem began as a result of prescription drug use. Some of these drugs were in fact administered for actual health problems; he had back pain, digestive troubles, and many eye afflictions, including glaucoma. Treatments for these conditions put Elvis in the hospital several times between 1973 and his death four years later. He also was hospitalized for throat ailments, pleurisy, and hypertension. Remember that during the 1960s and 1970s, a different attitude toward prescription drugs existed; drugs were prescribed much more freely. When Elvis went into the army, the stimulant Benedrine was actually a legal over-the-counter drug; during the 1970s, Valium was frequently prescribed for anxiety — before its addictive properties were discovered. So part of Elvis's rationalization for taking pills to relieve either physical or psychic pain was indicative of the times. Ironically, Elvis rarely indulged in alcohol and often spoke out against taking illegal drugs.

Some members of his entourage, including Red West, attempted to talk Elvis out of using so many drugs and even to prevent the drugs from getting to him, but their efforts were in vain. Elvis's primary physician, Dr. George Nichopoulos, sometimes gave his patient placebos, but if Elvis caught on, he went elsewhere for the drugs. Elvis's last long-term girlfriend, Linda Thompson, left him in 1976 after she tired of nursing him through dangerous drug episodes and of being fearful of the inevitable. Members of the Memphis Mafia disagree about the amount of drugs Elvis took, but the fact remains that he took more than his body could withstand. His drug abuse not only brought on a decline in his career, but it also led to his death.

In May 1973, Elvis's father, Vernon, and the Colonel hired a private investigator to discover the drug suppliers who were freely giving him prescriptions. When the suppliers (who turned out to be doctors) were uncovered, Elvis found other doctors to give him the drugs.

**TRIVIA**

Beauty queen Linda Thompson was Elvis's girlfriend from 1972 to 1976, staying with him during several difficult times in his life. Long after leaving Elvis, Thompson married gold medal champion Bruce Jenner and then record producer David Foster. An amateur poet, Thompson had impressed Elvis with her way with words. While married to Foster, she penned the words to several songs and received an Academy Award nomination in 1992 for her lyrics for "I Have Nothing" from *The Bodyguard*.

## Wrestling with a weight problem

Elvis's eating habits have been exaggerated over the years, because stories of his kingly excesses have become part of his myth. As early as 1955, when he was still considered an up-and-coming country-western singer, articles about the hot, young singer often mentioned that he liked to down several cheeseburgers at one sitting. An article in *Esquire* magazine in the late 1960s took a sarcastic but lighthearted tone when describing Elvis's favorite snack of peanut butter and mashed banana sandwiches washed down with several Pepsis. Prior to his death, stories about his food habits tended to be lighthearted or matter of fact.

Exaggeration aside, Elvis didn't eat a healthy diet by today's standards. Most of Elvis's favorite foods were traditional working-class Southern dishes, which lean heavily toward fried meats. Reporters and magazine writers who weren't familiar with Southern cooking felt that Elvis's eating habits were peculiar, but in reality many people in the South enjoyed the same foods. Other writers reported that the amount of food Elvis consumed was excessive. They told tall tales about Elvis eating so many Spanish omelets that he created an egg shortage in Tennessee. Rumors also have claimed that he once ate 30 cups of yogurt, 8 honeydew melons, and a hundred dollars worth of ice cream bars in one night. Elvis sometimes went on eating binges, particularly during his time off between projects, but stories about binges on such foods as bacon, ice cream, cheeseburgers, and pizza have been repeated so often that it seems as though Elvis ate that much every day. Elvis had many unhealthy eating habits and gained weight, but the stories about how much he consumed have been widely exaggerated.

**REMEMBER**

After Elvis's death, this kind of report on his eating habits took on a dark connotation. Stories of food consumption became sensationalized attempts to "prove" that Elvis was out of control, equating his appetite for food with his appetite for drugs. These attempts at armchair psychology didn't take into account that Elvis ate this way all of his life. His eating habits led to a weight problem in adulthood when he wasn't working and exercising, but his puffy, bloated look of the mid- to late 1970s wasn't due to overeating; it was due in part to the drugs he was consuming. (See Chapter 17 for more information on how the press covered Elvis's drug problems after he died.)

## Collecting extravagances

Not all of Elvis's extravagances were bad for his health, but they all suggested an inclination toward excess. He liked to collect ostentatious jewelry, fancy cars, and all kinds of guns. He also was fascinated by law enforcement and loved to collect authentic police badges. I describe his collections in the following sections.

### Accessorizing with rings and other flashy jewelry

At the start of his career, Elvis developed an image as an average, red-blooded, all-American male who would never wear any jewelry except a watch. Photographs of Elvis in the early days rarely show him wearing gaudy jewelry, but during the 1970s, Elvis began to wear rings on all his fingers while he was onstage and off. He also wore heavy medallions, gold-plated belts, and chain-link bracelets. On a gold chain around his neck, Elvis wore a gold Star of David and a crucifix. He also liked to carry walking sticks adorned with tops made of silver or gold. Elvis routinely bought expensive jewelry not only for himself but also for the Memphis Mafia, their wives, and his show business friends.

### Purchasing cars for himself and others

Elvis had a lifelong love affair with Cadillacs. During his career, he bought more than 100 Caddys for himself and the members of his entourage. One of the first cars Elvis purchased was a 1956 pink Cadillac sedan. He promptly gave the car to his mother, Gladys, despite the fact that she couldn't drive. This was the only Cadillac that Elvis kept throughout his life, and it's still parked at Graceland.

In addition to Cadillacs, Elvis bought unique foreign cars, such as a three-door Messerschmitt, as well as prestigious automobiles, including any number of Lincolns, a Mercedes limousine, a couple of Stutz Bearcats, and a Rolls Royce. Elvis's most outrageous vehicle was his 1960 Cadillac limousine that had been customized by George Barris, a well-known auto customizer. More of a promotional gimmick than a personal vehicle, the car was painted with diamond-dust gold paint and featured a motorized shoeshine kit, a wet bar, a television, and a record player. The car was too cumbersome and impractical to use every day, so Elvis eventually loaned the gold Cadillac to MGM to promote one of his movies. The car, which is worth more than $100,000, is now on display in the Country Music Hall of Fame in Nashville.

Collecting and buying cars in and of itself isn't particularly unusual, but buying them for complete strangers does suggest that there was more to these spontaneous gestures than meets the eye. Elvis was naturally generous. He gave freely to his friends and their families, and he also donated large amounts of money to charity. Once, while he was buying a couple of El Dorados for members of his entourage, Elvis noticed a young couple wandering around the dealer's lot trying to find a car that they could afford. Elvis told them to pick any car they wanted. Then he wrote out a check and left the salesman to do the paperwork.

Part of Elvis's penchant for giving away cars was his generous nature, but it also suggests an attempt to fill a void or to forge meaningful connections with people. These stories of his buying sprees and giveaways, which have become a part of his legend, also clearly suggest a life of excess and privilege.

### Packing a pistol

Elvis also collected guns and many other kinds of weapons. He owned thousands of dollars worth of guns. Elvis also lavished expensive guns on the members of the Memphis Mafia and on Priscilla. His bodyguards, particularly Red and Sonny West, often carried their weapons on them, which might be expected, but then so did Elvis and Priscilla. Priscilla frequently carried a dainty Derringer in her purse as a matter of course. And Elvis once boarded a commercial flight while packing a pistol. When the ticket agent followed him onto the plane to tell him he couldn't take a gun on board, Elvis left the plane in a huff. But the pilot came scurrying after him and apologized for the ticket agent, allowing Elvis to get back on the airplane.

During the 1970s, Elvis carried a gun with him at all times because he was concerned for his safety. After he returned to live performances in Las Vegas, Elvis received many death and kidnapping threats. He believed that assassins wanted glory through media attention. According to Elvis, they were so eager for the fame that would come from killing someone of his stature that they were willing to chance death or to live out their lives in prison.

In 1971, while Elvis was performing in Las Vegas, an anonymous caller got through to his hotel room and warned him that he faced an assassination attempt during that evening's performance. Later that day, Elvis received a hotel menu with his picture on the front. The picture had been defaced, and a handgun had been drawn near Elvis's heart. A message included with the menu read, "Guess who, and where?" The FBI was called in, which must have both thrilled and frightened Elvis, and the hotel management told him he didn't have to go on with the performance. But Elvis stuck a Derringer into his boot and a .45 into his belt and did the show anyway.

Over the next few years, Elvis received so many death threats that bodyguards Red and Sonny West became cautious about allowing strangers to get near Elvis. Their tactics were often rough, and they were frequently criticized by other entertainers and officials in the industry. At least three lawsuits were filed against Elvis in conjunction with the strong-arm tactics of his guards. Considering the fact that Elvis felt it was perfectly okay to carry a loaded pistol in his boot or belt, he was lucky he didn't shoot anyone himself.

**TRIVIA** According to legend, Elvis expressed his anger toward television sets. He supposedly shot out the TV screen when something came on that he didn't want to see. The number of times he actually shot out televisions has probably been exaggerated much like the stories about Elvis's eating binges, but he supposedly blasted at least one television set with the Derringer he kept in his boot because singer Robert Goulet appeared on the screen.

### Collecting badges of honor

Elvis was infatuated with law enforcement and collected police badges from whomever he could persuade to give him one. And, he didn't want an honorary badge or a replica; he always wanted the real thing. Elvis asked the sheriff of Shelby County, Tennessee, to get not just him, but also his father, his doctor, and most members of the Memphis Mafia, official deputy's badges. Elvis also had badges from the Palm Springs Police Department and police departments in other cities. Considering that Elvis once had an image as a rebel who opposed authority, it's ironic that he became so fascinated with law enforcement.

## Lost and Weary: Watching the King's Career Decline

Elvis's personal and professional decline became noticeable to the press and public around early 1974. He was unable to take off weight before his tours or Las Vegas engagements, and his behavior seemed increasingly erratic. By this time, Elvis was tired of the grind of performing live, and he grew increasingly disinterested in recording in a studio. Desperate to coerce Elvis into cutting new material, RCA helped their number-one singer turn part of his home into a makeshift recording studio. The material for Elvis's last album before he died, appropriately named *Moody Blue*, was recorded at Graceland.

---

### The end draws near: Elvis's final concert

Despite months of suffering digestive problems, bouts of vomiting, and head, stomach, and muscle pain, on June 26, 1977, Elvis and his entourage flew into Indianapolis, Indiana, for his 56th concert that year. When the plane landed, Elvis was so fatigued that members of the Memphis Mafia were concerned about his welfare. He rested at a local hotel before proceeding to Market Square Arena.

Backstage before the show, RCA presented Elvis with a special plaque commemorating the two billionth Presley record pressed by the company. The plaque featured a reproduction of his last album cover. That evening the show went on at 8:30 before a packed house of 18,000. Elvis gave one of his best performances in recent months. Unfortunately, no one knew it would be his last.

This section takes a look at Elvis's career during his last few years; it examines how his physical and spiritual decline affected his professional activities and vice versa.

## Paying the piper: The high price of the road

The grueling touring schedule and the month-long Las Vegas engagements took their toll on Elvis by 1973. What had once been a lifeline to a drowning singing career was now an exhausting chore; what had once been a challenge for Elvis was now routine. Elvis changed out the songs in the show so he didn't have to perform the exact same songs each night over the years. But, the format of the show didn't alter from about 1970, when he played Vegas for the second time, to the last performance he gave on June 26, 1977, at Market Square Arena in Indianapolis, Indiana.

Fans expected and still enjoyed the rituals that were part of the concert experience, and his shows continued to be popular. However, Elvis's increasing penchant for joking during the songs revealed his boredom with the show and the routine it had become. He seemed particularly unhappy with his long Vegas engagements. After his last show in the summer of 1973, he supposedly wanted to quit, but he continued to play Vegas until December 1976, which was his last engagement there.

Elvis bluntly revealed his feelings on stage in Sin City in late 1976, just about eight months before he died. He said to the crowd, "I hate Las Vegas."

Many have speculated as to why Elvis continued to tour and play such long engagements in Vegas after he was no longer challenged by them. Some blame the Colonel and his love of gambling. Parker loved Vegas, gambled frequently, and enjoyed the privileges of being the manager of the city's favorite son. According to some, he signed Elvis into long-term deals with the International Hotel because he enjoyed the Vegas lifestyle too much.

However, Elvis's situation was too complicated to blame his decline on business obligations. Increased drug use and personal disappointment led to a spiritual and personal malaise that made changing the act or accepting new challenges difficult for Elvis.

## Singing them moody and blue: Elvis records his last albums

Elvis's record output during the 1970s was extensive, making his recording schedule as grueling as his concert tours. Each year RCA typically released three to four studio albums, one or two live albums, and various singles. Because Elvis lost his enthusiasm for recording (just as he had for touring and performing in Vegas), this output diminished as the 1970s wore on. By 1976 and despite his contractual obligations, no one could get Elvis into the recording studio. And producer Felton Jarvis had the unenviable task of trying to release material on schedule for RCA.

To pacify Elvis by making the recording process as easy as possible, RCA sent their recording truck to Graceland in February 1976 so the reluctant singer could work in the convenience of his own home. Technicians set up a makeshift studio in the downstairs backroom known as the Jungle Room. (Flip to Chapter 19 for more on this and other Graceland rooms.) They made some technical compromises but, from this session and a later session in October, RCA got enough material to produce two albums: *From Elvis Presley Boulevard, Memphis, Tennessee* and *Moody Blue*. The October session, which resulted in only four completed tracks, was Elvis's last effort at studio recording before he died.

Critics and biographers often overlook these final LPs because they're hodge-podges of tracks. While neither album is a musical milestone, both tell us something about Elvis Presley at the very end of his life and career, and for that reason they deserve consideration and evaluation.

### From Elvis Presley Boulevard, Memphis, Tennessee

Released in April 1976, *From Elvis Presley Boulevard, Memphis, Tennessee* offers ten songs whose titles seem eerily reflective of Elvis's emotional state, albeit in hindsight. The song selection leans heavily to ballads of heartbreak and despair, and as such, they tell his story. Here's the list of songs on the album:

- "Hurt"
- "Never Again"
- "Blue Eyes Crying in the Rain"
- "Danny Boy"
- "The Last Farewell"
- "For the Heart"
- "Bitter They Are, Harder They Fall"
- "Solitaire"
- "Love Coming Down"
- "I'll Never Fall in Love Again"

The album reached number 1 on the *Billboard* country charts, but it reached only number 41 on the list of Top LPs. The ballad material was well suited to a country audience, who prefers songs of sentiment and raw emotion. The album remained on the charts for 17 weeks, eventually earning gold status.

### Moody Blue

Even though Elvis never wrote a song, one of his main talents was his ability to select material that spoke to him and personalize it through his interpretation. He had a talent for selecting material that suited him; it was his way of expressing himself. With a couple of exceptions, *Moody Blue* (1977) features mostly ballads of heartache, hopeless relationships, and lost love. The autobiographical relevance of the songs to Elvis's circumstances makes this album, released just a short time before his death, poignant and heartbreaking. Take a look at the tracks he chose for this last album:

- "Unchained Melody"
- "If You Love Me (Let Me Know)"
- "Little Darlin'"
- "He'll Have to Go"
- "Let Me Be There"
- "Way Down"
- "Pledging My Love"
- "Moody Blue"
- "She Thinks I Still Care"
- "It's Easy for You"

*Moody Blue* reached number three on the list of Top LPs, charting for 31 weeks. It was certified platinum on September 1, 1977.

The original pressing of *Moody Blue* produced 200,000 copies on blue translucent vinyl. RCA experimented with green, red, and gold vinyl, but they were quickly discarded for the blue — an obvious choice considering the album's title. After the initial pressing sold out, RCA chose the customary black vinyl for the next run, but then it later returned to blue. Fans referred to this LP as the "Blue Album," which is appropriate not only for its physical color but also for Elvis's frame of mind.

## August 16, 1977: Last Stop on the Mystery Train

Elvis Presley died at Graceland on August 16, 1977, at 42 years old. His last girlfriend, 21-year-old Ginger Alden, found him slumped over in the bathroom. She called for Elvis's longtime friend and right-hand man Joe Esposito, who phoned for the paramedics. Amidst growing chaos at Graceland, the paramedics failed to revive Elvis, and he was taken to Baptist Memorial Hospital where further attempts to resuscitate him failed. He was pronounced dead by his physician,

> ## Headlines from August 1977
>
> Elvis's death made headlines all over the world; some of them were almost poetic. Here are a few for you to consider:
>
> - "Death Captures Crown of Rock and Roll" — *Commercial Appeal*
> - "A Lonely Life Ends on Elvis Presley Boulevard" — *Memphis Press-Scimitar*
> - "The King Is Dead" — *Tupelo Daily Journal*
> - "All Roads Lead to Memphis" — *London Evening Standard*
> - "L'adieu a Elvis" — *France-Soir*
> - "Elvis: End of an Era" — *City Memphis*
> - "Elvis Has Left the Building" — *Stereo Review*

Dr. George Nichopoulos, who listed the official cause of death as "cardiac arrhythmia due to undetermined heartbeat," which is also known as erratic heartbeat. (Chapter 17 further discusses the cause of death.) Dr. Nick then took the long ride back to Graceland to find Vernon Presley and tell a father that his son was dead.

This section describes the immediate events surrounding the death of Elvis Presley and his funeral.

## Shocking the world with the news

Almost immediately after he died, rumors of Elvis's demise arrived at Memphis newspaper offices and radio and television newsrooms. However, the jaded local reporters took a wait-and-see attitude. Many of them had heard these rumors before. Over the years, many crank calls had come into the newsroom declaring that Elvis had been killed in a car accident or a plane crash, or that he had been shot by the jealous boyfriend of a woman who was hopelessly infatuated with the singer. Once, someone reported that Elvis had drowned in a submarine.

Elvis Presley was a hometown boy and a constant source of news, some of which was manufactured for or by the Memphis press. Newspaper editors and newsroom managers were cautious about sending out their reporters, because the rumor that Elvis was dead could be just another hoax. But when the staff of the *Memphis Press-Scimitar* learned from a trusted source that Elvis actually was dead, the newsroom grew unusually silent.

Dan Sears of radio station WMPS in Memphis made the first official announcement, and WHBQ-TV was the first television station to interrupt its programming with the terrible news. The story then reached the major networks who revealed the news to the rest of the country.

As reports of Elvis's death spread across the country, radio stations immediately began to play his records. Some stations quickly organized tributes to the singer while others simply played his music at the request of listeners, many of whom were in a state of shock by the announcement of his sudden death.

By the end of the day on August 16, fans had already begun to gather at the gates of Graceland to say goodbye. The next day, Vernon allowed as many fans as possible to file by the casket to view the body. Many who couldn't be there sent flowers, including the hundreds of fan clubs from all over the world. The fans sent a tremendous array of flowers, which were set out along the bank in front of the mansion. Besides the more traditional wreaths and bouquets, the arrangements were shaped like lightning bolts, guitars, hound dogs, and stars. Many of the arrangements were sent immediately to Forest Hill Cemetery, the site of the burial, where they shared space with more humble arrangements of wildflowers in Coke bottles.

Every blossom in Memphis had been sold by the afternoon of August 17, and so additional flowers had to be shipped in from other parts of the country. August 17 was the biggest day in the history of FTD, a florists' delivery service. FTD employees claim that more than 2,150 arrangements were delivered on that day.

## Preparing a Southern-style funeral

Elvis's body returned to Graceland on August 17 to lay in state in the living room. For the next two days, Shelby County sheriff deputies and Air National Guard sentries lined the driveway at Graceland as an honor guard — a gesture that Elvis would have appreciated.

Friends and family paid their respects in private that evening, while two members of the Memphis Mafia — Sam Thompson and Dick Grob — stood watch over Elvis's body. Among the many who paid their respects was soul singer James Brown, who had known Elvis since 1966. Brown took the death hard and sat alone with Elvis for a long time.

Elvis's funeral took place on August 18, 1977, in the living room at Graceland. A handful of celebrities attended, including Caroline Kennedy, country-music guitarist Chet Atkins, performers Ann-Margret and George Hamilton, former Sun Records owner Sam Phillips, and television evangelist Rex Humbard, who was one of the speakers during the service. Colonel Parker stood to the side dressed in a Hawaiian shirt for reasons known only to himself. Comedian Jackie Kahane, who had opened many of Elvis's concert performances, delivered his eulogy, and local minister C.W. Bradley conducted the religious service. Elvis's soprano Kathy Westmoreland sang during the service as did gospel performers Jake Hess, J.D. Sumner, and James Blackwood, along with their respective vocal groups.

A long motor cortege of 17 all-white automobiles escorted the casket to Forest Hill Cemetery, where a five-minute service officially concluded the funeral. Later, the bodies of Elvis and his mother would be reinterred at Graceland. (See Chapter 16 for more info on Elvis's final resting place.)

## The King is dead, long live the King

Throughout August, hundreds of editorials attempted to summarize Elvis's place in our culture. For the first time, the nation as a whole seemed to realize that Elvis was an important figure because he changed the way we looked, the music we listened to, the way we talked, and the image we identified with. At the time, many wrote that Elvis's death marked the end of an era, as well as the end of a legendary career, but this statement hasn't proved to be true. After Elvis died, the legend evolved into a mythology, which continues to grow with each new revelation about his personal life and each new reinterpretation of his contribution to popular culture. Elvis the man died on August 16, 1977, but Elvis the myth continues . . .

# Part IV
# From the King of Rock 'n' Roll to American Cultural Icon

The 5th Wave  By Rich Tennant

> I went into the Hall of Kings and saw paintings of Buckingham Palace, Holyrood, and the Palace of Versailles, but not a single picture of Graceland.

## In this part . . .

Elvis died on August 16, 1977, but he still hasn't left the building. In the aftermath of his death, fans instituted commemorative rituals and practices that kept the spotlight on the singer, resulting in continued interest in the man and his music.

A prosperous industry has developed around Elvis's home, Graceland, which opened to the public in 1982, giving fans and tourists a centralized location to gather and celebrate all things Elvis. In addition, albums and compilations of his music continue to be released to introduce Elvis to younger generations, while biographies, documentaries, and even college courses attempt to explain his significance and continued popularity.

In this part, I offer you an overview of the world of Elvis, including Graceland, the fans, recent album releases, biographies, and other parts of the phenomenon that help make Elvis the highest-earning celebrity almost every year.

# Chapter 16

# In the Aftermath of Death

## In This Chapter

▶ Noting the transfer of Elvis's body to Meditation Garden
▶ Considering the fan-based rituals that developed after Elvis's death

Though Elvis died on August 16, 1977, fans still wanted to feel connected to their idol. So they engaged in activities that were repeated regularly over time until they became rituals. These post-death rituals essentially replaced the in-concert routines enacted between the fans and Elvis during the 1970s. (See Chapter 13 for a complete account of the in-concert rituals.) These fan rituals represent one part of the Elvis Presley phenomenon that begins in the aftermath of his death and increases in scale and scope as the years go by. (The other chapters in this part introduce you to other aspects of the phenomenon.)

The most extensive fan ritual is the slate of activities known as Elvis Week. This celebration of Presley's life and music occurs every August on the anniversary of his death. The highlight of the week is a specific ritual known as the Candlelight Vigil, which is a moving tribute to Elvis in which fans solemnly walk by his gravesite in Meditation Garden with candles in hand.

Strangely enough, this ritual wouldn't have started without the odd event that occurred just after his funeral. Four people threatened to steal Elvis's body, resulting in the removal of the body from a mausoleum in Forest Hill Cemetery. The body was then buried behind Graceland in the small area known as Meditation Garden.

This chapter details the development of Elvis Week and its many celebrations and rituals, beginning with an event that was indirectly connected to the Candlelight Vigil.

> ## Meditation Garden
>
> Meditation Garden, a serene setting behind Graceland, was inspired by Elvis's interest in religion and spirituality, particularly after he attended the Self-Realization Fellowship in Los Angeles. The columns and arbor were already in place when the Presleys moved in, but Elvis commissioned the construction of the rest of the Garden in 1965. The plans called for a wall of Mexican brick with stained-glass windows, a small, round pool with fountains, sidewalks, statues, landscaping, and even a sound system. Elvis built Meditation Garden as a retreat for private prayer and contemplation; he had no idea that it would become his final resting place.

# Moving Elvis to Meditation Garden

On August 29, less than two weeks after Elvis died, four young Memphis men attempted to steal Elvis's body from the mausoleum in Forest Hill Cemetery and hold it for ransom. In a comedy of errors that probably would have made Elvis himself laugh, the culprits were caught in the act at the cemetery. Because of this incident, the bodies of Elvis and his mother were moved to the garden area behind Graceland. This new burial site eventually enabled the start of the Candlelight Vigil, which is now held annually on the eve of the anniversary of Elvis's death.

## Thieves in the night

The body-snatching escapade was foiled almost from the beginning when an informant tipped police that someone would attempt to steal Elvis's body. After learning of the tip, police staked out Forest Hill Cemetery for three nights. On one of those nights, they spotted four men investigating the mausoleum and the surrounding area, but the group didn't attempt a break-in.

However, the four returned two nights later just after midnight by climbing over a fence at the rear of the cemetery. As they tampered with the mausoleum, a car passed by on a nearby highway, inadvertently shining its headlights toward the suspects. The group freaked out and darted across the cemetery, racing over graves and monuments. Three of the would-be thieves jumped into a car and sped away, only to be picked up by the police waiting nearby. The fourth suspect scaled the fence but injured his leg in the process. Police nabbed him at a local hospital when he showed up for treatment.

The runaway suspect wasn't charged, but the other three were arrested and charged with criminal trespassing.

## Coming home to Graceland one last time

Elvis's father, Vernon Presley, originally wanted to inter his son on the grounds of Graceland, but the city of Memphis wouldn't grant the proper permits to allow it. (You can read more about Graceland and its significance in Chapter 19.) The attempted theft of Elvis's body helped changed the minds of city officials, however. The disturbance created in Forest Hill Cemetery by the thousands of fans trampling through the graveyard, causing congestion and destruction, also worked in Vernon's favor.

In the fall, Elvis returned home to rest in Meditation Garden just behind the house. Vernon ordered four graves to be dug, burying Elvis in one and his wife, Gladys, in another. Two years later, Vernon died and was laid to rest beside them. Finally, in 1980, Vernon's mother, Minnie Mae, who endured the deaths of her son, daughter-in-law, and grandson, was laid to rest in the fourth plot. The four family members are together in death just as they had lived together for much of their lives. To see the graves at Meditation Garden, refer to the color photo section.

The tiny family graveyard that takes up a large part of Meditation Garden proved to be the perfect place for fans to express their devotion, sadness, and feelings of loss. Vernon opened the Garden in November 1977 for fans to visit and pay their respects to Elvis, but the rest of Graceland wasn't open to the public until 1982.

# Establishing New Rituals

Fans planted the seeds for Elvis Week one year after his death when many of them informally met in Memphis to commemorate the one-year anniversary of his passing. Several random events were planned by different Memphis venues so that fans had something to do with their time, but none of these events were connected. As the years passed, the number of activities during Elvis Week grew in scope and complexity, which drew more and more fans to Memphis. For the most part, the activities weren't connected, and an informality marks the events during these formative years. Early on, fans referred to the commemoration as Elvis Week, and the name stuck.

Nothing jumpstarted the growth of Elvis Week like the opening of Graceland to the public in June 1982. Touring Graceland became a focal point for fan activities, culminating with the Candlelight Vigil. With access to Graceland, fans had a central location to rally around, and it soon became the place to organize their anniversary celebrations.

This section chronicles the development of Elvis Week from a simple informal celebration to a huge extravaganza of events and concerts.

## Gathering at the gates

While Elvis lived in Memphis, fans habitually gathered at the Music Gates at Graceland and waited to catch a glimpse of the King. When fans came from out of town, they immediately went to the gates to get the scoop on Elvis's whereabouts from other fans.

Within an hour of Elvis's death on August 16, 1977, fans began to flock to the gates not only to pay their respects but also to check in with each other. As the hours ticked by, fans from outside Memphis started to arrive. When they heard the news, they hurried their children into their cars and drove toward Graceland. Most fans hadn't made arrangements to stay in a motel after they arrived in Memphis; many hadn't even packed a change of clothes.

Reporters on the scene marveled at the growing crowd, repeatedly asking the fans why they had come. Most were unable to articulate an answer that would satisfy the dumbfounded reporters. They could only mutter that they had to come to be close to Elvis. By the next morning, the crowd numbered 20,000. The Memphis police repeatedly overestimated crowd totals until they were telling the press that the crowd consisted of 60,000 to 80,000 Elvis fans.

Elvis's body lay in state in the living room of Graceland, and Vernon opted for a public viewing. The doors opened in the morning and closed at 6:30 p.m., but so many mourners arrived that it was impossible for all of them to be admitted to Graceland. In fact, the mob grew so large that a carnival atmosphere developed. People hawking T-shirts and souvenirs worked the crowd. The hot Memphis weather and the close crush of people caused many people to faint. Luckily a medic was on hand to tend to the overheated. The fans who were unable to get inside Graceland consoled each other by exchanging anecdotes about Elvis.

## Returning to Memphis

A year after Elvis's death, many fans journeyed to Memphis to stand in front of Graceland. Led by the Texas Country Elvis Presley Fan Club, the group of fans lit candles by the gates to pay their respects. This impromptu event was the inspiration for the Candlelight Vigil. (Refer to the later section "Establishing Elvis Week" for more on this vigil.)

Several unrelated events were scheduled in Memphis to acknowledge the one-year anniversary of Elvis's passing. The Memphian Theater, which Elvis had frequently rented for after-hours showings of movies for his family and friends, offered a mini-retrospective of the most well-known Presley Travelogues. (Flip to Chapter 8 to read more about the Travelogues.) Pop artist Andy Warhol attended the opening of an art exhibition at the Brooks Memorial Art Gallery featuring his painting "Elvis Forty-Nine Times."

> ## The Colonel attempts to run the show
>
> Elvis's manager, Colonel Tom Parker, had controlled his client's career since 1955, and he was still managing it in death. A month after the first-anniversary debacle in Memphis (see the section "Returning to Memphis" for more), Parker attempted to launch an official celebration in Las Vegas called "Always Elvis." The highlight was the unveiling of a statue of the King by sculptor Carl Romanelli at the Hilton in front of their newly dedicated "Elvis Presley Showroom." Interspersed among the Elvis memorabilia were booths of souvenirs for sale at inflated prices. And fans could see Presley's plane, the Lisa Marie, at the Las Vegas Airport for a $5 fee. A weary Vernon Presley attended, looking lost as RCA presented him with 15 gold and platinum records in recognition of post-death sales.
>
> The Colonel had lost favor with the fans, so the event was poorly attended. A second "Always Elvis" festival never came to pass. Instead fans showed up in Memphis in August 1979 to commemorate the death of Elvis in their own way.

The week was marked not so much by these events but by unforeseen circumstances that made the first anniversary memorable for the wrong reasons. A strike by the police and fire departments forced the city to call out the National Guard, who instituted a curfew that caused the cancellation of some of the planned events. The high point of the week (or maybe the low point, depending on how you look at it) occurred when a drunken electric company employee accidentally knocked out the city's power supply.

Journalists were attracted to the chaos and descended on the city to report on the labor problems as well as the influx of Presley fans. The press painted a picture of obsessed fans who didn't want to accept the reality that Elvis was dead, and they depicted Memphis as a faded Southern city past its glory.

In August 1978, *The New York Times,* which has a long tradition of disparaging Elvis and his fans (a tradition that goes all the way back to 1956), smugly remarked, "Which will seem more absurd to students of our time, the nation-wide flap in the 1950's that kept Elvis Presley's gyrating hips from being televised or the hysteria with which his fans this week commemorated the first anniversary of his death?"

The second anniversary in Memphis was calm in comparison to the year before. Fans arrived to attend various memorial services, and Memphis State University presented a series of seminars on Elvis and his music. These seminars represented early academic efforts to put Presley's contributions to American history and culture into perspective. Fan clubs scheduled events for the week, but they didn't coordinate with each other in advance, so activities were disorganized and conflicted with each other. Fans were forced to choose one event over another.

After the second anniversary, fans, city officials, and the Estate of Elvis Presley realized that Memphis in August had become a mecca for Elvis devotees. At this point, the city and the Estate began to expect the fans each August, planning events and gearing up for an influx of people.

## Establishing Elvis Week

In 1980, a few fan clubs organized several events in mid-August as a way to commemorate Elvis Presley's life and music. These events became the real start of Elvis Week. That year, Bill Burk, a reporter for the *Memphis Press-Scimitar* who had often interviewed Presley, offered to help schedule the fan club events to avoid conflicts. The events ran smoothly, and Burk repeated his role as coordinator in 1981.

### The Estate jumps on the Elvis Week bandwagon

In May 1982, Graceland opened to the public. (See Chapter 19 for more information on the decision by Elvis Presley Enterprises, also known as the Estate, to open Graceland for public viewing.) The Estate hadn't been involved in any anniversary events up to that point, and it hadn't reached out to the fans since Elvis's death. Nonetheless, in 1982, the Estate attempted to take ownership of Elvis Week, noting that it was the fifth anniversary of Presley's death and that large crowds were expected. The Estate's attitude didn't sit well with the fans, who believed that Elvis Week belonged to them because their efforts had initiated it. To varying degrees, this hostility between the Estate and the fans still exists. The tension is caused by a combination of slights and miscalculations over the years.

The operations manager of Elvis's Estate called a meeting with the Memphis Convention and Visitors Bureau and reporter Bill Burk. In this meeting, the operations manager declared that from 1982 onward the anniversary week commemorating Elvis would be called Elvis Presley International Tribute Week (or EPITW). Considering that the name "Elvis Week" still stands, you can guess how well the Estate's idea went over.

Even though fans were less than enthusiastic about the Estate's involvement, opening part of the house and grounds to the public did pull the Estate into the anniversary celebration in a more high-profile way. After all, fans did want to see the place where Elvis lived and breathed. So touring Graceland became a central part of the Elvis Week experience.

### A tradition is formed

From about 1982 to the mid-1990s, Elvis Week was an inexpensive, informal, laid-back celebration for fans and anyone else who was attracted to the phenomena that Elvis was generating in death. Each year, the Estate staged a

Chapter 16: In the Aftermath of Death  **255**

few events and the fan clubs staged a few as well. The festivities lasted about five to seven days. If any of the events had an admission fee, the proceeds most likely went to charity, which was in keeping with Elvis's charitable nature. The pace of the week was leisurely, so participants had plenty of time and energy to participate in (and enjoy!) the many events.

Die-hard and casual fans alike attended Elvis Week. Fans were looking to connect with friends or to reconnect with Elvis through concerts, exhibits, and visits to Graceland, Sun Studio, his birthplace in Tupelo, and other familiar Elvis haunts.

If you were an Elvis fan who attended Elvis Week in 1992, you had this list of activities (and more!) to choose from:

- **Memphis Bandstand '92 Sock Hop:** Organized by the Estate, this huge concert at Mid-South Coliseum featured many acts from the 1950s and 1960s who were still performing, including the Shirelles, Dickey Lee, Billy Swan, Johnny Tillotson, and Andy Childs. Proceeds from the concert went to Goodwill Homes and Final Net.

- **A gospel concert:** J. D. Sumner and the Stamps Quartet and James Blackwood, gospel singers whom Elvis knew personally, headed the bill for this program designed as a memorial to Presley. Proceeds also benefited Goodwill Homes and Final Net.

- **An Elvis trivia contest:** This free two-day event sponsored by Graceland offered prizes to participants who showed off their knowledge of all things Elvis in Graceland Plaza, which was across the street from the main house.

- **Fan Appreciation Social:** Graceland hosted this free event at a local hotel to reach out to the fans in the way that Elvis and Colonel Tom Parker always had.

- **Elvis video nights:** No reservations were necessary for this series of free showings of concert films featuring Elvis.

- **Tours of Humes High School:** Tours of the high school that Elvis attended were offered by the school for a small fee of $2, which helped with upkeep of the building. Still in operation, Humes is now a junior high.

- **Elvis Presley Memorial Auction & Lunch:** A favorite event for fans, this auction and flea market–style sale of Elvis memorabilia was held to benefit Le Bonheur Children's Medical Center.

- ***Elvis World* breakfasts:** Hosted by Bill Burk of *Elvis World* magazine, these breakfasts featured talks by authors of books about Elvis. Attendees had the opportunity to have books autographed as well.

> ## Bill Burk and Elvis World
>
> Reporter Bill Burk knew Elvis Presley for almost 20 years, and he wrote close to 400 newspaper articles and columns about him for the *Memphis Press-Scimitar*. He made friends with most of Elvis's associates and family members, which gave him access to stories that most other publications didn't have. Vernon Presley once remarked that the best articles on his son had been written by Burk.
>
> In 1986, after six years of helping fan clubs coordinate events during Elvis Week, Burk launched *Elvis World,* a Memphis-based subscription-based newsletter for fans all over the world. Burk proudly proclaimed that his readership included former President Bill Clinton, Raisa Gorbachev (the wife of a Russian premier), former Russian Premier Boris Yeltsin, and Japanese President Junichiro Koizumi.
>
> Burk wrote more than a dozen books on Elvis, priding himself on uncovering original research that often changed popular misconceptions about Presley. He tracked down rare stories and photos from people who knew Elvis in childhood, some of whom had never been interviewed before. Burk debunked many myths about Elvis, including the story that he had been working as a truck driver when he recorded his first song at the Memphis Recording Service (see Chapter 2). Sadly, Burk passed away in 2008, and *Elvis World* ceased to publish. Both are sorely missed by the Elvis community.

In addition to the staged events, fans also migrated in the evenings to the outdoor pools at the Days Inn at Brooks Road and Howard Johnson's on Elvis Presley Boulevard. There they exchanged memories and renewed friendships. The Days Inn featured a window-decorating contest, in which visitors decorated the windows of their motel rooms with Elvis-related images. The contest became one of the most popular attractions of Elvis Week. To the fans, Elvis Week had become a social occasion with the feel of a family reunion. Seeing familiar faces and attending familiar events contributed to the relaxed, friendly atmosphere.

By 1982, the Candlelight Vigil had been established as the emotional high point of Elvis Week. This event still takes place in the same form each year. On the evening of August 15, fans gather in front of the Music Gates. Elvis's music is piped over a loudspeaker as people mingle and swap Elvis stories before lining up along the graffiti-covered wall. Around 11 p.m., two or more Graceland employees walk down to the gates with a torch that has been lit by the eternal flame near Elvis's grave. As the gates open, the fans, each with their own lighted candle, climb silently and reverently up the hill behind the house, where they walk single file past the grave site. The procession often takes as long as six hours to pass through Meditation Garden.

## The evolution of Elvis Week

Over the years, Memphis has taken advantage of Graceland and Elvis Week to promote its history, musical heritage, and rich Southern culture. In addition, each significant anniversary — such as the 20th in 1997, the 25th in 2002, and the 30th in 2007 — brought more extravagant programs and events from Graceland. The length of Elvis Week extended so that the occasion lasted seven to ten days, and the pace of the celebration picked up as more activities and larger-scale events were added.

Another shift in attitude and direction occurred in 2005 when controlling interest in Elvis Presley Enterprises (the Estate) was taken over by CKX, Inc., which is owned by financial wizard Robert F. X. Sillerman. (CKX also owns the *American Idol* television series along with other entertainment enterprises.) The corporatizing of Elvis Presley Enterprises has increased revenue by further commercializing Elvis's image on additional products, encouraging the broader marketing of his music, developing new videos and documentaries, placing more value on memorabilia, and creating plans to capitalize on Elvis's European fans.

The landscape of Memphis and the area surrounding Graceland also has changed over the years. The tourism revenue brought into Memphis by Elvis's fans revitalized the clubs and restaurants on Beale Street, creating a thriving night life where there wasn't one in the 1980s. (Chapter 2 discusses the infamous Beale Street in more detail.) The Estate bought out the motels, gift shops, and souvenir stands across the street from Graceland and replaced them with its own shops and museums. Sadly, the historic Days Inn and Howard Johnson's motel are no longer there.

The new sophistication and organization behind Elvis Week appeals to an international crowd, youthful fans who aren't interested in the family atmosphere of past years, and a broader range of tourists. However, higher-priced events, a faster pace, and a glitzy atmosphere have been difficult for traditional fans who miss the informality of the old days.

If you were a fan who attended the 2007 Elvis Week, you were likely overwhelmed by the nine days of activities and celebrations to choose from. While some of these activities were familiar fan club events, with an emphasis on charity donations, the scale and glamour of the new events signaled a contemporary approach to Elvis Week. Here's a rundown of some of the events:

- **Elvis Presley International 5K Run:** Almost 2,000 fans and runners participated in the race and the post-race party across from Graceland. Registration to participate was $25 with proceeds benefiting United Cerebral Palsy.

- **The premier of *Elvis Presley: His Home, His Story:*** Graceland premiered its new documentary at Memphis's Malco Theater. The event wasn't free, and proceeds didn't go to charity.

- **Meetup at Marlowe's Restaurant:** This fan-organized event, which benefits the Memphis Humane Society, is one of the oldest still on the schedule.

- **Elvis Gospel Breakfast:** Instead of live gospel performers, this event hosted by the Estate was held at Graceland Plaza across the street from the main house. For $33, fans enjoyed brunch and a morning of watching videos of Elvis singing gospel music.

- **Music and Movies at Graceland:** For two evenings, Elvis's movies were shown on the lawn at Graceland, including *Jailhouse Rock* and *Elvis: That's the Way It Is.* Admission for each Music and Movies at Graceland event was $44. A ticket for both nights cost fans $75.

- **Malco Theatre's Elvis Film Fest 5:** In contrast to Graceland's Music and Movie Nights, the budget-conscious fan could see five of Elvis's films for $5 per movie at the Malco Theatre. Proceeds went to a charity named after Todd Morgan, the late manager of Graceland who was well liked by fans. Morgan died unexpectedly in 2007.

- **Elvis Expo:** The memorabilia auction and flea market has been renamed Elvis Expo. It also was expanded to two days and moved to the Memphis Cook Conventions Center. Now dubbed a trade show, the expo features about 75 booths of Elvis merchandise — as opposed to true memorabilia.

- **Showing of *Elvis: From Broadway to Memphis:*** The Broadway cast of the hit play *All Shook Up,* which was based on Elvis's music, performed with the Memphis Symphony Orchestra. In addition, video footage of Elvis performing was accompanied by live music on the stage. Tickets ranged from $30 to $125, and nothing went to charity.

The evolution of Elvis Week from the fan-dominated era to the contemporary Estate-controlled extravaganza is evident when comparing events from the past and present. You can find virtues and disadvantages to both approaches to Elvis Week. The emphasis on professional entertainment brings in new fans and tourists, but the traditional fans feel pushed out of the commemorative occasion they began. No matter how you look at it, the highlight of this annual week-long celebration remains the Candlelight Vigil, which now streams live on the Internet. This moving tribute brings together the past and present and reminds all fans, tourists, and attendees what Elvis Week is all about.

# Chapter 17

# Examining the Jokes, Stereotypes, and Negative Influences

### In This Chapter
▶ Reviewing Elvis's treatment by the press
▶ Looking at the marketing of Elvis's image
▶ Assessing the personal biographies of Elvis
▶ Considering the Elvis impersonators

*E*ven long after his death, Elvis continues to attract a following from die-hard fans to casual enthusiasts. (You can read more about the depth of fan devotion to the singer in Chapter 16.) However, theirs is not the only perspective on Elvis Presley. Others, including the media, former friends and associates, and commercial marketers, have different perceptions of Elvis, and their perspectives affect the views of the general public — and often negatively.

Adding to the public's tendency to underestimate Elvis is the impression created by the impersonators, sometimes called "tribute artists." The impersonators love Elvis and most believe that they're honoring his memory, but many lack sufficient musical talent to perform his songs. The performances by those impersonators tend to reflect badly on Elvis's own talents and image, especially when the media exploits their unattractive traits.

This chapter offers an overview of the forces that have painted a negative portrait of Elvis over the years. This inaccurate portrait continues to interfere with the public's general understanding of the singer's amazing accomplishments and historical significance. No celebrity of Elvis's caliber and no figure of his cultural significance has been denied his due in the same way.

The influence of the media, the marketers, and the memoirs by former associates complicates the view of Elvis held by the mainstream public, infusing his image with doubt, reservations, and ugly stereotypes of bloated superstars past their prime. If this sounds like your perception of Elvis Presley, reading this book can help you understand why and perhaps change your mind.

## Bashing Elvis: The Press versus Presley

Mainstream newspapers and magazines, television news programs, talk shows, and other information outlets, have rarely treated Elvis Presley with the same reverence afforded other pop culture icons. (See Chapters 5, 7, 14, and 15 for detailed accounts of press coverage of Elvis over his career.)

In general, the press has been critical, clueless, or contemptuous when writing about Elvis Presley. In the 1950s, he was attacked for singing rock 'n' roll instead of pop; conversely in the 1970s, he was demeaned for singing melodramatic ballads that weren't in the rock style of the era. Some writers went beyond that level of criticism to be downright mean-spirited in their comments about the singer, his appearance, and his fans. In the 1950s, he was frequently called by the pejorative term "hillbilly" and described with words that equate him with animals — as when *Life* magazine called him a "21-year-old hillbilly, who howls, mumbles, coos, and cries. . . ." In the 1970s, writers seemed almost angry that Elvis and his fans were growing older. A low point was when his hometown newspaper, the Memphis *Commercial Appeal,* called him "fat and forty" and "sold out."

Just two weeks before Elvis died in 1977, an exposé by his former bodyguards — titled *Elvis: What Happened?* — accused Elvis of drug abuse and other image-busting transgressions. So when Elvis died, obituaries, columns, and other reactions to his untimely death were distracted by these negative revelations. Most of these post-death reactions failed to adequately assess Elvis's cultural contributions; instead, they exploited the scandal. The accusations seemed to "prove" the perspective that the media held about Elvis all along — that he was an anomaly in entertainment history who didn't deserve the attention and devotion of those who bought his records, went to his movies, or attended his concerts.

Drugs, weight, and other scandals had swirled around other superstars, including Judy Garland and Marilyn Monroe, but their problems were never used as fodder for jokes on late-night television or used to suggest that their star status wasn't deserved.

The negative perception by the media sharpened after Elvis's death as more revelations about his tragic lifestyle and drug abuse surfaced. As the years went by, fans and other followers continued to express devotion and appreciation, but the media tended to home in on any story that treated Elvis like he was the subject of a black velvet painting — tacky, superficial, and tasteless.

## Shaping early opinions: The bodyguard book

On August 1, 1977, just 15 days before Elvis died, Ballantine Books published a memoir put together by *New York Post* columnist and former National Enquirer reporter Steve Dunleavy. It consisted of interviews with three of Elvis's former bodyguards — Red West, Sonny West, and Dave Hebler. The three men were the first to come forward with stories of Elvis's bizarre lifestyle. *Elvis: What Happened?* included accounts of his mood swings, relationships with women, and excessive use of prescription drugs.

The book received little publicity until Bob Greene, a columnist for the *Chicago Sun-Times* and a lifelong Elvis fan, interviewed Sonny West for his syndicated column. Greene was curious about the book's allegations and wanted to know why the bodyguards had written it. He decided to go straight to the horse's mouth. By coincidence, the column ran on the day Elvis died (August 16, 1977). Greene's column provoked a lot of protest from fans across the country, and the "bodyguard book" (as it has since been dubbed) inspired the wrath of many, including Geraldo Rivera, who blasted Dunleavy on *Good Morning America* for smearing Elvis's name.

The bodyguards' story had been difficult to believe for several reasons. Nothing like it had surfaced on a wide scale before, because the Colonel had been able to keep Elvis's increasingly eccentric behavior out of the press. Also, Dunleavy lacked credibility as an objective biographer. He had been a reporter for the supermarket tabloid *The Star* when he started working on the book about Elvis, and he was working for the less-than-respected newspaper the *New York Post* when *Elvis: What Happened?* was published. Despite Dunleavy's less-than-stellar credentials, Elvis's death seemed to validate the bodyguards' book.

The bodyguard book influenced the coverage of Elvis's death and funeral, stealing the spotlight from the singer's legacy and historical significance — as evidenced by the NBC news documentary. Not every obituary, special edition newspaper, or follow-up article in the weeks to come made direct reference to drugs and scandal, but many did, tainting the coverage with accusation, morbid curiosity, and condemnation.

Contrary to most journalists, Charles Kuralt waxed eloquently about the meaning of Elvis Presley to America. Sadly, few others followed his lead. On a CBS news special that aired on August 18, 1977, Kuralt noted, "But it's hard to imagine Elvis Presley's success coming anywhere but here. He molded it out of so many American elements: country and blues and gospel and rock; a little Memphis, a little Vegas, a little arrogance, a little piety . . . How could we ever have felt estranged from Elvis? He was a native son."

## Media blunders after Elvis's death

The critically acclaimed book *When Elvis Died,* which was published in 1992 by Neal and Janice Gregory, chronicles the coverage of Elvis by the media in the days after he died. The book is a fascinating study of the media's handling of a major event in popular culture and a window into media prejudices and weaknesses.

One of the most revealing parts of the book details the way the news departments of the three major television networks reported the death of Elvis Presley on August 16. NBC and ABC chose to lead off with the story during their evening news programs and then to air a special late-night news documentary about the singer's life. However, the producers at CBS completely underestimated the importance of Elvis's death and ran the story after the second commercial break during the *CBS Nightly News.* Then the network chose not to prepare a special late-night documentary. CBS's evening news was the leading news program during the 1970s, but the show's ratings fell dramatically after viewers switched to the other networks when CBS didn't lead *Nightly News* with the story of Elvis's death. Executives realized they had miscalculated the importance of Elvis to his fans and underestimated the fascination of his death to the public, so they aired a special news documentary on the night of his funeral.

Other news organizations also undervalued Elvis Presley and his importance to the public. *The New York Times,* which prides itself on preparing prewritten obituaries on every prominent person in the world, had nothing for Presley. Editors asked one of the few Southerners on the staff, Molly Ivens from Texas, to write the obit because she talked with an accent. (After all, speaking with a Southern accent must mean that she knows something about Elvis. How's that for stereotypical?) Associated Press reporter Harry Rosenthal, who was working out of Washington, D.C., was denied the assignment to cover Elvis's death and funeral because editors told him that it was nothing but a "regional" story.

## Revealing the ugly truth: Elvis's drug abuse

Over the next two years, reports of Elvis's drug abuse and its role in his death surfaced occasionally, but no definitive ruling was established. Medical examiner Dr. Jerry Francisco had publicly declared that drugs hadn't played a part in Elvis's death, but the autopsy findings were kept private at Vernon's request. (See Chapter 15 for more information on the events related to Elvis's death.) Many fans refused to believe the sordid stories, and several show-business acquaintances, including producer Hal Wallis, came to his defense.

In 1979, controversial journalist Geraldo Rivera and his producer Charles Thompson, who also worked for the television news magazine *20/20,* aired a report titled "The Elvis Cover-Up." Rivera wanted to get to the bottom of all the rumors and hearsay regarding Elvis's life and death, though he didn't intend to further sully the singer's reputation. This report marked the first national media attention on the singer's drug use. Representatives of ABC and *20/20* filed a lawsuit to obtain a copy of the autopsy, but Dr. Francisco refused to comply. During the 1980s, the suit made it all the way to the Tennessee State Supreme Court, which ruled in Francisco's favor. In 1991, ABC went to court to force Francisco to surrender the autopsy report. Two years later, Shelby County officials also filed a lawsuit requesting that Francisco surrender the autopsy report. Eventually, Francisco was required to give up his autopsy notes, but not the report.

As a result of the publicity over the autopsy, Elvis's doctor, Dr. George Nichopoulos, was brought before the Tennessee Board of Medical Examiners on several charges involving overprescribing. In January 1980, the board suspended his license for more than three months. Unfortunately, the inquiry into the doctor's practices exposed several unsavory facts about Elvis, which confirmed his massive drug use. Consider these facts that came to light:

- Elvis was prescribed more than 12,000 pills and vials of potent drugs during the last 20 months of his life.
- He was hospitalized several times because he was swollen from head to toe due to drug misuse.
- He carried three suitcases full of pills and supplies when he toured, which everyone in his entourage used freely.

In November 1981, Nichopoulos, whom Elvis and his entourage called Dr. Nick, was officially charged with multiple felony counts of overprescribing drugs to numerous patients. News of the shocking number of pills prescribed to Elvis was difficult to believe, but Dr. Nichopoulos claimed that he also had given Presley placebos in an effort to control the medication. He noted that if he refused to give Elvis drugs, the singer simply got the medication from another doctor. Dr. Nick was acquitted of the charges. However, five new charges of overprescribing for Elvis and others were brought against him in 1992 by the state of Tennessee. In 1995, the State Department of Health permanently revoked his license.

## Caroline Kennedy covers Elvis's funeral

*Rolling Stone* hired Caroline Kennedy to write a piece related to Elvis's death, which was published in the September 22, 1977, issue. Kennedy wasn't a journalist, had never written for *Rolling Stone* before, and she didn't know the Presleys. The assignment was more like a stunt than a sincere effort to cover Elvis's funeral.

Apparently, no one at Graceland knew she was there on the magazine's behalf, and her celebrity status gained her access to Priscilla, some of the Memphis Mafia, and a brokenhearted Vernon Presley. Kennedy didn't write about Elvis's death nor of his funeral; instead, she offered impressions of the activities and people inside Graceland as though she were in a far-off land watching the strange rituals of an exotic (read "Southern") people.

**Part IV: From the King of Rock 'n' Roll to American Cultural Icon**

*REMEMBER:* After the autopsy findings, revelations by Dr. Nichopoulos on the witness stand, and statements by Dr. Eric Muirhead and Dr. Noel Foredo, who were present at the autopsy, it became impossible to deny the cause of Elvis's death: *polypharmacy,* or the interaction of several drugs.

## Weighing in on weight

The association between Elvis's weight and his drug use began almost immediately after his death, and connecting the two topics became a common practice. For instance, many magazines ran photos of an overweight Elvis with neighboring stories of his drug use, suggesting a bizarre lifestyle of excess and self-indulgence that led to artistic decline. The photos were always of Elvis on stage in his jumpsuits, because that was his costume style of choice during most of the 1970s.

Eventually, any shot of Elvis onstage in a jumpsuit began to signify his drug abuse, weight issues, and artistic deterioration. "Vegas Elvis" was often contrasted directly or indirectly with his image as a 1950s rock 'n' roll rebel, suggesting that Vegas Elvis was a musical disappointment in comparison to Rebel Elvis. By extension, those fans who liked this phase of Elvis's career were stereotyped as those "hysterical" women who had cried their hearts out at the gates of Graceland after Elvis died or as working-class stiffs who lacked taste and refinement. (Chapter 20 discusses the Vegas Elvis versus Rebel Elvis debate in further detail.)

During this time, the prejudice against Elvis's Southern identity came into play in media coverage just as it had in the 1950s. (See Chapter 5 for more information on Elvis's problems with the press during the 1950s.) Members of the mainstream media were reluctant to fully explore Elvis's unprecedented success or adequately describe his entire career. Acknowledgements of his accomplishments or importance were tempered with descriptions of his bizarre life in his Southern mansion in Memphis. In fact, sometimes his accomplishments were overlooked altogether in favor of jabs at his fondness for Southern-style food.

*TRIVIA:* One of the first major sources to exaggerate Elvis's Southern diet was a light-hearted but condescending book titled *Elvis World* by Jane and Michael Stern (published in 1987, and not to be confused with Bill Burk's *Elvis World* magazine). The tongue-in-cheek tone ridiculed Elvis more than it revealed anything about him when it included a recipe for his alleged favorite snack, a fried peanut butter and banana sandwich. Elvis did eat these sandwiches, but it was others who claimed the snack was his favorite.

## The bitter words of Albert Goldman

In 1981, biographer Albert Goldman published one of the first books about Elvis not penned by a former associate, family member, or showbiz acquaintance. Because of his distance from the star, the book received more attention than previous Presley books, and it was treated like an important biography. Titled *Elvis,* the book remains the most notorious account of Elvis's life, because Goldman openly disliked Presley and his music. Goldman speculated that Elvis had an unhealthy attachment to his mother as well as to his friends, the Memphis Mafia. He painted certain aspects of Elvis's lifestyle as bizarre, including his eating habits, his preference for young women, and his love of firearms. Goldman's view of Southern culture was particularly prejudiced, invalidating his opinions of Elvis's music.

Goldman's book was excerpted in *Rolling Stone,* which gave it further exposure during the period in which Geraldo Rivera and ABC were trying to get access to Elvis's autopsy. Sadly, Goldman's mean-spirited biography picked up where the "bodyguard book" (*Elvis: What Happened?*) left off in terms of setting the tone for media coverage of Elvis Presley.

Eventually, the book was dismissed by music historians and other Elvis biographers because Goldman was so clearly prejudiced against the singer and his Southern heritage. Unfortunately, inaccuracies and misinformation from the book are still repeated, particularly on the Internet. Goldman's book helped tarnish the perception of Elvis by the general public.

As time passed, it became almost obligatory for writers to mention Elvis's love of peanut butter and banana sandwiches, which was inevitably described as a Southern treat and discussed as though it were the exotic food of some lost native tribe. This type of coverage colored the general public's view of Elvis, robbing him of his legacy as a music pioneer and his potency as an icon who changed our social history. Instead he became fodder for bad jokes by stand-up comics, newspaper cartoonists, and late-night talk-show hosts.

## *Spreading rumors: Elvis is alive*

If you really want to anger one of Elvis's fans, ask him or her if the King is really dead. No other rumor, story, or fad has become more tiresome to fans than the saga of a burned-out Elvis faking his death to escape the burdens of his life. Similar legends and tall tales had surrounded other famous celebrities, including John Kennedy, James Dean, and Jim Morrison, but those stories were romanticized and mythologized in a way that turned the subjects into tragic heroes. In contrast, the "King is alive" rumors ridiculed Elvis and insulted his fans because of the claims that he was seen eating at the local fast-food restaurant or living in a trailer park — places working-class Southerners might be seen at.

**Part IV: From the King of Rock 'n' Roll to American Cultural Icon**

*REMEMBER*

The timing of these rumors couldn't have been worse, because the story hit around the tenth anniversary of Elvis's death. After years of negative stories about drug use and self-destructive behavior, serious discussions of his music and career were beginning to surface on a wide scale. But this reassessment was cut short because the media jumped on the "Elvis is alive" story.

Rumors about Elvis's faked death began to stir as early as 1979 when Gail Brewer-Giorgio published a fictional novel titled *Orion,* in which a Presley-like entertainer arranged his own death in order to find peace of mind. Similarly, in 1981, a book by Steven C. Chanzes claimed that an Elvis impersonator was interred behind Graceland — not the real King. Both books flopped.

The rumors were put to rest for a time, but in 1987, the stories circulated once again. This time they were fueled by Brewer-Giorgio's self-published book about the singer's faked death titled *The Most Incredible Elvis Presley Story Ever Told* and a song by Texas record producer Major Bill Smith called "Hey, Big E." Brewer-Giorgio took the premise of her fictional novel and tried to pass it off as the truth about Elvis's "death." The rumors of his faked death escalated in 1988 with supposed sightings of Elvis in fast-food restaurants, at cheap motels, and even at Chernobyl shortly after the nuclear disaster.

A legitimate publisher quickly republished Brewer-Giorgio's book and retitled it *Is Elvis Alive?* to take advantage of the media attention. As "proof" of Brewer-Giorgio's incredible claim that Elvis is alive, the publisher included an audiocassette of Elvis's voice with each book. The tape featured a voice that sounded like Elvis discussing events that occurred after 1977.

After Brewer-Giorgio released her book and audiocassette in 1988, Geraldo Rivera once again stepped into an Elvis controversy to uncover the "real" story. (See the earlier section "Revealing the ugly truth: Elvis's drug abuse" for details on how Geraldo stepped into another Elvis controversy.) Rivera exposed the author's tape as a phony on his television talk show by bringing on an Elvis sound-alike, who revealed that he had made the recording for a project that never materialized. The impersonator didn't know how the tape fell into Brewer-Giorgio's hands.

Ultimately, the authenticity of the tape and the accuracy of Brewer-Giorgio's theories mattered very little, because the story took on a life of its own. The media maintained the story as a lighthearted feature long after fans had become fed up with being accused of believing the story. Fans didn't believe it any more than most Americans did, but the press insisted that they did. Nothing painted the Elvis fan as a fringe element more than the "Elvis is alive" story.

**Chapter 17: Examining the Jokes, Stereotypes, and Negative Influences**

*REMEMBER*

The rumor that Elvis was still alive spawned years of jokes and tabloid tales at the expense of fans, but it also had a somewhat positive effect on Elvis's image. It inspired short stories by creative writers and original movies by clever filmmakers. (See Chapter 24 for more on Elvis-related films.) The treatment of fans aside, the rumor suggested that in a way, the American public wanted to keep Elvis alive. Unfortunately, it wasn't the historical figure who was being resurrected; instead it was Elvis, the icon of popular culture, who was being restored. In a backhanded way, the "Elvis is alive" rumor helped refigure Presley into an American folk hero endowed with cultural significance. (See Chapter 18 for more information about this phenomenon.) That said, 20 years of "Is Elvis alive?" jokes are enough.

## Treating Elvis with respect: It's about time

During the 1990s, time created a distance from the white-hot nature of the Presley scandals. Respected authors were finally weighing in on his music and career as much as on his personal life. Major anniversaries of his death, such as the 25th, inspired serious assessments of his cultural impact, and well-produced releases of his music introduced Elvis to new generations without all the hype surrounding them. (See Chapter 18 for more information on Elvis's post-death albums.) This newfound assessment of the singer countered some of the mainstream media's tendency to resist giving Elvis his due by focusing on the negative and the ridiculous. Unfortunately, that attitude still hasn't entirely disappeared.

## Marketing Elvis Presley: Would You Like to Buy Some Elvis Sweat?

The fans aren't alone in remembering the anniversary of Elvis's death. Each year, merchandisers, promoters, collectors, and manufacturers who market and sell memorabilia mark the passing of another year. Significant dates, such as the 25th anniversary of Elvis's death or his 50th birthday, increase the amount of merchandise that goes on sale.

The diversity of this merchandise is overwhelming and often amusing. From coats, underwear, liquor decanters, and shot glasses to lamps, clocks, wine, and shampoo, it's difficult to come up with something that hasn't featured Elvis's face . . . or pelvis! Even dirt from the grounds of Graceland and sweat supposedly from his body have been sold to willing consumers. This section offers a brief overview of the merchandizing of the King.

The King's things may be fun to consider, but in the past the enormous variety and incredible tackiness of some of the items have brought attention and ridicule to Elvis's name, further detracting from his music and accomplishments. Remember, the merchandise — no matter how ridiculous — has no bearing on Elvis's talent and cultural importance.

## Recognizing the Colonel's hand

The merchandizing of Elvis Presley goes as far back as 1956 when Colonel Parker entered into a deal with manufacturer Henry G. (Hank) Saperstein for the rights to manufacture several products with the singer's image on them. (You can read more about this deal in Chapter 5.)

The Colonel believed himself to be an expert at promotion, including merchandizing. Part of his arrangement with Elvis and any other business partners required him to be in charge of promotions and merchandise (which he called "exploitations").

During the 1950s, while "his boy" was tearing down the house in whatever venue he was playing, the Colonel could be found in the lobby selling photos of Elvis for a dime. During Elvis's film career, the Colonel was notorious for making quick deals with manufacturers of cheap novelties, who would slap the title of Elvis's latest film on any toy, gadget, or knickknack. The Colonel gave these trinkets to fan club presidents and members as promotions, but to Parker, nothing was free. In exchange, fan clubs were primed to attend Elvis's movies, generally more than once. Even in the 1970s, Parker paraded through the casino and lobby of the Hilton wearing a long duster emblazoned with Elvis's name as he sold photos, souvenir menus, and other small-priced items.

After Elvis died, Parker continued to manage the star's business. Legend has it that minutes after he heard about Elvis's death, he muttered, "Nothing has changed. This won't change anything." Whether he said it or not, by the time his client was laid to rest, the Colonel, a true businessman, had already made a deal with Factors, Inc., to market Elvis products. Parker got Vernon's signature to seal the deal on the day Elvis was buried.

In 1980, the executors of Elvis's estate, including Priscilla Presley (Vernon had died in 1979), petitioned the Tennessee court for approval of all the financial transactions made with Parker on behalf of the Estate. The executors wanted to establish a trust fund and make other long-term financial changes. In order to establish the fund, the Estate had to detail all the deals related to Elvis and the Estate, including those made with Parker. A court-appointed attorney, Blanchard E. Tual, investigated Parker's management of Elvis from the beginning of the singer's career to Parker's final deal with Factors, Inc. This inquiry resulted in a court case charging Parker with "enriching himself by mismanaging Presley's career."

The Colonel hadn't always mismanaged Elvis, but deals inked during the singer's final few years, in which he was affected by drugs, were definitely maneuvered to the Colonel's benefit at Elvis's expense. One such deal was made in 1976 when the Colonel arranged to take 50 percent of Elvis's income for managing his career, rather than his usual 15 percent. The standard percentage for a manager or an agent at the time was 10 percent. How the Colonel persuaded Elvis to go along with this deal is not known.

The judge ordered the Estate to stop all dealings with the Colonel and to sue him to recover at least part of the money the Colonel was responsible for losing. In 1983, the Estate attempted to sue Parker, who sought dismissal on the grounds that he wasn't an American citizen and couldn't be sued. For the first time, the Colonel admitted that he was Andreas Cornelis van Kuijk from Holland, not an American citizen. (See Chapter 4 for more details on the antics of Colonel Tom Parker.) The case was eventually settled out of court, and in 1984, Elvis Presley Enterprises (also known as the Estate) was granted the full rights to Elvis Presley's name and likeness. All rights and royalties went to the Estate.

## Valuing the Elvis merchandise: From trash to treasure

In the days after Elvis died, fans not only purchased products and souvenirs from manufacturers, but they also bartered and sold anything and everything that was connected to Elvis, including his broken guitar strings and clumps of grass from the lawn in front of the mausoleum where he was originally entombed. (See Chapter 16 for the complete story on Elvis's original burial and subsequent move to Meditation Garden.)

The media is often critical of Elvis memorabilia and merchandise, and generally focus their comments on the most ridiculous items, suggesting that everything related to Elvis is in bad taste. Fans take a different view, however; to them, memorabilia is a way to connect with each other or to the Elvis era that produced their favorite souvenirs. Many fans have become major collectors, parlaying their hobby into a moneymaking venture. Today, some memorabilia, including the last concert song list Elvis ever wrote or the jewelry he threw into the audience during his performances, is worth thousands of dollars. Rare, one-of-a-kind memorabilia is sold through the famous auction house, Sotheby's. The Colonel would approve!

**TRIVIA:** One of the most meaningful pieces of memorabilia for Elvis fans were the unused concert tickets for the tour the singer was about to start when he died. Promoters offered refunds for ticket buyers, but many chose not to return their tickets. Fans' reluctance to give up their one-of-a-kind souvenirs caused problems for promoters who had to account for their losses, pay cancellation fees, and so on. Of the $1,300,000 in tickets sold, an estimated $600,000 worth were kept by fans.

## Reading the Memoirs: Elvis, We Hardly Knew Ya

Elvis left behind no autobiography or definitive interview. If anything, interviews and press conferences were designed to conceal information rather than reveal it. So, for the first couple decades after his death, the only windows into his personal life were the biased remembrances of former associates, family members, and friends who published their memoirs about their relationship with the King. The almost continuous release of these types of biographies, in which the reader learned more about the writer than the subject, kept Elvis's name in the news. In the beginning, these books fell into two camps: those that supported the sordid stories of bizarre behavior and drug abuse and those that disputed them. However, the books' lack of information on Elvis's role in popular music and their highly personal nature fueled rumors of his drug abuse even while denying them.

Despite Elvis's enormous fame and following, very few biographies by professional writers were published about Presley until the 1990s. The exceptions were two separate books titled *Elvis,* which were released around 1981. One was a scathing account of Elvis's life written by Albert Goldman (see the sidebar "The bitter words of Albert Goldman" for more details), and the other was an assessment of his early music by rock historian Dave Marsh.

**REMEMBER:** In lieu of reliable biographies, the bookshelves instead were dominated by low-budget quickies written by hacks, coffee-table picture books, novelty books aimed at fans, and memoirs by those who knew him. Like Elvis's treatment by the media and his exploitation through merchandizing, these personal books seemed to stand in the way of a serious assessment of his music and his cultural significance. Their sensationalism and amateur chronicling limited the depiction of Elvis to scandal-ridden celebrity rather than musical pioneer or show business phenomenon.

In this section, I review the various memoirs written by former associates and family members. They're valuable as chronicles of Elvis's daily life and routines and as an inside view of stardom in another time, but each writer has an agenda, whether it be validation of his perspective, exploitation of his relationship for personal financial gain, a defense of Elvis or even the writer himself, and even payback. While each writer's point of view is valid, it's just that . . . point of view.

## The Memphis Mafia cash in

Many former members of the Memphis Mafia published their memoirs about their relationships with Elvis. (You can read more about the Memphis Mafia in Chapter 7.) Here are some of the memoirs:

- Jerry Hopkins wrote *Elvis: The Final Years* (1986), and Marty and Patsy Lacker collaborated on *Elvis: Portrait of a Friend* (1979). Both memoirs confirmed the stories from Steve Dunleavy's 1977 memoir *Elvis: What Happened?* about Elvis's drug use and destructive lifestyle (see the earlier section "Shaping early opinions: The bodyguard book" for more on Dunleavy's book).

- Lamar Fike drew the wrath of fans and former friends when he willingly cooperated with Albert Goldman on *Elvis,* which was published in 1981.

- Some members of the gang were loyal, refusing to write their own tell-alls, but their names were thrown around in other books, so eventually they felt the need to get their version of events down for posterity. Group foreman Joe Esposito, perhaps the most diligent and professional of the group, published *Good Rockin' Tonight* in 1994. Sonny West — one of the men behind the bodyguard book — took it full circle when he released his story *Elvis: Still Taking Care of Business* in 2007.

A cursory glance through the published memoirs of the members of the Memphis Mafia suggests that life with Elvis was one of perpetual adolescence. See Figure 17-1 to see the group posing together. The focus on fun, females, and freedom seemed normal for young men in their early 20s, but there was something irresponsible and rueful about men who pursued this credo when they were pushing 40. During the 1970s, when Elvis and his crew were either in Las Vegas or on the road, their insular lifestyle grew increasingly self-destructive. Infighting broke out among the group, and the members' personal relationships with wives and families suffered.

John Lennon once made an insightful statement about the ultimate destructive nature of Elvis's ever-present entourage of friends, family members, and personal employees: "The King is always killed by his courtiers. He is overfed, overindulged, overdrunk to keep him tied to his throne. Most people in the position never wake up."

**Figure 17-1:** The Memphis Mafia surround Elvis Presley just after receiving deputy badges from the Memphis sheriff.

## The cook, the stepfamily, the wife, and her lover

While the title of this section spoofs the title of a well-respected film called *The Cook, The Thief, His Wife, and Her Lover* (1989), it nonetheless describes the diverse group of "authors" who threw their Elvis memoirs into the biography ring. The following are a few of the bios:

- One of Elvis's cooks, Mary Jenkins, wrote a positive account of her employer called *Elvis, Memories Beyond Graceland Gates* in 1997.
- The singer's stepmother and stepbrothers have penned several books about their years as Presleys, including *Elvis, We Love You Tender* (1980).
- Priscilla wrote *Elvis and Me* in 1985 to combat the disgruntled musings about her by members of the Memphis Mafia.
- Male model Michael Edwards, one of Priscilla's boyfriends after Elvis, cobbled together *Priscilla, Elvis and Me* (1989), a long-forgotten book about his experiences.
- Several former employees and associates in passing, including publicist May Mann (*Elvis: Why Won't They Leave You Alone?* 1982) and secretary Becky Yancy (*My Life with Elvis,* 1977), penned books defending Elvis after the drug scandals, but their marginal relationships to Presley made for limited perspectives. Still, their positive portraits of Elvis, whom they obviously admired, were an important counterpoint to the outrageous tales in the books by the Memphis Mafia.

**Chapter 17: Examining the Jokes, Stereotypes, and Negative Influences**

✔ Among the most valuable memoirs are those by his former band mates, guitarist Scotty Moore and drummer D.J. Fontana, who were there from the beginning — actually, before the beginning — and are knowledgeable about Elvis's music. Moore's book is titled *That's All Right, Elvis* (1997), while Fontana has written two books, *D. J. Fontana Remembers* (1983) and *The Beat Behind the King* (2002).

## Imitating the King: From Impersonators to Tribute Artists

The politically correct term for Elvis impersonators is now *Elvis tribute artists,* or ETAs, and they're arguably the most curious offshoot of the collective desire to keep the singer's name and music alive.

Many are surprised to discover that Elvis tribute artists existed long before his death. As far back as 1957, a fanzine article listing 25 important facts about Elvis Presley mentioned that he was the most impersonated entertainer in the world. In 1958, *Life* magazine remarked on the increasing number of Elvis imitators in other countries, such as Germany and Japan. Elvis was said to have enjoyed the idea that professional Presley impersonators were at work. In fact, according to some sources, he would sneak into nightclubs to check out the acts of some of them.

After Elvis died, the impersonator phenomenon boomed. Eventually, the ETAs became so removed from the looks and skills of the real Elvis Presley that they developed into a phenomenon unto themselves. No longer do the impersonators have to look or sound like Elvis. You can find female Elvis ETAs, including Janice K.; black Elvis ETAs, such as Clearance Giddens; Asian ETAs, such as Hound Dog Fujimoto; and Hispanic ETAs, of whom El Vez is the most original and talented.

It's nearly impossible to accurately calculate the number of Elvis tribute artists around the world, but estimates range from 10,000 to 250,000.

Even though many in the media have taken to ridiculing the ETAs and, by extension, the fans who enjoy them, no fans expect the impersonators to be as talented or as charismatic as Elvis — or to even look exactly like him. Fans don't expect impersonators to take Elvis's place; they enjoy them as a way to remember and relive the excitement of one of Elvis's live performances.

A tribute artist's act consists entirely of imitating Elvis's singing and performing style, his costumes and hairstyle, and his mannerisms and speech patterns. Some of the impersonators even have had plastic surgery to make their faces and bodies resemble the real Elvis. Most imitators choose to emulate the Vegas Elvis, exaggerating the look of that era with coal-black hair, massive sideburns, and the ever-present jumpsuit. Very few imitators attempt to emulate the Elvis of the 1950s or 1960s, but there have been some, including Trent Carlini. Many have combined their names with one part of Elvis's name, such as Joe Elvis and Rick Presley.

At one point, the Estate attempted to bring legal action against the impersonators for violating the copyright on Elvis's name and image, but there were so many that the lawsuit was dropped. The Estate, like most Elvis fans, now accepts the impersonators as an indelible part of Presleyana. In fact, during the 30th anniversary festivities at Elvis Week in Memphis, the Estate sponsored the Ultimate Elvis Tribute Artist contest in the ultimate example of "If you can't beat 'em, join 'em."

Just after Elvis's death, most impersonators were professional entertainers with singing and stage experience. Nightclubs and stage reviews hired performers, such as Chicago's talented Rick Saucedo, because of their serious interpretation of Elvis's talents. As the years progressed, however, more amateurs joined the ranks of the impersonators. Many of these amateurs hold day jobs and never entertain beyond the confines of their hometowns. What they share is a desire to perform, a love of Elvis Presley, and the ability to bring a smile to the faces of those with open minds and good senses of humor.

# Chapter 18

# Appreciating Elvis as a Cultural and Historical Figure

### In This Chapter
- Exploring Elvis's music in the post-death era
- Considering Elvis as a character in movies
- Appreciating a good biography

As time erased the real Elvis Presley and replaced him with the cultural icon, Elvis's music was reissued in a way that showed his musical importance. He also continued to show up in the movies — first in made-for-TV biographical films and later as a character in big-screen dramatic features. The latter films present diverse interpretations of Elvis, which make his image far more nuanced than it ever was before. By depicting Elvis Presley as a larger-than-life symbolic figure with various connotations, these films contributed to a reevaluation of Elvis. Between the reissuing of his music and the emergence of his new symbolic status, he became mythic in stature — too big to be taken down by old jokes or old media criticisms.

This chapter chronicles the evolution of RCA's musical output after Elvis's death and offers a summary of the mythic use of his image in recent movies. The music and the movie-mythmaking point to an appreciation of Elvis Presley as a significant cultural and historical figure — finally.

## Taking Care of Elvis's Music: BMG-RCA

Elvis's death unleashed an outpouring of albums from RCA to take advantage of the sudden demand for the singer's music. However, those in charge of his catalog did little to take advantage of the renewed interest in Presley and squandered the opportunity to position him as a significant musical figure. With few notable exceptions, RCA merely repackaged the same material and reissued old albums.

In 1986, the Bertlesmann Music Group (BMG) absorbed RCA, and BMG formed an international restoration committee to research and restore the Presley catalog of recordings. The committee released well-planned CD compilations and albums in a way that fostered an appreciation for the significance of the singer's music.

Eventually the committee's efforts helped to shine a spotlight on Elvis's music rather than on his scandalous personal life, his bulging waistline, the tacky merchandise, or his fans. This renewed attention to his music led to cover recordings by other artists, soundtrack opportunities in Hollywood films, and musical plays based on his music. Most of all, this attention rehabilitated Elvis's reputation as an important musical influence.

## Cranking out the discs: RCA puts the pressing plants to work

Immediately after Elvis's death on August 16, 1977, record stores across the country sold out of his records. New orders for the singer's albums began pouring in, so RCA's pressing plants operated 24 hours a day to fill the orders. For a while, the record company even subcontracted other pressing plants to keep up with the demand. By September, RCA still hadn't caught up with all the orders. RCA's offices and pressing plants outside the U.S. found themselves in the same position. Pressing plants operated day and night. A factory in Hamburg, West Germany, produced only Elvis's records in an attempt to meet the demands of fans in that country. By October, sales were so high in the U.S. that several of Elvis's albums were on the charts again. This success set the tone for RCA's approach toward its most historically significant artist: Release as much product as quickly as possible.

Over the next few years, RCA continued to release Elvis Presley albums at the rate of two or three per year. As was the case while the singer was alive, some of the albums were worthy efforts, but others were inferior. (See Chapter 15 for more information on the decline in his recording output.) The following titles are a representative sampling of RCA's handling of the Presley catalog:

- *He Walks Beside Me — Favorite Songs of Faith and Inspiration* (1978) contained previously released material simply repackaged yet again.

- *Guitar Man* (1980) attempted to take advantage of developments in sound recording and enhancement to "improve" Elvis's sound, but any improvement in sound quality was debatable. However, the album charted well, reaching number 6 on the country lists and number 49 on the Top 200, indicating a noteworthy commercial success.

- Other albums seemed to be the result of RCA searching the vaults for any leftover tape with Elvis's voice on it. *Elvis — Greatest Hits Vol. 1* (1981) contained never-before-released live material from Las Vegas, Hawaii, and Nashville.

RCA was criticized by some purists for tinkering with the recordings of its most famous artist when it released several Elvis albums of older material that were enhanced for modern audiences. *Elvis: I Was the One* (1983) makes use of modern instruments that were overdubbed to accompany Elvis's vocals. Other albums consisted of original mono recordings with *rechanneled stereo* in which techniques such as filters to separate high and low frequencies are used to create the impression that the sound was recorded in stereo. Rock 'n' roll historians claim that any attempt to "improve" or "clean up" Elvis's early recordings doesn't necessarily illuminate his contributions to popular music; instead, it can distort them.

RCA stumbled across an unexpected treasure in 1983 when a producer found master tapes and records stored at Graceland. Some of the tapes were recordings of unreleased live performances and offstage conversations with Elvis. In 1985, RCA released much of the musical material on a six-album set that celebrated Elvis's 50th birthday.

## Developing new strategies to release Elvis's music

A new approach to marketing and releasing Elvis Presley's music began after RCA was sold to a German publishing group called Bertlesmann Music Group, or BMG, in 1986. Two years later, BMG formed an international restoration committee to research the Presley catalog of recordings and restore them to their former glory. Representatives from the United States, England, Germany, Denmark, and Asia comprised the committee, which was ultimately responsible for the high quality of the compilation and album releases from the late 1980s onward.

Ernst Jorgensen and Roger Semon, two of the most important members of the team, landed the job of listening to every minute of every tape with Elvis's voice on it. Over the years, the two tirelessly reordered, cataloged, and researched Elvis material.

Jorgensen and Semon's main contribution at BMG-RCA was to release Elvis's music in boxed sets and themed albums to introduce the singer to younger audiences. By grouping the music chronologically or by genre, they provided a context with which to learn about and appreciate Presley. The two-man team also hired music and popular culture historians to write informational booklets to further explain the importance of the music. These booklets were inserted inside the CD cases as bonus features. Jorgensen and Semon's work has gone a long way toward refocusing attention on Elvis's musical triumphs rather than on the personal tragedies of his life or the wacky aspects of his lifestyle.

**IN THEIR OWN WORDS**

In an interview with Record Collector magazine about his work, Jorgensen remarked, "I think my greatest challenge . . . was to get Elvis reestablished as a significant and important artist and not just a stupid joke in the *National Enquirer* because there was a tendency in the media to treat him like that. I think fifteen years later that has been achieved."

## Introducing the Masters Series to casual listeners and die-hard fans alike

Among the most important of the BMG-RCA productions was the Masters Series, which represents Jorgensen and Semon's efforts to not only release Elvis Presley's music commercially but to reframe it historically. Together, these three sets of CDs are a faithful audio documentation of Elvis's music from the beginning to the end. The tracks have been digitally remastered from old Sun and RCA recordings, but they maintain the integrity of the originals. (You can read about Elvis's association with Sun Records and RCA in Chapters 2 and 4, respectively.) Also included are the vocal exchanges and patter between Elvis and his musicians, which capture the camaraderie of the participants as well as the spontaneity of the sessions.

**REMEMBER**

Separately, each set suggests something about Elvis's career that defies a commonly held perception. Consider the following:

- By following the evolution of Elvis's work from 1954 to 1958, *Elvis: The King of Rock 'n' Roll — The Complete '50s Masters* (1992) proves that Elvis didn't "steal" the sound of black rhythm and blues artists and call it his own. Instead, the tracks reveal a blending of influences and an integration of musical genres that coalesced into a commercial sound and inched closer and closer toward a universal, mainstream style.

- *Elvis: From Nashville to Memphis — The Complete '60s Masters* (1993) shows that Elvis didn't entirely abandon his roots in country, gospel, and rhythm and blues after he achieved his pop style — an accusation hurled most often by rock-music critics. The smooth, mainstream pop stylings of Elvis's movie soundtracks did dominate this period, but his recordings of blues tunes — "Reconsider Baby" and "Such a Night" — and his gospel work later in the decade are declarations of his Southern heritage.

- *Elvis: Walk a Mile in My Shoes — The Complete '70s Masters* (1995) reveals that Elvis didn't grow lazy and rest on his laurels after his comeback to stage performances. He was a workhorse in the studio until his lifestyle caught up with him in the mid-1970s. (Chapter 15 discusses the effects of Elvis's lifestyle on his decline.)

An archival achievement as well as a musical one, the Masters Series also includes complete session credits and lengthy liner notes by music historians Peter Guralnik and Dave Marsh.

## Chapter 18: Appreciating Elvis as a Cultural and Historical Figure

**TRIVIA**

You can find a more concise treatment of Elvis's career in *Elvis Presley Platinum: A Life in Music* (1997), which charts the evolution of his style in a four-CD box set. *Platinum* contains 100 tracks, 77 of which were previously unreleased. The unreleased material represents mostly alternate takes of Presley classics or practice runs of various songs. However, it also includes the newly discovered 1954 demo of Elvis singing "I'll Never Stand in Your Way."

The chronological treatment of the music used in the Masters Series compels listeners to reevaluate the familiar and find a context for the unreleased material. In doing so, a new light is shined on Elvis's music, giving listeners a full appreciation for the impact of his career. This newfound appreciation rings true not only for young audiences, rock 'n' roll listeners, and Presley critics but also for Elvis fans, who remained faithful through the dark years of badly packaged rereleases.

### Digging for gold

To further shine light on Elvis's musical significance, the BMG committee researched the actual sales figures for the records and albums that Presley sold early in his career.

The Recording Industry Association of America (RIAA) is the official organization to which record companies report sales and request gold and platinum records for their artists. However, the RIAA wasn't formed until 1958, and Elvis had already sold millions of records by then. Even though RCA awarded Elvis various in-house gold records for his pre-1958 hits, they never asked the RIAA for retroactive certification of these records. Also, RCA rarely requested additional certification when Elvis's records went gold or platinum more than once. So the BMG committee used Colonel Tom Parker's extensive files to accurately research just how many records Elvis sold and which ones deserved gold, platinum, or multi-platinum status. (To read more about Parker, Elvis's long-time manager, refer to Chapter 4.)

After completing its research, the committee estimated that Elvis has sold more than a billion records worldwide. By August of 1992, the committee had updated the status of Elvis's albums and singles. As a result, he was awarded 110 gold, platinum, and multi-platinum albums and singles by the RIAA — the largest presentation of gold and platinum records in history.

As of 2005, the last date that BMG asked for a total accounting for all Presley releases, Elvis has earned 150 gold, platinum, or multi-platinum albums, singles, or extended-play albums (EPs). The RIAA first grants a hot-selling recording a gold disc when it meets the appropriate number of sales, and then a platinum disc, and then a multi-platinum disc. If Elvis had been receiving the RIAA certifications in the proper sequence all along instead of the all-in-one accounting in 1992, he would probably have around 270 gold, platinum, or multi-platinum albums.

## Marketing ELVIS: 30 #1 Hits

In 2002, to commemorate Elvis on the 25th anniversary of his death, RCA released a compilation of his number-one records titled *ELVIS: 30 #1 Hits*. The marketing campaign was designed around the tag line, "Before anyone did anything, Elvis did everything." A brilliant bit of phrasing, this line succinctly summarized Elvis's contribution to pop culture history while evoking the dynamism of his sound and the danger of his original image.

The world needed to be reminded of all of this — and it was. *ELVIS: 30 #1 Hits* debuted on the charts in the number-one position, meaning that it sold 500,000 copies in the first week of release. Debuting an album in the top spot on the U.S. charts was an accomplishment that Elvis hadn't managed while he was alive. In addition to the United States, *ELVIS: 30 #1 Hits* opened at number one in 16 other countries, including Canada, France, the United Kingdom, Argentina, and the United Arab Emirates. Marketing strategy aside, it was the music that accounted for the CD's success.

Arranged in chronological order, the compilation of hits covered Elvis's entire career at RCA — from "Heartbreak Hotel" in 1956 to "Way Down" in 1977. All the songs in the compilation reached number one on the charts either in the United States or the United Kingdom.

As a last-minute addition to *ELVIS: 30 #1 Hits*, the producers included a remix of "A Little Less Conversation," a song originally part of the soundtrack for the film *Live a Little, Love a Little*. (See Chapter 9 for more information on this film, which was released in 1968.) The Dutch deejay act Junkie XL reworked the song in early 2002 for a Nike World Cup commercial, but when it was released as a dance-mix single, it became Elvis's first top-ten single in decades. "A Little Less Conversation" was billed as a bonus track and was separate in concept from the rest of the cuts on the CD.

Jorgensen and Semon compiled and researched the tracks on *ELVIS: 30 #1 Hits*. BMG-RCA hired a group of expert engineers and mixers to optimize the sound in ways that remained true to the original recordings. This assignment proved to be difficult considering the condition of the original tapes. Stashed away at RCA's storage facilities in Iron Mountain, Pennsylvania, some of the original tapes hadn't been played in more than 40 years. Most were deteriorated to some degree, and the first goal was to transfer them onto a digital format for remixing or remastering. Some tapes, including the tape for "Way Down," were in such bad condition that they were baked in an oven to prevent the oxide from falling off the tape.

Elvis's songs from 1956 to 1961 had been recorded on a mono system and couldn't be remixed, only remastered. Those from 1961 to 1966 had been recorded on a three-track recording system and required an antique three-track machine to help in the remixing process. Only a few of these machines still exist, and the one the remixing team used tended to overheat, further aggravating the process. Later tunes had been recorded on 8 tracks, 16 tracks, and even 24 tracks and were considerably easier to remix. However, the goal was to produce a uniform quality to all the tracks and ensure that the quality remained whether the CD was played on a home stereo, on a computer, or in a car stereo. The efforts of these engineers and remixers resulted in a modernization that doesn't detract from Elvis's renditions of these songs. Instead this modernization restores the songs' vitality.

The vitality in Elvis's recordings comes in part from the way he worked in the studio. Consider the following:

- When Elvis entered the studio, he took down the partitions between performer and musician so he was in the same room as his band.
- Elvis sang each take of a song completely through as though it were a performance before an audience. Each take was enlivened — or, in some cases, ruined — by interaction between Elvis and the band in a kind of trial-and-error approach.
- All decisions regarding a song were made in the studio during the session — not beforehand. He generally didn't overdub, nor did he splice together various takes of a song to get a perfect "studio version."

The expert remixing and remastering of the songs on *ELVIS: 30 #1 Hits* captures the spontaneity of Elvis's unique approach to recording — one he never abandoned for easier, more technically driven methods. (See Chapters 4 and 11 for more information on Elvis's approach to recording.)

In 2004, BMG merged with Sony Music Entertainment to become Sony BMG. The company continues to use the RCA Record label for issuing Elvis releases, and Jorgensen and Semon still work with Sony BMG on showcasing the Presley catalog. In 2005, Sony BMG started a special Elvis collector's label called Follow That Dream Records, which releases special collector's material and reissues classic Elvis albums that are no longer part of the mainstream Sony BMG (RCA) catalog.

## *Mythologizing Elvis Onscreen*

Hollywood loomed large at every turn in Elvis's career. He turned to the movies in the 1950s in order to deflect negative publicity from his image as a notorious rock 'n' roller, and then he turned to an acting career in 1960 to increase his appeal to the mainstream audience. (See Part II for the complete story of Elvis's film career.) During the 1970s, two well-received documentaries showcased Elvis's concert act to millions who might not otherwise see the singer live. (Refer to Chapter 14 for information on these documentaries.)

> ### Kurt Russell's many connections to Elvis
>
> Actor Kurt Russell has experienced more than one brush with Elvis Presley during his career. The most distinguished example was his acclaimed performance in the TV biopic *Elvis* (see "Appreciating the first biopic" for details), but his career connection actually goes back to his childhood. In *It Happened at the World's Fair* (1963), 10-year-old Kurt had a walk-on as a bratty boy who kicks Elvis in the shins — a moment captured forever in a famous film still. In 1994, Russell also supplied the voice for the character Elvis Presley in *Forrest Gump*. Onscreen, Peter Dobson appeared as the young Presley, but it was Russell's voice that viewers heard. In 2001, Russell and Kevin Costner co-starred as a pair of Elvis impersonators who are also thieves in the violent R-rated film *3000 Miles to Graceland*.

After his death, documentaries and television miniseries and biographies explored different facets of his life, from his personal relationships to his career high points. By the end of the 1980s, a different cinematic depiction of the King of Rock 'n' Roll emerged. In this depiction, the figure of Elvis was used for its iconographic power to convey a variety of themes or ideas, turning him into a kind of a folk hero. This section offers a rundown of Elvis's post-death "career" onscreen.

## Busting the biopics

Elvis's last movie as a star opened in 1969, and his bitter remarks about his acting career at that time made it clear that he was through with Hollywood. But, Hollywood wasn't through with Elvis.

Beginning in 1979, a spate of miniseries and made-for-television biographies began rolling out, all claiming to offer a true slice of Elvis's real life. They range in quality from the thoughtful *Elvis* (1979), directed by the talented John Carpenter, to the ridiculous *Elvis and the Beauty Queen* (1981), featuring *Miami Vice*'s Don Johnson hopelessly miscast as the King. With the exception of Carpenter's biography and the ABC-TV series *Elvis,* produced in 1990, most of these efforts are neither dramatic nor well crafted. Yet, they share in common an attempt to reach beyond Elvis's life story in order to capture what made him tick.

### Appreciating the first biopic

On February 11, 1979, ABC-TV aired *Elvis,* the first biographical picture, or *biopic,* about the singer's life. Well crafted and sincere, this made-for-television feature was directed by John Carpenter, a respected filmmaker best known for his horror films (*Halloween* and *Escape from New York,* for example). It was produced by Dick Clark, a high-profile supporter of rock 'n' roll music since his show *American Bandstand* hit the airwaves in 1956. Airing 18 months after Presley's death, the biopic starred Kurt Russell, who offered a complex, sympathetic portrayal of Elvis during a time when controversy, scandal, and rumor were swirling around his drug use and excessive lifestyle. Russell received a much-deserved Emmy nomination for his portrayal of the King. (Check out the nearby sidebar, which explains Russell's other brushes with Elvis.)

### Dismissing the other biopics

The continued popularity of Elvis Presley among his fans spawned a number of TV biopics over the next 30 years, none of which surpassed John Carpenter's *Elvis* (which I explain in the preceding section). Most of the shows starred actors who were unsuited to the role; they tended to mimic Elvis's mannerisms and voice in lieu of depicting him as a three-dimensional character. Save yourself the disappointment of watching any of the following:

- *Elvis and the Beauty Queen* (1981), a syrupy account of the relationship between Elvis and Linda Thompson, his long-term girlfriend after Priscilla. This biopic suffered from the miscasting of Don Johnson, whose raspy tenor voice was the opposite of Elvis's deep, low tones.

- *Elvis and Me* (1988), a two-part miniseries based on Priscilla Presley's autobiography of the same title, which featured Dale Midkiff as the King. Even though Midkiff made for a distant, uncharismatic Elvis, 32 million viewers still watched and made it the highest-rated miniseries of that season.

- *Elvis and the Colonel* (1993), which starred the unknown Rob Youngblood as Elvis and Beau Bridges as Elvis's infamous manager Colonel Tom Parker. The biopic shared the same title as Dirk Vellenga's biography of Parker, but its fictionalized account is little more than a simplistic warning about the high price of fame.

- *Elvis,* a new biopic that was produced in 2005. The show was fully supported by Elvis Presley Enterprises and became the first to feature Elvis's master recordings. Starring Irish actor Jonathan Rhys Meyers, the two-part miniseries lacked sufficient insight to be anything more than a conventional biopic, and Rhys Meyers who knew little about Elvis, lacked any understanding of the American icon he was portraying.

### Remembering the best interpretation of the King's life and career

In the spring of 1990, ABC-TV launched *Elvis,* a television series based on the very beginning of Presley's career, from 1954–1955, before he became a national sensation. During this period, Elvis was a naive young truck driver hoping to begin a career as a singer. (Flip to Chapter 2 to read more about Elvis's early years.) The series, which was coproduced by Priscilla Presley and ex-Memphis Mafia member Jerry Schilling, was short lived, but it offered the public a thought-provoking interpretation of Elvis's life.

Starring Michael St. Gerard, the series was based on actual events in Elvis's life, but each experience was shaped so the episode pointed to a deeper significance. Some episodes were allegories that foretold Elvis's eventual impact on popular music and his legendary status as the King of Rock 'n' Roll; others commented on the effect that his childhood had on the rest of his life.

Shot on location, with stellar production values and a talented cast, *Elvis* the series remains the best interpretation of Presley's life and career because it reached beyond mere biography to express key themes and important ideas.

## Discovering the documentary: This Is Elvis

Produced, directed, and written by Andrew Solt and Malcolm Leo, the documentary *This Is Elvis* released in theaters in 1981. The film both re-creates scenes and combines news footage, television performances, and still photography to tell the story of Elvis's life and career. Informative, engaging, and fair, *This Is Elvis* offers a sensitive overview of the singer's life and career in a flashback structure, without suffering from the bad casting and sordid melodrama of the biopics.

The film opens with the shocking news of the singer's death and then flashes back to his childhood years in Tupelo, Mississippi. Four different actors portray Elvis at various points in his life, including his childhood, teen years when he performs in front of his high-school class for a talent show, his mature years when he's hospitalized for numerous ailments, and on the eve of his death at Graceland. Other events and phases of his career are depicted through news footage, home movies, concert material, and still photography. *This Is Elvis* was one of the first serious examinations of Elvis's life, and it holds up remarkably well today.

Documentaries are rarely released theatrically, but like the concert documentaries *Elvis — That's the Way It Is* (1970) and *Elvis on Tour* (1972), *This Is Elvis* became a box-office success. See Chapter 14 for a look at the concert documentaries.

## Turning Elvis into a symbol in fictional films

During the late 1980s, narrative films in which Elvis is a character — and not the subject of a biopic — began to emerge. Some were biographies based on other historical figures; some were complete fiction, often with outrageous story lines. All of them focused on the potent power of Elvis as an image to evoke ideas and move their audiences emotionally.

# Chapter 18: Appreciating Elvis as a Cultural and Historical Figure

No longer just a performer or a famous figure, Elvis Presley, the King of Rock 'n' Roll, now embodies a range of ideals, concepts, and values — from Elvis the great integrator of our society in *Hearts of Dixie* (1989) to Elvis the gaudy Vegas performer, who represents the excess and corruption of modern America, in *3000 Miles to Graceland* (2001). Though contradictory in meaning, both uses of Elvis as a symbol are valid in context of the films. These extremes suggest the diversity of Elvis representations in various fictional movies.

The following sections show a selection of some of the most interesting uses of Elvis's image in feature films. Some of the films are very good, some have good critical reputations, and some are flawed but worth a look. All provoke thought about Elvis as a cultural icon.

### Heartbreak Hotel: Elvis to the rescue

One of the first fiction films to prominently feature Elvis Presley as a character, the comedy *Heartbreak Hotel* (1988) involves a teenage boy in 1972 who kidnaps Elvis and brings him home to his single mother in a small Ohio town. The family has its share of problems. For one, they live in a ramshackle boarding house that has fallen into disrepair, which seems to reflect the disorder of their lives. Also, the members each have some issues of their own: The mother is depressed, lonely, and always falls for the wrong men; the son lacks self-confidence; and the daughter is afraid of the monsters that lurk in the dark.

Like a bona fide movie hero, Elvis "rescues" the family from its problems. As he repairs the fixtures on the house, mows the lawn, and even redecorates, he restores order within the family, fixing broken hearts and mending egos. At the same time, Elvis finds happiness in performing these everyday tasks and chores — something he never gets to do as the King of Rock 'n' Roll. The character of Elvis represents all of their fantasies come true, only to show them the beauty of their family and everyday lives.

Tuesday Weld co-starred as the mother in *Heartbreak Hotel*. Weld was also Elvis's real-life costar in *Wild in the Country* (1961).

### Heart of Dixie: Elvis and race relations

Released a year after *Heartbreak Hotel,* in 1989, *Heart of Dixie* dramatizes racial issues in Mississippi during the mid-1950s. An Elvis Presley concert is used to illustrate the state of race relations at the time. Elvis's remarkable but volatile music — a combination of white country western and black rhythm and blues — signifies integration. In the film, his concert draws both blacks and whites. Tension over this union of cultures erupts into violence at the concert when white audience members brutally attack a black couple who are dancing. The situation prefigures the tension that will surface over the announcement about the integration of the University of Mississippi.

### Mystery Train: Elvis in spirit

*Mystery Train* (1989), a unique film directed by independent filmmaker Jim Jarmusch, tells three seemingly unrelated stories. Here's a breakdown of the story lines:

- In the first story, a young Japanese couple hooked on American pop culture pass through Memphis as part of their vacation.
- The second story offers a look at an Italian widow on a layover who spends the night in a run-down Memphis hotel as she waits for the body of her dead husband to be sent home.
- In the third story, a trio of hapless thieves hole up in the same hotel while on the lam.

At the end of the film, the viewer discovers that the three stories are happening simultaneously, though the characters have little connection to one another. They remain isolated at the end of their experiences as victims of the dislocation and alienation that pervade the film.

The title, which is derived from one of Elvis's Sun recordings, and the Memphis setting cause the viewer to expect a film about Elvis Presley. Yet, Elvis, Graceland, and a recognizable Memphis are noticeably absent. Instead, tacky portraits of Elvis grace the rooms of the cheap, run-down Arcade Hotel where most of the action takes place; the hotel employees talk about Elvis trivia; guests admire their T-shirts from Graceland; "Blue Moon" plays on the radio in the background; and the confused ghost of Elvis appears briefly in one scene.

Like the characters in the film, the viewer experiences Elvis only as an icon of American pop culture. And also like the characters, today's fans buy souvenirs, listen to his oldies on the radio, and circulate mythic stories about his life; but, of course, these are poor substitutes for the authentic experience. To Jarmusch, Elvis has become an icon of a commercialized pop culture that's served up as a substitute for experience, compounding the isolation and alienation of modern society.

### 3000 Miles to Graceland: Violent Vegas impersonators

In *3000 Miles to Graceland* (2001), five impersonators try to rob a Vegas casino, but plans go awry when the head of the gang betrays his companions. In this film, Las Vegas is a dark, gritty town, and the seedy-looking impersonators with their extra-long sideburns and ultra-tacky jumpsuits are more than excessive; they're decadent and vulgar. In dressing the thieves like grubby impersonators, who are faux representations of a unique, authentic entertainer who changed the social history of our country, the director suggests that a corruption of sorts has infested America. *3000 Miles to Graceland* is rich in thought-provoking imagery, but its poor craftsmanship, nonstop profanity, and excessive violence distract from the film's strengths.

## Chapter 18: Appreciating Elvis as a Cultural and Historical Figure

---

### The King takes the stage

At least two musical plays have been written about Elvis's early music: *All Shook Up* (2005) and *Million Dollar Quartet* (2008). *All Shook Up* is a fantasy set in 1955 in which a cool, young drifter blows into a Midwestern town and sets hearts afire despite the town ordinances against anything fun. *Million Dollar Quartet* is a re-creation of the legendary afternoon that Johnny Cash, Elvis, Carl Perkins, and Jerry Lee Lewis jammed at Sun Studio. (Check out Chapter 19 for more details on this infamous story.)

---

#### Forrest Gump: Getting it wrong

Not all representations of Elvis Presley as a character in a fictional film successfully depict who he was. Some use him in such a superficial way that the character is wasted or amounts to little more than a weak joke. The Elvis character in *Forrest Gump* (1994) is the perfect example of getting it wrong, resulting in a complete waste of the singer's image.

*Forrest Gump* tells the story of a simpleton's epic journey through life in the latter half of the 20th century. Along the way, he encounters real-life historical figures and participates in actual historical events. The film's special effects team, headed by Ken Ralston, won an Oscar for the computer-generated imagery (CGI) that made it possible for Tom Hanks as Forrest Gump to interact with real historical figures in documentary news footage.

One of Forrest's earliest encounters in the film is with a young Elvis Presley in the mid-1950s; however, Elvis isn't re-created with CGI. Instead, he's played by actor Peter Dobson and voiced by Kurt Russell. It seems Elvis is a struggling singer staying at Gump's boarding house and hasn't yet stumbled onto his signature performing style. As a child, Forrest wears leg braces because of a spinal condition, so he walks and moves in an awkward, jerky gait as an adult. So when Elvis plays guitar and sings for him, Forrest begins to dance with herky-jerky movements. Inspired by Forrest, Elvis works these movements into his act, and the rest is history.

The idea that the most famous entertainer of the 20th century "borrowed" his unique performing style from such humble origins is quaint at best, but ultimately it robs Elvis's style of its sexual undertones and of its cultural significance as a fusion of black and white roots music — two factors that changed the course of popular music.

### Showing up in biopics of other celebrities

Biographical interpretations, or biopics, of real-life entertainers are a popular genre. So it isn't surprising that Elvis's peers at Sun Studio were given the Hollywood treatment just like Presley. Given that they all recorded for the same small studio, it's fitting that Elvis shows up in the biopics of these colleagues. In each of these films, Elvis is treated as a symbol of something rather than as a real-life historical figure.

### Great Balls of Fire: Goodness gracious, it's Jerry Lee Lewis

*Great Balls of Fire* (1989) was an interpretive biopic of Jerry Lee Lewis, a rockabilly singer who, like Elvis, had started with Sun Records in Memphis. In the film, Lewis is presented as the rock 'n' roller destined to follow in the footsteps of Elvis Presley, who's used as a symbol of the highest level of fame and fortune. Lewis's closeness to that goal is indicated in two scenes involving Elvis. As Lewis's star is rising, Elvis is shown in a brief scene alone and jealous of the immense fan adulation enjoyed by his new rockabilly rival. Later, just as Lewis is about to reach the pinnacle of success, Elvis is drafted into the army. He finds Lewis alone in Sun Studio and bitterly tells him, "Take it, take it all." Unfortunately, Lewis's sense of individuality and his freewheeling antics, which he refuses to curb, are scandalous to the mainstream public and prevent him from achieving Elvis's level of fame and fortune.

Michael St. Gerard, who plays Presley in *Elvis,* the TV series (see the earlier section "Remembering the best interpretation of the King's life and career" for details), portrays a brooding, sullen Elvis in *Great Balls of Fire*. St. Gerard also plays Elvis in the 1989 fictional film *Heart of Dixie.* Of all the actors who portrayed the young Elvis, Gerard looked the most like him and did a credible working-class Southern accent.

### Walk the Line: Johnny, Jerry, and Elvis

In 2005, a biopic of Johnny Cash — Sun Records's other legendary son — enjoyed critical acclaim and popular success. The biopic titled *Walk the Line* focuses mostly on Cash's romance with country singer June Carter. The first part of the film captures the earliest days of rockabilly, when Cash, Elvis, and Jerry Lee Lewis packed themselves into beat-up cars and drove from gig to gig, where they played to screaming girls in sold-out auditoriums and halls.

Star Joaquin Phoenix plays Cash, while newcomers Tyler Hilton and Waylon Payne play Presley and Lewis, respectively. Payne portrays Lewis as an out-of-control prankster who thinks of himself as a God-fearing Christian, an exaggeration of Lewis's persona. A walking contradiction, he likes to blow things up with dynamite and then remind the group that they're all going to hell for singing the Devil's music. Elvis is depicted as the object of unbridled lust for most of the girls in the audience. Together, the pair symbolize the sexuality and uninhibited spirit of rockabilly — a new sound for a new generation. The inclusion of Presley and Lewis as Cash's tour mates helps place Cash outside the mainstream of country music, a running theme in the film.

> ### Other films featuring Elvis
>
> Over the years, several films featuring Elvis as a character or using him as symbol have been released, including the following:
>
> - Bye Bye Birdie (1963)
> - Touched by Love (1980)
> - Eat the Peach (1986)
> - Leningrad Cowboys Go America (1989)
> - Wild at Heart (1990)
> - True Romance (1993)
> - The Woman Who Loved Elvis (1993)
> - Picasso at the Lapin Agile (1993)
> - Elvis Meets Nixon (1997)
> - Finding Graceland (1998)
> - Bubba Ho-Tep (2002)
> - Honeymoon In Vegas (2002)
> - Elvis Has Left the Building (2004)
> - Hounddog (2007)
>
> You can read about some of these films in further detail in Chapter 24.

**REMEMBER:** As a side note, *Walk the Line* serves as a reminder of Elvis's country roots, a part of his history and music too often neglected by pop-culture historians and critics who prefer to celebrate the rhythm and blues influence. (See Chapter 3 for more information on Elvis during this period.)

## Reading Some Worthy Elvis Biographies

Elvis was dead almost 20 years before an objective, thoroughly researched, comprehensive biography was written about him. The two-volume account written by music historian Peter Guralnik in the mid-1990s counts as the definitive Elvis biography. *Last Train to Memphis: The Rise of Elvis Presley* begins at birth and concludes with Elvis's departure for the army; *Careless Love: The Unmaking of Elvis* picks up the saga in 1958 and follows through to his death. Southern music is Guralnik's area of specialty, so he has written extensively about country music, blues, and rhythm and blues. His insightful analysis of Elvis's music is one of the strengths of his work.

More books have been written about Elvis Presley than about any other entertainer. The Elvis division of the National Popular Culture Association estimates that more than 1,700 books have been written about America's most famous performer. Of those, many have been biographies, including career accounts; personal memoirs by friends, associates, and former members of the Memphis Mafia; and dubious bios by those with personal agendas. The best books address his meaning as a cultural icon, analyze the complexities of his music, or offer an objective view of his career (rather than dwell on his personal life or misrepresent his movies). These solid biographies include the following:

- *Elvis Series* by Bill Burk, 1990–1994
- *In Search of Elvis: Music, Race, Art, Religion* edited by Vernon Chadwick, 1997
- *All Shook Up: Elvis Day-by-Day* by Lee Cotton, 1985
- *Elvis Atlas* by Michael Gray and Roger Osborne, 1996
- *Elvis* by Dave Marsh, 1982

# Chapter 19

# Visiting the Sites: The Elvis Tourist

### In This Chapter

- Taking a tour of Graceland
- Revisiting Sun Studio where it all began
- Considering a jaunt to other Elvis destinations
- Remembering Tupelo, Elvis's birthplace

A key to the continued popularity of Elvis rests with Graceland, his former home in Tennessee. Graceland provides fans with a tangible place to re-experience their appreciation of Elvis. Because Graceland was Elvis's home for most of his life, fans feel a personal connection to the property. Other popular cultural figures, such as Marilyn Monroe and James Dean, can't offer their fans the same type of visiting place. Elvis Presley Enterprises (the Estate) is based at Graceland, and from this centrally located site, the Estate organizes and generates events, products, and promotions to help keep Elvis's name alive. The desire of fans and visitors to experience Elvis makes Graceland the hub of a very successful business. Personal Elvis and corporate Elvis are all in one place.

Other locations related to Elvis hold a similar connotation for both die-hard and casual fans as well as interested visitors. For example, Sun Studio reminds the Elvis tourist and music fan where rockabilly began, and the Tupelo birthplace takes you back to Presley's roots, which are clearly an important part of his character. Additional Elvis destinations are as various as they are scattered, from Poplar Music, where he bought most of his records as a teen, to his homes away from home in the Los Angeles area.

In this chapter, I encourage you to take a tour of Elvis's world without leaving your chair by offering a look at Graceland and the other Presley-related sites.

## Graceland: Visiting the King's Palace

Over 600,000 people visit Graceland every year, making it the second most famous home in America after the White House. But, when the house was first opened to the public, no one knew whether the venture would be successful. The decision rested in part with Elvis's ex-wife, Priscilla, who was the executor of the will and a board of trustees member. Over the years, Priscilla Presley was instrumental in making the kinds of decisions that turned Graceland into a success. Later, Elvis's daughter, Lisa Marie, who still owns the house, the grounds, and her father's possessions, took over some of the hands-on decisions regarding the operations of the Estate. In 2005, she sold controlling interest in the Estate to CKX, Inc., but Lisa Marie and Priscilla are still involved in the decision-making process.

Graceland is located in Whitehaven, a few miles east of Memphis at 3764 Elvis Presley Boulevard. For fans, the idea of "going to Graceland" has changed over time. In the first few years after Elvis's death, it meant standing in front of the gates or mingling with friends at the strip mall across the way. When the house opened to the public, it meant touring the home where the key personal events of the singer's life unfolded. As time went by, the phrase referred to touring all of Memphis for a thorough Elvis experience.

Although additional Presley-related sites have been taken over by the Estate, the mansion, which you can see in the color photo section, remains the center of the experience. Reactions to the house depend on the visitor's own tastes and background. Some people find it gaudy and vulgar; others see it as a mansion befitting the King. This section offers an overview of Graceland — the first and most important stop on the Elvis Tour.

Graceland was more than just Elvis's home; it was his refuge from the pressures of making movies, recording music, and touring in concert. Having endured the death of his mother, his divorce from Priscilla, and two major career changes, Elvis found that Graceland was the only constant in his life.

## Still devoted: Looking at Priscilla's role in managing Graceland

Even though Priscilla was stashed away at Graceland for most of the 1960s, she had surprisingly little influence on Elvis's career. Young and inexperienced, she was Elvis's escape from his professional world, and she devoted herself to him. (See Chapter 7 for more on Elvis and Priscilla's relationship and marriage.)

In the post-death era, she has emerged as a savvy businesswoman who remains devoted to Elvis in a different way. She has her ex-husband's best interest at heart, and she has worked hard to ensure that his legacy remains fulfilled. Her involvement began when Elvis's father, Vernon, died in 1979. (You can read more about Elvis's father in Chapter 2.) The Estate was placed in the care of three coexecutors, or cotrustees, including Priscilla, accountant Joseph Banks, and the National Bank of Commerce. Though she and Elvis had divorced in 1973, she was Lisa Marie's mother and had remained close to the family.

Priscilla and the trustees soon realized that the Estate had a cash flow problem and that the mayor of Memphis was eager to purchase the house out from under them for the city. To help resolve the cash shortage, Priscilla and the others made the decision to open Graceland to the public. In 1981, they hired an investment counselor to plan and execute the opening of Graceland and then oversee the operation. The doors to Graceland opened for the first tour on June 7, 1982.

According to MSNBC, around 21,000 visitors descended on Graceland on opening day. Whether all of them were able to get inside that first day is not known.

Over the next few years, Priscilla and the other trustees worked to honor Elvis's memory and name by enhancing the Graceland experience. They not only generated revenue to preserve the Estate, but they also worked to improve Elvis's image by eliminating the less-than-dignified shops and attractions that exploited his name, image, and home. Here are some examples of the Estate's improvements:

- The Estate tracked down Elvis's two airplanes and added them as an attraction in 1984.
- The Automobile Museum opened in 1989 in Graceland Plaza.
- Elvis Presley's Heartbreak Hotel was developed from a nearby existing hotel in 1999.

## Walking through the house

You will see no antiques at Graceland; none of the decor is reminiscent of the distant past. All the furnishings were modern when Elvis purchased them, though some of them appear dated today. The dire poverty of Elvis's childhood, in which he was surrounded by used or handmade items, left him with a lifelong hatred of anything old.

Contrary to some reports, not *all* of Graceland is tasteless or tacky. Some rooms are ostentatious, even flamboyant, but the interior design of the main floor is no different from what was found in the homes of many wealthy Southerners in the 1950s and 1960s.

**TRIVIA**
When Graceland first opened to the public, the upstairs and kitchen remained off limits because one person still lived in the residence: Elvis's Aunt Delta Biggs. Aunt Delta moved into the house in 1967 with her dog, Edmond, and she remained there until she died in 1993. After her death, more of the house was opened up.

The main floor of Graceland includes the living room, the dining room, the music room, and the kitchen. The first three rooms are decorated with white or gilt-edged furniture, silky fabrics, elaborate drapes, crystal chandeliers, marble or mirror paneling, and wall-to-wall carpeting. Most of the walls are white as is the carpeting. The accessories in the main rooms are royal blue, which was Elvis's favorite color, and trimmed in gold. The rooms designed for recreation are located in the basement, and they're more flamboyant and personalized than the formal rooms upstairs. For a guided tour of Graceland's must-see rooms, read the following sections.

### Taking a peek into the living room

The living room features a stained-glass peacock that Laukhuff Stained Glass of Memphis designed for Elvis in 1974. Elvis supposedly liked peacocks because they symbolize eternal life. A few live birds even strolled the grounds of Graceland at one time. However, superstition has it that displaying peacocks inside a home will actually bring bad luck, adding an ominous note to the otherwise beautiful birds.

In 1974, Linda Thompson, Elvis's girlfriend, had the accessories in the living room and music room changed to bright red. However, when Graceland was opened to the public, Priscilla returned them to their original colors. Refer to the color photo section to have a look at the peacock-themed living room.

### Remembering the sounds from the music room

Elvis loved to play the piano and sing gospel tunes and other songs with his friends and family gathered around. So as soon as he purchased Graceland, Elvis converted the mansion's sunroom into a music room. The music room, which is shown in the color photo section, is predominantly gold and currently contains a black Story and Clark piano. This piano is one of three that were used at Graceland over the years.

The piano that stayed in the room the longest was a white and gold baby grand, which was replaced by a grand piano that Priscilla had covered with gold leaf for Elvis as an anniversary gift. The gold grand piano proved too large for the room, according to official accounts from the Presley estate, and it was replaced by the black Story and Clark.

### Gathering in the kitchen and dining room

The roomy kitchen is like a time capsule of the mid-1970s with its dark wood cabinets and avocado green, harvest gold, and maroon color scheme. Though the décor is from another era, it does create a warm, cozy atmosphere.

The kitchen was always open at Graceland. Friends, visitors, and staff passed through the house at all hours, and food was served at any time. Elvis appreciated the cooks' tolerance for the unusual hours, so he treated them well. For example, he bought televisions for the cooks so they could watch their "stories" (which is what Southern women called their soap operas) while working in the kitchen.

The dining room became a gathering place when several members of the Memphis Mafia were on hand. The guys sat around the long table, telling stories, eating snacks, and planning their next escapades. During the holidays, the dining room housed the Christmas tree.

### Relaxing in the TV room

The TV room, which was decorated in its present style in 1974, features mirrors on the ceiling and a wraparound mirrored bar with an old-fashioned soda fountain. A built-in jukebox from the 1950s fills one corner of the room. Much of Elvis's personal record collection is housed here, with some discs dating back to his high-school days. The TV room is predominantly navy blue and gold, with a bold graphic of a TCB lightning bolt emblazoned on one wall. (See Chapter 15 for an explanation of this symbol to Elvis's life.)

The focal point of the TV room is the bank of three televisions that are set side by side in a wall unit. Elvis got the idea for this arrangement from President Lyndon Johnson, who liked to watch the news simultaneously on all three networks. However, Elvis preferred watching sports.

### Playing games: Discovering the pool room

The pool room is across the hall from the TV room. In 1974, Elvis had it decorated with about 400 yards of rippled patchwork fabric, which still covers both the walls and ceiling. A large stained-glass lamp by Laukhuff Stained Glass hangs over the pool table, where Elvis enjoyed playing his favorite billiard game, eight ball. Interior designer Bill Eubanks helped decorate some of the rooms at Graceland, including the pool room and the TV room.

### Going ape in the Jungle Room

When Graceland first opened to the public, visitors dubbed one of the rooms the "Jungle Room," and the name stuck. This room was Elvis's favorite, though he referred to it as the den. The 40-foot-long room, which you can see in the color photo section, contains massive pieces of heavy furniture with fake-fur upholstery. The room is decorated in a Tahitian or Hawaiian motif, with hand-carved chairs and varnished, scallop-edged cypress tables that are accented with wooden lamps carved to resemble angry gods. Several monkey figurines pepper the Jungle Room, adding to the playful atmosphere. A figure of St. Francis, patron saint of animals, sits on a shelf by the waterfall wall, reflecting Elvis's love of animals.

The story behind the flamboyant room goes something like this: After Elvis saw a commercial for a Memphis furniture store called Donald's, he decided at the spur of the moment to drive down to the store and take a look at what was in stock. Within 30 minutes, he'd picked out enough furniture for the entire Jungle Room. Everything was delivered that same day. In other versions of the story, Vernon was the first to hear of Donald's, and he began talking about the strange furniture sold there. Elvis, however, had already seen the furniture and decided to buy it, much to Vernon's dismay.

In 1976, when Elvis couldn't bring himself to record new material, RCA helped turn the Jungle Room into a makeshift recording studio. (See Chapter 15 for more information on this temporary studio and Elvis's state of mind during the last months of his life.) The company parked a truck with recording equipment in the back and ran cables through the windows of the house. Two albums were recorded in the Jungle Room: *From Elvis Presley Boulevard, Memphis, Tennessee* (1976) and *Moody Blue* (1977), which featured Elvis's last single, "Way Down."

## Strolling the grounds

If the decor of his house reveals Elvis Presley the man, then the Exhibition Room and the Awards Exhibit herald Elvis the musical legend. Both of these exhibits are located on the Graceland property. While you're strolling the grounds, you also can walk past Elvis's barn and visit his final resting place.

### Viewing memorabilia in the Exhibition Room

Originally a four-bay garage in the north wing of Graceland, the space now called the Exhibition Room has taken many different forms over the years. In the 1960s it was turned into an apartment for guests. After Graceland was opened to the public, it became a bank of offices. In 2000, it was remodeled to become the Exhibition Room, which showcases collections of Elvis's belongings, including his costumes and personal clothing, firearm collection, and badge collection.

The enormous number of artifacts, mementoes, and pieces of memorabilia stored at Graceland make it impossible to show everything at once. The curators routinely rotate out parts of the collection so that fans can see something different each time they visit. In addition, special exhibitions group items together to offer new insights into the artifacts of Elvis's life.

### Showcasing Elvis's success in the Awards Exhibit

The Awards Exhibit, which is located in the racquetball court in the backyard, showcases Elvis's many awards, gold and platinum records, and famous costumes. The highlight of the exhibit is the wall of awards presented to Graceland by the Recording Industry Association of America (RIAA), featuring all of Elvis's gold and platinum records. Though presented in 1992, the wall is continually updated as Elvis continues to sell more records. (Flip to the color photo section to see the Awards Exhibit.)

### Visiting the King in Meditation Garden

The emotional high point of any visit to Graceland is seeing Elvis's grave in Meditation Garden behind the main house. A brick and white-columned peristyle encloses the small space in which Elvis, his parents, and his grandmother are buried. See the color photo section to view this memorable spot.

At the head of Elvis's grave burns an eternal flame, which sits atop a marble base marked by a bronze plaque. The plaque bears a touching epitaph commissioned by his father, Vernon, a quiet man who rarely expressed himself regarding the extraordinary life of his famous offspring. Vernon finally revealed his feelings in this poignant inscription in which he remembered his son as "A precious gift from God."

### Seeing the House of the Rising Sun

Visitors aren't allowed inside the barn, but the white structure and fences make a pretty picture alongside the green pastures where horses still graze. Elvis loved all animals, and throughout his life, he kept dogs, chickens, peacocks, horses, and even a chimpanzee at Graceland. In 1966, Elvis began keeping horses at Graceland. He and Priscilla became serious about horseback riding after he bought Priscilla a horse called Domino. Over the years, he purchased several horses for himself and his friends. Of all the horses, a stunning Palomino called Rising Sun is perhaps the most famous, and Elvis referred to his barn as the House of the Rising Sun. Rising Sun, who never missed a photo opportunity with visitors, died in 1993, outliving his master by 16 years.

In 2008, Priscilla continued the tradition of keeping horses at Graceland by arranging with animal rescue organizations to take in two horses that had suffered from neglect and cruelty and needed a new home.

## Where Legends Were Born: Stopping by Sun Studio

Called the "Cradle Where It Rocked," Sun Studio cultivated the exciting sounds of such rockabilly pioneers as Elvis, Jerry Lee Lewis, Carl Perkins, Johnny Cash, and Roy Orbison. Sun Studio, which was located on an oddly shaped corner on Union Avenue, sat next to a small restaurant called Taylor's, where Elvis, his producer Sam Phillips, and his band mates Scotty Moore and Bill Black often grabbed a bite to eat.

This section offers a description of the famous Sun Studio, where Phillips and Elvis cut the singer's first five singles. Come sit at Elvis's table at Taylor's (now called the Sun Café) and soak in the history of this tiny studio that changed the course of music history. Elvis's two years of recording at Sun Studio are detailed in Chapter 2. This section offers a look at the rest of the tiny studio's history.

## Sun before Elvis

In the early 1950s, Sam Phillips worked as an engineer for established recording studios. In 1951, he recorded what many consider to be the first rock 'n' roll recording, "Rocket 88," by Jackie Brenston and the Delta Cats.

Phillips launched the record company Sun Records in 1952 with the intention of recording the music of Memphis's African American rhythm-and-blues artists, who found it difficult to start recording careers because of the racism of the times. The discs were cut at Sun Studio, the small building on Union. Sun Records' first hit was Rufus Thomas's "Bearcat," which coincidentally was an answer to Willa Mae "Big Mama" Thornton's song "Hound Dog" (see Chapter 4 for more details on Thornton's song). In addition, he cut records with B.B. King, Little Junior Parker, Howlin' Wolf, and Ike Turner before expanding into the country music market. A lot of music history took place within the walls of Sun Studio.

Sun Studio also doubled as the Memphis Recording Service, which was where Elvis first headed when he decided to cut a disc for himself in 1953. (Flip to Chapter 2 for more on this historic recording.) Consisting of one recording room, a foyer, and a tiny control room in the back, the studio could only record one act at a time, and it was generally Phillips who served as engineer. Marion Keisker was Phillips's secretary and chief assistant, and his brother Judd helped out with promotion.

## Sun after Elvis

It could be said that Sam Phillips peaked after Elvis left Sun Records to sign with RCA. Around that time, Sam discovered Johnny Cash and Carl Perkins. Later he recorded albums for Jerry Lee Lewis and Roy Orbison. Lesser-known singers, such as Charlie Feathers and Charlie Rich, also signed with the company, making for a roster of high-powered talent.

## Studio B in Nashville

During the 1960s, Elvis cut the majority of his albums at RCA's state-of-the-art Studio B at 30 Music Square West in Nashville. His pop-rock stylings of the era were influenced by the highly polished sessions musicians hired by producer Chet Atkins. So many chart-topping singles and albums were recorded at Studio B that the facility was named the "Home of a Thousand Hits." Despite this distinction, the studio closed in 1977.

Shortly after the studio's closing, the Country Music Hall of Fame absorbed Studio B, and the facility was restored to its original décor and touted for its historical significance. In 2002, the Country Music Hall of Fame began conducting tours of Studio B for Music City's tourists. Occasionally a singer or act records at the studio for a special occasion.

Touring the studio can be insightful for the thoughtful Elvis fan: It points out the contrast between recording for Sun Records and recording for RCA. Sun Studio's tiny, intimate space and relaxed, informal atmosphere lent itself to experimentation and simply horsing around with different tunes. On the other hand, RCA's officious milieu and use of highly polished professional musicians promoted set agendas, tight schedules, and standardization.

On December 4, 1956, Elvis dropped by Sun Studio to see his old mentor, Sam Phillips. Carl Perkins was there cutting a new single, with Jerry Lee Lewis backing him on the piano. When Elvis started jamming with Perkins and Lewis, Phillips recorded the trio while someone phoned Sun's latest artist, Johnny Cash. Cash stopped in a short time later and added his talents to the mix. A local Memphis reporter who was there for this historic impromptu session dubbed the group the Million Dollar Quartet. In 2006, the definitive version of this famous impromptu session was issued. Called *The Complete Million Dollar Quartet,* it was released to mark the 50th anniversary of the event. In 2008, Colin Escott and Floyd Mutrux wrote a musical play titled *Million Dollar Quartet* to mythologize the event.

During the 1950s, the record industry began to change, with major recording companies jumping on the rock 'n' roll bandwagon and stealing talent from small regional labels. During this chaotic period, Phillips, his record company, and his studio also were in a state of flux. He moved Sun Studio from 706 Union to the larger 639 Madison. His brother, Judd, left the company to run his own label in 1958. Phillips later set up a second studio in Nashville. He lost his desire for producing records during the 1960s and pursued other interests, including investing in the Holiday Inn motel chain. In 1969, he sold Sun Records to Shelby Singleton, who moved the company entirely to Nashville.

The historic little yellow brick building on Union Avenue was eventually sold and became home to a plumbing company and later an auto parts store. In 1987, a decade after Elvis died, Grayline Tours purchased the building and partially restored it. Tours were offered so fans and music aficionados could see where it all started. The studio was furnished with musical instruments and recording equipment from the 1950s as well as photos of the legends who made history there. It also operated as a working music studio, with musicians cutting demos or recording tunes after the tours were over.

*REMEMBER:* Sun Studio became a National Historic Landmark in 2003; three years later, Elvis Presley Enterprises entered into a deal with Sun Studio in which the studio would be managed by the Estate. Though a major tourist attraction, it still operates a recording studio after hours. The inclusion of the studio in the Elvis experience placed a renewed emphasis on his rockabilly sound and the origins of his music, which was a much-needed step in raising awareness of the singer's cultural significance.

## Touring Other Elvis Sites in Memphis

In addition to Graceland and Sun Studio, other sites related to Elvis's life in Memphis attract fans and tourists who hope to better understand his life and music. Here are some of the highlights:

- **Lauderdale Courts:** Located at 185 Winchester Avenue, Lauderdale Courts was the federally funded housing project that the Presleys called home from September 1949 to January 1953. Even though it was a nicely run housing project, Lauderdale Courts is a reminder of the poverty that the Presleys struggled with.

- **Elvis's first home:** Elvis purchased his first house in the summer of 1956 at 1034 Audubon Drive, which unfortunately afforded him no privacy from fans. Neighbors complained about the constant stream of teenagers in their quiet neighborhood, so the Presleys moved to Graceland the following spring.

- **Poplar Tunes:** This record store, which is located at 308 Poplar Avenue near Lauderdale Courts, epitomizes the 1950s record store. Elvis purchased many of his favorite singles there, and when he became a local sensation, Poplar Tunes sold his records.

- **Humes High School:** Elvis attended Humes High School, located at 659 N. Manassas Street. The school is now a junior high — and a local hot spot. The school operates tours that include a look at the Elvis Room, which features Presley-related memorabilia, and the auditorium where he performed in the annual talent show.

You can read more about how these sites fit into Elvis's early life in Chapter 2.

## Making a Pilgrimage to Tupelo

Currently, Elvis's birthplace in Tupelo, Mississippi, consists of the original two-room shotgun shack built by Vernon and his family, the Elvis A. Presley Memorial Chapel, and the Elvis Presley Museum and Gift Shop. The grounds that these structures sit on is called Elvis Presley Park.

When Elvis's father, Vernon, built the family house during the Depression, it was an unpainted shotgun shack sitting on a dirt plot on Old Saltillo Road. However, after the city of Tupelo opened the house as a tourist attraction in 1971, they turned it into a quaint bungalow located on the newly renamed Elvis Presley Drive. City officials furnished the house with amenities that the Presleys could never have afforded, and they hung odds and ends on the doorknobs and pictures on the walls. Keeping a fresh coat of white paint on the house also gave the structure an external neatness that it didn't have when the Presleys lived there. Structural changes also were made to the little house, including the addition of a porch. The grounds were landscaped with new grass and were reorganized to include small dells with charming names like Gladys Glen and Lisa Lane. In effect, Tupelo's city officials turned the birthplace into a quaint tourist stop, a pleasant place with charm and coziness. However, in dressing up the shotgun shack, they robbed it of its historical accuracy.

Elvis's birthplace is a fascinating site because the shotgun shack is steeped in Elvis folklore. It's also a nostalgic glimpse back in time to a simple childhood in the rural South. The nearby Elvis Presley Memorial Chapel reminds visitors of the singer's strong faith and also offers a place of reflection and meditation for those who are so inclined. Also on the grounds are the Elvis Presley Museum and Gift Shop. The Museum features exhibits that focus on Elvis' childhood.

> **TRIVIA**
> While in Tupelo, be sure to drop by the Tupelo Hardware Company, Inc., where Gladys bought Elvis his first guitar. A signed affidavit by the store's owner, which includes the story of Elvis, Gladys, and the first guitar, rests inside a glass case for all to see.

## Exploring the California Hideaways

Making three films per year in Hollywood meant that Elvis and his entourage spent a fair amount of time in Los Angeles. So, the singer rented or owned several houses in Hollywood.

None of Elvis's homes in California achieved the mythic status of Graceland or the nostalgia of the shotgun shack in Tupelo, but two of them are interesting in their own ways.

- In 1961, Elvis rented a house at 565 Perugia Way in Bel Air. Elvis lived there off and on from 1961 to 1965. Originally called the Healy House, this residence was designed by Lloyd Wright in 1949 in the Southern California style. Wright was the son of famed architect Frank Lloyd Wright, and the house is often erroneously attributed to the elder Wright. It was once owned by the Shah of Iran, and before that movie star Rita Hayworth had possession.

- The only house that Elvis ever built for himself was located in Palm Springs at 825 Chino Road. Built in 1965, this single-story, Spanish-style, white stucco house featured 15 rooms and a swimming pool. Lisa Marie inherited the house when Elvis died, but when she became of age to receive her inheritance, she sold it. Among its other owners was Four Seasons singer Frankie Valli.

# Chapter 20

# Understanding Elvis Today

*In This Chapter*
- Blazing the trail with his regional style of music
- Molding a culture of receptive young people
- Breaking down Elvis's image into the parts people connect with

More than 30 years after his death, Elvis remains a prominent figure in our culture. Other cultural icons have been simplified in death, being reduced to their most obvious connotations or traits — John Wayne as the spirit of the independent western hero, Marilyn Monroe as the tragic sex goddess, or James Dean as the rebellious youth. Elvis, on the other hand, has expanded his significance, making him a complex figure with multiple meanings and connotations. Elvis signifies different things to different groups of people.

To Southerners, he's a local hero who "never got above his raising," as they say in the South. To his original fans, he's a figure who defined them as the first generation of teenagers to revel in youth culture. To academics, he's a multicultural icon who's rich in sociohistorical significance. To popular music enthusiasts, he's the Rosetta stone of rock 'n' roll. To his detractors, he's a joke in a jumpsuit. When assessing Elvis's importance, you must factor in this complexity of meaning.

Separate from the idea that Elvis Presley means different things to different people is an objective consideration of his true impact on American cultural history. Even those who harbor a negative attitude toward Elvis have to admit that he has a place in history.

This chapter attempts the difficult task of assessing Elvis for today's world. First, I offer a summary of the cultural importance of his music, and then I summarize his impact on the development of youth culture. To conclude, I comment further on the complexities of his multifaceted image, because Elvis truly does offer something for everybody.

Despite spending the bulk of this book explaining the significance of Elvis Presley, I can't help but recall an adage that fans are fond of quoting. Though attributed to Memphis Mafia member George Klein on the official Elvis Presley estate Web site, it's an oft-heard opinion: "If you're an Elvis fan, no explanation is necessary. If you're not, no explanation is possible."

# Innovator and History Maker: Elvis Changes the Music of the 1950s

Throughout his career, the music of Elvis Presley proved to be popular and financially successful. His music from the 1950s, however, actually made history on several counts. This section summarizes and reviews the reasons his music from this decade is so important.

## Integrating regional styles of music

Elvis's original rockabilly music combined the sounds and styles of regional, grass-roots music, including country, rhythm and blues, and blues. Even though the young singer was attracted to diverse styles of music, including pop and opera, his original sound combined the elements of these regional flavors. Lucky for Elvis, his personal musical tastes matched those of record producer Sam Phillips, who went on to groom the young singer to fit his goal of supporting the talents of regional performers. (See Chapter 2 for a full discussion of Elvis's early career and original sound.)

Elvis's rockabilly style and Phillips's goals as a producer represent an integration of white music and culture with African American music and culture. The fact that this musical integration occurred just prior to the movement for racial integration begs the questions: What is the relationship between popular culture and the society that produces it, and what can popular culture reveal about that society? In the case of Elvis, his music, and the tastes of his fans, scholars see a progression toward integration in our society before it was mandated by law. After scholars make a connection between pop culture and society, they tend to raise questions that aren't necessarily answerable but provoke thought and debate: Did Elvis have an effect on people's attitudes regarding integration? Did he help people accept it? Or, did he polarize the public further? As you can see, Elvis and rockabilly/rock 'n' roll aren't just part of a colorful fad like hula hoops and coonskin caps. Instead, they're windows into issues of race, class, and sexuality in our society.

## International Conference on Elvis Presley

In the summer of 1995, the University of Mississippi's Center for the Study of Southern Culture held the first annual International Conference on Elvis Presley. The purpose of the six-day event was to establish a forum for discussion among different experts who specialize in popular culture and how it relates to our society. The experts who were invited to the event included music critics, Elvis authorities, and scholars. These experts lectured on a range of subjects including "Elvis and Black Rhythm," "Country Elvis," "Elvis as Anthology," and "Elvis as Southerner."

## *Defying pop music standards*

As a fusion of regional sounds, Elvis's rockabilly-turned-rock-'n'-roll music defied the conventions of mainstream pop music as defined by the Tin Pan Alley tradition. (See Chapter 5 for more.) He then introduced this sound to a nationally based audience when he signed with RCA Victor and appeared on network television. As his popularity took off, so did the genre of rock 'n' roll. Eventually Elvis and this controversial genre were synonymous.

Regionally based music and rock 'n' roll, which had predominantly been the domain of small record labels, soon became enormously successful, proving to nationally based labels that they could make money from what many thought was a passing fad for a limited market. By making rock 'n' roll a financially lucrative sensation, Elvis helped changed the standards and conventions of what constituted popular music.

He also drew attention to the regional styles that made up his sound. During the 1950s, one of those styles, rhythm and blues, grew in stature and popularity among teenagers, partly as a result of the rise of rock 'n' roll. In interviews at the time, Elvis freely talked about the importance and influence of blues and R&B on his music, often naming singers that reporters had never heard of. Detractors have claimed that Elvis stole his music from African American blues and R&B singers, but his country-tinged sound, willingness to credit his influences, and quick evolution into a rock 'n' roll singer suggest otherwise.

In an interview with the *Charlotte Observer* on June 26, 1956, Elvis explained one of the origins of his music. Here's what he said: "The colored folks been singing it and playing it just like I'm doin' now, man, for more years than I know. They played it like that in the shanties and in their juke joints and nobody paid it no mind 'til I goose it up. I got it from them. Down in Tupelo, Mississippi, I used to hear old Arthur Crudup bang his box the way I do now, and I said if I ever got to the place I could feel all old Arthur felt, I'd be a music man like nobody ever saw." This quote is one of many in which Elvis credited his musical influences, and he was humble enough to acknowledge their superior musicianship.

> ## Elvis enters the Rock 'n' Roll Hall of Fame
>
> For his part in innovating rock 'n' roll and turning it into a financially successful genre, Elvis was one of the first inductees into the Rock 'n' Roll Hall of Fame in 1988. According to the Hall of Fame, Elvis "launched the rock and roll revolution with his commanding voice and charismatic stage presence."
>
> The Blue Moon Boys, Elvis's backup musicians, were also inducted into the Hall of Fame. Rhythm guitarist Scotty Moore was inducted in the Sidemen category in 2000, because he "[counterpointed] Presley's vocals with melodic yet forceful solos that helped launch the rockabilly revolution." Bassist Bill Black and drummer D.J. Fontana were inducted in the Sidemen category in 2009. Fontana was included because, according to the Hall of Fame, "his drumming built the foundation of rock and roll percussion influencing future players such as Ringo Starr, Charlie Watts and Max Weinberg," while "Black's bass playing had an extraordinary impact on rock and roll bass playing...."

## Influencing an important generation

Some of the music of Elvis and the other pioneer rock 'n' rollers, such as Jerry Lee Lewis, Chuck Berry, and Little Richard, sounds full of vitality after more than 50 years, especially if the listeners understand the innovative combination of styles and sounds they're listening to.

But, in the common cultural consensus today, the music of the 1950s has long carried a nostalgic connotation. In other words, today's generation automatically perceives it as music from a time long ago. Instead, in terms of a direct template for contemporary musicians, the music of the 1960s tends to be the model they return to for inspiration and influence. They look to artists such as Bob Dylan, The Beatles, the Rolling Stones, and James Brown.

However, one must remember that Elvis and his backup musicians — Scotty Moore, D.J. Fontana, and Bill Black — heavily influenced the 1960s generation. The rhythm, the beat, the sensuality, and the attitude of rock 'n' roll all began with Elvis and the Blue Moon Boys. That influence can't be underestimated.

Statements by 1960s musical legends acknowledge the role that Elvis played in their music. An oft-repeated quote by John Lennon attests to Elvis's influence on The Beatles: "Before Elvis, there was nothing."

## Shaping Youth Culture in the 1950s

Before the era of Elvis, teenagers latched onto entertainers, styles of music, and fashions and called them their own. However, the generation that grew up with Elvis in their lives experienced events, situations, and changes in society that previous generations hadn't. Something about this generation was different. For one, they had more money than previous eras of teenagers. They also grew up during the difficulties of social integration and were marketed to until they became a distinct demographic in the economic structure. This section offers some observations on how Elvis helped shape the identity of the 1950s generation.

## Forging an identity

Generally speaking, a prosperous economy during the 1950s helped turn teenagers of that era into solid consumers. Teens and young adults who held jobs no longer had to contribute all or part of their incomes to their families for survival. So with disposable income burning holes in their pockets, they purchased products, ate at restaurants, and sought entertainment marketed to their tastes and preferences. The teenagers of this decade emerged as a high-profile, identifiable group with their own fashion sense, hair styles, slang, tastes in music, preferences in movie stars, and other favorite pastimes. Their preferences for R&B music, rockabilly, and rock 'n' roll turned these genres into moneymaking ventures for record companies. Clearly this popularity made young people a desirable demographic to market to for the music industry. (Visit Chapter 5 for more information.)

Elvis became a focal point around which teenage fashions, slang, and music swirled. The controversy over his sensual performing style emphasized the gap in tastes and experiences between adults and teenagers, further alienating teens from their parents. More than any popular performer in any previous era, Elvis held the allure of forbidden fruit. He bonded together teens whose common goal was to experience their idol by buying his records, watching him on TV, or going to see his movies. Elvis and the sensation he created helped foster a strong sense of identity within the teenagers of the 1950s.

*Jailhouse Rock* best depicts the image of Elvis most beloved by teenagers of that period. His character, Vince Everett, is sullen, cynical, and cool on the outside but sensitive on the inside. He wears his hair in a long ducktail, speaks in slang, drives a Cadillac, and wears the hippest clothes. A scene in which Elvis admires his girlfriend's bathing suit captures the essence of the Rebel Elvis. Dressed in wide-legged pants and sporting a ducktail that stands tall on top of his head, Elvis looks his girl up and down, coolly remarking, "Flippy baby, really flippy."

## Smells like teen spirit

The youth of the 1950s may have been the first to have "teen spirit," and Elvis Presley was a major rallying point behind that spirit. Being an Elvis fan in the face of all the adult criticism against him bonded this generation. The criticism compelled teens to vocalize their support of Elvis and rock 'n' roll and reject the music and tastes of their parents' generation.

Since the 1950s, when teenagers became a distinct demographic targeted by marketers, each subsequent generation of young people has traveled the same road marked "Rite of Passage." Rebelling against the previous generation, these teens adopt their own fashions, favorites, and fads. They revel in their own controversies, and latch onto new subgenres of music, which are labeled "dangerous" or "threatening" much like Elvis's music was in 1956. Rebelling against their parents' world, or least drawing a distinction from it, is a liberating step for young people that's natural and necessary.

# Offering Something to Everyone

Elvis has become what academics like to call a "mutable cultural signifier." Don't let the academic jargon scare you; it simply refers to the many historical and social issues regarding class, race, and gender that revolve around Elvis's music, his career, and his personas so that his image conjures an array of diverse meanings and connotations, depending on who's looking at it. Since Elvis's death, these meanings have grown more varied and more complex. In fact, no other entertainer is so closely tied to so many of the issues and fissures that plague or disrupt society, including race, age, class, the American Dream, sex, excess, and success.

In other words, some people can look at a youthful Elvis and see the rebellious, threatening spirit of early rock 'n' roll; others see this image and feel nostalgia for a more innocent time. Similarly, some find Vegas Elvis of the 1970s a symbol of celebrity excess and decadence that led to an early grave; others see this image of Elvis as a betrayal of the musical innovation of the 1950s. Fans, on the other hand, remember the Vegas Elvis image fondly, because it reminds them of an era in which they seemingly had personal access to him in his concerts. Academics view Elvis as a fascinating study of race and class; certain officials in charge of the U.S. Postal Service called him a bad role model and a drug addict. All these assumptions are accurate.

This doesn't suggest that you can make the image of Elvis mean anything you want. It means that his image is so rich with cultural significance that it simultaneously holds diverse implications, interpretations, and connotations. Sometimes these meanings coalesce and parallel each other; other times they clash and contradict. This section offers an overview of the many meanings of Elvis and a reminder of why he's still an American icon of great significance.

## Comparing Rebel Elvis with Vegas Elvis

During the 1950s, the press skewered Elvis the rebellious rock 'n' roller in their columns, articles, and editorials. However, it's this image of a sexy, controversial youth blazing a musical trail across the blandness of the pop music landscape that appeals the most to the mainstream public today. (You can read about Elvis's treatment from the press in Chapter 5.)

## Return to sender: The Elvis stamp

The Rebel Elvis versus Vegas Elvis debate peaked in 1992 when the U.S. Postal Service allowed the public to vote on the final design for an Elvis stamp. It had taken years of lobbying by Elvis fans (led by fan Pat Geiger) before the Postal Service finally decided to issue a stamp featuring the singer. At the time, a public figure had to be dead ten years before the Postal Service considered a commemorative stamp. (The requirement was recently reduced to five years, however.) So Elvis would have been eligible in 1987, but officials within the Postal Service adopted an elitist attitude, declaring the singer a bad role model and a drug addict. Eventually, new administrators in the U.S. Postal Service changed this position, paving the way for the stamp.

Two designs were finalized in 1992 and were put to a vote by the general public. The Postal Service issued ballots that featured two illustrations — one of Rebel Elvis and the other of Vegas Elvis. Despite modeling Vegas Elvis after a photo from *Aloha From Hawaii,* when Elvis looked handsome and full of life, the jumpsuit he was wearing alluded to "the fat Elvis." (See Chapter 17 for more on the press and public's misperceptions of Elvis's weight.) The general public was asked to vote for one of the designs on the ballot and then mail the ballot to the U.S. Postal Service in Washington. After a voting period of several months, Rebel Elvis won.

Some culture critics couldn't let Elvis fans have their stamp in peace. Consumer advocate Ralph Nader remarked that the Postal Service was wasteful because it spent $300,000 on the "Decide Which Elvis Is King" contest. Nader said that to break even, the company would have to sell a million stamps to collectors who would then not use them. Like many non-fans, Nader underestimated Elvis. After the stamp was issued on Elvis's birthday in 1993, the Postal Service made a record profit of $31 million. As of 2009, the Elvis stamp remains the most popular stamp ever produced.

---

Even those who turn up their noses at Presley's overall career express appreciation for his role as a pioneer of rock 'n' roll. In this capacity, Elvis represents rebellion against the status quo; he's viewed as a nonconformist who disrupted the complacency of the 1950s. Full of vigor, confidence, and optimism, this is the Elvis who continued to rock his hips while the camera was filming him from the waist up, knowing that everyone was imagining what he was doing anyway. Mainstream America loves its mavericks, rebels, and antiheroes, and Rebel Elvis falls into this archetype.

Most remember Vegas Elvis as a middle-aged entertainer sporting a white jumpsuit who played to middle-aged audiences in Las Vegas or at huge arenas across the country. Elvis's original fans prefer this era of his career, and when they see this image, they're reminded of his charisma as an entertainer. They also remember the rituals and conventions of his 1970s concert performances in which he interacted with them directly. (See Chapter 13 for an overview of this era.) However, because the press rendered this Elvis as a fat, drug-rattled Vegas entertainer in a form-fitting jumpsuit, many people have a negative view of this phase of his career — a view that has only just begun to fade.

> **REMEMBER:** Vegas Elvis, who performs for middle-aged mothers in America's lower-middle-class playground (Las Vegas), is the essence of conformity and the polar opposite of Rebel Elvis. That one entertainer could connote such contradictory meanings and evoke such opposite responses is an example of Elvis's multifaceted image.

## Acknowledging his Southern roots

Elvis's identity as a member of the Southern working class has generated multiple interpretations of this aspect of his image. During the 1950s, his Southern heritage was directly and indirectly attacked, criticized, or ridiculed by the mainstream media as the reason for his "inferior" musical style, mode of talking, and tastes in clothing. (See Chapter 5 for more on this topic.)

This prejudice against his Southern working-class background dogged him throughout his career. To some degree, this bias has been transferred to his fans and is evidenced in the media's insistence on stereotyping the Elvis fan as a fawning, inarticulate Southern senior citizen in an oversized Elvis T-shirt. Tracking Elvis's treatment as an outsider to mainstream culture during parts of his career offers insight into the tension between the dominant culture and other grass-roots subcultures. Elvis was often positioned as the proverbial "other" by the media and the mainstream public. This position caused him to be an open target for accusations, criticisms, and misperceptions.

> **REMEMBER:** Southerners cast Elvis's heritage in a positive, even heroic light. The fact that Elvis maintained his primary residence in Memphis was a source of pride, because it indicated that he never "got above his raising." This phrase alone reveals the importance in the region of remaining close to Southern culture and roots. Elvis's expressed love of gospel music, country music, rhythm and blues, regional food, and regional pastimes reinforced his identity as a Southerner and further endeared him to Southern-based audiences.

Academics have recently embraced Elvis as a source of study. One reason for their interest involves his role as an integrator of musical styles indigenous to the South. As racial integration took hold all over the South, Elvis — a working class Southerner — fused the sounds of white country music with black blues and R&B, achieving musical and cultural integration. In studying Elvis, scholars of history and culture see a fascinating link between popular music and culture and social issues and problems.

## A taste of forbidden fruit: Examining Elvis's effect on his young female fans

Another side to Elvis's image during the 1950s involves his sensuality and sexuality, particularly his sexual appeal to young girls. (You can read more about his appeal in Chapter 5.) Drop-dead handsome, a major flirt, and naturally charming, Elvis Presley awakened the sexuality in his young female fans. And he did this without his controversial performing style in which he moved his hips and legs provocatively. Figure 20-1 shows a portrait of the handsome Elvis.

However, his performing style stirred the wrath of parents, educators, religious figures, newspaper editors, other entertainers, and local politicians. They were concerned about the effect that Elvis had on the girls in the audience. Though generally described with words such as "hysteria" or "frenzy," the reaction of the girls was more like a sexual awakening or expression, which was the real fear regarding Elvis.

Songwriter and publicist Mae Boren Axton, who cowrote "Heartbreak Hotel" especially for Elvis, was fond of quoting a teenage girl she once saw at an Elvis concert. The girl supposedly looked at Axton and exclaimed, "He's just one big hunk of forbidden fruit."

Elvis wasn't the first to elicit excited responses from adoring female fans. During the 1940s, Frank Sinatra crooned to the bobby-soxers, and 20 years before that, Rudy Vallee stirred up the passion of flappers. However, the girls' strong reactions combined with Elvis's provocative moves brought out the sexual nature of the dynamic between audience and performer in an obvious way. To women, especially those who saw him in concert, the image of a handsome Elvis from any stage of his career is a reminder of their awareness of their sexuality as women.

**Figure 20-1:** Elvis drove his female fans crazy, even without his provocative performing style.

## Considering other meanings of Elvis's image

Besides the main interpretations of Elvis's image and persona, which I explain in the preceding sections, you should also consider a few less-prominent ones held by various groups. Here they are in no particular order:

- On the surface, Elvis's rags-to-riches story is the personification of the American Dream, making him a working-class hero.
- Elvis's downward spiral into bizarre behavior and drug abuse make his decline a cautionary tale about the trap of celebrity and the road to excess.
- The Elvis tourist activities, particularly those during Elvis Week in Memphis, attract visitors from foreign countries who consider Presley and his fans to be indicative of the American experience.
- The tacky side of Elvis merchandizing, in which his name and image can be found on common household items, clothing, liquor decanters, license plates, and other objets d'art renders him a sort of folk hero.

# Part V
# The Part of Tens

The 5th Wave — By Rich Tennant

"Now this little plant is called Emma. Emma blooms best to the blistering rockabilly sound of Elvis Presley."

## In this part . . .

As an author of several books on Elvis Presley, I frequently have been asked to name, comment on, or list the best of Presley — including songs, singles, albums, films, and even jumpsuits. I discovered that constructing these types of lists provides an expedient way to measure and understand Elvis Presley's many accomplishments. In that spirit, I created this series of lists as a handy reference to the most acclaimed, influential, or just plain remarkable aspects of Elvis's career, along with my views and interpretations. You can read about Elvis's best songs, albums, and moments. I also include a list of fictional movies that show Elvis as a character or symbol.

Also note the appendix, which is an extensive list of the important people in Elvis's life and career.

# Chapter 21
# Ten Best Elvis Songs

**In This Chapter**
▶ Enjoying the ten best Elvis songs
▶ Discovering the details of each song

*I*n this chapter, I list ten of Elvis's best songs and offer background information on each. The best songs represent all phases of his career, including the movie era, which is the least respected era by critics and biographers. For each tune, I offer details about the songwriter, the era, and the chart status. Where relevant, I discuss the song's role in Elvis's career and anything else that might explain its importance.

The selections for this list were based on several criteria, including a song's significance to popular music, its importance in Elvis's career, and the statistics it generated (units sold, chart position, and gold or platinum status). In order to avoid complete repetition of songs discussed earlier in the book, I selected valid alternatives to some of the most well-known tunes. (See Chapters 4 and 13 for more examples of significant songs in Elvis's career.)

## "That's All Right"

"That's All Right," Elvis's first single, epitomized his rockabilly sound, which was a fusion of regional Southern styles, including country music, blues, and R&B. The song also featured the syncopation of the lyrics and the reverberation engineered by Sun Studio owner Sam Phillips, which produced an echo effect.

Elvis released "That's All Right," which was written and recorded previously by blues singer Arthur "Big Boy" Crudup, as a single on July 19, 1954, and it was a local sensation. Even though Elvis's version of the song didn't chart nationally, its importance is clearly linked to the fact that it launched the recording career of the 20th century's most important singer. In 1998, the song was elected to the Grammy Hall of Fame; in 2007, *Rolling Stone* declared it to be "the greatest song that changed the world."

## "Heartbreak Hotel"

"Heartbreak Hotel" became Elvis's first record to sell a million copies, and it was the first song written especially for him with his rockabilly style in mind. Composed in late 1955, just before Elvis appeared on the national canvas, the song reveals that the singer's style and image had permeated the music scene enough to be recognizable as his.

Songwriters Mae Boren Axton and Tommy Durden created the sexy, blues-influenced tune for Elvis. The idea for the lyrics came to Durden after he read a newspaper article about the suicide of an anonymous soul who had left behind a bittersweet note reading, "I walk a lonely street." Durden took his idea to Axton, a songwriter, TV personality, and publicist who had worked for Colonel Tom Parker, Elvis's manager. She told Durden they should write the song specifically for the hot new singer. The pair composed the lyrics and the music in about an hour. Then Glen Reeves, a local singer, recorded a demo record in the style of Elvis Presley. Axton took the demo to a disc jockey convention in Nashville, where Elvis and Parker were putting the finishing touches on Presley's deal with RCA Records. (See Chapter 4 for more information on his RCA deal.) She played the demo for a still-green Elvis who loved the song, exclaiming over and over, "Hot dog, Mae!"

Elvis recorded the song on January 10, 1956, during his first session at RCA in Nashville. The song exaggerated the echo that was associated with his Sun sound, creating a haunting, ghostly effect as Elvis sang the opening lines to each verse. Mournful and lonesome, the song captured the alienation of modern youth, Elvis's core audience.

"Heartbreak Hotel" was released as a single on January 27, 1956. On February 11, he sang it on national TV on Tommy and Jimmy Dorsey's *Stage Show*. He sang it on two more *Stage Show* appearances and on his first guest shot on *The Milton Berle Show*. The TV exposure helped propel the song to number one on the *Billboard* Hot 100, jukebox, and country charts. The song also climbed to number three on the R&B chart.

## "Don't Be Cruel"

"Don't Be Cruel" represents Elvis's side step away from Sam Phillips's rockabilly twang toward a purer rock 'n' roll style that was influenced by the smoother, urban sounds of big-city songwriters. The song's easygoing but fast-paced rhythm, light tone, and harmonious backup vocals by the Jordanaires indicate that Elvis had moved on from the Sun sound.

"Don't Be Cruel" was written by R&B singer-songwriter Otis Blackwell. In Chapter 4, I relate the story of Blackwell selling this hit song for just $25 on Christmas Eve, 1955. The song was Elvis's biggest-selling single of 1956, a year in which almost all his singles broke some kind of industry record. "Don't Be Cruel" was so popular that other singers borrowed it for their live acts, most notably Jackie Wilson, who was one of Elvis's favorite singers. Wilson's vocal mannerisms added a light, high-pitched touch to the song that Elvis liked. In his TV appearances, Elvis began singing it in Wilson's style, which is evident in the way he pronounced "telephone" as "te-lay-phone."

"Don't Be Cruel" topped the pop, country, and R&B charts. It sold steadily as a single for several years. By 1961, it had sold more than 6 million copies.

## "All Shook Up"

This charming rock 'n' roll hit from 1957 tends to be overshadowed by Elvis's other singles from that year, but "All Shook Up" racked up some impressive statistics in its time. The song remained at the top of the *Billboard* Top 100 chart for 30 weeks — the longest of any Presley single. At the end of the year, it was named the Number One Single for 1957. "Heartbreak Hotel" had been the Number One Single for 1956, making Elvis Presley the first rock 'n' roll singer to top the year-end charts for two consecutive years.

Otis Blackwell, who wrote "Don't Be Cruel," also penned "All Shook Up." His inspiration for the title came from an ordinary conversation in the workaday world, though the tale has undoubtedly been exaggerated through retellings over the years. While working for Shalimar Music as a songwriter, Blackwell was sitting in the office attempting to compose a new powerhouse tune. Al Stanton, one of the owners of Shalimar, dropped in while drinking a bottle of soda. He shook up the bottle so the contents fizzed, casually remarking, "Why don't you write a song called 'All Shook Up'?" A couple of days later, Blackwell surprised Stanton with a draft of the song.

Blackwell didn't write the song for Elvis. Two other singers, David Hill and Vicki Young, recorded it before him. When cutting his version in Hollywood in January 1957, Elvis overdubbed himself slapping the back of his guitar, recalling some of the effects of his Sun singles. While Elvis was moving on from the rockabilly of Sun Records, he didn't turn his back on it completely.

## "Jailhouse Rock"

Penned by the legendary rock 'n' roll songwriters Jerry Leiber and Mike Stoller, "Jailhouse Rock" was commissioned as the title tune for Elvis's third movie, which was designed to reflect the notorious side of Elvis the Pelvis — the Elvis that shook his leg, swiveled his hips, and made the girls scream. The 1957 film needed a title song that suggested the scandalous nature of rock 'n' roll, and Leiber and Stoller nailed it with this tune. The production number for this song in the movie also became an iconic image in film history. "Jailhouse Rock" topped the pop, country, and R&B charts. In England, it became the first single to ever enter the charts at number one.

Leiber and Stoller wrote hard-driving R&B tunes with satiric or hip lyrics that could be interpreted on more than one level. At first, they weren't interested in writing for Elvis, because they felt he was too sentimental and too sincere. A bit snobby, the pair felt that Elvis's musical foray into R&B was a fluke, and they were suspicious of his interest in the blues. The three met during an April 1957 recording session, and Leiber and Stoller changed their minds about Elvis after they realized his passion for music. The pair took over the recording sessions for the film's music, serving as unofficial producers of "Jailhouse Rock," "Treat Me Nice," "Baby I Don't Care," and other songs.

## "It's Now or Never"

No one could have guessed that a reworked version of the 1901 opera-style song "O Sole Mio" with a cha-cha arrangement would become the King of Rock 'n' Roll's biggest-selling single. An oddity with little influence on future singers, 1960's "It's Now or Never" was nonetheless an important song in Elvis's career. It reflected his ability to conquer yet another genre of music — pop music. It also helped Elvis move away from the rock 'n' roll sound and image that he was no longer interested in after he was discharged from the army.

Elvis's interest in the song goes back to the original Italian version, which had been recorded by Mario Lanza, an opera singer and movie star whom Elvis admired. Elvis also had heard the English version "There's No Tomorrow," which had been recorded by pop singer Tony Martin. While he was still in the army, Elvis asked his music publisher to find someone to write new lyrics for the song. Aaron Schroeder and Wally Gold composed the new lyrics in less than half an hour. Elvis was challenged by the operalike style, and he was attracted to the drama of it.

"It's Now or Never" charted for 20 weeks holding the number-one slot for five weeks. Worldwide sales of the tune reached 20 million copies.

## "Return to Sender"

Otis Blackwell cowrote "Return to Sender" with Winfield Scott for the 1962 romantic comedy *Girls! Girls! Girls!* making the catchy pop tune the third on the list by Blackwell. Elvis's music publishing company Hill and Range discouraged him from recording the work of the most talented songwriters, because most of them refused to sign over the rights and half the credit to

Elvis. Blackwell was an exception, at least until the early 1960s. The African American songwriter was attuned to the pop-rock side to Elvis's style, and he successfully wrote in that direction. Blackwell penned seven songs for Elvis.

RCA released "Return to Sender" in October 1962, and it quickly sold 1 million copies. The clever pop tune belies the accusation that none of Elvis's movie music was worthy.

The song figures into Elvis lore in another way as well. In the 1960s, fans regularly sent letters to Elvis at nonexistent addresses so they would be marked "Return to Sender" and sent back. In 1993, when the Elvis postage stamp was launched, fans revived this practice so their letters addressed to Elvis with Elvis stamps on them would come back to the fans marked "Return to Sender." Chapter 20 talks more about the controversy over the Elvis stamp.

## "How Great Thou Art"

Originally a 19th-century Swedish hymn by Carl Boberg, "How Great Thou Art" was translated into English in the 1940s. George Beverly Shea first recorded the tune, and then the gospel quartets the Blackwood Brothers and the Statesmen created their own versions. Elvis became familiar with the song through the Blackwood Brothers.

Elvis recorded his version of the hymn in 1966 as the title track for one of his gospel albums. Not only did the song reflect his Southern roots and love for gospel music, it also sparked his interest in recording music that wasn't related to movie soundtracks. Over the years Elvis had become disillusioned with the movie music he produced and lost all interest in recording, but gospel music helped bring him back to life. Legend has it that Elvis became so deeply involved in recording "How Great Thou Art," stretching his voice to cover the necessary range, that he almost fainted.

In 1974, a live version of "How Great Thou Art" from the album *Elvis Recorded Live On Stage in Memphis* won a Grammy for Best Inspirational Performance.

## "If I Can Dream"

"If I Can Dream" was the incredibly poignant song that Elvis sang as the closing number for *The '68 Comeback Special,* the critically acclaimed NBC television program that changed the course of Elvis's career. (You can read more on the special and this point in Elvis's life in Chapter 11.) The song was written by the special's musical director, W. Earl Brown. He composed the song in response to the assassinations of Martin Luther King and Bobby

Kennedy, which had occurred in 1968 — one of the most tumultuous years of the 20th century. Elvis, who was upset by the assassination of King in his hometown of Memphis, believed in the song's message of tolerance and understanding and sang it with great passion and conviction. The large scale of the song, with its monumental ending, prefigures Elvis's music of the 1970s.

## "Suspicious Minds"

"Suspicious Minds" written by Mark James, represents the typical Presley song from the last phase of his career. A fast-paced heart stopper with a hard-driving bass line, "Suspicious Minds" blends horns, strings, and drums with the voices of Presley and a choir of female backup singers. The song gallops forward at a breakneck speed until it reaches a peak, and then it slows down to a quiet lull before bursting wide open once more. Elvis introduced the song in 1969 during his comeback to live performances at the International Hotel in Vegas. "Suspicious Minds" had yet to be released as a single, so the Vegas audience was unfamiliar with it. Elvis's six-minute performance of the song on that hot July night brought down the house.

Recorded at American Sound Studio in 1969, the song was produced by Chips Moman, who was responsible for what is arguably Elvis's best album, *From Elvis in Memphis.* However, some music historians may not include this song on a list as one of Elvis's best. That's because the version released as a single in late 1969 was altered by Felton Jarvis after Moman had finished it, causing some friction with Moman's camp.

"Suspicious Minds" became Elvis's first number-one single since 1962 and the last number-one single of his career. Because these statistics make the song a significant one in his career, it deserves its place on a list of his best.

# Chapter 22
# Ten Best Elvis Albums

*In This Chapter*
- Checking out a list of Elvis's best albums
- Considering the variety of his song selection

*P*aring down Elvis's hundreds of albums into the ten best is a difficult task and requires a set of criteria to do it effectively. My criteria include cultural significance, career impact, and popularity, which together make for a fairly standard set of measures. However, I also use other criteria that are more meaningful to me. For example, I consider how an album reflects Elvis's strengths as a singer and cultural figure, and I make sure that my picks showcase the diversity of his song selection. I also like to include the story behind the album if it offers insight into the music.

In discussing some of Elvis's biggest-selling albums, the temptation to rely on figures, numbers, and statistics is overwhelming. But, stats can be misleading, inaccurate, and difficult to validate. Besides, the inclusion of too many numbers spoils their effectiveness. Keeping that in mind, I avoided relying on too many statistics, preferring to stick with those that are reliable, permanent, and not subject to diverse interpretations. Without further ado, I present my list of the ten best albums by Elvis Presley.

## Elvis Presley: The First Album

A mix of rock 'n' roll, ballads, and rhythm and blues, *Elvis Presley* reveals a red-hot 21-year-old singer who's exploring his musical tastes. This debut album, which was released March 13, 1956, marked Elvis's first recordings for RCA, and it represented a step away from the five rockabilly singles he had released through Sun Records earlier in the decade. The album hinted to fans that Elvis was at home with other musical genres and that he intended to break from the Sun sound by recording a variety of song types.

The album's monster single, "Heartbreak Hotel," is most like the Sun sound because the RCA engineers managed to re-create the echo effect that had been Elvis's trademark under Sam Phillips's guidance. But, his renditions of

"I'm Counting on You," "Blue Moon," and "I Was the One" reveal a powerful ballad singer, while his interpretation of Ray Charles's "I Got a Woman" shows that he was comfortable with R&B. Elvis's eclectic influences clearly helped him master different types of music, which was one of his key strengths as a singer. RCA filled out the album with five tracks previously recorded at Sun, though never released as singles. (You can read more about Elvis's time with Phillips and his early musical influences in Chapter 2.)

The album, which cost $3.98, made $1 million for RCA less than a month after it was released. It reached number one on the *Billboard* list of Top LPs, remaining there for ten weeks.

## Elvis's Christmas Album: Rock 'n' Roll Controversy

*Elvis's Christmas Album,* which includes the now classic "Blue Christmas," is more than a collection of carols. It combines the new with the old, the radical with the traditional. Released in December 1957, this holiday album debuted during a time when Elvis was still generating controversy with his live performances. (Check out Chapter 5 to read more about this controversy.) Recording the album may have been part of a strategy to counter the bad publicity over accusations that he was degenerate. Unfortunately, the strategy had uneven results. The album stayed in the top spot of the *Billboard* list of Top 100 LPs for three weeks, but some music-industry people and entertainment journalists were offended that a notorious rock 'n' roller had the nerve to cut a Christmas album.

Several disc jockeys even refused to play cuts from the album, and those who did risked repercussions. At KEX in Portland, Oregon, deejay Al Priddy was fired for playing Elvis's "White Christmas," the Irving Berlin classic made famous by Bing Crosby. Elvis sang the carol in his style, slurring the words and dragging out individual words with a succession of different notes. Some stations banned the entire album outright, while WCFL in Chicago got carried away and banned all records by Elvis.

## Elvis Is Back! Home from the Army

Released in 1960, *Elvis Is Back!* was the singer's first LP after his discharge from the army. The album reveals maturity and confidence in his voice, and it features an eclectic assortment of songs, from a sentimental duet between Elvis and his friend Charlie Hodge called "I Will Be Home Again" to the pop stylings of "Fever" to the bluesy "Such a Night." Unfortunately, as the 1960s progressed, diversity and variety would become sorely lacking in Elvis's albums, because he was kept busy pumping out soundtrack albums filled with pop tunes in the same easygoing style.

Critics and skeptics assumed his two-year absence from the music scene because of his army service would hurt his popularity, but sales from *Elvis Is Back!* proved them wrong. The album charted for 56 weeks, peaking at number two. (See Chapter 5 for more information about Elvis in the army.)

## Blue Hawaii: The Movie Music

The soundtrack for the movie *Blue Hawaii* proves that not all of Elvis's movie music was mediocre (see Chapter 7 for more about *Blue Hawaii* and Chapter 8 for details on the mediocre movie music). The material was far removed from the rockabilly that made Elvis famous, but it's a solid example of the blend of pop and rock that defined his movie music. Like the movies themselves, this musical style was designed to attract a mainstream audience — and to that end, this album was successful.

The title track of this album had been a hit for Bing Crosby back in 1937 and was later recorded by Gene Autry and Billy Vaughn. Recording the song positioned Elvis in a mainstream pop tradition. Several other songs on the soundtrack had also been previously released by pop singers, including "Moonlight Swim," "Hawaiian Wedding Song," and "Aloha Oe." The romantic ballad "Can't Help Falling in Love" was penned especially for the movie, but its tune was borrowed from an 18th century French song called "Plaisir d'Amour." Very little rock 'n' roll made its way onto the soundtrack; even "Rock-a-Hula Baby" is a playful takeoff on rock 'n' roll dance crazes rather than a hearty rock number.

The goal of attracting a broad audience for the movie music worked, at least for this album. Issued in 1961, *Blue Hawaii* became Elvis's biggest-selling LP during his lifetime. It reached number one on the *Billboard* list of Hot 100 LPs, and it remained in the top spot for five months. This record held out until 1977 when Fleetwood Mac's *Rumors* finally surpassed it.

## How Great Thou Art: Gospel Roots

The first Elvis album produced by Felton Jarvis, *How Great Thou Art* (1967), reveals Elvis's lifelong passion for gospel and reflects the influence of this music on his career. Elvis held his own alongside the gospel quartets who backed him on the album, including Jake Hess and the Imperials and the Blackwood Brothers. *How Great Thou Art* came along to boost Elvis's spirits at a low point in his career when he was disappointed in his film career and disillusioned with recording movie soundtracks.

As a singer born and raised in the South, Elvis had loved gospel music since his childhood in Tupelo, Mississippi. Listening to or singing gospel always soothed his soul during times of difficulty, and it reminded him of who he was. The album held a special place in Elvis's heart not only because he was proud of his singing on this LP but also because he won his first Grammy Award for *How Great Thou Art*. (Chapter 11 provides more information on *How Great Thou Art* and Elvis's comeback.)

## From Elvis in Memphis: Back in the Groove

*From Elvis in Memphis,* which was produced by Chips Moman at American Sound Studio in 1969, was instrumental in forging Elvis's musical style of the 1970s. The large scale of the sound, the blend of musical genres, and the superior material by up-and-coming songwriters became hallmarks of Elvis's music. (Flip to Chapter 11 to read more about *From Elvis in Memphis*.)

The album sold very well at the time of release, staying on the LP charts for 24 weeks. It also was critically acclaimed; *Rolling Stone* declared it equal to the best music Elvis had ever done. The album continues to be popular among subsequent generations of fans. In 2000, *From Elvis in Memphis* was remastered and rereleased with bonus tracks, including some of the other famous songs recorded at American Sound that aren't on the original album.

## That's the Way It Is: Elvis's Heartsongs

Despite the title, *That's the Way It Is* (1970) isn't the soundtrack from the 1970 documentary film of Elvis in concert. Instead, most of the songs on this album are about love. The album captures one of Elvis's strengths as a mature singer: his ability to express the various moods of love, which include joy, sorrow, and loss.

Many of the songs on this album had been recorded by other singers, but Elvis's heartfelt interpretations made them his own. For example, B.J. Thomas enjoyed a modest hit with the joyful "I Just Can't Help Believin'" in 1970, but Elvis offered a light, smooth version that gives the song a sense of intimacy. Other selections on the album expose the darker side of love, including "How the Web Was Woven" and "You've Lost That Lovin' Feeling."

Elvis's version of Paul Simon's "Bridge Over Troubled Water" resonated with such pain and loss that Simon supposedly remarked, "It was a bit dramatic but how the hell am I supposed to compete with that."

*That's the Way It Is* did modestly well, eventually reaching gold status in June 1973. Sadly, the album may have been the last one to thoroughly explore Elvis's talent as a passionate ballad singer and sincere chronicler of love and loss. Beginning in 1971, his manager, Colonel Tom Parker, and the folks at RCA had difficulty coming up with decent material to record because of their insistence on controlling publishing rights. So, many of Elvis's albums were reduced to a hodgepodge of leftover tracks, b-sides, and the occasional new song. (See Chapter 15 for an overview of the difficult personal and professional issues Elvis faced in the 1970s.)

## Reconsider Baby: Ain't Nothin' But the Blues

Some of Elvis's best albums were released after his death, including *Reconsider Baby* (1985), a blistering collection of blues and R&B tunes that Elvis recorded over the years. Of the hundreds of Elvis albums, this one is my personal favorite for several reasons:

- It reveals his appreciation for blues-related music, which goes back to his days as a Memphis teenager with an extremely eclectic record collection.
- Because he's absolutely comfortable with the songs and music, he interprets tunes by Arthur "Big Boy" Crudup, Lonnie Johnson, and Smiley Lewis in his own style without destroying the characteristics of the genre.
- He knows the songs, the original singers, and the Southern culture where blues and R&B came from.

His deep connection to blues and R&B music is evident in his interpretations of "One Night of Sin," "Reconsider Baby," "High Heel Sneakers," and more. He isn't merely visiting these African American–based musical genres, like so many pop-based singers did. Instead, he's completely at home with them. And, that's the key to understanding Elvis and his significance to American culture. Read more about Elvis's early life in the South in Chapter 2.

## The Masters Series

When BMG purchased RCA in 1986, it formed an international committee of record executives with a background in music history to clean up the Presley catalog. Interested in positively presenting Elvis's musical legacy, the committee's long-term goal involved restoring and reissuing the music as close to its original form as possible. The committee compiled the music in a series of releases called the Masters Series, and fans appreciated the thorough approach to Elvis's music. Each release in the Masters Series consists of five discs of material from one decade of Elvis's career:

- *Elvis, the King of Rock 'n' roll: The Complete 50s Masters* (1992), which was BMG's first significant restoration effort, contains all of Elvis's released recordings from this most popular Presley era.

- *Elvis Presley: From Nashville to Memphis: The Essential 60s Masters* (1993) bears witness to Elvis's mature pop stylings of the 1960s, but it doesn't include songs from the movie soundtracks that he recorded during this time.

- *Walk a Mile in My Shoes: The Essential 70s Masters* (1995), helps to dispel the stereotype of a garish Elvis in his white jumpsuit belting out Vegas-style tunes. The singer's output during this time wasn't handled well by RCA, who issued albums chaotically to say the least. However, the 120 songs in this Masters Series set show Elvis to be an all-around entertainer who mastered many musical genres.

# ELVIS: 30 #1 Hits

In 2002, on the 25th anniversary of Elvis's death, RCA-BMG released a collection of his number-one songs called *ELV1S: 30 #1 Hits*. Compiling the number-one hits into one streamlined package on a significant anniversary reminded everyone — fans, the press, music historians, cultural pundits — of why Elvis is an important figure in American culture. And, the fact that the songs were arranged chronologically proved that Elvis was a significant entertainer during his entire career, not just in the 1950s.

In order to review the album, critics were forced to revisit the songs, and their updated or reassessed interpretations of Elvis's career created new interest among young generations and non-fans. The success of the album generated feature articles putting Elvis in a historical and cultural context. The press, the mainstream media, and culture commentators have rarely given Presley his due, but this compilation directed their attention to what was most important about Elvis.

The record label capped its strategy with the best promotional line of Presley's career: "Before anyone did anything, Elvis did everything." The line succinctly summarized Elvis's importance while evoking the dynamism of his sound and the danger of his original image. *ELV1S: 30 #1 Hits* rocketed to number one when it debuted in 2002 — a feat Elvis hadn't managed while he was alive.

# Chapter 23
# Ten Best Elvis Moments

**In This Chapter**
- Reflecting on memorable moments in Elvis's career
- Understanding how those moments are part of our culture

In this chapter, I list ten memorable moments from Elvis's career. These are key points — or flashbulb moments — from public appearances, songs, television appearances, or movie roles that influenced popular music, made an impact on the future, or challenged our culture to the point of change. Many of these moments are so familiar they have become iconic.

In the case of most entertainers, singers, actors, or performers, it would be difficult to come up with just two or three moments. The fact that this chapter lists ten is a testament to the cultural significance of Elvis Presley.

## Performing "That's All Right" at the Overton Park Shell, July 30, 1954

Just days after recording "That's All Right," Elvis was hastily added to the bill for a show starring country yodeler Slim Whitman at Memphis's Overton Park Shell. Elvis was so new to the scene that the newspaper ad for the event misspelled his name as "Ellis Presley." Elvis had only one single to his credit, and more than likely he sang both "That's All Right" and the flip side, "Blue Moon of Kentucky," on July 30, 1954, at the Overton.

According to Elvis's rhythm guitar player, Scotty Moore, the young inexperienced singer exhibited signs of extreme nervousness while singing. He moved constantly on the stage as he sang and played his guitar. Halfway through "That's All Right," the girls in the audience began to scream, stomp, and clap. After their performance was over, Elvis asked Moore what the girls were "hollerin'" at, and Moore replied, "It was your leg, man. It was the way you were shakin' your left leg."

From that point on, Elvis began to finesse his movements on stage in order to elicit responses from the girls. His onstage movements became his trademark and the core of the controversy surrounding him — and it all started at the Overton. (See Chapter 2 for more information on this concert.)

## Performing "Hound Dog" on The Milton Berle Show, June 5, 1956

The controversy swirling amorphously around rock 'n' roll music and Elvis Presley during the first half of 1956 came to rest squarely on Elvis's shoulders when he performed "Hound Dog" on *The Milton Berle Show* on June 5, 1956. Specifically, it was the last verse of the song that caused the trouble.

Elvis had appeared throughout the show in the comedy sketches before stepping in front of the camera to sing "Hound Dog." Performing the song for the first time, he sang it without his guitar. Without his guitar to clutch, swing, or hang onto, Elvis grabbed the microphone throughout his performance, bending it over and straddling it between his legs. At times he stopped, dropped his head, and then cast his eyes upward to point his finger at the studio audience, which resulted in full-volume screaming.

For the climax of the song, Elvis slowed down the tempo to repeat the chorus. While belting out this final verse to a blues beat, he turned his body in profile to the audience and thrust his pelvis back and forth. Accentuating the pelvic movements was the fact that his hand was positioned next to his crotch.

This memorable moment of Elvis singing this specific verse of "Hound Dog" on national television outraged a nation, centered the criticism of rock 'n' roll on Elvis, and excited teenagers across the country. (You can read more on this television appearance in Chapter 4.)

## Defying Authority Onstage in Jacksonville, August 11, 1956

Elvis had been playing across the South without incident since 1954, including in Jacksonville, but in 1956, his reputation as a notorious rock 'n' roller suddenly made him seem like more of a threat. His act had not changed that much, but the perception of his act had changed a lot. Mainstream audiences thought him to be crude, unsophisticated, and an assault on the tastes of the status quo; teenagers saw him as exciting, sexy, and rebellious — and that worried the mainstream audience even more.

Elvis seldom gave in to the rebellious side of his image; his performance in Jacksonville, Florida, on August 11, 1956, was one exception. Juvenile Court Judge Marion W. Gooding attended Elvis's first show on August 10. After the show, Gooding met with Elvis and his manager Colonel Tom Parker, warning the singer to tone down his act. The police attended the next show to make sure Elvis obeyed the judge's order. In a clever act of defiance, Elvis reacted to the directive by wiggling only his little finger during the entire performance. The gesture instigated squeals from the audience, which almost defeated the purpose of the judge's order. (Flip to Chapter 4 for more information on this incident.)

## Getting Censored on The Ed Sullivan Show, January 6, 1957

Perhaps the most famous moment in all of Elvis's career was his third appearance on *The Ed Sullivan Show* in which the CBS censors allowed him to be shown only from the waist up. The controversy over his hip-swiveling performing style had come to a head, and the result was the waist-up edict.

In retrospect, this historic appearance on January 6, 1957, has come to represent the fears, mores, and conservative tastes of the status quo during the 1950s in the face of an outsider who threatened to liberate us from them. (Chapter 4 provides more information on this appearance.)

## Performing the Title Song in Jailhouse Rock, 1957

The most iconic musical number in Elvis's film career is the high-energy title song from *Jailhouse Rock,* which was released in 1957. Even those who have never seen the film know this production number, which captures Elvis in his most popular incarnation — as the young rebel who gave a generation an identity and an attitude.

When preparing this production number, choreographer Alex Romero first attempted to teach Elvis some standard steps for a more conventional movie-musical number. When Elvis had problems mastering them, Romero decided to try another approach. He watched Elvis move to his music and then developed steps and moves based on Elvis's own performing style.

**Remember:** Some books insist that Elvis did his own choreography for the "Jailhouse Rock" number, but that's a distortion of his contribution. Ultimately, however, the extent of Elvis's contribution is irrelevant, because it's his image as a notorious rock 'n' roller that people respond to. (Visit Chapter 6 for more on *Jailhouse Rock*.)

## Swinging with Ann-Margret in Viva Las Vegas, 1964

In recent years, the reputation of *Viva Las Vegas* (1964) has improved, partly because Bruce Springsteen covered the title song but also because of the revelation that Elvis and Ann-Margret had a love affair on the set. The obvious chemistry between the two, along with the sparkling talent of Ann-Margret, elevates this Presley musical beyond the level of most of his movie vehicles.

Ann-Margret's sexy, high-energy dancing style seemed to match Elvis's hip-swiveling performing style. As a matter of fact, she was dubbed the "Female Elvis Presley" during the early 1960s. The pair exhibited unbounded energy and a sexy charisma in their *Viva Las Vegas* production numbers together, particularly "C'mon Everybody." Later in the film, Elvis and Ann-Margret danced the Climb, a wacky rock 'n' roll dance not unlike the Jerk, the Pony, the Twist, and the Watusi, which were dance crazes popular during the early 1960s. The pair's youthful exuberance, stylish dress, and hip attitude as they danced the Climb epitomize the pre-hippie Swinging Sixties. (Refer to Chapter 7 to read more on *Viva Las Vegas*.)

## Mesmerizing a Live Audience on The '68 Comeback Special, December 3, 1968

One of Elvis's finest moments occurred when he sang and reminisced about his career before a live audience during *The '68 Comeback Special*. Looking handsome with his long jet-black hair and sideburns, Elvis was dressed in black leather from head to foot, recalling the 1950s without waxing nostalgic for them.

Throughout the late 1960s, the counterculture's psychedelic music, protest songs, and musical pleas for peace, love, and understanding were hailed as anti-establishment, suggesting a cultural rebellion against the status quo. But, during *The Comeback Special* when Elvis prowled across the stage in his black leather ensemble growling the words to "Tiger Man," he was rebellion incarnate. Raw, rough, and full of attitude, Elvis's look and sound reminded everyone of just who started it all. (See Chapter 11 for more information on this television special.)

## Opening with "Blue Suede Shoes" at the International Hotel, July 31, 1969

After an eight-year absence from live performances, Elvis returned to the stage on July 31, 1969, at the International Hotel in Las Vegas. He burst onto the stage, grabbed his guitar, struck a pose, and launched into "Blue Suede Shoes." The crowd jumped to their feet for the first of many standing ovations during the exhausting 90-minute performance.

This entire show at the International represents a true high point in Elvis's career, but the opening number was the exact moment that he snatched back his crown as the King of Rock 'n' Roll from the pretenders who thought he had given it up. (I discuss this concert in more detail in Chapter 12.)

## Shaking Hands with Richard Nixon, December 21, 1970

On December 21, 1970, Elvis made a spontaneous decision to go to Washington, D.C., to visit Deputy U.S. Narcotics Director John Finlator. Even though Elvis said he was going to Washington to volunteer his help in the antidrug campaign to be a sort of "federal agent at large," he was really hoping to obtain a federal narcotics badge and a complete set of credentials to add to his collection. Director Finlator turned down Elvis's request for a badge, but this didn't stop Elvis. He immediately decided to go over Finlator's head, and with a couple of members of the Memphis Mafia, Elvis went to call on President Nixon at the White House. It took Elvis only a few minutes of laying on the charm to talk Nixon into giving him an authentic narcotics agent's badge, but by then Elvis was on a roll, so he convinced the President to give him souvenirs inscribed with the presidential seal for his bodyguards and their wives.

The meeting between Elvis and Nixon resulted in a famous photograph session featuring the two shaking hands and posing together. Reproduced on postcards, T-shirts, and posters, the photos are rife with connotation and have been used to illustrate different facets of the Elvis Presley myth.

For example, critics use the photos' connotation to "prove" that Elvis held conservative beliefs and was therefore a traitor to the rebellion that he symbolized in the 1950s. Others use it as a kitschy monument to the gaudy 1970s, particularly considering Elvis donned an outrageous purple velvet suit to greet the President. Still others see it as a portrait of two iconic celebrities who faced disgrace at the end of the decade. None of these interpretations are necessarily accurate, but they're all true.

# Performing for the World: Aloha from Hawaii, January 14, 1973

In a one-of-a-kind event, Elvis performed at the Honolulu International Center Arena in a concert that was broadcast via satellite to countries all over the world. Eventually, more than 1 billion people in 40 countries saw this concert. The concert typified Elvis's act in the 1970s: He wore a gem-encrusted jumpsuit and cape, sang a diverse repertoire of contemporary and classic songs in a variety of genres, and performed with a huge musical ensemble that included a rock band, a female backup group, a gospel quartet, and an orchestra.

The moment in the show that captures the essence of Elvis from this era is one that thrills the fans and fuels the criticism of his detractors. At the end of the final song, "Can't Help Falling in Love," Elvis drops to one knee and bows his head. Then he grabs the ends of his cape in both hands, snaps his head up, and lifts his arms into the air in a sublime gesture that is everything you want it to be — corny, thrilling, gaudy, theatrical, and utterly Elvis. (Check out Chapter 14 to read more information about this concert.)

# Chapter 24
# Ten Best Elvis-Related Movies

*In This Chapter*
- Reviewing movies with Elvis as a character or a symbol
- Seeing how fictional films portrayed Elvis's cultural significance

Just two years after Elvis's death, film and television producers began to develop miniseries, made-for-TV films, and other projects based on the life and career of Elvis Presley. Elvis was given the *biopic* treatment, meaning his life story was turned into biography pictures. He also became the subject of documentaries. (Read Chapter 18 for more information on these films.) After sufficient time had passed and the mythology surrounding Elvis expanded and evolved, films and projects began to emerge featuring the King as a character in a fictional story or as a symbol in someone else's biopic. In these films, Elvis either interacts with fictional characters during the course of the story or he acts as a potent symbol, icon, or metaphor. The figure of Elvis Presley is so rich with cultural meaning that each of these films can refer to different facets of his image or career without duplication.

In this chapter, I list ten of the most interesting cinematic depictions of Elvis as a character, icon, or symbol. Some of these movies may not be the best-quality films, but their representations of Elvis are thought provoking or appealing and among the best examples of using Elvis's image as a symbol.

## Bye Bye Birdie

Perhaps my selection of *Bye Bye Birdie* cheats the concept of this chapter, because it was released in 1963 (before Elvis died). But, it's an early example of spoofing Elvis's larger-than-life image, and it offers a window into the era that launched Presley-mania. Based on a Broadway play from 1960, the narrative centers on the efforts of a songwriter to get the country's most popular singer, Conrad Birdie, to record one of his tunes, "Just One Kiss," before the singer is inducted into the army. Teenage girls all over the country are upset to lose their idol to the army, and they demonstrate their devotion by screaming, fainting, and swooning.

Conrad Birdie and the antics of the teenagers spoof Elvis and the hysteria that surrounded him in 1958 when he was drafted into the army. The name Conrad Birdie is possibly based on Conway Twitty, a real-life rock 'n' roll singer who was marketed like Elvis (and who later became a beloved country music crooner). In addition to the army and the hysterical teenagers, Conrad reminds the viewer of Elvis in other ways. He enunciates and exaggerates each syllable of each word in "Just One Kiss," like critics accused Elvis of doing when he spoke and sang, and he rotates his hips in an exaggerated swivel. Birdie even is scheduled to appear on *The Ed Sullivan Show*.

## Mystery Train

In this uniquely structured independent film from 1989, director Jim Jarmusch tells three separate stories about non-Americans stuck in Elvis's hometown of Memphis, Tennessee. At the end of the third tale, the viewer realizes that the stories are happening simultaneously, though the characters have little connection to each other. They're alienated outsiders who are isolated from each other and from the city's permanent residents. (See Chapter 18 for more information on the plot and theme of this film.)

Jarmusch references Elvis throughout the film without ever showing him or discussing him in the dialogue. Instead, Elvis exists only on the periphery of the story, vaguely referred to through bits and pieces of his music, the commercialization of his image, and the presence of his rock 'n' roll peers who have been forgotten. Note these examples from the film:

- The title of the film reminds viewers of the most haunting of Elvis's Sun recordings, while the lonesome strains of "Blue Moon" are heard occasionally in the film as well. Viewers recognize these songs as Elvis's, but they're only vague references to him.

- Tacky pictures of the King hang in the rooms of the rundown Arcade Hotel, the film's principal setting, but they're only poor likenesses.

- The film shows souvenirs from Graceland but doesn't show the mansion.

- A creepy stranger relates an urban legend about picking up the ghost of Elvis hitchhiking, but a ghost story is far removed from the original.

- Two musical figures from the 1950s, Rufus Thomas and Screamin' Jay Hawkins, have roles in the film, but few viewers will recognize them as R&B and rock 'n' roll pioneers of Elvis's generation.

These examples indicate that the myth of Elvis — not the authentic figure — permeates the film. In director Jarmusch's eyes, Elvis has been exploited to the point where the real singer and his artistry no longer belong in our culturally bankrupt society — an idea suggested by the scene in which the ghost of the "real" Elvis appears for a brief moment. He looks confused and then disappears, perplexed by the world he's no longer a part of.

## Leningrad Cowboys Go America

*Leningrad Cowboys Go America,* a 1989 Finnish film by internationally acclaimed director Aki Kaurismäki, tells the story of a Russian rock 'n' roll band called the Leningrad Cowboys that travels to the United States to seek fame and fortune. A wry comedy that exploits Kaurismäki's strange sensibilities, *Leningrad Cowboys Go America* offers a unique look at America through the eyes of outsiders.

The Leningrad Cowboys wear wigs that are combed into exaggerated black pompadours with long black sideburns. This hairstyle is clearly a takeoff on Elvis's coif from the 1970s. His look from that era is so iconic that even when one facet of it is isolated, we still recognize it as a reference to Elvis. Like Presley, the Cowboys achieve a large-scale sound by combining the talents of orchestras, folk musicians, dancers, and others. By referencing Elvis, the Cowboys are channeling his image as a larger-than-life show-business legend.

## Wild at Heart

David Lynch, one of America's most imaginative filmmakers, directed *Wild at Heart* in 1990. This bizarre road film stars Nicolas Cage and Laura Dern as Sailor Ripley and Lula Pace Fortuna, a young couple on the run from her vindictive and possessive mother. As a character, Sailor recalls Elvis, with his dark hair, sideburns, gold jacket, and penchant for singing ballads to Lula, including "Love Me" and "Love Me Tender." By relating Sailor to Elvis, Lynch is referencing the myth of Elvis Presley as America's premier rebel — a creative force who disrupted the status quo and pushed the limits of taste and expression. Much like Elvis, Lynch has strived to push the boundaries of standard conventions and tastes; not surprisingly, he's an Elvis fan.

Cage, who leapt at the chance to play this character, is also a major Elvis fan. He even married Elvis's daughter, Lisa Marie, though the two later divorced.

## Honeymoon in Vegas

In this 1992 romantic comedy, Nicolas Cage plays a marriage-phobic man who finally agrees to wed his long-suffering fiancée played by Sarah Jessica Parker, as long as they tie the knot in Vegas. While there, Parker's character is put off by the city's surreal atmosphere, which is emphasized by the legion of ridiculous Elvis impersonators of all sizes, races, and ages who humorously pop up in the background. The recurring joke culminates with the Flying Elvises, a group of 34 impersonators who sky-dive onto the Vegas Strip as part of their act. The impersonators are used to help show that Vegas is extreme, bizarre, and completely alien to Parker's character, who misses her normal life consisting of her friends, family, and job as a schoolteacher.

Original and engaging, *Honeymoon in Vegas* boasts a soundtrack of Elvis's best tunes reworked by a variety of prominent pop, rock, and country singers, but the film paints the impersonators as farcical, which indirectly and unfairly suggests that Elvis's Vegas era was akin to a circus act.

## True Romance

*True Romance* (1993) launched the career of Quentin Tarantino, who wrote the screenplay for this quirky action romance but didn't direct it. The story of two misfits on the lam from violent criminals is deceptively simple; the film's real artistry, however, is the smooth direction by Tony Scott and the pop culture homages that Tarantino uses in the screenplay. Tarantino has a talent for weaving pop culture references and iconography into the fabric of his narratives, which adds new meaning and depth to those references. It's a part of his style that's often emulated but never matched.

In *True Romance,* Tarantino uses Elvis as a symbol of rebellion against authority, rugged male individualism, and cool hipness. Whenever geeky protagonist Clarence needs to be assertive, Val Kilmer's character, who looks a lot like Elvis, appears to him in his trademark sunglasses to advise Clarence to stand up for himself. Like everyone who draws strength from pop culture heroes who represent ideals and values they admire, Clarence draws strength from the rebel Elvis, though the King is never referred to by name.

## Picasso at the Lapin Agile

Despite much interest, *Picasso at the Lapin Agile,* a play written by Steve Martin in 1993, has yet to be made into a movie. However, its interesting use of Elvis as a cultural figure warrants a place on this list. *Picasso at the Lapin Agile* finds the characters of Albert Einstein and Pablo Picasso having drinks at a cafe-bar called the Lapin Agile (or the Nimble Rabbit) in the artists' quarter of Montmartre in Paris. Set on October 8, 1904, each genius is on the verge of a breakthrough in their respective fields; Einstein the scientist will reveal his theory of relativity in 1905, and Picasso the artist will paint *Les Demoiselles d'Avignon* in 1907. The two discuss at length the importance of genius and talent, the roles of art and science, commercialism, and other related issues.

Near the end of the play, an unidentified man known only as the Visitor drops in from the future. The Visitor doesn't have a name, but his clothes and appearance make up a visual iconography that identifies him as Elvis Presley. Elvis adds another dimension to Picasso and Einstein's debate, representing the idea that great genius in one's field isn't always the product of academic study or philosophical understanding.

## 3000 Miles to Graceland

Violent, crude, and populated by unlikable protagonists, *3000 Miles to Graceland* (2001), directed by newcomer Demian Lichtenstein, is a controversial selection for this list, because it isn't particularly well crafted, and its nonstop profanity and gratuitous violence angered many Elvis fans. But, to its credit, the film is thought provoking in its use of Elvis iconography. Flip to Chapter 18 for more on the film's plot and theme.

The film makes use of the negative connotations of Elvis's Vegas image in order to paint a downbeat portrait of degenerate characters in a corrupt society. Elvis's detractors associate the jewel-encrusted jumpsuits, long sideburns, and big sunglasses of the Vegas image with the uncultured, kitschy tastes of fans and the squandered talent of a once-great rock 'n' roller. The film plays on this connotation by dressing its violent, unsavory protagonists like the most decadent of Elvis impersonators. No wonder Elvis fans dislike this film so much. But, by using an American icon like Elvis, who at the end of his career had become a drug-addicted, bloated Vegas performer (in the eyes of his detractors), the filmmakers underscore their theme about failed values in a greedy society. Viewers can disagree with the filmmakers' assessment of Elvis's Vegas image, but they do use it symbolically.

## Walk the Line

*Walk the Line,* the 2005 biopic of Johnny Cash — Sun Records' other pioneering rockabilly star — focuses mostly on his relationship with June Carter, who eventually became his wife. (See Chapter 18 for more on the film's plot.) However, the first part of the film offers a wonderful portrait of the early days of rockabilly when Cash, Elvis, and Jerry Lee Lewis were at the beginning of their careers, introducing a new sound for a new generation. Elvis and Jerry Lee are used to represent the sexuality, vitality, and Southern flavor of the music. Waylon Payne portrays Lewis as a destructive prankster who is also a God-fearing Christian. A walking contradiction, Lewis revels in lighting dynamite sticks and then reminding the group that they're all going to hell for singing the Devil's music. Tyler Hilton plays Elvis as the object of unbridled lust for the girls in the audience.

The use of Elvis in this film is the opposite of *3000 Miles to Graceland,* and not just because the former uses Rebel Elvis and the latter Vegas Elvis. *Walk the Line* uses Elvis and Jerry Lee to paint an exuberant portrait of rockabilly as the expression of uninhibited Southern spirit and raw sexuality. *Graceland* is a dark, pessimistic vision of sleazy corruption.

That one cultural figure could be used to symbolize opposing ideas is a testament to Elvis's complexity as an icon.

# Hounddog

Directed by Deborah Kampmeier, *Hounddog* (2007) is about an adolescent girl coming of age in the rural South in the 1950s. Dakota Fanning stars as Lewellen, a poor girl with a dysfunctional family who's unaware of her burgeoning sexuality until she's assaulted. She turns to her African American neighbor for compassion and to his music for comfort.

Filled with imagery and themes associated with Southern Gothic literature — such as snakes, the uplifting power of music, and the burden of class — the film was critically dismissed by mainstream reviewers from the North. Many viewers also were put off by the assault scene. But, Lewellen's devotion to Elvis offers an interesting depiction of his Southern-based fans, who, in retrospect, are among his most devoted. Lewellen becomes obsessed with getting tickets to an Elvis concert, but a cruel trick robs her of this dream. One moonlit night, she sees Elvis, played by Ryan Pelton, driving by in his mythic pink Cadillac, and the singer blows her a kiss.

To his rural Southern fans who were born in the same grinding poverty as he was, Elvis represents more than a sensational singing idol from the past. He was one of their own who escaped the poverty and the ugly class system that continually keeps them down. Elvis's "blessing" of the blown kiss represents hope for Lewellen that she will escape, too.

# Appendix

# Cast of Characters

*I*f you can't keep the members of the Memphis Mafia straight, or you need a reminder of who Minnie Mae Presley was, a quick glance at this cast of characters will help you out. Beyond that, the list is an accurate, unbiased reference to key people in Elvis's life and career that isn't often found in other books. Many of these people have been misrepresented in previous books; others overlooked. This is a handy resource to the many friends, family members, and associates who passed through the life of the King of Rock 'n' Roll.

**Jean and Julian Aberbach:** The Aberbach brothers owned Hill and Range music publishing, which was the publisher of Elvis's entire repertoire of recorded music under the names Elvis Presley Music and Gladys Music. Hill and Range entered this arrangement with Elvis in 1955 as part of the complicated deal that Presley's manager, Colonel Tom Parker, made with RCA Victor. The Hill and Range deal has been criticized in retrospect for coercing Elvis into recording inferior songs by the company's staff writers because it was more lucrative for all parties than using those penned by independent songwriters.

**Ginger Alden:** Alden was Elvis's last long-term girlfriend. She was likely the first person to discover his body when he died on August 16, 1977, though new reports at the time claimed Joe Esposito had been the first.

**Ann-Margret:** When red-headed singer-dancer Ann-Margret co-starred with Elvis in *Viva Las Vegas* in 1964, their onscreen chemistry soon gave way to an off-screen romance. Though Elvis had dated many of his movie costars, his relationship with Ann-Margret grew very serious despite the fact that a young Priscilla was sequestered in Memphis as his secret girlfriend. However, Elvis broke off the relationship because he decided that he didn't want a wife who had a career. Instead, he intensified his relationship with Priscilla, marrying her on May 1, 1967. A week later, Ann-Margret married Roger Smith.

**Chet Atkins:** Atkins was a legendary country-music guitarist who also worked for RCA as a producer and engineer. He helped create the Nashville Sound, a smooth, pop-influenced style of country music that dominated the country scene during the 1960s. Atkins became Elvis's record producer when the young phenomenon signed with RCA. They continued to work together until the mid-1960s.

**Bill Belew:** A Hollywood costume designer, Belew created Elvis's black leather outfit for *The '68 Comeback Special.* Elvis liked it so much he asked Belew to create his stage wardrobe when he returned to live performances in 1969. Working from a basic sketch by Elvis's wife, Priscilla, Belew created the first of the famous jumpsuits. He then went on to design each and every costume Elvis wore in concert.

**Delta Mae Presley Biggs:** When Elvis's Aunt Delta became a widow in 1966, the singer moved her to Graceland as a companion for his paternal grandmother, Minnie Mae. Aunt Delta was the last Presley to occupy Graceland, remaining there until her death in 1993.

**Steve Binder:** Binder, a television producer-director, developed the concept for *The '68 Comeback Special,* which presented a vibrant, invigorated Elvis Presley to the public in December 1968. The special revived Elvis's interest in recording new material and paved the way for his return to live performances. In 1980, Binder produced a television special about Graceland for Elvis Presley Enterprises (the Estate).

**Bill Black:** An original Blue Moon Boy, Black was the bass player who was part of Elvis's backup group from the very beginning. He played with Elvis from 1955 to 1957. Unhappy with the low wages he was receiving compared to Elvis, Black quit in 1957 to form his own group, the Bill Black Combo. He died of a brain tumor in 1967.

**Otis Blackwell:** Blackwell, an African American songwriter of rock 'n' roll songs, composed a handful of Elvis's biggest hits, including "Don't Be Cruel," "All Shook Up," and "Return to Sender."

**The Blackwood Brothers:** The members of the Blackwood Brothers gospel quartet belonged to the same Assembly of God church that the Presleys did in Memphis during the 1950s. Elvis supposedly tried out for the group's junior quartet of young singers called the Songfellows but didn't make it. Elvis retained his acquaintance with the Blackwoods, and the quartet sang at Gladys Presley's funeral in 1958 and at Elvis's funeral in 1977.

**Joe Esposito:** Esposito was Elvis's road manager and foreman of his entourage, the Memphis Mafia. He worked for Elvis from 1960 to 1977. His memoirs of his life with Elvis are titled *Elvis: Straight Up.* As foreman of the entourage, he was informally in charge of organizational details and doling out duties to other members of the Memphis Mafia (except for the bodyguards, who took care of their own duties). Elvis and Vernon dubbed Joe's position "foreman," because it is hard to define or describe with other words. He was more than an assistant or valet, but he wasn't a manager.

**Lamar Fike:** A member of the Memphis Mafia, Fike worked for Elvis over the years as a bodyguard, lighting systems operator, and tour organizer. Fike even worked for Hill and Range for a while. He incurred the wrath of Elvis fans forever when they learned he had told all to controversial biographer Albert Goldman.

**D.J. Fontana:** An original Blue Moon Boy, Fontana was Elvis' drummer on stage from 1955 to 1958 and from 1960 to 1961. He also served as Elvis's primary drummer in recording sessions from 1956 through the early 1960s. He returned to the fold to be Elvis's drummer for *The '68 Comeback Special*.

**Alan Fortas:** A Memphis Mafia member, Fortas had been a local football hero when he joined Elvis's entourage in 1958 as a bodyguard. His memoirs about his life with Elvis are titled *My Friend Elvis*.

**Larry Geller:** Geller was Elvis's hairstylist during the mid-1960s, but he also influenced Elvis in philosophical and religious matters. Geller turned Elvis on to the occult, parapsychology, Eastern religions, and other non-mainstream beliefs. Elvis became obsessed with these ideas, which eventually prompted the Colonel to ban Geller from further communication with the singer.

**Dick Grob:** A member of the Memphis Mafia, Grob served as security chief for more than seven years.

**Lowell Hays:** Hays was Elvis's jeweler from the late 1960s through the 1970s. He designed the TCB ring and other TCB jewelry for Elvis and the Memphis Mafia. TCB was Elvis's motto and stood for "Takin' Care of Business."

**Dave Hebler:** A martial arts expert, Hebler worked as Elvis's bodyguard from 1974 to 1976, when he was fired by Elvis's father, Vernon. Hebler coauthored *Elvis: What Happened?* the infamous "bodyguard book" that exposed Elvis's bizarre behavior and drug abuse, with Red and Sonny West.

**Charlie Hodge:** Hodge, one of Elvis's most loyal friends, met the singer in 1956 and remained close to him until he died in 1977. He became Elvis's aide and later one of his guitarists and backup singers. During Elvis's performances in the 1970s, Hodge was the person who kept scarves around Elvis's neck so the singer could give them to audience members. More importantly, Hodge was there during Elvis's most personal moments. He drove Priscilla and Elvis to the hospital when Lisa Marie was born, he played bit parts in a few of Elvis's movies, and he witnessed Elvis's will.

**The Imperials:** The Imperials were a group of vocalists who worked with Elvis on the *How Great Thou Art* and *He Touched Me* albums. They also backed him on stage from 1969 to late 1971. Throughout the years, the quartet has experienced many personnel changes, but an active Imperials group still exists and records.

**Felton Jarvis:** Jarvis became Elvis's producer at RCA in 1966, and he helped revitalize Elvis's recording career by convincing him to record music not related to movie soundtracks. Jarvis left RCA in 1970 to devote his attention to Elvis's career full time. He died in 1981.

**The Jordanaires:** This gospel quartet was Elvis's primary male backup vocal group from 1956 to the end of the 1960s. They worked with Elvis in the recording studio, onstage, and in his movies. The quartet has experienced some personnel changes over the years, but an active Jordanaires group still exists.

**Jackie Kahane:** Kahane was the comedian who opened for Elvis during the 1970s. He also delivered the eulogy at the singer's funeral.

**Marion Keisker:** Keisker worked as Sam Phillips's assistant, secretary, and Girl Friday. When Elvis came into Phillips's American Recording Service to cut an acetate disc of his voice, Keisker felt the boy had talent. She taped him while he cut his disc so Phillips could listen to him later. Her hunch about the odd-looking kid with the shy manners and long ducktail haircut paid off.

**George Klein:** Klein is a popular Memphis entertainment and media personality. He and Elvis became friends while attending Humes High School together, and he became a member of the Memphis Mafia, though he didn't work directly for Elvis. He maintained a separate career as a disc jockey. He introduced Elvis to two of his girlfriends, Linda Thompson and Ginger Alden.

**Marty Lacker:** A member of the Memphis Mafia, Lacker worked for Elvis from 1960 to 1967 as his personal secretary and bookkeeper. Along with Joe Esposito, Lacker was best man at Elvis's wedding. He and his wife, Patsy, wrote their memoirs about life with Elvis in a book entitled *Elvis: Portrait of a Friend.*

**Bernard and Guy Lansky:** The Lansky Brothers owned a clothing store on Beale Street in Memphis where Elvis bought his clothes during the 1950s. Lansky's Clothing Emporium catered to the hipsters, the rhythm-and-blues artists, and other unconventional customers. Lansky's fitted Elvis with his last suit, which he was buried in.

**Abe Lastfogel:** Lastfogel was Elvis's personal agent at the William Morris talent agency in Los Angeles. Lastfogel represented Elvis in Hollywood and worked with Colonel Tom Parker to turn Elvis into a successful leading man in Hollywood.

**Mississippi Slim:** Born Carvel Lee Ausborn, this traditional country singer befriended Elvis when Presley was a boy in Tupelo, Mississippi. Slim had his own radio show on the local station WELO, and he allowed Elvis to sing on his show on at least one occasion. Elvis got a sense of what a musical career was like because of his friendship with Slim.

## Appendix: Cast of Characters

**Chips Moman:** The owner-operator of American Sound Studio in Memphis, Moman produced Elvis's album *From Elvis in Memphis* in 1969. The album of new material by legitimate songwriters helped focus positive attention on Elvis for the first time in years and paved the way for his return to live performances.

**Scotty Moore:** An original Blue Moon Boy, Moore was Elvis's lead guitarist on stage from 1954 to 1958 and from 1960 to 1961. He recorded with Elvis on his very first releases for Sun Records, and then continued with the singer when he signed with RCA Victor. He returned to work with Elvis on *The '68 Comeback Special*. Moore's rhythm guitar solos on Elvis's Sun recordings became the backbone of his rockabilly sound.

**Bob Neal:** Neal was the country-music disc jockey who managed Elvis in 1955 before the singer hooked up with Colonel Tom Parker.

**Dr. George Nichopoulos:** Called Dr. Nick by Elvis, Nichopoulos was charged with overprescribing medication to Presley, Jerry Lee Lewis, and Marty Lacker in 1980. After years of accusations and charges by various Tennessee medical authorities, Nichopoulos eventually lost his license.

**Ed Parker:** A member of the Memphis Mafia and a karate champion, Parker served as Elvis's bodyguard during the 1970s. Parker's book about his relationship with Elvis is titled *Inside Elvis*.

**Colonel Tom Parker:** Elvis's manager from 1955 until after the singer's death, the Colonel was a colorful ex-carny who was a walking contradiction. Seemingly crass, uneducated, and uncouth, Parker managed to steer Elvis clear of career-hampering controversy during the 1950s, make him the highest paid actor in Hollywood during the 1960s, and secure him lucrative deals in Vegas during the 1970s. Their complex relationship was one of the most unusual in show business with extreme highs and rock-bottom lows.

**Dewey Phillips:** One of early rock 'n' roll's most colorful disc jockeys, Phillips was the first deejay to play an Elvis record. He played "That's All Right" several times in a row in early July 1954, launching Elvis's career. Phillips lost his status as an important tastemaker when he could no longer hold a job after turning to alcohol and drugs. He died in 1968.

**Sam Phillips:** Phillips was the owner-operator of the American Recording Service in addition to Sun Records and Sun Studio, where Elvis Presley cut his first five singles. Phillips mentored Elvis and helped cultivate the singer's rockabilly sound. Phillips, who was dedicated to recording the regional sounds of local Memphis musicians, also recorded local rhythm-and-blues musicians, such as Rufus Thomas, and other rockabilly singers, such as Jerry Lee Lewis, Carl Perkins, and Johnny Cash.

**Dee Stanley Presley:** Dee became Elvis's stepmother in 1960. Their relationship was strained from the beginning, but Elvis seemed to genuinely like her sons, Rick, David, and Billy Stanley. Dee and Vernon divorced in late 1977.

**Gladys Love Smith Presley:** Elvis and his mother, Gladys, were deeply devoted to one another. Though she was supportive of his singing career, and proud of her son, she longed for him to stay in Memphis, find a local girl, and settle down in marriage. Unfortunately, she didn't live to see that. She died of a heart attack, complicated by liver failure, in 1958.

**Lisa Marie Presley:** Elvis's only offspring, Lisa Marie was born on February 1, 1968. After her parents divorced in 1973, Lisa lived with her mother, Priscilla Presley, in California, and frequently visited her father at Graceland. Priscilla shielded Lisa from the limelight for most of her life until she became of age to take her place as head of Elvis Presley Enterprises, also known as the Estate. In 2005, Lisa and Priscilla sold control of the Estate to CRX Enterprises, though both continue to make decisions regarding the Estate. Lisa, a singer in her own right, is one of the few female rock 'n' rollers working today.

**Minnie Mae Hood Presley:** Elvis's grandmother, Minnie Mae, joined her son Vernon Presley's family in Memphis in the late 1940s after her husband left her. She lived with them from their days in tiny apartments in the low-rent areas of the city through Elvis's years at Graceland. After Gladys died, she became the woman of the household, moving to Germany with Elvis and Vernon when the former was stationed there during his army service. Sadly, she outlasted both her son and grandson, dying in 1980.

**Priscilla Beaulieu Presley:** Elvis's only marriage was to Priscilla, from 1967 to 1973, though they were together for many years before marriage. Elvis met Priscilla during his final months in the army while stationed in Germany. She came to live in Memphis in the early 1960s, though few knew of her existence until she and Elvis were married. After Vernon Presley's death in 1979, Priscilla was named one of the executors of the Estate until Lisa Marie Presley came of age. She was instrumental in opening Graceland to the public and in making other decisions to maintain Elvis's legacy.

**Vernon Presley:** Vernon was Elvis's father. He also served as the singer's financial manager. Most of his job entailed keeping Elvis's spending in check, and many have joked about Vernon's thriftiness. Quiet and low key, Vernon preferred the background to the limelight of his famous son. But, no father could have loved his son more, and the death of his only child brought on his own passing less than two years later in 1979.

**Vester Presley:** Elvis's uncle and Vernon Presley's brother, Vester had fooled around with the guitar when he was younger. He supposedly showed Elvis a few chords when the boy first got his guitar. In his later years, Vester worked as a guard at the gates of Graceland, becoming a fan favorite over the years.

**Jerry Schilling:** A member of the Memphis Mafia, Schilling worked in creative capacities related to Elvis's music. He also served as the manager of the Sweet Inspirations, Elvis's female backup group, before striking out on his own as the manager of the Beach Boys. Since Elvis's death, Schilling has worked for Elvis Presley Enterprises as a creative affairs director. He coproduced the ABC television series *Elvis* in 1990, among many other ventures.

**Steve Sholes:** Sholes was the RCA Victor executive who was instrumental in getting the label to sign Elvis. He closely monitored the production of Elvis's first albums, fearful of the singer's organic approach to recording. Eventually, he left the creative decisions to Elvis and his producers, resting on his laurels as the man who exposed Elvis to a national audience.

**Gene Smith:** Junior, Gene, and Billy Smith were Elvis's cousins from his mother's side of the family. Elvis grew up with Gene Smith, and the pair became good friends in addition to being cousins. When a young Elvis began touring the Southern circuits in 1954, Gene went with him to help out on the road. Elvis and Gene were very close until 1962, when they experienced a falling out. Later, however, Gene returned to visit Graceland regularly. Gene chronicled his life with Elvis in *Elvis's Man Friday* in 1994.

**Rick, David, and Billy Stanley:** Elvis gained three stepbrothers when his father, Vernon Presley, married Dee Stanley in 1960. Rick and David worked security at Graceland when they grew up and traveled with Elvis as part of the entourage. Billy did odd jobs and ran errands. With their mother, Dee, they cowrote *Elvis: We Love You Tender*. They also each wrote individual memoirs of their relationships with Elvis.

**J.D. Sumner & the Stamps Quartet:** J.D. Sumner & the Stamps Quartet was Elvis's backing vocal group from 1971 to 1977. Sumner's friendship with Presley began in the 1950s, when Sumner, then a member of the Blackwood Brothers Quartet, allowed a young Elvis to get into the Ellis Auditorium gospel sings for free. The Stamps Quartet has changed over the years, but a configuration of the group still performs today.

**The Sweet Inspirations:** The Sweet Inspirations served as Elvis's female backup group from 1969 to 1977. The group included Cissy Houston, mother of Whitney Houston.

**TCB Band:** Elvis's rhythm group from his concert years in the 1970s was called the TCB Band and included James Burton (lead guitar), Glen D. Hardin (piano), Jerry Scheff (bass guitar), Ronnie Tutt (drums), and John Wilkinson (rhythm guitar). TCB stands for "Takin' Care of Business."

**Linda Thompson:** A Memphis-born beauty queen, Thompson was Elvis's first serious relationship after his breakup with Priscilla. At the time she was a college student, but she gave up her studies to stay with Elvis from 1972 to 1976.

**Hal B. Wallis:** Wallis was a well-respected film producer who made Elvis Presley a movie star when he signed him to a personal contract in 1956. Wallis thought Elvis had charisma that could transfer to the big screen, so he cast him in musical vehicles to showcase his talents as an entertainer. Wallis didn't try to push Elvis into dramatic roles; he was content to star him in musical vehicles until they ran their course in terms of popularity. The producer opted not to pick up Elvis's contract after *Easy Come, Easy Go* in 1967.

**Red West:** One of the original members of the Memphis Mafia, West was a star football player at Humes High School when Elvis attended. In 1956, he began working as a bodyguard for Elvis. During the 1960s, when Elvis became a Hollywood leading man, West carved out a second career for himself as a stunt man and then a bit player. He also cowrote some songs that Elvis eventually recorded, including "If Every Day Was Like Christmas" and "You'll Be Gone." West cowrote the notorious "bodyguard book," *Elvis: What Happened?* with Dave Hebler and his cousin, Sonny West. Red later studied acting and became a sought-after character actor in films directed by such talents as Francis Coppola and Robert Altman. West's performance in 2008's *Goodbye Solo* earned him critical acclaim.

**Sonny West:** The cousin of Red West, Sonny became a member of the Memphis Mafia in the early 1960s, working as Elvis's bodyguard. With Red and Dave Hebler, Sonny cowrote *Elvis: What Happened?* the book that first revealed Elvis's bizarre behavior and heavy drug use. In 2005, West wrote his memoirs about Elvis in a book titled *Elvis: Still Taking Care of Business.*

**Kathy Westmoreland:** Westmoreland backed Elvis onstage and on recordings from 1970 to 1977. She's the soprano vocalist Elvis referred to in his band introductions as "the little girl with the beautiful high voice."

# Index

## • Numerics •

*20/20* (news magazine), 262–263
20th Century Fox (movie studio), 149–151
*3000 Miles to Graceland* (movie), 282, 286, 337

## • A •

"A Big Hunk o' Love" (song), 224
"A Cane and a High-Starched Collar" (song), 151
"A Little Less Conversation" (song), 133, 155, 280
Abel, Robert (filmmaker), 228
Aberbach, Jean and Julian (music publishers), 339
accent, 86, 91
acetate disc, 37–38
acting, Method approach to, 164
Adidge, Pierre (filmmaker), 228
African Americans
　dealings with record publishers, 74
　musical influence, 36–37, 41
　popularity of Elvis with, 58–59
　racism, 90
　segregation, 36
　Sun Records recording artists, 298
"After Loving You" (song), 186
after-hours lifestyle, 232
AIP (American International Pictures), 167
airplane, 253
Albright, Lola (actress), 153
albums. *See also specific album titles*
　extended play, 72, 133
　marketing by RCA, 145
　soundtrack, 133–134, 138, 140–141, 144–145, 148
Alden, Ginger (girlfriend of Elvis), 25, 243, 339
"All My Trials" (song), 207
*All Shook Up* (play), 287
"All Shook Up" (song), 183, 214, 317
Allied Artists (production company), 141
*Almost in Love* (album), 155
Aloha Eagle (jumpsuit), 211
*Aloha from Hawaii* (album), 226
*Aloha from Hawaii* (DVD), 226
Aloha from Hawaii (jumpsuit), 211
*Aloha from Hawaii* (TV special), 202, 223–225, 332
*Aloha from Hawaii via Satellite* (album), 226
*The Alternative Aloha* (album), 226
"Always Elvis" festival, 253
"Always on My Mind" (song), 208
American International Pictures (AIP), 167
amphetamines, 235
"An American Trilogy" (song), 207, 222
animals, Elvis's love of, 296, 297
Anka, Paul (singer-songwriter), 208–209
Ann-Margret (singer-dancer)
　relationship with Elvis, 130, 339
　in *Viva Las Vegas,* 125–126, 138, 168, 330, 339
"Are You Lonesome Tonight?" (song), 132
*Arizona,* benefit for U.S.S., 134
army
　deferment, 95
　discharge and return home, 96, 117
　*G.I. Blues* (movie), 116, 119–120
　housing arrangement, 96, 117
　image of Elvis reshaped by service, 116–117
　induction into, 15–16, 95, 117
　special services, 16, 95, 117
Asner, Ed (actor), 153
Astrodome, Houston, 189, 195–196
Astroworld (amusement park), 196
Atkins, Chet (guitarist-producer), 69, 176, 299, 339
Atkins, Thomas (activist), 220
Audubon Drive, Elvis's home on, 300
Ausborn, Carvel Lee. *See* Mississippi Slim
Austin, Pam (actress), 169

Avalon, Frankie (singer), 131, 163, 164, 165, 167
Awards Exhibit, Graceland, 297
Axton, Mae Boren (songwriter), 71, 311, 316

## • B •

"Baby I Don't Care" (song), 110
"Baby Let's Play House" (song), 43–44
backstage musical, 170
badges, 240, 331
Baker, Joby (actor), 169
Ballard, Lucien (cinematographer), 227
"Barefoot Ballad" (song), 145
barker, 64, 65
"Battle Hymn of the Republic" (song), 207
beach movie, 167
Beale Street, 11, 35–36, 51–52, 257
Bear Claw (Sabre Tooth) (jumpsuit), 212–213
*The Beat Behind the King* (Fontana), 272
The Beatles, 192, 193, 306
Beaulieu, Captain John Paul (father of Priscilla), 97–98
Belew, Bill (costume designer)
  black leather outfit, 184, 340
  black mohair karate suit, 192
  cape, 225
  jumpsuit, 194, 209–213, 340
belt, gift from International Hotel, 194, 222
Berman, Pandro (producer), 15, 105, 108–109
Berry, Chuck (singer), 131, 165, 195
Bertlesmann Music Group (BMG), 276–281
Bertrand, Michael T. (*Race, Rock, and Elvis*), 59
"Big Boss Man" (song), 177, 183
Biggs, Delta Mae Presley (aunt of Elvis), 294, 340
Bill Haley and the Comets, 195
Binder, Steve (producer-director), 20, 180–183, 340
binges, eating, 237
biographers, 162–163
biographies of Elvis, 289–290
biopics
  on Elvis, 282–284
  on other celebrities, 287–289

birth, of Elvis, 10, 28
birthplace, of Elvis, 28, 301
Bishop, Joey (entertainer), 118
Black, Bill (musician)
  Bill Black's Combo, 186
  biographical information, 340
  dislike of Tom Parker, 67
  early work with Elvis, 40–42, 46, 50–57
  in movies, 106, 108, 110, 111
  performance style, 50
  RCA recording sessions, 69, 71
  Rock 'n' Roll Hall of Fame, 306
  salary-versus-percentage arrangement, 66–67
Black Conquistador (jumpsuit), 213
Blackman, Joan (actress), 131
Blackwell, Otis (songwriter), 73–74, 316, 317, 318–319, 340
Blackwood Brothers (gospel quartet), 35, 97, 201, 319, 340
Blondell, Joan (actress), 168
Blossoms (vocal trio), 183
Blue Album, 243
*Blue Hawaii* (album), 121, 144, 323
*Blue Hawaii* (movie), 18, 121–123, 131, 134, 168–171
Blue Moon Boys, 50–57. *See also* Black, Bill; Moore, Scotty
"Blue Moon of Kentucky" (song), 40, 54
"Blue Suede Shoes" (song), 71, 183, 191, 331
blue-eyed soul, 186
blues, influence on Elvis, 35–36, 43, 88, 305
BMG (Bertlesmann Music Group), 276–281
bodyguard book. *See Elvis: What Happened?* (Hebler, West, and West)
bodyguards, 239, 260, 261. *See also* Memphis Mafia
body-snatching escapade, 250
bootleg records, 87
Bradley, C.W. (minister), 245
Brando, Marlon (actor), 164
Brewer-Giorgio, Gail (writer), 266
"Bridge Over Troubled Water" (song), 199, 206
Bridges, Beau (actor), 283
Bronson, Charles (actor), 153
Brown, Estelle (singer), 202

Brown, James (singer), 245
Brown, W. Earl (musical director), 183
Bucha, Captain William (Medal of Honor winner), 220
Burk, Bill (reporter), 254–256
Burning Love (jumpsuit), 211
"Burning Love" (song), 206, 224
Burton, James (guitarist), 191, 198–199
Burton, Richard (actor), 161
*Bye Bye Birdie* (movie), 333–334

• C •

Cadillac cars, Elvis's taste for, 105–106, 107, 109, 111, 238
California homes, Elvis's, 234, 301–302
Candlelight Vigil, 252, 256, 258
"Can't Help Falling in Love" (song), 121, 134, 192, 205, 225
cape, tossing, 225
Capecchi, Dr. Mario (molecular geneticist), 220
*Careless Love: The Unmaking of Elvis* (Guralnik), 289
carnivals, Colonel Tom Parker and, 64, 65
Carpenter, John (director), 282
cars, Elvis's taste in, 238–239
Cash, Johnny (musician), 44, 56, 288, 298–299
censorship, 14, 81–82
*Change of Habit* (movie), 134, 153, 154, 157, 168
charity, 134, 238, 255
charms, 234
*Charro!* (movie), 156–157
Cherry, Harry (businessman), 220
childhood
  birth, 10, 28
  in Memphis, 11, 32–36
  in Tupelo, 10, 28–31
Christman, Gene (drummer), 186
church choir, 31
CKX, Inc., 257, 292
*Clambake* (movie), 124, 141, 169, 234
The Clam (dance), 126
Clapton, Eric (musician), 199
Clark, Petula (singer), 191

Claude Thompson Dancers, 182, 183
Clayton, Rose (*Elvis Up Close*), 203, 213
The Climb (dance), 330
clothing
  black leather suit, 184, 210
  criticism of, 91
  Hillbilly Cat, 51–52
  iconography of Elvis's, 105, 109
  jumpsuit, 22–23, 194–195, 209–213
  for Las Vegas performances, 192, 194–195
  movie star, 128–129
  in *The '68 Comeback Special,* 184
"C'mon Everybody" (song), 134, 330
Coll, Edward Thomas (humanitarian), 220
Colonel, title of, 64
comeback, Elvis's
  American Sound Studio recording sessions, 185–188
  *From Elvis in Memphis,* 184–187
  live performances, 189–196
  role of producer Felton Jarvis, 176–179
  *The '68 Comeback Special,* 179–184
  sound and quality improvements, 177–178
concerts, Elvis's 1970s
  *Aloha from Hawaii,* 223–226, 332
  "An American Trilogy," 207
  "Bridge Over Troubled Water," 206
  documentaries, 202, 226–228
  dramatic movements, 216
  entrance onstage, 214
  exchanging gifts, 214–215
  final, 25, 240, 241
  interactive nature of, 197, 214–215
  jumpsuits, 209–213
  leaving the building, 216–217
  Madison Square Garden, 222
  musicians joining Elvis, 198–203
  "My Way," 208–209
  new singles, 205–206
  opening acts, 216–217
  "Polk Salad Annie," 206–207
  Priscilla Songs, 208
  revamped old favorites, 204–205
  rituals and ceremonies, 213–217, 241
  romancing the audience, 215
  song selection, 23, 204, 208, 224

controversy surrounding Elvis
  countering bad publicity, 92–93
  generational conflicts, 85–87
  hillbilly heritage, 89–91
  image reshaped by movies, 94, 101, 112–114
  negative press coverage, 85–86, 90–91
  Southern accent, 86, 91
  Tin Pan Alley versus rock 'n' roll, 87–89
Corey, Wendell (actor), 114
Corman, Gene (producer), 167
costumes. *See* clothing
Country Music Hall of Fame, 299
country-western music
  costumes, 52
  musical influence on Elvis, 35, 43, 88, 305
  promotion of Elvis by RCA, 68, 69
  touring circuit as Hillbilly Cat and the Blue Moon Boys, 53–62
  versatility and elasticity of genre, 58
Craig, Yvonne (actress), 131, 169
Cramer, Floyd (pianist), 69
Crosby, Bing (singer-actor), 103
Crosby, Gary (actor), 169
Crosby, John (reviewer), 78
Crudup, Arthur "Big Boy" (singer)
  as musical influence on Elvis, 305
  "My Baby Left Me," 71
  "That's All Right," 40, 45, 50, 315
"Crying in the Chapel" (song), 144
cultural icon, 9–10, 303
Curtis, Tony (actor), 120

## • D •

Darby, Ken (songwriter), 104
Darin, Bobby (singer), 131, 164
Dave Clark Five (musical group), 167
Davis, Mac (songwriter), 187
Davis, Sammy, Jr. (entertainer), 116
Days Inn, Memphis, 256
Dean, James (actor), 164
death, of Elvis
  autopsy findings, 264
  body-snatching escapade, 250
  discovery of, 243
  Elvis Week, 251–258
  faked death rumors, 265–267
  funeral, 245, 263
  news of, 244, 262
  viewing of body, 245, 252
death threats, 239
Del Rio, Delores (actress), 17, 151, 168
Demerol (narcotic), 235
Denny, Jim (manager of *Grand Ole Opry*), 53–54
Denver, John (singer), 199
"Devil in Disguise" (song), 133
Dilaudid (narcotic), 235
divorce, of Elvis and Priscilla, 25, 196, 231
"Dixie" (song), 207
Dixon, Luther (songwriter), 177
*D.J. Fontana Remembers* (Fontana), 272
"Do the Clam" (song), 145
Dobson, Peter (actor), 287
documentaries
  *Elvis on Tour*, 24, 202, 228
  *Elvis: That's the Way It Is*, 24, 202, 226–227
  *This Is Elvis*, 284
Dodger. *See* Presley, Minnie Mae Hood
"Don't Be Cruel" (song), 73, 80, 316–317
"Don't Leave Me Now" (song), 110
Dorsey, Tommy and Jimmy (TV hosts-musicians), 13, 76, 102
*Double Trouble* (movie), 124, 169
Douglas, Donna (actress), 131
drug abuse, 235–236, 262–264, 312
ducktail, 52, 105
Dunleavy, Steve (writer), 261
Dunne, Philip (director), 152
Durden, Tommy (songwriter), 71, 316

## • E •

*Easy Come, Easy Go* (movie), 124, 142, 170, 234
eating habits, 237, 264
echo effect, 11, 71, 72
*The Ed Sullivan Show* (TV program), 14, 79–82, 93, 193, 329
Eden, Barbara (actress), 151
Edgren, Stig (producer), 202
Egan, Richard (actor), 104

Elliot, Jane (actress), 168
*Elvis* (album), 72
*Elvis* (Goldman), 265, 270
*Elvis* (TV biopic), 282–283
*Elvis* (TV series), 283–284
*ELV1S: 30 #1 Hits* (album), 155, 280–281, 326
*Elvis: Aloha from Hawaii* (TV program), 24, 223–225
*Elvis and Kathy* (Westmoreland), 203
*Elvis and Me* (Priscilla Presley), 21, 192, 272
*Elvis and Me* (TV biopic), 283
*Elvis and the Beauty Queen* (TV biopic), 283
*Elvis and the Colonel* (TV biopic), 283
*Elvis as Recorded at Madison Square Garden* (album), 222
*Elvis by Request* (album), 133
*The Elvis Encyclopedia* (Victor), 117, 122, 200, 224, 230, 231
*Elvis: From Nashville to Memphis: The Essential 60s Masters* (album), 278, 326
*Elvis: Greatest Hits Vol.1* (album), 276
*Elvis: His Love for Gospel Music* (Sumner), 201
*Elvis: I Was the One* (album), 276
*Elvis Is Back* (album), 132, 322–323
*Elvis on Tour* (documentary), 24, 202, 228
*Elvis: Portrait of a Friend* (Lacker), 342
*Elvis Presley* (album), 72, 321–322
Elvis Presley Enterprises (the Estate), 254–255, 268–269, 291–293, 300
Elvis Presley Music (songwriting company), 74–75, 177
*Elvis Presley Platinum: A Life in Music* (album), 279
*Elvis: Still Taking Care of Business* (Sonny West), 271, 346
*Elvis: Straight Up* (Esposito), 340
*Elvis: That's the Way It Is* (documentary), 24, 202, 226–227
Elvis: The Concert (tour), 198, 199, 202, 203
*Elvis: The Ed Sullivan Shows* (DVD), 62, 82
*Elvis: The King of Rock 'n' roll: The Complete 50s Masters* (album), 278, 326
Elvis the Pelvis, 85, 87, 96, 101, 115
*Elvis Up Close* (Clayton and Heard), 203, 213
*Elvis: Viva Las Vegas* (TV special), 229

*Elvis: Walk a Mile in My Shoes: The Essential 70s Masters* (album), 278, 326
*Elvis: We Love You Tender* (Stanley), 345
Elvis Week
 Candlelight Vigil, 252, 256, 258
 described, 251
 Estate involvement in, 254–255
 evolution of, 257–258
 list of activities (1992), 255
 list of activities (2007), 257–258
 one-year anniversary, 252–253
*Elvis: What Happened?* (Hebler, West, and West), 236, 260–261, 341
*Elvis World* (Stern and Stern), 86, 264
*Elvis's Christmas Album* (album), 322
*Elvis's Favorite Gospel Songs* (album by Sumner), 201
*Elvis's Man Friday* (Gene Smith), 345
Eminem (rapper-actor), 171
Emmons, Bobby (organist), 186
entourage. *See* Memphis Mafia
EP (extended-play album), 72, 133
Erickson, Leif (actor), 168
Esposito, Joe (foreman of entourage)
 army service, 340
 biographical information, 340
 on cape tossing, 225
 death of Elvis and, 243
 *Elvis: Straight Up,* 340
 *Good Rockin' Tonight,* 271
Estate. *See* Elvis Presley Enterprises (the Estate)
"Everybody Loves Somebody Sometime" (song), 194
Exhibition Room, Graceland, 296
exploitation, 14, 140, 268
extended-play album, 72, 133

## • F •

Fabares, Shelley (actress), 126, 169
Fabian (singer), 131, 163, 164
Factors, Inc. (marketer), 268, 269
faked death rumors, 265–267
fame, downside of, 232

"Fame and Fortune" (song), 118
fans
  African Americans, 58–59
  country music, 59
  death of Elvis and, 245–246, 252
  downside of fame, 232
  female, 59–62, 76, 78, 310–311
  hysterical, 61, 86, 311
  at Jacksonville concert (May 13, 1955), 61
  loyalty of, 140, 146, 197, 215
  memorabilia, 269–270
  of movies, 140, 146
  post-death rituals, 249–258
  romancing during concert, 215
  at television appearances, 76, 78, 80
  young, 59, 61, 69, 78, 86
fanzines, 113, 117
Feathers, Charlie (singer-songwriter), 44
"Fever" (song), 132
Fike, Lamar (member Memphis Mafia), 341
Finkel, Bob (producer), 180–181
*Flaming Star* (movie), 17–18, 121, 150–151, 168
"Flaming Star" (song), 151
*Follow That Dream* (movie), 152–153, 168, 170
Follow That Dream Records, 281
Fontana, D.J. (drummer)
  *The Beat Behind the King*, 272
  biographical information, 341
  *D.J. Fontana Remembers*, 272
  joining Elvis, 55
  in movies, 106, 108, 110, 111
  RCA recording sessions, 69, 71
  Rock 'n' Roll Hall of Fame, 306
  in *The '68 Comeback Special*, 183
Forest Hill Cemetery, 245, 250, 251
Forrest, Steve (actor), 151
*Forrest Gump* (movie), 282
Fortas, Alan (member Memphis Mafia)
  biographical information, 341
  *My Friend Elvis*, 341
Francisco, Dr. Jerry (medical examiner), 262–263
*The Frank Sinatra Show* (TV program), 118
*Frank Sinatra's Welcome Home Party for Elvis* (TV program), 118
*Frankie and Johnny* (movie), 124, 131, 141

*From Elvis in Memphis* (album), 20–21, 184–187, 204, 242, 324
*From Elvis Presley Boulevard, Memphis, Tennessee* (album), 242, 296
*From Memphis to Vegas/From Vegas to Memphis* (album), 187
FTD (floral delivery service), 245
Fuller, Dolores (songwriter), 145
*Fun in Acapulco* (movie), 124
funeral, 245–246, 263
Funicello, Annette (actress), 167
"Funny How Time Slips Away" (song), 208

## • G •

generational conflicts, 85–87, 307
*G.I. Blues* (album), 119, 144
*G.I. Blues* (movie), 17, 116, 119–120, 130, 168
"G.I. Blues" (song), 119
gifts
  exchanging during concerts, 214–215
  watches, 221
*Girl Happy* (movie), 124, 126, 131, 134, 168
*Girls! Girls! Girl!* (movie), 124, 134, 169
Gladys Music (songwriting company), 74–75, 177
Goetz, James B. (media mogul), 220
gold records, 196, 253, 279, 297
Goldman, Arthur (*Elvis*), 265, 270
Good, Jack (TV producer), 192
*Good Rockin' Tonight* (Esposito), 271
"Good Rockin' Tonight" (song), 42
Gooding, Marion (judge), 84, 329
gospel music
  *How Great Thou Art* (album), 176, 178–179, 323–324
  musical influence on Elvis, 35
  in *The '68 Comeback Special*, 182–183
  as warm up in RCA recording sessions, 71
Graceland
  Awards Exhibit, 297
  barn (House of the Rising Sun), 297
  decor, 293–294
  den ("Jungle Room"), 242, 295–296
  described, 291–292

# Index

Exhibition Room, 296
grounds, 296–297
kitchen and dining room, 295
living room, 294
Meditation Garden, 97, 250–251, 256, 297
Music Gates, 94, 252, 256
music room, 294
opening to public, 254, 293, 294
original owners, 94
pool room, 295
Priscilla's role in managing, 292–293
purchase of, 94–95
recording studio, 240, 242, 296
TV room, 295
*Graceland* (album by Paul Simon), 206
Graham, Billy (director), 157
Grammy Award, 179
*Grand Ole Opry,* 53–54
Grant, Cary (actor), 191, 192
Grant, Currie (friend of Elvis), 98
graves, 250, 251
*Great Balls of Fire* (movie), 288
Greene, Bob (columnist), 261
Gregory, Neal and Janice *(When Elvis Died),* 262
Griffith, Andy (actor-comedian), 57, 79
Grob, Dick (member Memphis Mafia), 245, 341
Guercio, Joe (orchestra director), 203
guitar
　Elvis's first, 301
　learning to play, 31
*Guitar Man* (album), 276
"Guitar Man" (song), 19, 177, 178, 182, 183
guns, 239–240
Guralnik, Peter
　*Careless Love: The Unmaking of Elvis,* 289
　*Last Train to Memphis,* 50, 70, 289

## • H •

hair
　color, 120
　cut for army induction, 95
　ducktail, 52, 105
　in G.I. Blues, 120
　iconography of Elvis's, 105, 107, 109

Hamilton, Roy (singer), 221
Hardin, Glen D. (musician), 199–200
Harris, Wynonie (R&B artist), 42, 47
Hart, Dolores (actress), 108
*Harum Scarum* (movie), 124, 131, 138, 143–144
"Hawaiian Wedding Song" (song), 169, 171
*Hayride. See Louisiana Hayride*
Hays, Lowell (jeweler), 341
*He Touched Me* (album), 179
*He Walks Beside Me–Favorite Songs of Faith and Inspiration* (album), 276
Heard, Dick (songwriter)
　*Elvis Up Close,* 203, 213
　"Kentucky Rain," 188
*Heart of Dixie* (movie), 338
*Heartbreak Hotel* (movie), 338
"Heartbreak Hotel" (song), 70, 71, 72, 76, 316
Hebler, Dave (bodyguard)
　biographical information, 341
　*Elvis: What Happened?,* 261, 341
Herman's Hermits (musical group), 165, 167
Hess, Jake (singer), 35, 47, 178, 202, 245
"Hey Jude" (song), 192
High School, L.C. Humes, 32, 33, 300
Hill and Range (music publisher), 67, 73–75, 145, 339
hillbilly, use as derogatory term, 89–91
Hillbilly Cat, 12, 50–56
Hilton, Tyler (actor), 288
hip gyrations, 57, 80, 81, 84, 86
Hodge, Charlie (friend of Elvis), 117, 191, 215, 341
*Hollywood Reporter,* 227
homes, Elvis's
　California, 234, 301–302
　first in Memphis, 300
　Graceland, 291–297
　shotgun shack in Tupelo, 10, 29, 301
*Honeymoon in Vegas* (movie), 335–336
horses, at Graceland, 297
"Hound Dog" (song), 73, 77–81, 183, 192, 328
*Hounddog* (movie), 338
Houston, Cissy (singer), 202–203
Houston Astrodome, 189, 195–196
*How Great Thou Art* (album), 176, 178–179, 323–324
"How Great Thou Art" (song), 179, 319
Howe, Bones (musical engineer), 181

Humann, Walter (business leader), 220
Humes High School, 32, 33, 300
Humperdinck, Engelbert (singer), 229, 230
"Husky Dusky Day" (song), 152
*Hy Gardner Calling* (TV program), 92–93

## • I •

"I Don't Care if the Sun Don't Shine" (song), 42
"I Forgot to Remember to Forget" (song), 44
"I Got a Woman" (song), 76
"I Slipped, I Stumbled, and I Fell" (song), 152
"I Was the One" (song), 70
Ice Cube (rapper-actor), 171
Ice-T (rapper-actor), 171
iconography, 105–106, 107–108, 109–110, 111, 210
icons, used in text, 6
"If I Can Dream" (song), 183, 205, 319–320
"If the Lord Wasn't Walking by My Side" (song), 178
"I'll Remember You" (song), 224
"I'm Counting on You" (song), 70
"I'm Left, You're Right, She's Gone" (song), 43–44
"I'm So Lonesome I Could Cry" (song), 224
image of Elvis, 312
  as forbidden fruit, 310–311
  Rebel Elvis, 264, 308–309
  as Southerner, 310
  Vegas Elvis, 264, 309–310
impact on American culture
  musical, 304–306
  youth culture, 306–308
the Imperials (vocalists), 178, 191, 341
impersonators, 259, 273–274, 286
"In My Way" (song), 152
"In the Ghetto" (song), 187, 188, 205
*Inside Elvis* (Ed Parker), 343
integrated musicals, 170–171
integration, 10, 41, 304
International Conference on Elvis Presley, 305
International Hotel, Las Vegas, 21–22, 189–195, 331
*It Happened at the World's Fair* (movie), 124, 128, 169, 282
Italian western, 156–157
"It's Now or Never" (song), 132–133, 318
"I've Got a Woman" (song), 70
Ivens, Molly (reporter), 262

## • J •

Jacksonville concerts
  August 1956, 84, 328–329
  May 13, 1955, 61, 65
Jaeckel, Richard (actor), 151
Jagger, Dean (actor), 114, 168
*Jailhouse Rock* (movie), 108–110, 113–114, 130, 307
"Jailhouse Rock" (song), 113, 317–318, 329–330
Jamboree Attractions, 65, 67
James, Mark (songwriter), 320
Jarmusch, Jim (director), 286
Jarvis, Felton (producer), 175, 176–179, 242, 342
Jaycees' Outstanding Young Men of America, 220–221
jewelry, 238
Johnson, Don (actor), 283
Jones, Carolyn (actress), 110, 114, 168
Jones, Tom (singer), 229
the Jordanaires (gospel quartet)
  backup vocalists for Elvis, 70, 73, 178, 342
  on *The Ed Sullivan Show,* 81
  in Elvis movies, 106, 111
Jorgensen, Ernst (BMG), 277–278
jumpsuit
  Aloha from Hawaii (Aloha Eagle), 211
  as autobiography, 210–213
  Bear Claw (Sabre Tooth), 212–213
  Black Conquistador, 213
  Burning Love, 211
  in Las Vegas performances, 23, 194–195, 209, 210
  list of, 213
  Memphis, 212

Peacock, 212
Tiger (Mad Tiger), 212
white, 194–195, 209, 210, 222, 225
"Jungle Room," Graceland, 242, 295–296
juvenile delinquency, linked to rock 'n' roll, 85, 165

## • K •

Kahane, Jackie (comedian), 217, 245, 342
Kanter, Hal (director-writer), 107
Katzman, Sam (producer), 138, 142–144, 166
Kefauver, Estes (Senator), 118
Keisker, Marion (assistant to Sam Phillips), 37–38, 50, 298, 342
Kennedy, Caroline (celebrity), 263
"Kentucky Rain" (song), 188
Kerkorian, Kirk (International Hotel owner), 190
Kesler, Stanley (songwriter), 44
*Kid Galahad* (movie), 131, 153, 168, 170
*King Creole* (movie), 95, 110–111, 113–114, 168, 170
*Kissin' Cousins* (album), 144
*Kissin' Cousins* (movie), 129, 131, 138–139, 142–143, 168
Klein, George (disc jockey), 233, 304, 342
Kuiokalani Lee Cancer Fund, 224
Kuralt, Charles (journalist), 261

## • L •

Lacker, Marty (secretary/bookkeeper)
  biographical information, 342
  *Elvis: Portrait of a Friend,* 342
Landau, Jon (critic), 184
Lane, Jocelyn (actress), 141
Lange, Hope (actress), 151, 168
Lansbury, Angela (actress), 168
Lansky, Bernard and Guy (clothiers), 36, 51, 342
Lanza, Mario (singer-actor), 103, 131, 133
Las Vegas
  "Always Elvis" festival, 253
  attendance records, 194
  congratulations after first concert, 193
  influence of Elvis on other entertainers, 228–230
  International Hotel appearances, 21–26, 189–196
  New Frontier booking, 77
  opening night, 191–192, 331
  Tom Parker's enjoyment of, 241
  preparation for first concert, 191
  residency contracts, 230
  tablecloth deal, 193
*Last Train to Memphis* (Guralnik), 50, 70, 289
Lastfogel, Abe (agent), 103, 342
Lauderdale Courts, 32, 33, 300
law enforcement, Elvis's fascination with, 240
Lawford, Peter (entertainer), 118
L.C. Humes High School, 32, 33, 300
Lee, Peggy (singer), 132
Leiber, Jerry (songwriter), 73, 317–318
leitmotif, 182, 183
*Leningrad Cowboys Go America* (movie), 335
Lennon, John (musician), 271, 306
Lewis, Jerry Lee (musician), 131, 165, 195, 288, 298–299
Lewis, Marlo (TV producer), 82
Lime, Yvonne (actress), 108, 130
"Little Egypt" (song), 134, 183
Little Richard (singer), 131, 165
*Live a Little, Love a Little* (movie), 155, 280
Long, Shortly (pianist), 71
*Louisiana Hayride,* 52, 54–55, 107
"Love Letters" (song), 145
"Love Me" (song), 224
*Love Me Tender* (album), 72
*Love Me Tender* (movie), 80, 103–104
"Love Me Tender" (song), 80–81, 104, 118, 205, 215
*Loving You* (movie), 106–108, 113, 114, 130
Luman, Bob (singer), 12

## • M •

Mad Tiger (jumpsuit), 212
Madison Square Garden, 24, 222
Marcus, Greil (rock-music historian)
  criticism of Elvis's movies, 162–163
  *Mystery Train,* 184
marriage, of Elvis and Priscilla, 134–135

Marsh, Dave (rock-music historian), 162–163, 270
Martin, Dean (actor-singer), 194
Martin, Tony (singer), 132
Masters V (gospel group), 202
Matthau, Walter (actor), 110, 114, 168
McIntire, John (actor), 17, 151, 168
"Mean Woman Blues" (song), 107
Meditation Garden, Graceland, 97, 250–251, 256, 297
melodrama, 151–152
memoirs, 270–273
memorabilia, 269–270
"Memories" (song), 183
Memphis
  Beale Street, 11, 35–36, 51–52, 257
  Elvis's teenage years in, 11, 32–36
  Graceland, 291–297
  Sun Studio, 297–300
  tourism, 257, 300
Memphis (jumpsuit), 212
Memphis Mafia. *See also specific individuals*
  after-hours lifestyle, 232
  arrested emotional development, 233–234
  behavior during movie production, 130, 234–235
  careers of, 233
  compensation and gifts to, 233
  described, 129–130
  drug use, 235–236
  Elvis's indulgences and, 232–233
  fraternity-like environment, 233
  members, 129, 233
  memoirs, 271–272
  no-wives rule, 196
  photograph of, 272
  TCB symbol, 234
Memphis Recording Service, 37–39, 298
merchandising Elvis, 93–94, 267–270
Method approach to acting, 164
Meyers, Jonathan Rhys (actor), 283
middle name, 29
Midkiff, Dale (actor), 283
"Milkcow Blues Boogie" (song), 43
Million Dollar Quartet, 287, 299
*The Milton Berle Show* (TV program), 14, 77–78, 328
Mirisch brothers (producers), 149, 153

Mississippi Slim (country singer), 10, 28, 31, 342
Mississippi-Alabama Fair and Dairy Show, 31
Mobley, Mary Ann (actress), 131
Mockridge, Cyril (composer), 151
Moman, Chips (music producer), 21, 185–186, 320, 343
"Money Honey" (song), 70
Montenegro, Hugh (composer), 157
*Moody Blue* (album), 240, 243, 296
Moore, Mary Tyler (actress), 157, 168
Moore, Scotty (guitarist)
  biographical information, 343
  early work with Elvis, 40–42, 44, 46–47, 50–57, 62
  on Elvis's first public performance, 327
  in movies, 106, 108, 110, 111
  performance style, 44, 50
  RCA recording sessions, 69, 71
  Rock 'n' Roll Hall of Fame, 306
  role as manager, 53
  salary-versus-percentage arrangement, 66–67
  in *The '68 Comeback Special*, 183
  *That's All Right*, 273
Moretti, Nick *(My Life Before, During, and After Elvis Presley)*, 201
Morris, Bill (Memphis Sheriff), 220
Morrow, Vic (actor), 114
motto (Takin' Care of Business), 198, 234
movies
  Elvis-related, 333–338
  fanzines, 113, 117
  integrated musicals, 170–171
  production values, 169
  show business success myth in, 111–112
  teen musical subgenre, 165–171
  vehicles, 105, 167, 171–172
movies starring Elvis. *See also specific movie titles*
  acting ambitions of Elvis, 103, 149
  as autobiography, 105–111
  behavior during filming, 234–235
  contracts with Hal Wallis, 15, 102, 116, 119
  criticism of, 162–165
  dances in, 126, 330
  defense of, 161–172

disappointment of Elvis with, 144, 146, 149, 153, 160–162
dual roles in, 138, 143
final films, 153–157
formula for, 121–125
iconography used in, 105–106
image reshaped by, 94, 101, 112–114
integrated musicals, 170–171
leading ladies, 130–131
multicultural aspects, 169
performance style of Elvis in, 106, 108, 110, 111, 113–114
Presley Travelogues, 125–126, 138, 140–142, 147, 167–170
production costs, cutting, 138–142
production values, 169–170
publicity and promotion, 127–128
screen test, 102
shooting schedules, 140, 142–143
vehicles for Elvis, 105–111, 122
Muhoberac, Larry (keyboard player), 191
Murphy, Eddie (actor-comedian), 171–172
Music Gates, Graceland, 94, 252, 256
musical
  backstage, 170
  integrated, 170–171
  teen, 165–171
musical comedy, 18, 123–125, 159, 161
musical drama, 153
musical influences on Elvis
  blues and R&B, 35–36, 43, 88, 305
  for concerts of the 1970s, 204
  country western, 35, 43, 88, 305
  credited by Elvis, 305
  gospel, 35
  Memphis radio stations, 34
  Mississippi Slim, 10, 31
  record collection, 34
  soul music, 204
  Southern musical genres, 36–37
  swamp rock, 204
musical plays, 287
musical style, Elvis's
  in movies, 113–114
  musical establishment's resentment of, 87
mutable cultural signifier, 308
"My Baby Left Me" (song), 71
*My Friend Elvis* (Fortas), 341

*My Life Before, During, and After Elvis Presley* (Wilkinson and Moretti), 201
"My Way" (song), 208–209, 224
*Mystery Train* (Greil), 184
*Mystery Train* (movie), 286, 334–335
"Mystery Train" (song), 44, 227

• *N* •

Nader, Ralph (consumer advocate), 309
narcotics, 235
narcotics agent's badge, 331
Neal, Bob (disc jockey/manager), 55–56, 65–67, 343
Nelson, Gene (director), 142
Newbury, Mickey (songwriter), 207
Neyland, Anne (actress), 130
Nichopoulos, Dr. George (physician to Elvis), 25, 236, 243, 343
Nixon, Richard (President), 331
Noel, Chris (actor), 169
Noone, Peter (singer), 167
"Nothingville" (song), 183

• *O* •

O'Connell, Arthur (actor), 153, 168
Odets, Clifford (writer), 152
O'Toole, Peter (actor), 161
Outstanding Young Men of America, 220–221
Overton Park Shell (first performance), 46–47, 53, 327–328

• *P* •

Paget, Debra (actress), 104
*Paradise, Hawaiian Style* (movie), 124, 169
Parchman Prison, 30, 36
Parker, Colonel Tom (manager)
  "Always Elvis" festival, 253
  background of, 64–65
  biographical information, 343
  controlling media access to Elvis, 96, 127, 135, 162
  countering bad publicity, 92–93

Parker, Colonel Tom *(continued)*
  deal making on films, 139–141
  early interest in Elvis, 65
  Elvis's army induction, 15–16, 95, 117
  Elvis's drug use, 236
  fan loyalty, promoting, 140, 146
  at funeral for Elvis, 245
  gambling by, 241
  *Harum Scarum* and, 143–144
  Hill and Range deal, 67, 74–75, 339
  Jamboree Attractions, 65, 67
  Las Vegas deals/performances, 189, 192, 193, 241
  Madison Square Garden deal, 222
  marketing ploys, 140
  merchandising deal with Hank Saperstein, 93, 268
  mismanagement by, 269
  movie deals turned down, 17
  movie production costs and, 138–142
  NBC special deal, 180, 181
  New Frontier booking, 77
  percentage of Elvis's monies, 139
  RCA Victor deal, 13, 67–68
  soundtrack albums, 145, 148
  as "special advisor," 66
  sued by the Estate, 269
  television bookings, 14, 75–76, 80
  true identity, 65, 269
Parker, Ed (bodyguard)
  biographical information, 343
  *Inside Elvis*, 343
Pasetta, Marty (producer-director), 224
"Peace in the Valley" (song), 81, 93
Peacock (jumpsuit), 212
Peer, Ralph (music recorder), 91
performance style of Elvis
  censorship, 81–82
  in concerts of the 1970s, 22, 204, 214–217
  controversy over, 14, 83–92
  development/evolution of, 60–61
  dramatic movements in concert, 216
  film footage of, 61–62
  iconography of, 106, 108, 110, 111
  influences on, 47
  in movies, 113–114
  post-army, 118
  in RCA recording sessions, 70–71
  romancing the audience, 215
  sensual/sexual connotations, 78, 84, 85, 86, 113
  television appearances, 76, 78, 80–81
  touring as Hillbilly Cat and the Blue Moon Boys, 12, 57, 58, 60–62
performances. *See also* concerts, Elvis's 1970s
  benefit for U.S.S. *Arizona,* 134
  final, 25, 240, 241
  first public (Overton Park Shell), 46–47, 53, 327–328
  as "hard act to follow," 56
  Jacksonville concert (August 1956), 84, 328–329
  Jacksonville concert (May 1955), 61, 65
  Las Vegas, 21–22, 189–196, 331
  Madison Square Garden, 24, 222
  in *The '68 Comeback Special,* 20, 183, 330
  television, 14, 76–82
  Texas Livestock Show, 189, 195–196
Perkins, Carl (musician), 298–299
Perkins, Millie (actress), 151, 168
philanthropy, 220, 224
Phillips, Dewey (disc jockey), 11, 12, 45–46, 343
Phillips, Judd (music producer), 298, 299
Phillips, Sam (music producer)
  advice to Elvis, 70
  advice to Steve Sholes, 71, 72
  biographical information, 39, 343
  early work with Elvis, 11–12, 37–43, 45–46, 53–54
  at Las Vegas comeback performance, 191
  sale of Elvis's contract, 66, 67, 68
  Sun Studio/Records, 38–44, 88–89, 297–299
*Picasso at the Lapin Agile* (movie), 336–337
pluggers, 88
"Polk Salad Annie" (song), 206–207
polypharmacy, 264
pop music
  ballads, 88
  promotion of Elvis by RCA, 68, 69
  rock 'n' roll charted as, 89
  rocking pop style of 1960s Elvis, 131–132, 164
  Tin Pan Alley, 87–89
Poplar Tunes (record shop), 36, 300
postage stamp, Elvis, 319
practical jokes, 234

prescription drugs, abuse of, 235–236
Presley, Dee Stanley (stepmother of Elvis), 344
Presley, Gladys Love Smith (mother of Elvis)
 biographical information, 344
 Cadillac gift, 238
 dealings with Colonel Tom Parker, 66, 67
 death, 16, 97
 early life, 28–29
 during Elvis's childhood, 29–30–33
 Elvis's first guitar, 301
 Elvis's radio debut, 45
 Graceland purchase, 94
 in *Loving You* movie, 108
Presley, J.D. (grandfather of Elvis), 28
Presley, Jessie Garon (brother of Elvis), 10, 28
Presley, Lisa Marie (daughter of Elvis)
 biographical information, 344
 birth, 21, 135
 "In the Ghetto" remix, 188
 role in managing the Estate, 292
Presley, Minnie Mae Hood (grandmother of Elvis), 33, 91, 251, 344
Presley, Priscilla Beaulieu (wife of Elvis)
 biographical information, 344
 divorce, 25, 196
 *Elvis and Me,* 21, 192, 272
 guns, 239
 marriage to Elvis, 21, 134–135
 meeting Elvis in Germany, 16, 97–98
 producer of *Elvis* TV series, 283
 role in managing Graceland, 292–293
Presley, Vernon (father of Elvis)
 at "Always Elvis" festival, 253
 on Bill Burk, 256
 biographical information, 344
 dealings with Colonel Tom Parker, 66
 death, 251, 292
 early life, 28–29
 during Elvis's childhood, 28–33
 Elvis's death, 245, 251, 252
 Elvis's drug use, 236
 Elvis's grave inscription, 297
 Elvis's radio debut, 45
 in Germany with Elvis, 91
 interments at Graceland, 251
 in *Loving You* movie, 108
Presley, Vester (uncle of Elvis), 31, 344

press coverage
 bodyguard book, effect of, 261
 during comeback years, 193
 controlled media access to Elvis, 96, 127, 135, 162
 death of Elvis, 244, 262
 drug abuse, 262–264
 of Elvis's performing style, 85–86, 90–91
 Madison Square Garden concerts, 222
 movie publicity and promotion, 127–128
 post-death, 260–265
 of *The '68 Comeback Special,* 184
 weight problem, 264
Priscilla Songs, 208
production values, movie, 169–170
property, movie, 103
Prowse, Juliet (actress), 130, 168
public appearance, first, 46–47
publishing companies
 Hill and Range, 67, 73–75, 339
 setting up Elvis's, 74–75

• R •

Rabbitt, Eddie (songwriter), 187, 188
*Race, Rock, and Elvis* (Bertrand), 59
racism, 90
radio stations
 Elvis's debut on *Red Hot and Blue,* 45–46
 Memphis, 11, 34
 rock 'n' roll, 89
rap artists, in movies, 171
Rat Pack, 118, 229
R&B music
 musical influence on Elvis, 35–36, 88, 305
 promotion of Elvis by RCA, 68, 69
RCA
 Aloha albums, 226
 changes in Elvis's sound, 72–73
 colored vinyl albums, 243
 first album releases, 72
 Madison Square Garden concert recordings, 222
 marketing soundtrack albums, 145
 plaque presentation, 240
 promotion of Elvis, 68–69
 purchase of Elvis's contract, 13, 67–68

RCA *(continued)*
  recording sessions for Elvis (1956), 69–71, 73
  recording sessions for Elvis (1960), 132–133
  recording sessions for Elvis (1967), 177
  releases after Elvis's death, 275–281
  Studio B, 299
"Ready Teddy" (song), 80
rechanneled stereo, 277
*Reconsider Baby* (album), 325
"Reconsider Baby" (song), 278
record collection, Elvis's, 34, 295
Recording Industry Association of America (RIAA), 279, 297
recording sessions
  American Sound Studio, 185–187
  Elvis's approach to, 176
  at Graceland, 242
  for *How Great Thou Art*, 177
  Memphis Recording Service, 37–39
  RCA (1956), 69–71, 73
  RCA (1960), 132–133
  RCA (1967), 177
  Sun Studio, 40–41
recording studio
  American Sound Studio, 185–187
  at Graceland, 240, 242, 296
  Studio B, 299
  Sun Studio/Records, 38–44, 297–299
records. *See also specific album titles; specific song titles*
  bootleg, 87
  Elvis's first, 46
  gold, 196, 253, 279, 297
*Red Hot and Blue* (radio program), 11, 12, 45–46
Reed, Jerry (singer-songwriter), 177, 178, 182, 187
residency contracts, Las Vegas, 230
"Return to Sender" (song), 134, 318–319
reverberation, 11, 40, 72
reviewers
  description of Elvis's sound, 51
  of television appearances, 78
RIAA (Recording Industry Association of America), 279, 297
Rich, John (director), 142, 234
Richards, Keith (guitarist), 44

Rising Sun (horse), 297
Rivera, Geraldo (journalist), 261, 262, 265, 266
rock 'n' roll
  charted as pop music, 89
  Elvis's association with, 85–86, 89, 305, 306
  generational conflict and, 85, 87
  linked to sex and juvenile crime, 85, 165
  movement of Elvis's sound toward, 69
  Soviet Union ban on, 87
Rock 'n' Roll Hall of Fame, 306
rockabilly
  Elvis and, 9, 41, 77, 304
  features of, 41, 42, 58
  Sam Phillips and, 39
"Rock-a-Hula Baby" (song), 145
Romanelli, Carl (sculptor), 253
Romero, Alex (choreographer), 114, 329
Rosenthal, Harry (reporter), 262
*Roustabout* (movie), 124, 126, 134, 140–141, 161, 168
royalties, 73, 74, 75, 177
"Rubberneckin" (song), 134, 157
Russell, Kurt (actor), 282–283, 287

## • S •

Sabre Tooth (jumpsuit), 212–213
Sanders, Denis (director), 227
Saperstein, Hank (merchandiser), 93, 268
satire, 152–153
*Saturday Night Live* (TV program), 171
Savage, John (actor), 142
"Saved" (song), 183
scarf, tossing into audience, 215
Scheff, Jerry (bassist), 191, 199, 200
Schilling, Jerry (member Memphis Mafia), 283, 345
Scott, Lizabeth (actress), 106, 114
screen test, 102
Sears, Dan (radio host), 244
"See See Rider" (song), 214
Semon, Roger (BMG), 277
"Separate Ways" (song), 208
"Shake, Rattle, and Roll" (song), 76
Shalimar Music (music publisher), 73
Sharnik, John (writer), 87
Shaughnessy, Mickey (actor), 108, 114

Shemwell, Sylvia (singer), 202
Shigeta, James (actor), 169
*Shindig* (TV program), 199, 200
Sholes, Steve (RCA Victor executive), 68–72, 345
Shore, Sammy (comedian), 217
shotgun shack, 10, 29, 301
show business success myth, 111–112
sideburns, 95, 105, 107, 109, 111
Sidney, George (director), 138
Siegel, Don (director), 150–151
Sillerman, Robert F.X. (owner of CKX), 257
Simon, Paul (singer-songwriter), 206
Sinatra, Frank (singer-actor), 103, 116–119, 209, 311
Sinatra, Nancy (singer), 117, 118, 126, 169, 229
Singleton, Shelby (music producer), 299
*The '68 Comeback Special*
   clothing, 184
   description, 179–180
   importance for redefining Elvis, 184
   live segments, 20, 183, 330
   production numbers, 20, 182–183
   production of, 180–181
   ratings, 184
Smith, Al (songwriter), 177
Smith, Billy (cousin of Elvis), 231
Smith, Gene (cousin of Elvis)
   biographical information, 345
   *Elvis's Man Friday*, 345
Smith, Myrna (singer), 202
Snow, Hank (singer), 54, 65, 66, 67
songs. *See specific song titles*
songwriters. *See also individual songwriters*
   credit sharing, 73–74, 177
   employment by Hill and Range, 75, 145
   royalties, 73, 74, 75, 177
   for soundtrack albums, 145
   of Tin Pan Alley, 88
soul music, 204
soundtrack albums, 133–134, 138, 140–141, 144–145, 148
Southern heritage of Elvis, 265, 310
Southern musical genres, 36–37
*Speedway* (movie), 124, 126
Speer, Ben and Brock (gospel singers), 69
*Spinout* (movie), 124, 131
St. Gerard, Michael (actor), 284, 288

stage fright, 47
*Stage Show* (TV program), 13, 76, 102
stamp, Elvis, 309
Stamps Quartet (gospel group), 201–202, 345
"Stand by Me" (song), 178
Stanley, Rick, David, and Billy (stepbrothers of Elvis)
   biographical information, 345
   *Elvis: We Love You Tender*, 345
Stanwyck, Barbara (actress), 126, 168
Starlite Wranglers (country group), 40, 50, 51, 53
*Starmaker* (Wallis), 102
the Statesmen (gospel quartet), 35, 47
*Stay Away, Joe* (movie), 124, 168, 234
"Steamroller Blues" (song), 224
Stern, Jane and Michael (*Elvis World*), 86, 264
*The Steve Allen Show* (TV program), 14, 78–79
stilyagis, 87
Stoker, Gordon (vocalist), 70
Stoller, Mike (songwriter), 73, 317–318
Streisand, Barbara (singer-actress), 190
striptease, Elvis's performing style compared to, 78, 85, 86
"Stuck on You" (song), 118, 132
Studio B, 299
"Such a Night" (song), 278
Sumner, J.D. (vocalist)
   *Elvis: His Love for Gospel Music*, 201
   *Elvis's Favorite Gospel Songs*, 201
   at funeral for Elvis, 245
   Masters V, 202
   Stamps Quartet, 201–202, 345
Sun Records, 38–39, 66, 72, 88, 298–299
Sun Studio
   after Elvis, 298–300
   before Elvis, 298
   Elvis's recordings at, 11–12, 39–44
   location, 297–298, 299
   mainstream music compared, 88–89
   management by the Estate, 300
   sale of Elvis's contract at, 67
"Suspicious Minds" (song), 187, 192, 205, 224, 320
swamp rock/pop, 186, 204, 206–207
the Sweet Inspirations (vocal group), 191, 202–203, 345
syncopation, 40

## • T •

tablecloth deal, International Hotel, 193
"Takin' Care of Business" (motto), 198, 234
talking bridge, 132
Taurog, Norman (director), 122
Taylor's (Sun Café), 298
TCB Band, 198–201, 345
TCB lightening bolt symbol, 234, 295
"Teddy Bear" (song), 205
teen musical
　beach movie, 167
　characteristics of, 166–167
　integrated musicals, 170–171
　as music subgenre, 165
　Presley Travelogues as, 167–170
teen spirit, 307
teenagers
　disposable income of, 307
　Elvis merchandise marketed to, 93–94
　identity, 307
　Russian, 87
　young fans of Elvis, 59, 61, 69, 78, 86
　youth culture, 86–87, 306–308
television
　coast-to-coast broadcasting, 75
　first worldwide live satellite broadcast, 223–224
television appearances by Elvis
　*The Ed Sullivan Show* (1956 and 1957), 14, 79–82, 93, 329
　*Elvis: Aloha from Hawaii* (1973), 223–225
　*Hy Gardner Calling* (1956), 92–93
　*The Milton Berle Show* (1956), 14, 77–78, 328
　*The '68 Comeback Special* (1968), 179–184
　*Stage Show* (1956), 13, 76, 102
　*The Steve Allen Show* (1956), 14, 78–79
　*The Timex Special* (1960), 118
Texas Livestock Show, 189, 195–196
*That's All Right* (Moore), 273
"That's All Right" (song), 40, 45–46, 50–51, 214, 315, 327
*That's the Way It Is* (album), 324–325
"The First Time Ever I Saw Your Face" (song), 207

*This Is Elvis* (documentary), 284
Thompson, Linda (girlfriend of Elvis)
　biographical information, 345
　drug use by Elvis, 236
　Graceland decor and, 294
　life after Elvis, 237
Thompson, Sam (member Memphis Mafia), 245
Thornton, Willa Mae "Big Mama," 73, 77
threats, 239
*3000 Miles to Graceland* (movie), 282, 286, 337
*Tickle Me* (movie), 124, 141, 235
Tiger (Mad Tiger) (jumpsuit), 212
"Tiger Man" (song), 183, 227, 330
*The Timex Special* (TV program), 118
Tin Pan Alley, 88–89
Todaro, Dr. George (researcher), 220
touring
　during comeback years, 22, 196
　country-western circuit (1954-1956), 12, 53–62
　importance of, 56–62
　price of grueling schedule, 241
tourist sites
　California homes, 301–302
　Graceland, 291–297
　Memphis highlights, 300
　Sun Studio, 297–300
　Tupelo, 301
towel, tossing into audience, 215
Travelogues, Presley, 125–126, 138, 140–142, 147, 167–170
tribute artists, 259, 273–274
"Trouble" (song), 182
*The Trouble with Girls* (movie), 155–156
Troy, Doris (singer), 202
"True Love Travels on a Gravel Road" (song), 186
*True Romance* (movie), 336
Tupelo, Mississippi (birthplace of Elvis), 10, 28–31, 301
Tutt, Ronnie (drummer), 191, 200
"Tutti Frutti" (song), 71
*20/20* (news magazine), 262–263
20th Century Fox (movie studio), 149–151
Tyler, Judy (actress), 108, 114

# • U •

Ukelele Ike (blues musician), 47
underwear, tossing in concert, 214
United Artists (movie studio), 149, 152–153
"Up Above My Head" (song), 183
"U.S. Male" (song), 177, 178

# • V •

van Kuijk, Andreas Cornelis. *See* Parker, Colonel Tom
Vegas throat, 194
vehicle, movie, 105, 167, 171–172
vibrato technique, 178
Victor, Adam (*The Elvis Encyclopedia*), 117, 122, 200, 224, 230, 231
*Viva Las Vegas* (movie), 124–125, 130, 134, 138–139, 330

# • W •

Wagoner, Porter (singer), 60
waist-up rule, 81–82
*Walk the Line* (movie), 288–289, 337–338
Walley, Deborah (actress), 131
Wallis, Hal B. (film producer)
  biographical information, 102, 346
  *Blue Hawaii,* 121–123
  contracts with Elvis, 15, 102, 116, 119
  ending relationship with Elvis, 142
  *G.I. Blues,* 116, 119
  on Presley picture success, 161
  production values, 169–170
  *Roustabout,* 140, 141, 161
  *Starmaker,* 102
  vehicles for Elvis, 105, 123–125
wardrobe. *See* clothing
Warhol, Andy (artist), 252
Warren, Charles Marquis (director), 156
Warwick, Dee Dee (singer), 202
watch, as gift, 221
weight problem, 237, 264
Weisbart, David (producer), 150
Weld, Tuesday (actress), 18, 130, 151–152, 168, 285
*WELO Jamboree,* 31
"We're Gonna Move" (song), 104
Werheimer, Albert (photographer), 107
West, Red (member Memphis Mafia)
  biographical information, 346
  on drug use by Elvis, 236
  *Elvis: What Happened?,* 236, 261, 346
  guns, 239
  stuntman, 233
West, Sonny (member Memphis Mafia)
  on *Aloha from Hawaii* concert, 224
  biographical information, 346
  *Elvis: Still Taking Care of Business,* 271, 346
  *Elvis: What Happened?,* 261, 346
  guns, 239
western, 150–151, 156–157
Westmoreland, Kathy (vocalist)
  backing up Elvis, 203, 346
  *Elvis and Kathy,* 203
  at funeral for Elvis, 245
Wetherington, Jim (singer), 47
"What'd I Say" (song), 134, 192
*When Elvis Died* (Gregory and Gregory), 262
"Where Could I Go But to the Lord" (song), 183
White, Tony Joe (musician-songwriter), 206
White House, Elvis's trip to, 331
"The Wiffenpoof Song" (song), 156
*Wild at Heart* (movie), 335
*Wild in the Country* (movie), 18, 121, 130, 151–152, 168
"Wild in the Country" (song), 152
Wilkinson, John (guitarist)
  *My Life Before, During, and After Elvis Presley,* 201
  TCB Band, 191, 200–201
will, 292
William Morris Agency, 64
Williams, Ann (singer), 203
Winters, David (choreographer), 125, 126
Winters, Roland (actor), 153
"Witchcraft" (song), 118
"Wolf Call" (song), 134
"The Wonder of You" (song), 199
"Wooden Heart" (song), 119
Wright, Early (disc jockey), 58–59

## • Y •

"Yesterday" (song), 192
"You Gave Me a Mountain" (song), 208
Young, Gig (actor), 153, 168
Young, Reggie (guitarist), 186
Youngblood, Rob (actor), 283
"You're a Heartbreaker" (song), 43

youth culture
  impact of Elvis on, 306–308
  rise of, 86–87

## • Z •

Ziegler, Ron (presidential press secretary), 220

## BUSINESS, CAREERS & PERSONAL FINANCE

**Accounting For Dummies, 4th Edition*** 
978-0-470-24600-9

**Bookkeeping Workbook For Dummies†** 
978-0-470-16983-4

**Commodities For Dummies** 
978-0-470-04928-0

**Doing Business in China For Dummies** 
978-0-470-04929-7

**E-Mail Marketing For Dummies** 
978-0-470-19087-6

**Job Interviews For Dummies, 3rd Edition*†** 
978-0-470-17748-8

**Personal Finance Workbook For Dummies*†** 
978-0-470-09933-9

**Real Estate License Exams For Dummies** 
978-0-7645-7623-2

**Six Sigma For Dummies** 
978-0-7645-6798-8

**Small Business Kit For Dummies, 2nd Edition*†** 
978-0-7645-5984-6

**Telephone Sales For Dummies** 
978-0-470-16836-3

## BUSINESS PRODUCTIVITY & MICROSOFT OFFICE

**Access 2007 For Dummies** 
978-0-470-03649-5

**Excel 2007 For Dummies** 
978-0-470-03737-9

**Office 2007 For Dummies** 
978-0-470-00923-9

**Outlook 2007 For Dummies** 
978-0-470-03830-7

**PowerPoint 2007 For Dummies** 
978-0-470-04059-1

**Project 2007 For Dummies** 
978-0-470-03651-8

**QuickBooks 2008 For Dummies** 
978-0-470-18470-7

**Quicken 2008 For Dummies** 
978-0-470-17473-9

**Salesforce.com For Dummies, 2nd Edition** 
978-0-470-04893-1

**Word 2007 For Dummies** 
978-0-470-03658-7

## EDUCATION, HISTORY, REFERENCE & TEST PREPARATION

**African American History For Dummies** 
978-0-7645-5469-8

**Algebra For Dummies** 
978-0-7645-5325-7

**Algebra Workbook For Dummies** 
978-0-7645-8467-1

**Art History For Dummies** 
978-0-470-09910-0

**ASVAB For Dummies, 2nd Edition** 
978-0-470-10671-6

**British Military History For Dummies** 
978-0-470-03213-8

**Calculus For Dummies** 
978-0-7645-2498-1

**Canadian History For Dummies, 2nd Edition** 
978-0-470-83656-9

**Geometry Workbook For Dummies** 
978-0-471-79940-5

**The SAT I For Dummies, 6th Edition** 
978-0-7645-7193-0

**Series 7 Exam For Dummies** 
978-0-470-09932-2

**World History For Dummies** 
978-0-7645-5242-7

## FOOD, GARDEN, HOBBIES & HOME

**Bridge For Dummies, 2nd Edition** 
978-0-471-92426-5

**Coin Collecting For Dummies, 2nd Edition** 
978-0-470-22275-1

**Cooking Basics For Dummies, 3rd Edition** 
978-0-7645-7206-7

**Drawing For Dummies** 
978-0-7645-5476-6

**Etiquette For Dummies, 2nd Edition** 
978-0-470-10672-3

**Gardening Basics For Dummies*†** 
978-0-470-03749-2

**Knitting Patterns For Dummies** 
978-0-470-04556-5

**Living Gluten-Free For Dummies†** 
978-0-471-77383-2

**Painting Do-It-Yourself For Dummies** 
978-0-470-17533-0

## HEALTH, SELF HELP, PARENTING & PETS

**Anger Management For Dummies** 
978-0-470-03715-7

**Anxiety & Depression Workbook For Dummies** 
978-0-7645-9793-0

**Dieting For Dummies, 2nd Edition** 
978-0-7645-4149-0

**Dog Training For Dummies, 2nd Edition** 
978-0-7645-8418-3

**Horseback Riding For Dummies** 
978-0-470-09719-9

**Infertility For Dummies†** 
978-0-470-11518-3

**Meditation For Dummies with CD-ROM, 2nd Edition** 
978-0-471-77774-8

**Post-Traumatic Stress Disorder For Dummies** 
978-0-470-04922-8

**Puppies For Dummies, 2nd Edition** 
978-0-470-03717-1

**Thyroid For Dummies, 2nd Edition†** 
978-0-471-78755-6

**Type 1 Diabetes For Dummies*†** 
978-0-470-17811-9

\* Separate Canadian edition also available 
† Separate U.K. edition also available

Available wherever books are sold. For more information or to order direct: U.S. customers visit www.dummies.com or call 1-877-762-2974. 
U.K. customers visit www.wileyeurope.com or call (0) 1243 843291. Canadian customers visit www.wiley.ca or call 1-800-567-4797.

**WILEY**

## INTERNET & DIGITAL MEDIA

**AdWords For Dummies**
978-0-470-15252-2

**Blogging For Dummies, 2nd Edition**
978-0-470-23017-6

**Digital Photography All-in-One Desk Reference For Dummies, 3rd Edition**
978-0-470-03743-0

**Digital Photography For Dummies, 5th Edition**
978-0-7645-9802-9

**Digital SLR Cameras & Photography For Dummies, 2nd Edition**
978-0-470-14927-0

**eBay Business All-in-One Desk Reference For Dummies**
978-0-7645-8438-1

**eBay For Dummies, 5th Edition*
978-0-470-04529-9

**eBay Listings That Sell For Dummies**
978-0-471-78912-3

**Facebook For Dummies**
978-0-470-26273-3

**The Internet For Dummies, 11th Edition**
978-0-470-12174-0

**Investing Online For Dummies, 5th Edition**
978-0-7645-8456-5

**iPod & iTunes For Dummies, 5th Edition**
978-0-470-17474-6

**MySpace For Dummies**
978-0-470-09529-4

**Podcasting For Dummies**
978-0-471-74898-4

**Search Engine Optimization For Dummies, 2nd Edition**
978-0-471-97998-2

**Second Life For Dummies**
978-0-470-18025-9

**Starting an eBay Business For Dummies, 3rd Edition†**
978-0-470-14924-9

## GRAPHICS, DESIGN & WEB DEVELOPMENT

**Adobe Creative Suite 3 Design Premium All-in-One Desk Reference For Dummies**
978-0-470-11724-8

**Adobe Web Suite CS3 All-in-One Desk Reference For Dummies**
978-0-470-12099-6

**AutoCAD 2008 For Dummies**
978-0-470-11650-0

**Building a Web Site For Dummies, 3rd Edition**
978-0-470-14928-7

**Creating Web Pages All-in-One Desk Reference For Dummies, 3rd Edition**
978-0-470-09629-1

**Creating Web Pages For Dummies, 8th Edition**
978-0-470-08030-6

**Dreamweaver CS3 For Dummies**
978-0-470-11490-2

**Flash CS3 For Dummies**
978-0-470-12100-9

**Google SketchUp For Dummies**
978-0-470-13744-4

**InDesign CS3 For Dummies**
978-0-470-11865-8

**Photoshop CS3 All-in-One Desk Reference For Dummies**
978-0-470-11195-6

**Photoshop CS3 For Dummies**
978-0-470-11193-2

**Photoshop Elements 5 For Dummies**
978-0-470-09810-3

**SolidWorks For Dummies**
978-0-7645-9555-4

**Visio 2007 For Dummies**
978-0-470-08983-5

**Web Design For Dummies, 2nd Edition**
978-0-471-78117-2

**Web Sites Do-It-Yourself For Dummies**
978-0-470-16903-2

**Web Stores Do-It-Yourself For Dummies**
978-0-470-17443-2

## LANGUAGES, RELIGION & SPIRITUALITY

**Arabic For Dummies**
978-0-471-77270-5

**Chinese For Dummies, Audio Set**
978-0-470-12766-7

**French For Dummies**
978-0-7645-5193-2

**German For Dummies**
978-0-7645-5195-6

**Hebrew For Dummies**
978-0-7645-5489-6

**Ingles Para Dummies**
978-0-7645-5427-8

**Italian For Dummies, Audio Set**
978-0-470-09586-7

**Italian Verbs For Dummies**
978-0-471-77389-4

**Japanese For Dummies**
978-0-7645-5429-2

**Latin For Dummies**
978-0-7645-5431-5

**Portuguese For Dummies**
978-0-471-78738-9

**Russian For Dummies**
978-0-471-78001-4

**Spanish Phrases For Dummies**
978-0-7645-7204-3

**Spanish For Dummies**
978-0-7645-5194-9

**Spanish For Dummies, Audio Set**
978-0-470-09585-0

**The Bible For Dummies**
978-0-7645-5296-0

**Catholicism For Dummies**
978-0-7645-5391-2

**The Historical Jesus For Dummies**
978-0-470-16785-4

**Islam For Dummies**
978-0-7645-5503-9

**Spirituality For Dummies, 2nd Edition**
978-0-470-19142-2

## NETWORKING AND PROGRAMMING

**ASP.NET 3.5 For Dummies**
978-0-470-19592-5

**C# 2008 For Dummies**
978-0-470-19109-5

**Hacking For Dummies, 2nd Edition**
978-0-470-05235-8

**Home Networking For Dummies, 4th Edition**
978-0-470-11806-1

**Java For Dummies, 4th Edition**
978-0-470-08716-9

**Microsoft® SQL Server™ 2008 All-in-One Desk Reference For Dummies**
978-0-470-17954-3

**Networking All-in-One Desk Reference For Dummies, 2nd Edition**
978-0-7645-9939-2

**Networking For Dummies, 8th Edition**
978-0-470-05620-2

**SharePoint 2007 For Dummies**
978-0-470-09941-4

**Wireless Home Networking For Dummies, 2nd Edition**
978-0-471-74940-0